Land, Property, and the Environment

Land, Property, and the Environment

EDITED BY JOHN F. RICHARDS

 **PRESS**

INSTITUTE FOR CONTEMPORARY STUDIES
OAKLAND, CALIFORNIA

Copyright © 2002 by John F. Richards.

Printed in the United States of America. All rights reserved. No part of this book may be used or reproduced in any manner without express written permission, except in the case of brief quotations in critical articles and reviews.

This book is a publication of the Institute for Contemporary Studies, a nonprofit, non-partisan public policy research organization. The analyses, conclusions, and opinions expressed in ICS Press publications are those of the authors and not necessarily those of the Institute or its officers, its directors, or others associated with, or funding, its work.

Inquiries, book orders, and catalog requests should be addressed to ICS Press, Latham Square, 1611 Telegraph Avenue, Suite 406, Oakland, CA 94612. Tel.: (510) 238-5010; Fax: (510) 238-8440; Internet: www.icspress.com. For book orders and catalog requests, call toll free in the United States: (800) 326-0263.

0 9 8 7 6 5 4 3 2 1

Library of Congress Cataloging-in-Publication Data

Richards, John F.
    Land, property, and the environment / edited by John F. Richards.
        p. cm.
    Includes bibliographical references.
    ISBN 1-55815-516-3 (paper)
    1. Land use—Enviromental aspects. 2. Land use—Planning.
3. Right of property. I. Title.

HD108.3.R53 2001
333.7—dc21   2001026391

Contents

Tables and Illustrations

A Note from the Publisher

There is no better place to study modern life than the nexus of land, property rights, and the environment.

As I write this note, looking out on San Francisco Bay from Pt. Richmond, my community is in the midst of a protracted legal and political dispute with local developers, the city of Richmond, and regional planners over the quality of life and over density issues. The strange mix of people on each side of this conflict suggests that the old political categories no longer apply. Many of those fighting against the development are clearly free-market advocates standing for strong property rights, yet they also assert the strong rights of the community to have a real voice in development.

At the center of this dispute, as this book suggests, is the issue of property rights. Who has the right to make decisions about land use and for what purposes? The distinction between government and private makes less and less sense in our modern, globalized world. Few will accept as tolerable the notion of a world czar for land-use decision making, just as few would accept a purely private system.

In a world increasingly dedicated to participatory democracy we will increasingly face demands that decisions about property rights be subject to the reflection and choices of diverse communities of men and women. If we are to bypass the age-old reliance on accident and force for such decisions, we must have access to well-reasoned alternatives about property rights and how they are allocated. Where can we use free-market allocations of land? Where are common-property regimes appropriate and with what mix for private activity? What roles should communities play, involving what rights and responsibilities? Should the "state" hold all natural resources in common, as in Alaska?

At the most fundamental level these are constitutional issues. How a community decides to use land, who has the right to use land, and how these claims are adjudicated are constitutional issues in terms of fundamental law and how we constitute ourselves. This book provides historical background as well as insights into current issues that will allow scholars, policy makers, and citizens to deepen their discussion and reflection about how to address the fundamental issues of property rights. These rights, after all, lie at the heart of self-governance. Property rights and issues of governance are merely two sides of the same coin.

—ROBERT B. HAWKINS, JR.
President and CEO,
Institute for Contemporary Studies

Preface

This book results from the work of the Committee on Global Environmental Change of the Social Science Research Council (SSRC) and formed part of that committee's examination of human land use and environmental change in a comparative global perspective. The project on Landed Property Rights assembled the authors contributing to this volume and other experts to reflect upon the complex issue of property rights in land and human-induced ("anthropogenic") environmental change in a global context. The project members—political scientists, anthropologists, historians, legal scholars, and economists—assembled for six workshops over the period 1991 to 1998. Most of the essays included in this book were first presented at a workshop held in August 1994 in Stowe, Vermont.

Each workshop generated intense discussion and fruitful examination of property rights in land from a theoretical, comparative, and always an empirical perspective. As the organizers had hoped, sequential workshops, interspersed with continuing communication by the new medium of e-mail, fostered steadily growing understanding, comprehension, and more powerful analysis of land and different property rights regimes. As the discussions occurred and recurred, often with new members at each workshop, we moved freely in time from the present to the early modern centuries and from the most familiar of American/European property rights in land to the most conceptually distant in Asia and Africa. As we proceeded, it became clear that we were grappling with concerns more profound than merely comparing and analyzing complex systems and rules for access to land and its benefit. We invariably engaged the most pervasive institutions and the most powerful forces in human society. We confronted no less than the collision of state, market, and, above all, community and place when we analyzed human land use rights and their effect upon environmental change.

Those scholars who were part of the original working group and who contributed much to all the workshop discussions, but who are not among the volume contributors include: Steven Sanderson, Karen Polenske, and Margaret McKean. Other participants in one or more workshops are Arun Agrawal, Omar Razzaz, Anne Osborne, Paul Greenough, Robert Repetto, Karen Wigen, Martin Lewis, David Ludden, and N. S. Jodha.

Funding for this project came from the National Science Foundation and the Ford Foundation. We are conscious of our debt to Stanley Heginbotham, former vice president of the Social Science Research Council, for negotiating our Ford Foundation funding and to Walter Coward, who served as the project officer.

Finally, we must acknowledge the supportive atmosphere provided by the Social Science Research Council for interdisciplinary ventures such as this. The research committee structure of the council fosters group creativity and innovative thinking and analysis in unmatched fashion. B. L. Turner II, head of the Committee on Global Environmental Change working group on land use, offered support and many ideas for the property rights project. We are grateful to the staffpersons for the Committee on Global Environmental Change—Richard Rockwell, David Major, and Sarah Gordon—for the enthusiasm and care with which they helped us organize the meetings and report on their results. The editor is especially appreciative of David Major's drafting of a jointly authored project report and theoretical statement for *Items*, the SSRC newsletter.

Introduction

Nearly all our present and future environmental concerns ultimately return to questions of land use. The world's lands must be managed for food and industrial production and human settlement in a sustainable manner. Humankind must also maintain aesthetically appealing, pollution-free landscapes—some of which might even be "wilderness" tracts untrammeled by direct human intervention. How, on a local to regional to global scale, do we encourage and reward appropriate stewardship over land and its resources and ensure that land managers do not ignore long-term goals for short-term rewards? How do we fix societal rules for land use that meet these needs? These questions immediately plunge us into the labyrinth of property rights regimes and their effect on land use and the environment.

All societies must resolve a fundamental question: Who has the right to do what with the land for how long? Rights to land are defined and redefined by an ongoing process of challenge, negotiation, and conflict. Local, regional, and international elites struggle over who controls land for what purpose. How land is used is a crucial variable in the life and identity of a community of any size. Bitter and protracted conflicts over these issues—both legal and extralegal—are common to nearly all societies.

Property rights over land are a social construction, a set of rules that express human territoriality, that is, "an attempt by an individual or a group to affect, influence or control people, phenomena and relationships, by delimiting and asserting control over a geographic area." Property rights regimes classify and demarcate a spatial area, a piece of land, and define strategies by which owners of those rights can control access to and the use of that area. To remain viable, property rights in land "require constant effort to establish and maintain" by vigilant demarcation and defense the bounded limits of one's land.[1]

There exists a widely accepted taxonomy of property rights in land based on categories of ownership. Social scientists distinguish between unowned or open-access land; state property (both public property held in trust and state property); the property of groups or individuals (jointly owned or common); and individually owned private property. Property rights consist of complex "bundles" of rights that may or may not reside in a single owner. At one extreme landowners possess a high proportion of conceivable rights to land: They may exclude others from occupancy or use of their precisely measured and bounded land; they may occupy, cultivate, clear, pave, or otherwise transform the holding; they may consume, extract, and sell all subtractible resources above or below the land surface, that is, soil, water, minerals, grass, trees and other vegetation, and wildlife; they may alienate part or all of their holding (by sale or gift), lease part or all of the ownership rights, offer their land as security on a loan, and bequeath all these rights to heirs. Any or all of these rights (and many others) may be taken out of the bundle and sold, leased, or assigned by the owner. In other regimes these rights may be unbundled and divided in complicated patterns among various persons and organizations by nonmarket mechanisms. Conflicts over these issues—both legal and extralegal—are common to nearly all societies.

Two questions occur: First, does the form of property rights formally and informally exercised over land matter for environmental outcomes? The obvious answer is yes. Rules of property and their acceptance and enforcement by community and state do matter. Property regimes do exclude certain land uses and permit others in certain places. Property regimes whose rules have been long established may constrain present-day land use in an unforeseen way. Second, is one form of land ownership—individual, corporate, common property, or state—superior to others in shaping favorable environmental outcomes? There is not an obvious and clear-cut answer to this question. It is not so certain that any particular mode of landownership, private or public, determines whether or not environmental degradation occurs. Theoretical debates over this issue, often ideologically driven, sometimes obfuscate more basic considerations. The primary issue when considering environmental outcomes is not the form that landownership takes. It is instead whether and to what degree a market in land exists in any specified time and place.

As land markets around the world become more effective, they accelerate the speed and lower the cost of transactions in land. Market pressures fracture those social forces that constrain versatility in land use in the interests of social stability. Everywhere land markets crash against social barriers in order to free more land for conversion to the most profitable economic use. Everywhere land in commercial and industrial areas changes ownership and use with extraordinary velocity. This is by no means a solely western idea or a process driven solely by westerners, but is a global phenomenon.

Landowners and land managers are pressured to place their land under the most economically productive use as reflected in land prices.[1] As desirable land becomes scarce, pressures on landowners to sell and take their profits spiral upward. In the most extreme conditions of economic expansion and free land markets, the velocity of transactions and the rate at which land use changes also spiral upward. As this process continues, the usual effect is to increase intensity of human land use.

Increasing intensity invariably means reduced biomass and biodiversity on the land in question as land managers seek to increase production. Whatever the form of production, whether agricultural, industrial, or even human settlement, the land manager's fixed aim is to diminish natural change, natural diversity, and natural hazard. To take only simple examples, the land manager must control and, if necessary, divert stormwater that intrudes on his productive land. He must prevent natural fire from encroaching upon his domain; or if it cannot be stopped, he must find ways to benefit from its presence. He must exclude wild animals, birds, and insects whose behavior threatens production by declaring them vermin. He must eliminate spontaneously growing plants that interfere with production by declaring them weeds. In short, the land manager seeking the highest form of production must reduce the velocity and capacity of natural change on his land.

Land scarcity as expressed in price-driven land markets elicits steadily rising human effort aimed at reducing natural change in favor of accelerating human interventions at faster and faster rates. A freely functioning land market has a profound appeal to deep human concerns for steadily increasing production and material well-being. The swirling effect of booming land markets also touches human aesthetic needs for novelty, for play, and for nearly irresistible gambling on the future. Intensified land use draws in new people to a region and releases new energies and new synergies as population grows.

The basic issue for those concerned with environmental issues is exactly opposite. The goal of the land manager under this ethic is to reduce the pace and intensity of human intervention so as to allow natural change to progress. In order to accomplish this, the land market must be constrained, vitiated, or even completely eliminated for certain tracts of land. This goal can be achieved under any form of ownership—individual/household, corporate, or state.

Restraining the pace of change by circumscribing the land market makes a different, but equally powerful, emotional appeal in every society. Land is immovable; land conveys a sense of place. Property rights in land frequently confer identity and confirm the cultural heritage of the owner(s). Landownership may carry with it preferred membership in a community, lineage, or other corporate identity. For all societies the broad principles governing land use constitute a central trope deeply grounded in its moral order. Particular pieces of land acquire a sacred quality either from religious beliefs or from the great people and events of the past. These landed rights are often nonnegotiable and nontransferable outside the community or nation and must be defended by extreme means. Linking the spilled blood of warrior forbears and the soil of the nation or community is a common expression of this sentiment. Love of the land need not be fascist or ultra-nationalist. It can be expressed in more benign ways in a shared sense of purpose. Rather than scientific or utilitarian arguments, environmentally sound land use rests upon emotion and sentiment: a sense of place, strong attachment to a city or townscape, to a neighborhood, to a park or greenery, to a landscape, to a forest, or to animals, birds, and waterways.[2]

OVERVIEW OF CHAPTERS (A HEAD EXAMPLE)

The scholars contributing chapters to this volume, although writing from differing disciplinary, theoretical, historical, and comparative perspectives have shared interests in land use, property rights, and human impacts on the natural world. Each contributor has grappled with the complex interaction between market, state, and community whenever human use of the land is in question. Each has patiently sifted through the intricate terminology that every society employs in the discussion of property rights in land. Each is sensitive to the complex, and often unexpected, consequences of land use decisions. Each contributor has participated in an extended and wide-ranging series of discussions of these issues from a global perspective. The essays assembled in this volume are a sobering testimony to the difficulties of resolving the tension between human productivity and the health of the land. Even the most carefully planned sets of rules embedded in landed property rights will not ensure wise land use if a balance of power does not exist between state, market, and community. If one of these spheres is overly dominant, the results are likely to be environmental distortion.

The opening chapter, "Toward a Global System of Property Rights in Land" by the editor, argues that property rights in land around the world have become more uniform in a slow process of convergence. Looking back over several centuries, one can identify shared cumulative processes of change that cross national lines and world regions. Intensified land use encouraged by centralizing states is a common human experience in the early modern and modern worlds. As land use intensifies, markets in land extend their reach, efficiency, and capacity. As property rights in land converge in the early modern and modern eras, at least three massive, shared changes have occurred. First was "the obliteration of localized property rights regimes"—usually variants of communal landholding—as tribal or indigenous peoples lost the struggle against intruding pioneer settlers. Second was the "erosion of community property rights in land exercised by peasants in agrarian societies." Third was the assertion of property rights in urban land by "an ever-more compressed and ever-growing urban lower class." While not coterminous in origin, the struggles characteristic of each of these changes can still be seen in progress in various parts of the world today.

In Chapter 2, "Harvests of Chance: Corporate Control of Arable Land in Early Modern Japan," Philip Brown describes an unusual system of corporate land rights widely employed by peasant villages in Tokugawa Japan. Under this *warichi* system, each peasant cultivator owned a share in the village corporation that gave him and his family access to a stipulated amount of cultivable land but not to a specified plot of land. These shares could be freely sold, rented, or bequeathed to outsiders willing to take up residence in the village. Under this system the village community periodically redistributed cultivable lands by lottery or by fixed rotation. This system seems to have risen in part because rural villages under the Tokugawa faced joint or corporate responsibility for payment of land taxes and periodic redistribution of cultivable fields helped to ensure equitable distribution of the tax burden. The warichi system also offered security in the form of basic maintenance for all households in the village. The system also distributed labor, risk, and interest equally when village lands were improved or when they suffered devastation. The village community continued to manage woodlots, grazing areas, and other village lands as common property resources. The warichi system faltered in some areas and in others persisted until today. Its longevity is a testimonial to village cooperation and sense of community in managing the land.

In "Property Rights on Imperial China's Frontiers," Peter Perdue objects to a longstanding Orientalist tendency by both Western and Chinese scholars to assume universal and unchanging principles of property rights in land in premodern China based on readings of law codes and other normative texts. This approach leads to a notion of an unchanging "Asiatic despotism" in which the state owned the land and individual property rights remained merely customary and hence insecure. State control enfeebled individual property rights and retarded investment and growth in agriculture. Perdue instead argues that the Qing empire, as had its predecessors, was intensely interested in intensifying land use and agricultural productivity. Two case studies of eighteenth-century frontier expansion—Taiwan and the north-west steppe regions—illustrate how the Qing empire converted a shifting cultivation economy and a pastoral economy to intensive cultivation by Han settlers who obtained secure property rights in land. Chinese property rights in land did not change as radically as did European land rights in the seventeenth to the nineteenth centuries. Common property resources managed by lineages persisted. So also did customary law in such matters as the right of redemption by a seller of land for the original price even after an extended period of time. The Qing state struggled to reconcile ever-more insistent market forces with its longstanding notion of stability and harmonious relations in the countryside.

Anna Tsing challenges the view, put forward by John Richards in his essay, that uniform modern property rights in land will inevitably prevail. She argues that even the most powerful landed property rights regimes are, after all, sets of social relationships that are unstable, context specific, and the product of ongoing "debates, struggles, and negotiations." In "Land as Law: Negotiating the Meaning of Property in Indonesia," she traces the creation of a dual system of landed property rights—the European and *adat*, or native, systems—codified by the Dutch for the Dutch East Indies in their 1870 Agrarian Act. Lands, not people, were classified in this manner. European lands could be bought, sold, or mortgaged freely. Adat lands could only be leased and were held on varying types of communal tenures. After independence a new piece of legislation, the Basic Agrarian Law of 1960, set out a unified Indonesian land law, based on adat first principles of social responsibility, but which also established "Dutch principles of land ownership and disposal" that expanded the reach of land markets. As development proceeded, adat law became increasingly irrelevant to economic development and to metropolitan culture. Recently, however, environmental activists have returned to the never-abandoned principles of adat law to establish property rights for marginalized forest peoples threatened by forest clearing for transmigration settlement schemes and plantation agriculture.

Like the Dutch in Indonesia, British colonial rulers in East Africa tried to segregate lands between those held by Europeans with private property rights and those occupied by Africans with customary, corporate rights. James Giblin in "Land Tenure, Traditions of Thought about Land, and Their Environmental Implications in Tanzania" reconstructs precolonial customary land tenures in the farming regions of northeastern lowland Tanzania. Although grounded conceptually in shared matrilineage identities, land tenure and land management in the precolonial period relied on the authority of strong patron-chiefs who offered security to dependent kin and clients in the lands they occupied. Strong chiefs successfully imposed corporate discipline on their communities to maintain disease-free environments for cattle. Trypanosomiasis, spread by blood parasites in tsetse fly, and theilerosis (East Coast Fever), spread by parasites in ticks, could be controlled by burning and clearing brush and woods that harbored wildlife and insects. When droughts occurred, chiefs supplied hoarded food to keep their client-farmers on the land and keep up measures of environmental control. After colonial conquest, British ideas of African communal property owned by corporate matrilineages justified giving individual alienable private property rights to European settlers, but withholding them from Africans living in reserved areas. In theory, chiefs retained their power to control their dependent client farmers; but in fact they lost the all-important power to seize holdings. Weakened chiefs could not impose the social discipline necessary for disease control—especially in times of drought—and epidemics of cattle disease followed. Having traced the transition from precolonial systems of land tenure to the conceptions of customary law introduced by the British, Giblin concludes that forms of land tenure were less important than political relationships in determining the environmental outcome of land use. David Feeny reaches a similar conclusion in the next chapter.

Market pressures and population increase also generated changes in independent Thailand in the nineteenth and twentieth centuries. In "The Coevolution of Property Rights Regimes for Land, Man, and Forests in Thailand, 1790–1990," David Feeny describes a shift from a land-abundant, labor-scarce economy to a land-scarce, labor-abundant economy as the world market demand for rice stimulated a rice export boom in nineteenth-century Thailand. Pioneer settlement and land clearing continued at a brisk pace. The state defined and strengthened existing customary private use rights in agricultural land to reduce growing land disputes. Property rights in human beings—corvée and slavery—gradually eroded and were finally abolished. Land instead of people could then be used as collateral for credit. Largely uncontrolled open access to forested land—owned by the king—encouraged land clearing and settlement. By the end of the nineteenth century, the Thai monarchy actively asserted royal man-

agement and ownership of the royal forests to restrain commercial timber-
ing and conserve the forested lands remaining. Employing counterfactual
examples, Feeny suggests that neither the option of creating firm private
property rights in forests or fostering of common-property regimes for village lands would have substantially altered the land transformation that
did occur in Thailand over the past two centuries.

"Tragedies of Privatization: Land, Liberty, and Environmental Change
in Spain and Italy, 1800–1910," John R. McNeill's essay, reviews the land
use and land tenure history of Southern Europe when liberal reform movements succeeded in the nineteenth century. After the unification of Italy
in 1860, liberal reformers succeeded in passing national legislation that
permitted sale of millions of hectares of church, public, and village
common lands to private buyers. Most of the new owners promptly cleared
and plowed any lands that could be sown with wheat as a cash crop.
Similarly in Spain, liberal, anticlerical regimes sold at a minimum 5 million hectares of church, military order, municipal, and village lands to
private owners throughout the nineteenth century. Privatization resulted
in massive nineteenth-century woodland clearances in Iberia.

In India, colonial British officials followed similar liberal principles as
they encouraged agricultural expansion and the unfettering of land markets
throughout the subcontinent. Meena Bhargava and John Richards's joint
essay "Defining Property Rights in Land in Colonial India: Gorakhpur
Region in the Indo-Gangetic Plain" illustrates these tendencies by means
of a district-level case study. Despite the bewildering complexity of land
tenures and land taxes found in each region, East India Company officials
slowly realized that agriculture on the subcontinent shared important
common features: an armed rural aristocracy acting as intermediaries
between the state and peasantry; a stratum of peasant smallholders; and a
labor-scarce and land-abundant countryside. The East India Company rapidly stripped the rural aristocracy of its weaponry and reduced its status to
that of revenue intermediaries and rent receivers. As they gained experience, East India Company officials favored direct state relations with
smallholding peasants holding property rights in land as an option to early
views that favored large landlords. To improve agricultural production, and
thereby state revenues, British officials left rural production in private
hands; established well-defined, stable, and legally-enforceable property
rights in land; encouraged the growth of land markets; disciplined delin-
quent taxpayers by selling off their land; and provided incentives for the
cultivation of so-called wasteland. This bias carried over into independent
India and Pakistan to the extent that post-1947 land reforms virtually abolished large landed estates.

Ronald J. Herring in "State Property Rights in Nature (with Special Reference to India)" acknowledges that the Indian state has failed to protect many of its richest national parks and world heritage areas from degradation and depletion of wildlife and flora. For example, Manas, in northeastern India, is a World Heritage Center in which guerillas of the Bodo ethnic national insurgency sought refuge. With the loss of central control, local inhabitants moved in quickly to harvest wildlife and fell timber. Reoccupation of the tract by the center and augmented forest guards with better weapons have restored some measure of control. But the damage is substantial. Herring rejects the view that because of this and other less dramatic failures to protect natural sites efforts by the government of India should be abandoned in favor of local communities. He argues that the current rush to condemn state landownership and resource management as ineffectual or worse in sustaining ecosystems is misguided. The problem does not lie in the state's property claims over land, but in the state's capacity to govern. In India creation of property rights in local offices—such as forest and park guards—has been part of growing political decay and has contributed to degradation of sequestered reserves. The answer does not lie in transfer of power to local communities. Localism and devolved local property rights regimes cannot inspire effective and environmentally sound land management without state backing. Too often state property claims in land have weakened and destroyed local governance. Moreover, communities necessarily operate on a restricted territorial scale and often have parochial visions. "What is globally scarce may be locally commonplace, even pesky," Herring writes. Institutions and procedures of governance must surround and support institutions and procedures of property rights in land for both the nation-state and the community.

The use of fresh water in its many forms—rainfall, groundwater, soil moisture, and bodies and streams of water—is certainly one of the most valuable and most contested among varied property rights in land. When the state creates new sources of water by means of large-scale irrigation projects, social tension and conflict follow. Whatever the distributive mechanisms adopted—whether market or allocation—the state and its water bureaucracy invariably clash with local communities over disposal of irrigation water. Individual landowners frequently clash with other landowners. In "Water Rights in South Asia and the United States: Comparative Perspectives, 1873–2000," James Wescoat traces mutual influences and diverging practices for two of the world's largest irrigation regimes. In nineteenth-century California, officials and planners, deeply impressed by their understanding of forceful control over water rights and irrigated land by an autocratic colonial state in British India, applied the same principles to the design of large-scale water projects in that state. State power could be employed for the public good instead of for private profit. After 1947, newly independent India and Pakistan borrowed notions of multilateral river basin water control projects from the United States. Both countries retained tightly centralized state control over water and land in these projects with little consideration for community partici- pation. More recently, pressed by international and environmental organizations, India and Pakistan have become more concerned with "water management" practices harmonious with and reliant upon local communities.

In "Property Regimes for Sustainable Resource Management," Daniel W. Bromley argues that local natural resource management regimes— whether common, private, or state property—require "internal authority" derived from shared social expectations and enforcement of regime rules in order to survive and operate effectively. They also require "external legiti- macy" in the eyes of the state to protect the community's property claims against legal and extralegal intrusions by outsiders. Both state and commu- nity must act in concert to encourage responsible resource management.

Stephen Gudeman and Alberto Rivera in their chapter, "Sustaining the Community, Resisting the Market: Guatemalan Perspectives," look closely at the intricate interaction between community ("mutuality") and market ("self-interest") in contemporary Guatemala. They acknowledge that market transactions offer the appeal of efficient, unencumbered exchange, often anonymously accomplished. Nevertheless, the "commu- nity realm of economy" retains valuable characteristics that deserve recognition and encouragement. Communities have a shared base or com- mons that is the legacy and shared identity of that group and that they maintain over time. Goods and services from the commons circulate by "processes of allotment that encode and ensure enduring moralities." Transactions are marked by a bias toward self-sufficiency. Communities favor situational or contextual reasoning that stresses nurture of social rela- tionships as an essential aspect of well-being.

Eric T. Freyfogle's essay, "Community and the Market in Modern American Property Law," surveys American property rights in land from the nineteenth century to the present. Over the course of the nineteenth century, landowners gained rights to use land more intensively, and social controls diminished. By century's end, nature was primarily viewed as a fragmented collection of resources, with private owners largely immune from liability for the disruptive external harms they caused. Driven by widespread public support for industrialization, the United States increas- ingly embraced a "simple vision of land as a secure, clearly defined, transferable commodity, vested in a single private owner." But the costs of such freedom and fragmentation, especially in the despoliation of natural environments, generated a reaction that brought constraints on landown-ership. The twentieth century, Freyfogle concludes, has been a story largely of increased communal control, with control exercised not just at the local level but at the state and national levels as well. Landowners face greater restrictions on their intensive land uses, and land development is subject to detailed regulation covering larger and larger geographic scales. In many ways, landowner rights are becoming dependent on surrounding social and natural contexts, with rights more vaguely defined and subject to formal processes of negotiation. Moreover, ownership rights in particular parcels of land are increasingly fragmented rather than held by a single owner, and land is more often held by groups of individuals in ownership forms that mix the public and the private.

NOTES

1. The notions of land manager and land management are central to this study. A land manager is that person or group of persons who decides how and when natural processes of change on the land will be altered by human intervention. See Piers M. Blaikie and H. C. Brookfield, 1987, *Land Degradation and Society*, London, New York: Methuen, 74–83.

2. See Edward S. Casey, 1993, *Getting Back into Place: Toward a Renewed Understanding of the Place-World*, *Studies in Continental Thought*, Bloomington: Indiana University Press.

1

Toward a Global System of Property Rights in Land

JOHN F. RICHARDS

T he global landscape existing in the late fifteenth century has been transformed in the past half-millennium by human action.[1] Land, formerly abundant in most parts of the world, has become relatively scarce and valuable as human numbers have increased twelve times (from one-half billion to six billion) in the past five centuries. Land use for agriculture, pastoralism, resource extraction, industrial production, commerce, and human settlement has become more specialized and capital intensive. Intensified land use, in conjunction with the discovery and use of fossil-fuel energy, has caused massive changes in the natural environment throughout the world. The total standing biomass in the world today is considerably less than it was in 1500. Biodiversity has been much reduced in each region of the world.

During the early modern and modern centuries, humans have raised their knowledge, control, and use of the world's lands to an unprecedented level. Before the turn of the millennium, every hectare of the world's land surface was known, recorded, demarcated, mapped, and claimed as part of the territory of a particular nation-state (or a consortium of states, as in Antarctica). Cascading technical advances in astronomy, navigation, mathematics, geography, and cartography as well as dramatic improvements in maritime and land transport have made possible this sort of territorial control and access. Today's world is truly a unified and largely inhabited unit divided into precisely measured tracts of land.

In the past few centuries, every human society has moved toward what is becoming an increasingly similar landed property rights regime.

Bewilderingly complex, particularized local systems of property rights in land have been altered, transformed, or replaced by simplified, more uniform sets of rules in a remarkably similar fashion across all world regions. Paradoxically, however, these converging property rules have helped to establish more precise, exact, nuanced, and complex rights over individual parcels of land. This trend reflects the intensifying manipulation and use of smaller and smaller units of land within land markets of increasing transparency and efficiency.

How do we detect and analyze those processes and structural changes that have produced converging property rights regimes in land across the globe? One approach, that taken here, is to look for similar large-scale processes of change over longer periods of time.[2] In this effort, our interest is in detecting similarities across comparative cases rather than identifying differences. This paper examines three massive changes in land use and property rights over the past six centuries: first, the displacement or extinction of indigenous peoples and the consequent obliteration of localized property rights regimes; second, erosion of community property rights in land exercised by peasants in agrarian societies; and third, as part of the massive process of global urbanization in the past two centuries, the struggle of an ever-more compressed and ever-growing urban lower class for stable property rights in urban land. Although the last change begins later in time, all three processes proceed simultaneously today.

THE CENTRALIZING STATE

Early modern and modern states have been the principal agents of intensified human land use and land management. Intensifying land use is essential to state centralization and modernization. Today all land areas are claimed as ultimate property by a nation-state (or sometimes more than one). Each state does its best to demarcate and defend its national boundaries located precisely on maps and on the ground.[3] Behind these lines each state exercises territorial strategies to control its national land surface. Some portion, often quite large, remains under active ownership and management by official agencies. In most nation-states, the remaining land is relinquished to the active ownership of private, individual, or corporate landowners. Part of the nation-state's credibility rests with its guarantee of predictable and stable private property rights in land. The modern state as ultimate owner can and does take private property, usually with compensation, by right of eminent domain for public purposes ranging from highways to creation of artificial lakes. In times of emergency or crisis, states act ruthlessly to seize land for purposes of national defense and survival. However, confidence in private property depends upon assurances that the state will not arbitrarily or needlessly seize lands. The state itself must be constrained by rules and statutes that guarantee landownership.

The state's assertion of complete property rights over all land within its boundaries is an essential aspect of modern nationalism, national identity, and the nation-state. The growth of nationalism has been coterminous with growth in state control over land. Construction of a national territory is vital to national identity and community. The nation-state uses territoriality to define membership (for example, by birthright citizenship) and to build a shared national culture aimed at uniformity everywhere within its boundaries. Lacking a secure national territory, nationalisms remain incomplete and unfulfilled movements, not nations. Ultimate landownership expressed in sovereign control over a fixed territory is an essential step in nation building. Simultaneously, nationalism validates the sweeping property claims of the nation-state as ultimate landlord. Every bit of land within the national boundaries is the inheritance of the national community. The nation-state has a solemn responsibility to manage its lands for the present and the future. Which vision suffuses this stewardship and how lands are to be managed remain matters of dispute and controversy.

Centralizing states—both early modern monarchies and modern nation-states—with their ever-extending territorial reach have destroyed or swept aside hundreds, perhaps even thousands, of indigenous peoples.[4] From the Tupi Indians of coastal Brazil in the sixteenth century to the Meratus Dayaks of South Kalimantan, Indonesia, in the late twentieth, every century claimed its roster of victims.[5] Hunter-gatherer, shifting cultivator, or nomadic pastoralist peoples have never been satisfactory revenue-producing subjects for aggrandizing states. Often such "primitive" or "savage" peoples have been elusive and difficult to count and tax; usually they are subsistence producers with little usable surplus; often they are the inconvenient occupants of lands bearing timber or minerals of great value; and generally they are objects of great suspicion, fear, and hatred. Deficient in numbers, technology, and literacy, these marginal peoples can only resist for a time the onslaught of civilized powers.

States open frontiers to expand into "wild" or "empty" or "desolate" space inhabited by savages or nonpersons. As it does so, the state announces new overriding claims of ownership over lands viewed as waste or wilderness. State-encouraged frontier expansion destroys systems of landholding and land use employed by each indigenous group. New property rights in land support more intensive, market-oriented production by the new settlers. Population density increases with settlement and

sedentary cultivation. Generally, in the most common scenario, the con-
quering state gives or sells settlers individual property rights over arbitrarily
assigned tracts of land. These lands are seized from the indigenous peoples
whose rights of occupancy and use are either disregarded or taken by force
or bartered for trivial compensation. Whether these pioneer owners have
only smallholdings or whether they are allowed to claim large estates is
largely a matter of structural forces and dominant ideology in the period
and region in question. Depending on local ecology, the settlers engage in
plow agriculture, commercial pastoralism (ranching), or mining. Forests
are cleared; swamps drained; grasslands plowed; and dangerous wildlife
killed off as the frontier presses forward.

Frontier expansion confiscates land from loosely demarcated community-managed land employed by indigenous peoples for shared hunting
and gathering, for grazing, or for shifting horticulture.[6] If they survive the
initial shock of contact, indigenous groups may remain on their original
settlements or habitations and retain their individually occupied homesteads and garden plots and community space; but the total lands accessible
to their use are sharply reduced and compressed. Moving to new unde-
pleted lands for horticulture, grazing, or hunting becomes difficult as more
and more lands are occupied and claimed by settlers. Often new diseases
accompany political and cultural pressures that further weaken indigenous
resistance to settler pressure. As the frontier moves forward, new lands are
surveyed and demarcated.

As early as the sixteenth century, the early modern governments of
the Netherlands revived cadastral mapping as a tool of state land management.[7] Techniques employed by professional surveyors improved to the
point that land could be precisely named, located, and represented on a
map. Surveyors became more proficient at determining from published
astronomical observations their exact positions. From known locations and
heights, surveyors could do transects over previously unmapped lands and
obtain the data for accurate topographical mapping. After baselines were
established, surveyors could begin detailed cadastral mapping of the new
lands. (Of course, detailed cadastral mapping did not depend upon precise
location by longitude and latitude and had been carried out to divide lands
long before this). Land maps are intended, as James Scott reminds us, to be
"a geometric representation of the borders or frontiers between parcels of
land."[8] They are intended to link the landowner precisely with his property
primarily for tax purposes. Often in frontier circumstances, surveyors map
and lay out parcels of land in anticipation of occupation and ownership by
settlers. Their official land maps establish a new, usually gridded landscape
comprehensible to arriving settlers, but opaque to indigenous peoples.

The state as ultimate landowner confirms the property rights of the new settlers by written documentation preserved in official archives. The original claims for land with their crude bounds marked by natural features, trees, or streams are gradually superseded by new precisely measured plats from cadastral surveys. In most instances these new settlers hold individual proprietary rights over their lands. For a time at least, the state is willing to concede virtually the full bundle of ownership rights to its hardy pioneers. The centralizing state will, if necessary, adjudicate disputes over ownership and use in the courts, and will back up properly registered ownership claims by force.

Most centralizing states encourage the development of an open land market in agricultural land in these newly settled areas. The state frees land from the constraints of community and the slow-paced cyclical change of indigenous land use. The new property rights system is aimed at speeding ownership transfers and easing changes in land use. As land becomes a commodity with a price, it is readily transferred from one owner to another and subject to the most productive use determined by the market. As villages and towns are settled and expand, suburban and urban lands become fungible and available for any use in an urban context. Urban land use changes become even faster and easier as transaction costs move downward in booming land markets.

States also retain active ownership and management of portions of newly annexed lands. A common practice has been to establish territories for indigenous peoples—usually less desirable and productive tracts—so that they may be more easily controlled and kept from contact with settlers. On the "reservations" or "native lands," group property rights over land may be tolerated by the conquest state. Generally, however, these rights are also determined, measured, recorded in written documents, and thereby frozen in place in a newly static system of land tenure. Keeping them out of any form of land market preserves native lands. Outsiders are prohibited from acquiring property rights on these reservations. Native peoples caught up in these territorial systems face the worst of both worlds: Their older systems of production are less effective under the new conditions, and they have no capital and often no legal way to improve production on their reserved lands. Not surprisingly, state demarcation of reserved "tribal" territory has contributed to new, more unified composite identities and far greater cohesion among the peoples so bounded.[9]

The centralizing state often bars pioneer settlement in large areas of potentially valuable natural resources—especially forests. Continually rising timber prices in the early modern and modern world economy have encouraged states to retain at least some portion of unsettled forest lands for revenue purposes. In defining such spaces, the universal tendency has been to discourage and remove indigenous peoples living on these lands. Fear of the use of fire as an ecological tool by shifting cultivators has been one of the primary motives for removals along with stereotypical concerns about savage violence. The effect has been to depopulate those forests designated as state property. Punitive military expeditions have been followed by creation of quasi-military patrolling and guard systems to keep people away from the resource. Under some regimes and in some periods, however, local people living adjacent to the forest have been permitted to graze animals; gather fuelwood, thatch, berries or other forest products; and even hunt and fish to a limited extent. Access has always been contingent and regulated by the state as landowner.

In some forested lands, little or no management occurred as officials simply leased timber-cutting rights to private contractors (often for illegal compensation and bribes) with scarcely any thought for sustainable development. Often an influx of settlers followed, either legally or as squatters. Elsewhere in national or state forest lands, forestry agencies employed professionally trained foresters and scientists as land managers. Globally accepted standards for forest science and management have been coalescing since the eighteenth century.[10] Timber harvesting on state forest land, usually by leases and permits to private contractors, generated a revenue stream for the treasury. Foresters have, however, consistently fought for the territorial integrity of their bounded state-owned forest lands. Sometimes they have prevailed against powerful public and private groups seeking to clear and develop state forest lands for profit; sometimes they have not.

By and large foresters have been more concerned with generating usable timber supplies than with maintaining the ecological integrity of forests. Concern for sustainable use and for replanting tends to vary according to the morale, political support, state financial needs, and timber needs of the regime. For example, under wartime supply pressures, state-run forests universally suffer intense cutting and exploitation. Generally, even in normal circumstances, the pressures for over-exploitation have led to overcutting in most state-owned forests worldwide.[11] Scientific theories and threats of financial loss have encouraged obsessive concerns with wildfire in forest, brush, and grassland settings.[12]

One way to measure intensifying land management around the world is to look at the steadily growing effort and resources put into suppressing fires that occur naturally or by human action. Fire has changed from a commonly employed tool to a hazard to be suppressed. The use of fire has been stripped from the bundle of ownership rights by the centralizing state. In most twentieth-century societies, firing state-owned lands is a criminal offense. Employing fire on private property is strictly regulated and more often than not prohibited by official edict.

It is primarily the state, rather than local society, that condemns the use of fire as a threat to order and that suppresses burning. Since firing the woods is an essential process for shifting cultivators, this puts them on a collision course with officials. Foresters, engineers, and scientists have universally condemned the use of fire by indigenous peoples as a tool of ecological management to encourage game or to promote soil fertility. That intimate ecological knowledge and sense of place that permitted local folk to employ fire successfully is disparaged and ignored.

State claims to ultimate landownership extend to nearly all natural resources. Rights to consume wildlife, for example, are extracted from the bundle of property rights attached to land. Wildlife—animals, birds, fish—are claimed as property by the state, which may or may not permit individuals to hunt, fish, trap, or otherwise make use of these resources. (Of course, state interest in regulating hunting is mixed with its concern to regulate the use of firearms by its citizenry.) Even on lands long conceded to private or corporate ownership, the state regulates treatment of wildlife by its rules regarding hunting, taking, or disturbing of animal, fish, or bird populations. Specialized wildlife and fishery agencies evolve that try to regulate the taking of wildlife and often intervene in natural processes by breeding and stocking favored species, by manipulating the physical environment, and by exterminating species considered vermin because they harm preferred wildlife. Frequently these agencies fix bounded territories whose sole purpose is to protect wildlife from human depredation. In these reserves, humans are excluded save for regulated excursions to view wildlife.

Some state-owned lands become potent symbols of national identity. The monuments, sites, gardens, and walks of the national capital; the carefully maintained terrain of major battles; or the grounds of a vast military cemetery are all bounded areas sacred to the nation and its history. So also are the state-owned natural parks that surround and protect dramatically appealing natural features: active volcanoes, steam geysers, immense river canyons, glaciers, mountains, coral reefs, and so on. Such features have come to be viewed as part of the national property and are to be made accessible to all by the nation-state. The national parks system in the United States is among the most developed and extensive in the world, but other nations have their own versions of this territorial definition of nature. The nation-state's proprietorial rights in these areas are to be maintained in perpetuity. Citizens have tightly controlled rights of access to these sites, but nothing beyond that. Almost all forms of natural resource exploitation and economic production on these sites—save tourism—are prohibited. Sacral qualities are to be retained by preservation, by change-lessness. The transformations of the market and capitalist development are to be excluded and restrained by this categorization.

PEASANT SOCIETIES AND LAND MARKETS

Freely transferable landed property rights often threaten community iden-tity, social stability, and sense of place—especially if these permit outsiders to capture control of community land. On the other hand, market forces may serve to open up opportunities for members of local elites to acquire land and hence gain more power within their community.

Community struggles with land markets have been a central theme in the recent history of the agrarian societies of Europe and Asia. During the late medieval and early modern centuries, peasant communities across Europe, Asia, and parts of Africa developed strong, resilient organizational structures that controlled land use and restricted membership in the village. The village and its lands constituted a defined territorial unit. In these hierarchical societies, village elites or notables held dominant power—power that early modern states found useful to foster and support. Headmen and councils from dominant families and households gathered and paid land taxes, negotiated with landlords and tax farmers, kept order, dispensed justice, and organized village defenses when regimes collapsed. Kinship ties between dominant peasant households expressed in shared lineage or caste idioms facilitated operation of these institutions.

Depending upon the intensity of land use and modes of cultivation, individual property rights in land remained with individual families or households in peasant societies. These rights did not depend upon prior recognition from the state but emerged when "land is a scarce good that can be made to yield continuously and reliably over the long term by intensive methods."[13] Well-tended, irrigated, manured garden plots, for example, were passed down from one generation to the other in most peas-ant societies. Individual property rights did not, however, generally confer the right of alienation beyond the community or lineage, but did permit temporary use, borrowing, or leasing among households of the same lineage or community.

Beyond intensively cultivated garden lands, dominant peasant elites acted as managers of village lands and natural resources under common property institutions. As population densities increased in areas of seden-tary cultivation, individual communities found it useful to restrict access to and control resource extraction from village pastures, irrigation works, forests, and wastes. Local elites devised organizational structures, rules, and enforcement mechanisms that ensured sustained land use and provided access (usually unequal) to all members of the community. Access to these lands was an important income supplement to all, but especially to the poorer members of each community.

The overall trend has been for market forces to weaken and ultimately destroy common property regimes and to weaken the territorial powers of village elites. Vigorous demand and efficient land markets have made it more difficult for village elites to regulate landownership and occupancy within the village. This change has not been carried out without contestation, protest, and at times violence. The transition to individualized property rights in community lands has varied in space, time, and speed. Pro-market policies by states have hastened this transition. Anti-market policies sometimes have slowed the process, but have never stopped it completely. Today, local common property regimes are vestigial and close to extinction.[14]

Descriptions of this process form a staple of the historical literature for agrarian societies. The question of enclosure and the commons informed the theorizing of the classical economists. In early modern Europe, common property controls over village lands and resources were ubiquitous both west and east of the Elbe River.[15] The protracted process of peasant emancipation involved commutation or freedom from manorial obligations; partition of common lands among those who had previously held rights of access; and concentration of scattered plots of arable land under one owner.[16] As these legal reforms occurred, markets in land penetrated the countryside and commercialization of agriculture followed. As early as the sixteenth century, the peasant communal institutions in the manorial villages of southern England felt market pressures and began to be subject to enclosure.[17] On the continent, it was not until the early nineteenth century that the French Revolution triggered legal reforms in France and then in Germany by mid-century.[18]

The major exception is Russia. By the seventeenth century, the Russian *mir*, or commune, had evolved into "the most extreme form of communal control over agrarian terrain anywhere in Europe." Nothing resembling the enclosures to the west occurred in Russia.[19] The abolition of serfdom in 1861 left legal control of land under the commune, which periodically repartitioned land among its members. Challenges to the collective authority of the commune over its members and lands came with new migratory labor opportunities and with some modest consolidation of lands by wealthier peasants who could control repartition. However, the mir remained impervious to land markets until the Stolypin reforms of 1909.[20]

Asian agrarian societies went through similar processes. In the mid-seventeenth century, the victorious Manchus dismantled the manorial social formation of the Ming dynasty with its landlords and serfs and reapportioned land to newly enfranchised village communities of smallholding peasants.[21] To increase rural production and state revenues, the Qing regime actively supported and encouraged peasant smallholding ownership rights. The state also actively encouraged land reclamation to increase production. Nevertheless in the later Qing, corporate landholdings of lineages and village common property lands became increasingly vulnerable to active land markets as internal settlement frontiers closed.[22] A brisk land market emerged despite continuing rights of preemption on sales of land. Sellers retained the right to recover the land by repayment of the sale price or, if the value of the land had gone up, to seek an additional payment from the buyer. This was a reflection of the deep-seated Chinese belief that land was held in trust for a family. There was also a longstanding division of subsoil and surface rights, each of which could be pawned, sold, or mortgaged.[23]

In Tokugawa Japan, where land was formally inalienable, one estimate puts communally managed village forests and meadows at 12 million hectares. When formal rights of alienation in land were introduced, village lands were steadily reduced to approximately 3 million hectares today.[24]

In early modern India, sedentary peasant communities vigorously expanded cultivation throughout the subcontinent.[25] As they did so, they constructed village communities that actively managed village lands and resources. Rural land markets for rights of occupancy and cultivation remained relatively undeveloped and village common property institutions unchallenged until the British colonial period. Thereafter, brisk markets in land developed in nearly every region of sedentary cultivation in the subcontinent, and communal property rights declined accordingly.[26]

In North Africa the same patterns emerged. In early modern lower Egypt, for example, land markets, circumscribed by tight elite control over the transfer and working of cultivated lands in each village, were freed and extended by liberal reforms under Khedive Ismail in the 1860s.[27]

Sub-Saharan East Africa followed a slightly different path in the absence of strong, centralizing early modern indigenous states. Population growth, land intensification, and peasantization took place under more loosely organized chieftaincies and patrilineages. It was only after colonial conquest in the late nineteenth century that land markets appeared. The experience of the cattle-keeping, horticultural Chagga peoples on the slopes of Mount Kilimanjaro or the Kipsigis of western Kenya illustrates this process.[28]

The loss of community-managed lands to expanding cultivation and private landownership in modern agrarian societies removed an important asset for all, but especially for poorer peasant families. Peasant communities lost a significant buffer against scarcity. Those commodities and amenities found beyond the cultivated fields of the village, in the interstitial spaces of woods, grassland, and wetland were a significant part of household resources. Readily gathered fuelwood that provided cheap energy for domestic cooking and heating purposes was but one of the many resources accessible to the poorest rural family. Supplemental foodstuffs, medicines, and building materials were literally at hand.[29] These products coupled with grazing for a few animals and the produce of small plots of land offered modest subsistence despite the vagaries of the local labor market.

LAND, PROPERTY RIGHTS, AND URBAN SPACE

One of the most significant global social processes since 1800 has been massive growth in the size and number of large cities. Rural-to-urban migration and natural increase have placed a rising percentage of the world's population into city life. Over the last half century since 1950, this trend has accelerated. In 1985 the percentage of the world population living in urban areas had reached 2 billion persons or just over 43 percent of the total (up from 726 million and 29 percent in 1950).[30] At present several metropolises have populations of over 10 million; and one, Mexico City, is over 20 million. The number of cities with over half a million in population has risen to nearly a thousand.

The world's cities have also expanded steadily in territory, although not proportionate to their growth in human numbers. There has been a continuing compression of urban space as a result. More and more people have been crowding into proportionately less space. Urban land has been increasingly needed simply for buildings with a consequent decline in open or green space. In Mexico City, a population of over 20 million today is crowded into 2,700 square kilometers of land, only 6 percent of the land area is not occupied by buildings and roads. The average green space available to each Mexico City inhabitant is just 5 square meters.[31]

This process has had obvious implications for global land use and for converging systems of property rights in urban land. Property rights regimes in cities, despite local peculiarities, are remarkably alike. Cities have expanded in territory, although not proportionate to their growth in human numbers. In every growing city, urban land generally has risen sharply in value as demand for urban space has increased. In every growing city, land markets have proved to be extraordinarily powerful forces. The struggle over access to and control of urban lands became one of the most contested areas in modern and post-modern life. Speculation in land just prior to urban expansion or improvement has been a primary avenue to the accumulation of wealth and capital. Ownership of prime urban properties is generally a guarantee of rising revenue streams and appreciating capital values for both buildings and land. The twin forces of capitalism and industrialism require a continuing creative process of construction, alteration, destruction, and movement in the use and configuration of urban space.

Nevertheless, cities generally are resistant to change in land use. Capital invested in the built environment with its fixed buildings, streets, and other infrastructural elements has its own inertia, its own trajectory once established. Urban land market forces generally operate within the larger spatial configuration of each city. As David Harvey puts it, the contemporary city "forms what we might call a *palimpsest*, a composite landscape made up of different built forms superimposed upon each other with the passage of time."[32] Cities become more and more "sclerotic" as incremental changes are made in their physical fabric generation after generation.

Occasionally, extraordinary political agreement permits radical changes in cityscapes. Examples of such moments include the British Indian colonial regime's authoritarian power to drive wide boulevards through crowded lower-class neighborhoods (slums) in early twentieth-century Bombay and Calcutta. Rhetorical appeal to the sanitation virtues of opening up the high-density, crowded slums of the city to light and air was coupled with fears of Indian political unrest in slum areas.[33]

Population growth arising from economic growth in cities exacerbates the problem of land markets. Urban elites invariably were torn between the temptations to profit from unrestricted operation of land markets—as rentiers, as developers, as speculators—and the need to resist and control market forces. Elites in every industrial city have resorted to territorial strategies to control land use and to tame the urban land market. Their continuing effort to attain some level of social and political stability and to foster a sense of place and urban identity leads to the sequestering of urban land from the market. As with national territory and the nation-state, cities retained control of municipal property to meet the space needs of city government, to create streets and other spaces for public transit, and to reserve land for monuments and other sacred sites.

The new nineteenth-century sciences of urban planning, city management, and public health drew their strength from the practice of zoning urban land for specific purposes.[34] Within each zoned area, municipal codes set out detailed rules for land use and buildings that would be consistent with that use and with the public welfare. Particular attention was paid to segregating and securing residential space for upper-class and elite residents of the city from intrusion by the lower classes.

The greatest strain in urban land use and property rights has been that caused by poor migrants to the cities seeking space in which to live. Aside from earning a living, their greatest struggle has been to obtain tolerable, affordable housing within reasonable proximity to their work. Access to housing involves some form of property rights in urban space—whether as tolerated squatters or as tenants and even eventually as owners. Tenement and slum dwellers could and did organize themselves to press for concessions from landlords and from the municipality. These ranged from due process protections for tenants, to provision of basic amenities, to occupancy rights, to rent control. In other words, they sought protection from the untrammeled land market. In this struggle a sense of place and strong community identities emerged over time. These were reinforced by the tendency of migrants to cluster in areas according to ethnic and regional origin.

Somewhat paradoxically, the interests of poor, lower-class urbanites in gaining rights to a modicum of living space coincided with the interests of most members of urban elites. The economic health of the city demanded cheap labor in industry and service sectors. The political health of the city required relative contentment among the lower classes. Extreme poverty and inadequate sanitation among its poorer inhabitants threatened the public health of the city. Crowding and crime among the urban poor threatened the physical security of the upper classes.

Between 1850 and 1950, the cities of the industrial age absorbed vast numbers of migrants, put them to work, and provided housing in tenements. In city after city, the same process occurred. Across Europe, Asia, Africa, and the Americas, the migratory flow began. Whether located in imperial countries or in the colonial world, industrializing cities took in migrants from the surrounding countryside. Whether they were primate cities like New York or provincial centers like Cleveland, steady inflows of migrants had to be accommodated within the territory of the city.[35]

Slowly, in each city municipal reformers and lower-class people themselves generated a series of entitlements and reforms that gave meaningful property rights to tenants of the urban lower class.[36] Rights of occupancy and standards of amenities began to coalesce in municipal codes in cities around the world. Various municipal projects to build and subsidize worker's housing came to fruition by the 1920s. Driven in part by the concern for public health, slum clearance projects often preceded the construction of new public housing schemes. Under varying mixes of private and public ownership, lower-class dwellers in the industrial cities of the world obtained legally recognized rights to urban living space.

Bombay illustrates this global process. The founding of what proved to be profitable cotton textile mills in Bombay by Indian entrepreneurs launched the city's industrial base as early as the 1860s. Rural migrants in search of work poured into the city from its surrounding agricultural districts. Between the first census in 1872 and that in 1941, the population more than doubled from 644,000 to 1.5 million.[37] Often rural migrants worked seasonally in between the busiest times of the agricultural year and returned home. To keep good jobs, however, required full-time residence in the city. Many migrants practiced circular migration. Male workers from as far away as 200 miles from Bombay kept their families in their villages, remitted their surplus pay, returned on holidays, and retired to the village.[38] The pattern of circular migration from the countryside encouraged retention of strong intercaste ties with fellow villagers in Bombay. Groups of single men from the same village rented living space and ate together.[39]

Because land in colonial Bombay was limited by its island configuration (about the size of Manhattan), urban living space near the textile mills was scarce. Wealthy property owners had already constructed five- to seven-story dwellings, many of which were converted into tenements with one-room accommodations per family. The textile mills built additional multi-story tenements to rent to their workers. Private developers built two-story structures to accommodate shops on the ground level and tightly packed tenants on the second floor. What came to be called *chawls* might have as many as 500 persons living in a single structure. Each family had a room 10 feet by 10 feet, opening onto a communal veranda with shared bathrooms on each level connected to a single shaft and a single standpipe for water. Late nineteenth-century population densities in these slum districts went as high as 1,200 per acre. The 1911 Census reported that over 80 percent of Bombay's population lived in chawls.[40]

Housing for textile workers was concentrated in a working-class neighborhood known as Girangaon. In spite of intense rural ties, working-class life in Bombay developed its own distinctive character. Community organizations, such as chawl committees, wrestling gymnasia (*akhadas*), and Muslim neighborhood societies (*melas*) flourished. Neighborhood bosses (*dadas*) headed gangs and operated protection rackets, but also protected their neighborhoods from street violence and rioting. Jobbers who contracted with the mills for labor and trade union leaders became spokespersons for community interests.[41]

Rent control, imposed as early as 1918 and retained permanently after World War II, had the effect of giving protected tenants substantial property rights. The mills and other owners of rent-controlled chawls abandoned any investment in the buildings because the rents were so low.

As a result, sitting tenants were free to sell their rights for thousands of rupees to new tenants, who would then pay minuscule rents to the mills or other landlords.[42]

As populations stabilized in these neighborhoods, residents developed a strong sense of place and an attachment to the intimacy and community life of the chawl.[43] As Norma Evenson comments: "Over the years the chawl was to become part of the image and legend of Bombay, even spawning writers who celebrated the intimate and supportive social life engendered by shared balconies and courtyards. Like many city neighborhoods despised by planners, the chawl districts could inspire deep affection and loyalty among their inhabitants."[44]

After World War II, as the colonial world disintegrated, these relatively harmonious arrangements in Bombay and other industrial cities around the world were superseded by vast new waves of urban migration. Only in North America and Europe have suburbanization, upper-class and elite flight, and the automobile culture caused relative decline of many industrial cities such as Baltimore and Liverpool.[45] As is well understood, over the last half-century most world cities have grown in size at a pace previously unknown in human history.

In present-day Bombay, for example, close to half of the inhabitants of the city, an estimated 6 million or more people, live in squatter settlements or slums, not chawls. These people are not destitute, like the 100,000 or more pavement dwellers so visible in the city; rather they have some resources and income. Most are migrant families in Bombay; some recent; some back two or even three generations.[46] Almost all are employed in either service or industry. They work as servants in the high-rise buildings for the middle- and upper-class residents of the city. They are carpenters, mechanics, orderlies, or even clerks in offices and in factories. Many work in industrial establishments within the slum itself, such as in small metal fabricating shops, welding operations, paint mixing, metal foundries, leather tanneries, or plastic recycling operations (to make plastic sheets sold to slum dwellers). Men, women, and children work long hours in these establishments. Many women do handwork, sewing, and assembling in the home. These are working-class and lower–middle class people who have dignity and aspirations for the future.

As soon as a family occupies a few square meters of land and puts up a few flimsy wooden sticks, plastic film, and a few boards, it has established informal ownership rights to that plot. Formal landowners find it impossible to evict hut dwellers by going through the courts once they are established. Their only recourse is to informal coercion. Often the easier course of action is to employ criminal gangs who collect regular rent from each slum dweller. Payment of protection money permits the slum family to remain and to improve their home. Frequently absentee landowners simply ignore the situation and cede control of the land to the gangs, who have no formal legal title.

Bombay slums are crowded; the slum dweller has only the space occupied by his or her hut. Connecting lanes are really footpaths so narrow that even motor scooters cannot be ridden but have to be pushed. Lacking stormwater drainage, Bombay's slums are often flooded in the rainy season. As time passes, the inhabitants make improvements: They build with corrugated iron and brick; they connect to electricity legally or more often illegally; they pay to have water piped to their homes. They decorate; buy appliances, TVs, and videocassette players; and buy electric fans. In the older Bombay slums, the majority of the inhabitants have electricity.

Slum dwellers develop informal property rights over time that can be bought and sold on an emerging land and housing market. In established slums an improved house can be sold for more than Rs. 100,000. A continuing threat to their tenure lies in the possibility of a more valuable use for the land. If private owners are determined, they can buy off the gangsters and drive off the slum dwellers. Or the state can clear a slum in the name of urban improvement. Generally, however, older slums serve as massive vote banks for Indian politicians who prevent demolition. Indian social reformers also campaign against slum clearance.[47] In a final stage, an improved slum can be recognized as fit for human habitation by action of the state of Maharashtra, and its dwellers receive formal rights and recognition of their property. When this happens, community latrines, water taps, public lighting, schools, and welfare centers appear.

Bombay's experience was shared by other cities in Latin America, Africa, the Middle East, and Asia. The sheer volume of migration to the cities overwhelmed previous arrangements for creating and sustaining rights to urban living space. By and large urban elites in these postcolonial cities have been unable and unwilling to accommodate or to control the vast numbers of newcomers. Migrants have acted spontaneously to move beyond the territorial constraints of bounded neighborhoods, house lots, and the formal land market. Instead, they have built audacious squatter settlements, without tenure and without permission, upon any accessible urban land and have created their own property regimes.[48]

Although subject to sporadic demolition and removal, most squatter settlements survive over years and decades to develop coherent community identities and consciousness. Residents make incremental improvements in their homes, improve water supplies, and even find ways to obtain electrical power. As time passes, an informal property market emerges in which prices paid for improved dwellings and lots can rise to substantial heights. The state may formally recognize and record the property rights of slum dwellers in some cases.[49] In democratic, but even in authoritarian, regimes, slum dwellers begin to have a political voice that helps to stabilize their tenure through their resistance to slum clearance. Social reformers, rather than supporting destruction of working-class slums and rebuilding of public projects as in the older industrial city model, organize slum dwellers to fight off such attempts and to press for incremental improvements in their situation.[50]

This has been true even for socialist states that have attempted to control migration and that, in theory, permitted no land markets or private property. Today nascent land markets have appeared in Russia, China, and Eastern Europe. In Soviet Russia industrialization and collectivization of agriculture unleashed 23 million Soviet peasants to move to cities between 1926 and 1939. Despite imposition of internal passports, the Soviet authorities failed to control and direct this flow. Soviet urban planners failed to build anywhere-near-adequate workers' housing, to provide transportation, or to regulate the shantytowns that sprang up around Soviet cities. Russian peasant migrants to the cities retained their communal organization in workers' *artels* despite heavy official indoctrination aimed at creating a worker's consciousness.[51] Migrants living in shantytowns developed their own occupancy rights over urban space.

For the first three decades or so of its existence, the People's Republic of China succeeded in controlling urban growth and migration from the countryside to the city. The post-1949 government planned and built uniform, extensive low-rise cityscapes consisting of three- to five-story buildings with mixed residential, health, educational, industrial, and commercial activities in each spatial unit. These walled wards, organized by work unit, offered facilities for living, recreation, shopping, and work within walking distance. The guarded and gated inhabitants were tightly controlled and monitored. Without work permits that also provided registration and a place to live, rural folk could not easily migrate to the city.[52]

After 1980, however, in a new era of reform, these controls were relaxed. From 50 million to 70 million peasants officially domiciled in the countryside have moved to the cities illegally and form a "floating population." Earning their living in the most arduous and ill-paid of urban work, these migrants are still not able to obtain urban certification and are denied access to official housing. They live with relatives, in small workers' hotels, and in various forms of shanties and shantytowns. Contemporary China now has the same sort of slum population found in other countries around the world.[53]

PLACE, ELITES, AND THE NATION-STATE

Since the fifteenth century, land markets in every world region have dissolved the constraints imposed by states and local communities and converged toward a shared world system. Steady population increases, economic growth, and technological advances over these centuries have imparted economic value to a greater and greater share of the earth's land surface. In spite of the vicissitudes of political struggles and shifting ideologies, the long-term trend is toward more transparent, accessible markets in private property rights in land. (Currently, the People's Republic of China is the most significant exception to this trend.) In these markets land use shifts rapidly and suddenly to meet economic incentives. A unified, price-fixing world market in land is still subject to the obstacles of nation-state territorial control, but the numbers of transnational land transactions continue to rise.

Nation-states, and behind them the international order, provide guarantees for long-term stability of ownership, for the validity of contracts, and for monetary stability. Scarcities of suitable lands lead to rising prices and rising demand. Landed property rights permit rapidly changing land use aimed at the highest economic benefit for each parcel of land bought or sold. This is by no means a solely western idea or a process driven solely by westerners, but is a global phenomenon.[54]

From one perspective, human management of land everywhere has become more centralized, more intrusive, and more instrumentally effective. Large-scale capitalist forms of agriculture and resource extraction are prominently visible throughout the world. Land use decisions increasingly reflect the narrow interests of large-scale, complex organizations and the professional interests of the land managers they employ. Often these managers have little or no direct knowledge of the tracts that they control. Over the early modern and modern centuries, the intimate, personal tie formerly seen between the land manager and his or her lands (even on the largest estates) has been altered, attenuated, or eliminated altogether.[55]

Intensifying land markets fostered ambivalent reactions. The centralizing state as ultimate owner has acted decisively to set aside bounded tracts of land from the market to meet national objectives. Simultaneously, political elites in both early modern and modern states have concluded that relatively unconstricted land markets stimulate economic growth. (The twentieth-century socialist attempt to suppress land markets and private property in land in the former USSR, Eastern Europe, Cuba, and the People's Republic of China demonstrated the costs of this policy.) A surprising number of sharply contested national issues arise from these conflicting notions of appropriate land use.

All nation-states concern themselves with the long-term stability of land rights and their recording and demarcation. But more than this, ultimate control of land use is absolutely key to the centralizing state and helps to define national values and character. Print and new electronic communications permit visual images of land use to be deployed. They engender an intimate sense of shared management and concern for the national territory. It is at this juncture that the interests of local elites and the territorial state coincide. National identities and local identities are formed from converging territorial interests.

The triumph of converging forms of alienable private landownership does not end the preoccupation of local elites—both rural and urban— with land. They struggle to control the allocation of property and the rules by which it is to be used. The worldwide tension between the local community and land markets and between the local community and the state continues. Property rights in land remain a central point of conflict, negotiation, compromise, and tension in every community. The formal arena for this struggle lies in the law, litigation, and courts or in administrative offices of the nation-state. Modern land use is controlled by territorial strategies of planning, classification by area—that is, zoning—and development codes. Local governments, guided and limited by state and national laws and regulations, try to control and tame land markets by demarcation of both urban and rural lands for specific purposes: residential, commercial, recreational, industrial, and municipal, among others. Zoning of course also permits various forms of social, political, and ethnic segregation by territory as well. These approaches mirror territorial segregation practiced by the nation-state. The informal arena for conflict lies in devices such as social and economic pressure, extralegal violence, or other coercive measures undertaken by elites.

Behind this territorial strategy lies the deeply emotional connection of people with land and their physical environment. The sense of place engendered by occupancy and use of land is an important source of community identity. Landscape and cityscape are part of the power of place. Nothing is so disorienting as displacement from previous implacement. The pathology of displacement, of refugeeism, includes "disorientation, memory loss, homelessness, depression and various modes of estrangement from self and others."[56] Land is one of our most deeply felt concerns, among those that affect our immediate sense of security and resonate with our deepest moral, aesthetic, and religious attitudes. The physical environment of early childhood imprints a profound and indelible impression on personality. Our earliest memories contain images of space and land use that are part of our identity. Nostalgia for a past land use and configuration of space is an important, often unacknowledged force in human affairs.[57] It is also important to note that strong emotive ties to place are not necessarily a product of childhood memories or long residence. In today's mobile societies, new residents frequently find themselves rapidly invested in a sense of place as they engage issues of land use.

Those most involved in the struggle over property rights in land continue to be the elite members of the village, town, city, county, or its equivalent administrative unit who control land and its uses. Elites engage in personal interaction in various circumscribed social spaces under accepted rules. Local elites, despite the size of the territorial unit—even a very large city—by and large have face-to-face contact. These conflicts elicit a discourse based upon varying ideologies of belief and morality in which desirable land uses are debated. Local elite stability rests in large measure on its capacity to control and dominate this discourse. Nevertheless, local notables are constrained from applying a pure calculus of rational advantage or profit to land transactions. Prevailing ideologies and metaphors by which they legitimate their power shape their calculations. The long-term health and interest of the community must be a consideration for local elites. Long-sighted policies are often the privilege of the privileged when it comes to land.

Improved communications have made the boundaries of the community more permeable than ever before. New ideologies and new values intrude easily and quickly into the community and contribute to the debate and struggle. Increasingly, elite struggles over land use and management spill over into public debate and assessment. Participatory politics force expansion of local elites to accommodate new members in a more diverse and enlarged dominant group. Simultaneously, prices in modern land markets are fixed by ever-widening and enlarging market areas.

Perhaps the most typical conflict over property rights in land—evoked in numerous literary accounts—is that over the exploitation of a natural resource that has become valuable and marketable. Prices for certain tracts of land soar. Should this exploitation be permitted? Issues of stability, tradition, and nostalgia are pitted against the excitement of new wealth and productivity in internecine elite conflict. In recent decades a new environmental or ecological ethic has entered the ideology of appropriate land use among elites.

NOTES

1. See John F. Richards, "Land Transformation," in *The Earth As Transformed by Human Action: Global and Regional Changes in the Biosphere over the Past 300 Years*, ed. B. L. Turner (Cambridge and New York: Cambridge University Press with Clark University, 1990); and John F. Richards, "World Environmental History and Economic Development," in *Sustainable Development of the Biosphere*, ed. R. E. Munn and William C. Clark (Cambridge, Cambridgeshire, and New York: Cambridge University Press, 1986).

2. For a similar approach to world history, see David Hackett Fischer, *The Great Wave: Price Revolutions and the Rhythm of History* (New York: Oxford University Press, 1996). Fischer's Appendix O, "Economics and History," contains a stimulating discussion of the value of descriptive history and the benefits of framing a *problematique* or a set of empirical questions.

3. For an example of renewed interest in territoriality, nationalism, and the nation-state, see Winichakul Thongchai, *Siam Mapped: A History of the Geo-body of a Nation* (Honolulu: University of Hawaii Press, 1994).

4. For a recent comparative treatment of this process, see Richard John Perry, *From Time Immemorial: Indigenous Peoples and State Systems*, 1st ed. (Austin: University of Texas Press, 1996). See also John F. Richards, "Only a World Perspective Is Significant: Settlement Frontiers and Property Rights in Early Modern World History," in *The Humanities and the Environment*, ed. Jill Conway, Kenneth Keniston, and Leo Marx (Cambridge: MIT Press, 1998). Fernand Braudel, *Civilization and Capitalism, 15th–18th Century*, vol. I, 1st California paperback printing, (Berkeley: University of California Press, 1992). *The Structures of Everyday Life*, makes a similar point (pp. 98–103).

5. John Hemming, *Red Gold: The Conquest of the Brazilian Indians*, rev. ed. (London: Papermac, 1995) for the Tupi; and Anna Lowenhaupt Tsing, *In the Realm of the Diamond Queen: Marginality in an Out-of-the-Way Place* (Princeton, N.J.: Princeton University Press, 1993) for the present-day Dayak.

6. See, for example, Linda S. Parker, *Native American Estate: The Struggle over Indian and Hawaiian Lands* (Honolulu: University of Hawaii Press, 1989).

7. R. J. P. Kain and Elizabeth Baigent, *The Cadastral Map in the Service of the State: A History of Property Mapping* (Chicago: University of Chicago Press, 1992).

8. James C. Scott, "State Simplifications: Nature, Space, and People," *The Journal of Political Philosophy* 3 (1995): 191–233.

9. For one example of this process, see Peter Robb, "The Colonial State and Constructions of Indian Identity: An Example on the Northeast Frontier in the 1880s," *Modern Asian Studies* 31 (1997): 245–83. In this essay Robb describes the demarcation of the Naga Hills of southeastern Assam by British administrators and the subsequent definition of the Nagas as imperial subjects.

10. Henry E. Lowood, "The Calculating Forester: Quantification, Cameral Science, and the Emergence of Scientific Forestry Management in Germany," in *The Quantifying Spirit in the 18th Century*, ed. Tore Frängsmyr, Robin E. Rider, and J. L. Heilbron (Berkeley: University of California Press, 1990), 315–42.

11. See Paul W. Hirt, *A Conspiracy of Optimism: Management of the National Forests since World War Two, Our Sustainable Future* 6 (Lincoln: University of Nebraska Press, 1994), for the United States national forests.

12. The scholar most responsible for bringing the issue of fire to our attention is Stephen Pyne. His global synthesis is *World of Fire: The Culture of Fire on Earth* (New York: Henry Holt and Company, 1995). See also Stephen J. Pyne, *Vestal Fire: An Environmental History, Told through Fire, of Europe and Europe's Encounter with the World*, (Seattle: University of Washington Press, 1997).

13. Robert McNetting, *Smallholders, Householders: Farm Families and the Ecology of Intensive, Sustainable Agriculture*, (Stanford, Calif.: Stanford University Press, 1993), 158.

14. This is not to deny that those peasant-run systems which survive—high mountain pastures and local irrigation systems—are not important for the lessons that they can teach us. See Elinor Ostrom, *Governing the Commons: The Evolution of Institutions for Collective Action*, (Cambridge and New York: Cambridge University Press, 1990).

15. Werner Rösener, *The Peasantry of Europe* (Oxford and Cambridge: Blackwell, 1994), "Neighbors and Village Communities," 157–70. Rösener maintains that the authoritarian regimes of the estates east of the Elbe did not succeed in eliminating a resilient village community in Eastern Europe.

16. Rösener, 172.

17. The enclosure and commons literature on early modern England is gigantic. See Robert C. Allen, *Enclosure and the Yeoman* (Oxford and New York: Clarendon Press with Oxford University Press, 1992); and J. M. Neeson, *Commoners: Common Right, Enclosure, and Social Change in England, 1700–1820* Past and present publications (Cambridge and New York: Cambridge University Press, 1993).

18. Rösener, 174–84.

19. Rösener, 168.

20. The clearest description of the commune is to be found in Christine D. Worobec, *Peasant Russia: Family and Community in the Post-Emancipation Period* (Princeton, N.J.: Princeton University Press, 1991), 1–41. See also the following: Ben Eklof and Stephen Frank, *The World of the Russian Peasant: Post-Emancipation Culture and Society* (Boston: Unwin Hyman, 1990); Esther Kingston-Mann, Timothy Mixter, and Jeffrey Burds, *Peasant Economy, Culture, and Politics of European Russia, 1800–1921* (Princeton, N.J.: Princeton University Press, 1991); Roger P. Bartlett, *Land Commune and Peasant Community in Russia: Communal Forms in Imperial and Early Soviet Society* (New York: St. Martin's Press, 1990).

21. Sucheta Mazumdar, *Sugar and Society in China: Peasants, Technology, and the World Market*, Harvard-Yenching Institute monograph series 45 (Cambridge, Mass.: Harvard University Asia Center, 1998) 216–17.

22. Mazumdar, 217–30. Peter C. Perdue, *Exhausting the Earth: State and Peasant in Hunan, 1500–1850*, Harvard East Asian monographs 130 (Cambridge, Mass.: Council on East Asian Studies, Harvard University, 1987).

23. Perdue, 136–40. Also, Anne Osborne, "Highlands and Lowlands: Economic and Ecological Interactions in the Lower Yangzi Region under the Qing," in *Sediments of Time: Environment and Society in Chinese History*, ed. Mark Elvin and Liu Ts'ui-jung (Cambridge: Cambridge University Press, 1998), 203–34; and Anne Osborne, "The Local Politics of Land Reclamation in the Lower Yangzi Highlands," *Late Imperial China* 15 (1994): 1–46; and Tai-Shun Yang, *Property Rights and Constitutional Order in Imperial China* (Bloomington, Indiana, Ph.D. dissertation, 1987).

24. M. A. McKean, "Management of Traditional Common Lands (*Iriachi*) in Japan," in *Proceedings of the Conference on Common Property Resource Management, April 21–26, 1985*, ed. National Research Council (U.S.) Panel on Common Property Resource Management (Washington, D.C.: National Academy Press, 1986), 553–89. See also J. Mark Ramseyer, "Political Economy of Institutions and Decisions," *Odd Markets in Japanese History: Law and Economic Growth* (Cambridge and New York: Cambridge University Press, 1996).

25. For an example of an early modern settlement frontier, see Richard M. Eaton, *The Rise of Islam and the Bengal Frontier, 1204–1760* (Berkeley: University of California Press, 1993).

26. See Minoti Chakravarty-Kaul, *Common Lands and Customary Law: Institutional Change in North India over the Past Two Centuries* (Delhi: Oxford University Press, 1996). For a discussion of the colonial state's destruction of communal lands in nineteenth-century Sri Lanka, see Nihal Perera, "Transitions—Asia and Asian America," *Society and Space: Colonialism, Nationalism, and Postcolonial Identity in Sri Lanka*, (Boulder, Colo.: Westview Press, 1998).

27. See Kenneth M. Cuno, *The Pasha's Peasants: Land, Society, and Economy in Lower Egypt, 1740–1858*, Cambridge Middle East Library 27 (Cambridge and New York: Cambridge University Press, 1992).

28. Sally Falk Moore, *Social Facts and Fabrications: "Customary" Law on Kilimanjaro 1880–1980* The Lewis Henry Morgan Lectures, 1981 (Cambridge, Cambridgeshire, and New York: Cambridge University Press, 1986); and Michael Donovan, "Capturing the Land: Kipsigis Narratives of Progress," *Comparative Studies in Society and History* 36 (1996): 658–86.

29. For an eloquent argument to this effect for England, see Neeson, *Commoners*, especially pp. 158–84, "The Uses of Waste."

30. Brian J. Berry, "Urbanization," in *The Earth as Transformed by Human Action: Global and Regional Changes in the Biosphere over the Past 300 Years*, ed. B. L. Turner

(Cambridge and New York: Cambridge University Press with Clark University, 1990), Table 7.5, "The World's Urban Population, 1950–1985," 116. See Ali Madanipour, *Tehran: The Making of a Metropolis*, World Cities Series (Chichester and New York: John Wiley, 1998), 137–40 for the disappearance of green space in Tehran in the last half of the twentieth century.

31. Adrian Guillermo Aguilar et al., "The Basin of Mexico," in *Regions at Risk: Comparisons of Threatened Environments*, ed. Jeanne X. Kasperson, Roger E. Kasperson, and B. L. Turner II (Tokyo: United Nations University Press, 1995), 327.

32. David Harvey, *Justice, Nature, and the Geography of Difference* (Cambridge, Mass.: Blackwell Publishers, 1996), 417.

33. Norma Evenson, *The Indian Metropolis: A View toward the West* (New Haven, Conn.: Yale University Press, 1989) 113–45.

34. Brian Ladd, *Urban Planning and Civic Order in Germany: 1860–1914* (Cambridge, Mass.: Harvard University Press, 1990) discusses Germany's lead in this innovation.

35. Kenneth A. Scherzer, *The Unbounded Community: Neighborhood Life and Social Structure in New York City, 1830–1875* (Durham, N.C.: Duke University Press, 1992); and W. Dennis Keating, Norman Krumholz, and David C. Perry, *Cleveland: A Metropolitan Reader* (Kent, Ohio: Kent State University Press, 1995).

36. See, for example, J. A. Yelling, *Slums and Slum Clearance in Victorian London*, The London Research Series in Geography 10 (London and Boston: Allen and Unwin, 1986).

37. Rajnarayan Chandavarkar, *The Origins of Industrial Capitalism in India: Business Strategies and the Working Classes in Bombay, 1900–1940*, Cambridge South Asian Studies 51 (Cambridge and New York: Cambridge University Press, 1994), 30.

38. Hemalata C. Dandekar, *Men to Bombay, Women at Home: Urban Influence on Sugao Village, Deccan, Maharashtra, India, 1942–1982*, Michigan Papers on South and Southeast Asia 28 (Ann Arbor, Mich.: Center for South and Southeast Asian Studies, University of Michigan, 1986), 219–21.

39. Dandekar, 233.

40. Evenson, 139–42. In less-crowded Calcutta, by contrast, jute mill owners bought up empty land adjacent to their factories and leased large plots to their Indian labor contractors so that they could build lines of thatched-roof, mud-packed bamboo huts clustered around ponds for water. The labor contractors rented cubicles in these huts to the factory workers they recruited for work in the jute mills. These settlements became the *bustees* of Calcutta. Frederic C. Thomas, *Calcutta Poor: Elegies on a City above Pretense*, (Armonk, N.Y.: M. E. Sharpe, 1997), 63–65.

41. Chandavarkar, 168–238.

42. V. S. Naipaul interviewed a chawl resident who in 1985 paid Rs. 35,000 for the lease to a unit and whose rent was only 12.5 Rs. per month. V. S. Naipaul, *India: A Million Mutinies Now*, 1st American ed. (New York: Viking, 1991).

43. Naipaul, 60–69.

44. Evenson, 142.

45. Harvey, *Justice, Nature, and the Geography of Difference*, 404.

46. Jeremy Seabrook, *Life and Labour in a Bombay Slum* (London and New York: Quartet, 1987).

47. See Seabrook, 84–110, for a description of one protest against slum clearing. A documentary film made by Anand Patwardhan, *Bombay, Our City* (First Run Icarus Films, 1990), interprets these events.

48. Joe Lugalla, *Crisis, Urbanization, and Urban Poverty in Tanzania: A Study of Urban Poverty and Survival Politics* (Lanham, Md.: University Press of America, 1995), on p. 43 reports that 70 percent of the total population of Dar es Salaam, Tanzania, are squatters.

49. For example in 1979, Tunis revised its urban code and gave formal approval to established illegal settlements around the city. Elizabeth Vasile, "Devotion as Distinction, Piety as Power: Religious Revival and the Transformation of Space in the Illegal Settlements of Tunis," in *Population, Poverty, and Politics in Middle East Cities*, ed. Michael E. Bonine (Gainesville: University Press of Florida, 1997), 113–40.

50. See Robert Gay, *Popular Organization and Democracy in Rio de Janeiro: A Tale of Two Favelas* (Philadelphia: Temple University Press, 1994).

51. David L. Hoffmann, *Peasant Metropolis: Social Identities in Moscow, 1929–1941*, Studies of the Harriman Institute (Ithaca: Cornell University Press, 1994).

52. Piper Rae Gaubatz, "Urban Transformation in Post-Mao China: Impacts of the Reform Era on China's Urban Form," in *Urban Spaces in Contemporary China: The Potential for Autonomy and Community in Post-Mao China*, ed. Deborah Davis (Washington, D.C.: Woodrow Wilson Center Press; Cambridge and New York: Cambridge University Press, 1995), 28–60.

53. Dorothy J. Solinger, "The Floating Population in the Cities: Chances for Assimilation?" in Davis, et al., 113–39.

54. Douglass North and Paul Thomas make a similar point for property rights in land in Europe and its dominions in *The Rise of the Western World*.

55. See Piers M. Blaikie and H. C. Brookfield, *Land Degradation and Society* (London and New York: Methuen, 1987), for a discussion of this point.

56. Edward S. Casey, *Getting Back into Place: Toward a Renewed Understanding of the Place-World*, Studies in Continental Thought (Bloomington: Indiana University Press, 1993), 38.

57. M. H. Matthews, "Developing Body and Mind," *Making Sense of Place: Children's Understanding of Large-Scale Environments*, (Hemel Hempstead, Hertfordshire and Lanham, Md.: Harvester Wheatsheaf with Barnes and Noble, 1992).

2

Harvests of Chance: Corporate Control of Arable Land in Early Modern Japan

PHILIP C. BROWN

Unstable farming conditions, especially frequent flooding, have been seen as the impetus for Japanese farmers and regional rulers (daimyo) to develop an unusual system of land tenures, one that I will refer to simply as *warichi*. In reality, there was not a single system, but myriad systems with many local names and variant practices. But all of them shared two core features. First, the tie between the so-called landowner and the land he cultivated or managed was indirect. As in a modern joint stock company, what was owned was a "share" of the village agricultural corporation, not a specific asset. That share gave his family the right to manage a certain amount of land, but—with some exceptions—not the right to farm a given piece of land until it was sold or bequeathed to someone else. Second, who farmed what piece of land was determined by chance, not personal choice. Some villages held lotteries on a periodic basis or used a fixed rotation of cultivation rights; others waited until a consensus developed—usually stimulated by loss of a substantial amount of arable land due to flood or landslide—to reassess village land and to reallocate rights to use it. This latter circumstance has suggested to scholars that the system originated as a means for sharing the costs of natural disasters in those areas that were particularly prone to such events. In addition to the normal risks of agriculture, the farmers in warichi areas coped with the consequences of chance in an additional sense—they could not, by their own purchases and sales, determine for more than a brief time which plot of land they would farm.

The existence of these redistributional systems raises two broad questions for students of the relationship between property rights and the environment. On the one hand, standard explanations for the origin of redistribution stress the role of flooding and other environmental factors. On the other, modern scholars often see regimes of corporate tenure such as warichi as the site of inevitable environmental degradation and "tragedy of the commons."

While under attack, the "tragedy of the commons" model remains powerful and the critique continues.[1] The critiques levied against the "tragedy of the commons" model—while effective in noting that commons, private landownership, and public ownership are all subject to resource failure, and while helpful in delineating circumstances in which "commons" has succeeded in the past—are limited in the type of case study they examine. Overwhelmingly, these scholars are concerned with "fugitive resources" (game, water, or fish) or "common lands" used for grazing, fuel, fertilizer, or other products that supplement the main business of farming in rural communities. Studies of medieval European "open field" agriculture represent something of an exception. Clearly off-season uses of the land for pasture were well integrated into the agricultural regime, providing manure for fertilizer and requiring some degree of cooperative management. Yet this common use does not directly control who farms what piece of land nor does it directly take land away from one cultivator to give to another or in other ways suggest the community exercises full use rights (assuming the manor lord is the actual owner) in the land.

The redistribution systems I discuss here involve more than just a part-year community intrusion in farm regimes. They involve direct exercise of community control over who cultivates which particular plot in some, or more commonly all, of the arable land in a village. The land at issue here is not forest or "common lands," but the land on which villagers grew their most important crops. Redistribution practices involve the kind of land in which we expect to find villagers making heavy investments to increase their ability to support their families.

In the remainder of this essay, I will briefly sketch the parameters of variation of these redistribution systems, discuss factors that seem to play a role in the origins and maintenance of them, look more closely at warichi in one region to illustrate its operation, and then make a preliminary attempt to assess the impact on field degradation.

Just what the full range of consequences of this lottery was is the focus of my current research and many questions are yet to be explored. Nonetheless, it is important to state clearly what two of the consequences were not. (1) The system did not, as the open field system did in Europe, impose a system of fairly uniform cropping patterns[2]; (2) Nor did it generally require that the village be "closed." Shares were rented, sold, bequeathed, and so on to nonvillagers in many areas that practiced warichi.[3]

GENERAL OBSERVATIONS

By the end of 1590, all of Japan had sworn allegiance to Toyotomi Hideyoshi; and although Hideyoshi himself would attempt to conquer China in two continental invasions during this decade and although the Tokugawa family would replace him at the start of the seventeenth century, Japan had embarked on more than two centuries of nearly complete domestic peace. Two large, but very localized battles would still be fought among contenders for national power by 1615; but domestic peace enabled domain lords (daimyo) and villagers alike to invest in reestablishing arable lands that had fallen into disuse during the preceding centuries of nation-wide disorder and civil wars.

The political order established by Hideyoshi and his Tokugawa succes-sors was largely an amalgam of quite autonomous baronial (daimyo) domains. While the Hideyoshi and the Shoguns could compel daimyo to provide military service, for example, there was no system of regular, national taxation. Regular duties were not extracted from daimyo, nor were hegemons able to extract taxes from the residents of daimyo domains. The financial foundations of the Shoguns were restricted to those they could tap within the boundaries of their own domains.

The question of determining land tenure systems falls into the same category as taxation: The Shoguns were not capable of determining a national policy. The direct impact of Shogunal laws on land were greater than those of other daimyo by virtue of the area that they administered through their own bureaucratic subordinates—more than one-eighth of Japan. Shogunal policies echoed in other domains as daimyo used them as models for their own administration, but the Shogun could not compel daimyo to adopt a particular policy. At no time during the late-sixteenth to nineteenth centuries did the central political authority have any nation-wide concern with the definition of individual private land rights.[4]

What is striking in regard to Shogunal policies on arable land is the largely hands-off attitude that they reveal even within its own lands. With the exception of a limited effort to restrict the sales of arable land in whole or in part, the Shoguns made no effort to establish a uniform system of tenures within the confines of their own directly administered territories.[5]

In some regions, such as Shogunal lands in Echigo (modern Niigata prefecture) province, warichi was practiced; in other regions it was not. In effect, a village local option was in effect. The villages in Echigo, without Shogunal leadership or regulation, implemented redistribution on their own initiative and designed the detailed regulations to suit the perceived needs of village leadership.

This same phenomenon, the "local option" for villages, was present within daimyo domains as well. That option was common, for example, in Kaga domain for most of the early modern era. Villages chose the circumstances and manner in which they would implement warichi on their own.

This is not to say that domains always left the forms of tenure to villages. From the beginnings of the early modern era, Satsuma (modern Kagoshima prefecture) in Kyushu implemented its own domainwide form of warichi. Tosa (modern Kochi prefecture) in Shikoku also chose to implement a domainwide system of warichi.

This political system, with its substantial autonomy for both domains and villages in the determination of land tenure regimes, resulted in considerable diversity of practice nationally, and sometimes even within a domain. This makes generalization, even within one general type of tenure system such as warichi, very difficult.

Within this political context, the establishment of peace brought a transformation in agriculture and a consequent expansion of Japan's early modern population. The seventeenth-century expansion of arable land was remarkable even when we consider that many lands were being restored after the disruption of a century of civil wars. When daimyo or whole districts cooperated, hundreds of acres of land were opened or converted from dry field to more-calorie-productive rice paddy. By the end of midcentury, the great majority of such large-scale projects had been completed. While some large-scale projects were undertaken later, most were much smaller scale. Individual villages and even individual cultivators continued small-scale reclamation and conversions.

The reduction in scale reflected the margins to which arable lands had been extended. Increasingly, villages debated about conversion of the commons to arable land and pushed into less stable land, exploiting old riverbeds and diluvial deposits, draining swamps, filling in lagoons, and the like. When Japan's first truly national administration was established in the mid–nineteenth century and tax policies changed, cultivation of the most marginal lands was simply abandoned by families that favored other economic activities.

The expansion of cultivated land and the conversion to paddy were sufficient to help support a dramatic increase in both overall population and the expansion of urban areas. Estimates of early seventeenth-century population vary from 12 million to 18 million souls. By the eighteenth century, population had leveled off at roughly 28 million to 30 million. Urban populations exploded. The onset of peace allowed the domain capitals to expand many times their late sixteenth-century populations. Kanazawa, a small village of a few thousand at the time it became the headquarters of the Maeda domain, grew to about 100,000 by the end of the seventeenth century. A swampy village in 1590, Edo became the headquarters of the Tokugawa family and later the Shogunal capital. Its population soon reached three-quarters of a million. Given that there were more than 250 domain lords, all concentrating their armies, support, and administrative staff in similar castle towns, readers can readily imagine the breadth of urban growth even where it was not as dramatic as in Kanazawa and Edo.

Intemperate weather, blight, and insect infestations could be widespread enough to induce Malthusian crises on a broad scale in the Kan'ei era (1640s), the Kyōhō era (1720s), the Tenmei era (1780s), and the Tempō era (1830s). The geographic scope of these crises appears to have been more restricted later in the era than in the seventeenth century. Regardless of scope, the impact of these crises was exacerbated by the lack of a national administration or other device for coordinating interregional trade.

While none of these crises seem to have had long-term impact and populations seem to have recovered quite rapidly, the conclusion that Japan could not afford a reduction in the quality of arable land is inescapable. In other words—given the level of agricultural development and population growth—by the late seventeenth century, Japan faced pressures on resources similar to those faced by many places in the world today.

Even in areas of Japan that practiced land tenure arrangements other than warichi, by its nature rice cultivation relied extensively on green manures and water control thereby imposing cooperation with their regime on villagers. While eighteenth- and nineteenth-century pressures on villagers created conflicts over common lands, from the seventeenth century through the nineteenth century, common lands were a widespread part of village economies. They provided grasses for manuring of seed and vegetable plots; light timber for construction; kindling; rushes and reeds for manufacture of thatch or mats; and even marginal lands for cultivation of coarse grains, red beans, and similar crops. Rather than open-access lands, these common lands were highly regulated by the villagers themselves.[6] Long before the dawn of the early modern era (the seventeenth to nineteenth centuries), many decades of experience with detailed regulations designed by villagers and tailored to local circumstances, embodying mechanisms for policing and backed by finely graded punishments for infractions, prepared villagers to cooperate in the corporate management of village resources.

The heavy reliance on irrigation also encouraged cooperation among villagers. As arable lands were extended in the seventeenth century, and as efforts to improve yields per hectare continued over the next two centuries, irrigation works—trunk lines and branches—were constructed, extended, and improved. Construction alone required cooperation within and between villages, sometimes over extended territory. The need for routine maintenance of streams, gates, and reservoirs sustained those cooperative mechanisms. Just as importantly, however, the heavy use of irrigation called for extensive and cooperative planning in the distribution of water among villages, and within villages among villagers themselves. As with common lands, villagers developed systems of monitoring responsibility and tables detailing how irrigation water was to be shared.

While early modern Japanese villages were often economically stratified, upper-class villagers, even those who owned sufficient acreage to comprise several villages, could not blithely ignore those below them. Large landholders often held the position of village headman or the positions immediately below headman, the "peasant representatives" (*hyakushō* and "group leaders" (*kumichō*) who lead the village neighborhood associations. But land taxes, the major tax villagers bore, were assessed on villages as a whole, not on individuals. Villagers divided the tax among themselves through their leadership councils. If one villager could not bear his tax burden, other villagers had to make up the deficit from their own income. This system provided a constraint that encouraged village leadership to be reasonably fair in the way they allocated access to the fruits of the commons and irrigation waters. Not to do so was to put their own wealth and that of others in the village at risk.

WARICHI: SCOPE

Because of the variation in the level of control and the patterns of document survival, it is impossible to completely document the extent of warichi. Map 2.1 shows the distribution of warichi regions where both domain-mandated and village-based warichi existed. In certain provinces we can verify that warichi was practiced in some areas, but not all. Since we can't clearly identify the scope of the practice, this map represents only a rough approximation of the distribution of warichi.

The areas where domains mandated the practice comprise about one-third the putative value (*kokudaka*) of all arable land. How effective

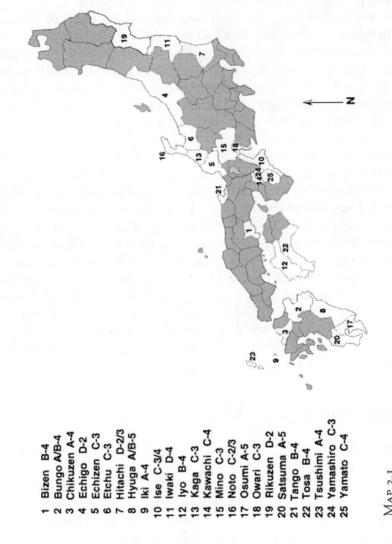

1 Bizen B-4
2 Bungo A/B-4
3 Chikuzen A-4
4 Echigo D-2
5 Echizen C-3
6 Etchu C-3
7 Hitachi D-2/3
8 Hyuga A/B-5
9 Iki A-4
10 Ise C-3/4
11 Iwaki D-4
12 Iyo B-4
13 Kaga C-3
14 Kawachi C-4
15 Mino C-3
16 Noto C-2/3
17 Osumi A-5
18 Owari C-3
19 Rikuzen D-2
20 Satsuma A-5
21 Tango B-4
22 Tosa B-4
23 Tsushimi A-4
24 Yamashiro C-3
25 Yamato C-4

N

MAP 2.1
Warichi Distribution in Early Modern Japan (by province)

enforcement of domain ordinances was is open to some question, but at least in principle, warichi operated throughout these regions for some or all of the early modern era.

Many regions which at one time witnessed the development of domain regulations for warichi first experienced redistribution at a strictly village level. We may know from references in domain regulations that village-level warichi existed before domain involvement; we may know that in some sense domain regulations were based on earlier practice, but still have no surviving direct evidence of how widespread the practice was. Even where villagers practiced warichi without domain encouragement or regulation, the practice frequently was reported to be widespread; but we have a hard time verifying the breadth of its use. In some places, the practice was apparently based only on oral tradition; I have also encountered cases of private documentation of which there is no public knowledge.[7] The practice continues today in some areas as a completely oral tradition, without public or private documentation. In other areas, related documents were disposed of when the system was abandoned—most often in the late nineteenth century but also sometimes during the early modern era as local conditions changed, or under the impact of the postwar land reform.[8] Given these conditions, I think that it is fair to say that even more land was affected by redistribution than I have suggested above. One-third of putative land value seems to be a conservative estimate.

This picture of varied local control permitted considerable flexibility and adaptability in redistributional systems. We see much variation in the scope of the practice within different villages. Some villages applied redistribution to all of a village (practically speaking); others to only part of a village (paddy only; dry field only; *honden* [old fields] only but not reclaimed land; a part of paddy or dry field [often set aside for purposes of social welfare or, in modern times, recreational gardening]). Furthermore, there was substantial variation in the degree to which the systems were specifically aimed at redistributing wealth. Some practices aimed at equal partition of affected land; most, however, were based on purchase of shares without any restraint on the size of one's total holdings. Some regions permitted outsiders to buy into redistributional lands; others excluded them.

Most explanations of warichi origins suggest a single purpose, usually that it arose in easily flooded regions in an era of mutual responsibility of the village corporation for payment of land taxes (the standard practice in rural areas of seventeenth-century Japan) or its utility in cooperative land reclamation. Yet even the brief enumeration of redistributional patterns above suggests the potential for a wide range of motives for employing warichi. Several historical considerations suggest a complicated and probably complex set of stimuli.

During the mid-1870s, the new central government under the Emperor Meiji introduced a system of land taxation and ownership that, in principle, outlawed this system of corporate land tenures. Ownership of all farmland was privatized, and certificates of ownership were distributed to those the state deemed to be the owners.[9] Yet many areas that had relied on warichi heretofore continued to do so. Some continued the practice up through the land reform laws of the U.S. Occupation in the late 1940s, when once again the practice was made illegal in principle. However, once more a number of villages chose to ignore the laws of the state or to manipulate them in such a way as to defeat their purpose. In scattered areas warichi is practiced even today.[10]

This persistence alone suggests the inadequacy of any explanation for the origin and maintenance of warichi practices that relies solely on environmental factors, and that impression is reinforced by the fact that flooding and landslides were common in many parts of Japan that did not rely on warichi, even in the heyday of the practice, ca. 1600–1870. The resolution of this particular mystery is not close at hand, but as a beginning hypothesis I suggest efforts to find a single impetus be abandoned; we should recognize that there were likely several stimuli, operating individually or in combination, that spurred the development of warichi. Although providing a form of insurance against the catastrophic impact of natural disasters or the desire to spread the risks of local microclimates and soil variation may have provided a motive for warichi, that alone or in combination with corporate village responsibility for payment of major taxes is insufficient to explain warichi origins.[11] Even if these conditions were sufficient to explain the origins, they are inadequate to explain maintenance of these practices where they persist in the modern era. Some set of special social or economic factors was also critical in the decision to begin and maintain this complex system of land reallocation.

At this stage in my work, I can do no more than suggest the possible human factors which underlay warichi. One factor in its origins appears to be the poor development of a day labor market. Areas in the most commercialized parts of Japan generally (though not exclusively) did not practice warichi. In less densely populated areas where natural calamities destroyed irrigation and water control facilities and inundated fields, labor demands to repair facilities and clear fields of debris may have peaked well above the ability of a small group of farmers to marshal the necessary labor in a day labor market. Where villagers had to assume the tax obligations of those who could not pay their share of taxes, other villagers, however grudgingly, had an interest in helping neighbors restore water control facilities and land to maximum potential operation even if their fields were not affected directly by the damage. Warichi often reinforced this interest by giving all shareholders some land rights in each risk category of village land.

A second factor seems to have been the lack of a single individual capable of commanding sufficient labor to develop certain land reclamation projects. Warichi provided a system for proportionally sharing the benefits of new farmland created by their labor. In accord with their contributions, all participants were assured that they would share in access to land of all qualities without discrimination. Each family's land use rights would provide access to the same ratio of superior, good, and poor quality land as a reward for investing labor in the project.[12]

A third element involved placing part of a village's land under warichi as a form of "social security." For example, in the ōaza of Seiriki (Kumayama-machi, Okayama prefecture), warichi was employed during the nineteenth and twentieth centuries in the Shimizu section to provide land for newly formed branch households (*bunke*) as well as main households (*honke*) and originally applied to dry field only to assure that all had vegetables to eat. In the Abushima section of the Abusaka area of Tokamachi-shi, warichi was used during the same period (and even today) to provide access to rice land with priority given to those who had no other paddy or arable land. In Kudakajima, Okinawa, access to land (all of which was dry field) was provided by a form of warichi to provide basic sustenance for women and children while the men sailed off to engage in trade, fishing, and piracy. In this latter case in particular, there was no association whatsoever between frequent flooding and the presence of warichi.

Although warichi was a widespread phenomenon, the decision to implement it was never taken at a national level but de facto was taken at a local or regional (daimyo domain) level. Consequently, the interests involved must include those of domain lords as well as the villagers on whom our discussion has focused thus far. In many instances the involvement of the domain came after villagers had independently developed local systems. In these cases, the role of domain policy was usually to standardize some key aspects of the process and to extend the system to all villages in the domain. Kaga domain in western central Japan represents one example of this type of domain involvement.[13] Until the early nineteenth century, the domain only licensed those who measured land for redistribution and required unanimity before implementing warichi; thereafter, it attempted to enforce a twenty-year maximum interval between redistributions. Less typical were domains like Tosa and Satsuma, which attempted a top-down implementation of warichi-type systems. Such domain interest seems to have focused on two issues: retaining adequate labor in villages to farm and take care of domain public works projects, and assuring that village tax payments were paid as regularly and fully as possible.

Finally, respondents in interviews, when asked why the tradition continued so long in their villages, replied that their area was made up of people who generally got along better than folks in nearby villages. While this is something of a stock reply in "in-group"–conscious Japan, I think that in reality there may just be an important element of truth here. That is not to deny the possible role of effective persuasion, including threats; but ultimately even when there was the potential to marshal outside support for nonparticipation, people acceded to the old ways.[14] There are other indications of tension with villages practicing warichi; but if we conceive of harmony as agreement on the rules by which disputes are resolved—a George Simmel perspective on social conflict—then these villages managed to find ways to resolve conflicts and patch up rifts while maintaining the system pretty much intact. Within this context, villagers managed to adapt their redistributional practices to a variety of changing circumstances—conversion of dry land to paddy, the implementation of new national tax and land laws, changes in the surrounding social and economic context, and so forth.

As these circumstances changed, the ends which warichi served were sometimes dramatically altered. In the Tokamachi case mentioned above, privately owned land was flooded, and the land was converted to public land when the landholder could not recultivate it through his own efforts in the mid–nineteenth century. Warichi was employed initially as a means to bring together sufficient labor to reclaim the land. Over several decades this land came to have primarily the social security function mentioned earlier—a function that has continued despite the development of effective water control facilities that have eliminated flooding as a frequent concern.

A CASE STUDY: ECHIGO

Echigo (virtually coterminous with modern Niigata prefecture) was an elongated province on the Japan Sea side of northern Japan. Like many examples of land repartition, the origins of repartition in Echigo are not entirely clear. The frequent administrative changes in the late sixteenth and early seventeenth centuries as well as flooding, fires, civil war, and American bombing have reduced the number of early documents substantially. Two gazetteers, *Echigo fudo kō* and *Onk ōno shiori*, suggest that the first repartitions were associated with the 1610 land surveys of the Shibata domain. The authors indicate that the decisions to redistribute were the outcome of village efforts to reduce quarrels that resulted from inequities in the land tax burden following the survey.[15] Repartition practices became a widespread, permanent feature throughout many Echigo villages during the early seventeenth century, spreading across domain boundaries and finding a home in such diverse domains as local Tokugawa house lands, the Nagaoka and Mineyama domains, as well as those of the Shibata family, for example.

In terms of geographical features—especially the presence or absence of broad, easily flooded river plains, the region is quite diverse, with the central coastal areas being dominated by the influence of Japan's longest river, the Shinano. The river has its headwaters in faraway Nagano prefecture, and it is quite possible for localized storms there to cause flooding in Niigata. Consequently, local residents watch not only the weather forecasts for their own area, but also those for the Japan Alps. They know too well that (depending on where they live) eight, ten, or twelve hours after a storm there they will witness rising waters or flooding locally. Coastal lagoons are also common, formed by flood deposition. Farmers gradually reclaimed a number of these marshlands over the centuries.

If warichi were limited to the Shinano river basin and coastal lagoons of central Echigo, we could readily conclude that the primary stimulus to redistribute arable lands periodically was to provide insurance against floods. Yet warichi is also commonly found in southern Echigo, where there are no large rivers like the Shinano. In northern Echigo, however, evidence of warichi is quite rare.[16]

Economically, the Echigo region was primarily agricultural, just like the vast majority of Japan up to the mid–twentieth century. While the greatest crop value lay in rice production, a variety of other products like soybeans were produced on the margins of rice-farm enterprises. Unlike some areas to the south, double cropping was not possible in most of the province. Nonetheless, the presence of a major gold mine on Sado Island and the movement of daimyo from their local headquarters to the Shogun's capital (Edo, modern Tokyo) biannually assured a good flow of big-spender traffic through central Echigo and lay one of the cornerstones for commercial development in the region. The southern regions faced Osaka and the Kinai region, and trade moved quite freely in that direction, too. With the development of Japan's western coastal route (*nishi-mawari sen*), coastal trade opened up with many other regions of Japan. All in all, by the late eighteenth century, commercialization was changing agriculture and in some cases exerting substantial pressures on traditional agricultural practices. Among those pressures were newly wealthy farm families who pushed for a greater voice in village affairs, the rise of absentee landlords who wished to extend the practices of their native villages in the areas where they acquired new land, and the purchase of arable land by prospering merchants who often were unfamiliar with local practices. Whether merchant or absentee landlord, some factions within the village resented their presence, and frictions sometimes turned into longstanding disputes.

Politically, Echigo was highly fragmented after the early seventeenth century. During the late sixteenth century, all of Echigo and parts of neighboring provinces had been under the control of the very powerful Uesugi family, once contenders for national political preeminence. However, in 1598, the nationally hegemonic Toyotomi Hideyoshi transferred them out of Echigo. In their place, Hori Hideharu was enfeoffed with the entire province. By 1610, the Hori family, too, had been transferred elsewhere; and henceforth Echigo was divided among a number of different lords, including small to medium-sized daimyo and some lands directly administered by the Tokugawa shogunate. Even these political units were subject to frequent changes. Domain sizes increased or decreased, and parts of one domain were entrusted to the governance of a neighboring lord although the initial lord still remained the nominal ruler. (By comparison with other areas of Japan, this administrative instability was not particularly unusual; it represents a common, if not "average," experience in domain administration.)

There is no need to sketch changes in local rulership in any detail; for our purposes, it is enough to note that these changes made it very difficult for any consistent land tenure system to be created "from above." To date, I have seen no evidence that such an attempt was made in Echigo, but the political fluidity of the region posed substantial obstacles to doing so.[17] The primary initiative for determining the nature of land tenures in the Echigo area lay at the village level.

Supravillage authorities became involved in shaping land tenure systems in Echigo only indirectly, in a case-by-case treatment of appeals from villagers who could not resolve disputes about redistribution among themselves. On these occasions, supravillage authorities were first contacted to investigate and act as mediators. This process might be repeated several times before there was a satisfactory resolution or the dispute moved into more formal legal channels. During the mediation and adjudication process, supravillage officials could push the operation of redistribution in one direction or another; but their decision or the resulting compromise affected that one village only.[18]

Under the circumstances, village-level decisions were the most significant in determining land tenure regimes. While supravillage authorities did not try to manage or destroy the warichi system, neither did they take actions to promote its spread or more frequent implementation. In contrast to Elinor Ostrom's argument that higher-level administrators must provide a "constitutional" framework, which protects local regulation of common pool resources, what we seem to have here is a de facto recognition of warichi, a kind of neglect, not always "benign" but often effectively reinforcing local tradition.

Yet external administrative practices may have had an indirect impact on tenures through an entirely different mechanism, the land tax system. Warichi was conducted with substantial frequency in the Echigo region. One possible reason for this lay not only in the susceptibility to flooding, landslides, and so forth, but also in the apparent lack of flexibility of administrative practice in adjusting land taxes to new conditions of agriculture. When there was a poor harvest, taxes would, in principle, be lowered. In much of the Echigo region, taxes would be lowered only if yields fell 30 percent below normal. In neighboring Kaga domain, yields 20 percent below normal received special consideration. Thus, Echigo farmers were forced to shoulder a greater share of crop risk than in some other regions. In addition, since both land taxes and relief measures for crop failures were distributed based on local records of land management—that is, documents closely associated with the redistribution process, villagers had a substantial incentive to keep them up to date and to be sure that frequent adjustments were made as the condition of the land changed.

Despite warichi's widespread presence in diverse geographic and economic settings in Echigo, there is surprisingly little in the way of direct description of the rules for conducting a redistribution. For the most part, the practices were transmitted orally, rather than in writing. Consequently, the underlying principles, limitations, and scope often must be inferred from redistributional "notebooks" that leave much unsaid. This is not simply an issue for scholars: It is clear from dispute settlement cases that the lack of documentation was sometimes the source of disputes among villagers, too. This was troublesome for supravillage authorities as well, for district and domain officials often had to contend with competing verbal assertions that they could not verify in any way. In general outline, the system functioned as follows.

The unit of repartition usually was the village, although in some instances it was applied only to jointly reclaimed farmland or some section of a village where land had changed substantially or where there had been a dispute over the equity of the previous reallocation. As already noted, this did not mean that participants were residents of the village.[19]

Land subject to redistribution was surveyed, graded, and divided into units of uniform productive value.[20] Each was given an identifying label—

a local section name or a number—that was written on paper or a stick of bamboo that would be used in the blind draw for land. This evaluation process made it possible to account for changes that had occurred in the amount of arable land and in soil fertility since the last repartition.

Villagers, too, had to be organized. All participants were assembled into lottery groups (*kuji kumi*). When the actual allocation of cultivation rights began, a representative from the group (*kuji oya*) would draw lots on behalf of the group members. Each lottery group received rights to the same amount of land. Each shareholder, however, did not; he maintained the same proportion of the village rights after redistribution as he had before it. Since this right to manage land represented a proportion of the total rather than a fixed area of land, families were said to hold whole or partial "shares" (in Japanese, *kenmae* or some similar expression). The absolute amount of land represented by a "share" might increase if there was reclamation or decrease if there was a flood or other natural disaster, but the proportion remained constant.

After all preparations had been made, the group representatives drew lots for fields in each category of land. If the group was comprised of a single household, the process was now complete. If several households formed a group, they would hold their own lottery to further subdivide the land into smaller shares and hold another drawing among themselves. If needed, some shares were subdivided into fractional shares. By the final drawing, each household held rights to cultivate lands comprised of the same proportions of superior, average, and poor quality land as any other household.[21] Table 2.1 presents a hypothetical case, which illustrates these processes. Consequently, although the size of each family's land rights varied, each family's holdings would be comprised of one-third superior land, one-third average land, and one-third poor land (for example) if that were the ratio of these grades of land in the village as a whole.

Once the land was apportioned among households, they were able to dispose of their cultivation rights as they saw fit. They could buy, sell, rent, bequeath, or inherit these tenurial rights as well as work the land on their own. In effect, these rights were roughly comparable to holding shares of stock in the village.

This brings us to a very interesting point in the discussion of warichi. The general sense among Japan specialists is that there is traditionally a strong sense of attachment felt by Japanese farmers for a given piece of land (*aichakushin*). If the practice of warichi itself is not sufficient reason to raise questions about that shibboleth, then the evidence scattered throughout land certificates and warichi documents (registers or dispute records) provides more: There we find a very substantial number of instances where

Table 2.1

Hypothetical Allocation of Cultivation Rights to Twenty-two Share-holding Families in Ten *Kuji* Groups under Echigo Warichi

Family	Share	*Kuji* Group	Family	Share	*Kuji* Group
1	1.25	A, B	12	.50	H
2	1.00	C	13	.50	I
3	.50	D	14	.25	I
4	.50	D	15	.25	I
5	.50	E	16	.25	J
6	.50	E	17	.25	J
7	.50	F	18	.25	J
8	.50	F	19	.25	J
9	.50	G	20	.25	B
10	.50	G	21	.25	B
11	.50	H	22	.25	B

In this example, only one family would participate in just a single drawing. Family 1 would participate in two first-round drawings (as the sole member of *Kuji* Group A and as co-participants in Group B with families 20–22). All others (including families 20–22) would participate in a single first-round drawing and a second, intragroup drawing. Adapted from Philip C. Brown, *Central Authority and Local Autonomy in the Formation of Early Modern Japan*, 104.

farmers simply swapped the rights to cultivate specific pieces of land. Sometimes they may have swapped land to gain plots closer to home or other fields; in other instances, they may have imagined a more valuable alternative use for the land than the current holder (for example, planting a cash crop rather than rice or another food crop). In several instances we can document such transfers right after a reallocation had taken place. The villagers may have retained a sense of identity with the village as a whole, but the attachment to specific plots was absent.

The aftermarket may also hold a key to why the warichi system functioned for so long: A noncash aftermarket permitted people to make adjustments while still staying within a framework that fostered equitable access to different grades and types (for example, dry field/paddy) of land.

Such a conclusion is necessarily tentative because the extent of such after-markets is uncertain. The fact that the practice was fairly common in Echigo province suggests that it may have been present in other regions, too.

There was substantial variation in the period between redistributions. It is tempting to suggest that the more frequent flooding or landslides were in an area, the shorter the interval between redistributions. However, dispute documents make it clear that villagers did not see such a direct relationship. Because implementation of warichi was such a time-consuming practice, there were efforts to minimize the frequency of implementation and to use alternative measures (generally lumped together under the general term for mutual assistance, yonai). All interim measures to compensate for land lost to cultivation or that suffered reduced productivity due to flood or landslide damage involved either transfer payments within the village, reduction of tax and related burdens, or division of donations from the domain rather than redistribution of land. Villages able to reach such accommodation could tolerate longer intervals between redistribution. Two possibilities, yet to be investigated, are that the shorter intervals between redistributions occurred in smaller villages or villages where the person-land ratio was high and where the challenges of valuing and measuring land were less of a burden on the laborers involved.

How longstanding crops with potential commercial value were treated is of particular interest, both from the standpoint of warichi's potential to retard economic growth or to accommodate commercial crops without permitting them to overwhelm the tenurial and agricultural system. If investments in such crops were discouraged by warichi, then the system acted at least in part to discourage the growth of commercialized agriculture and the expansion of a cash economy. For example, crops such as the lacquer tree grew for a number of years before reaching maturity and harvest. Certain varieties could produce sap that would be refined and used to make lacquerware. Other varieties produced wood for construction, kindling, charcoal, and so on. Although primarily for local consumption, even these trees had commercial potential.

The Yoshikawa region, which I have studied most intensively, sprouted only one such crop, urushi, or lacquer. The variety produced here was that used for construction and other purposes, not for the production of sap. While this lacquer tree's commercial value might be considered less than the sap-producing trees, the treatment of land producing lacquer trees is suggestive of the degree to which warichi could accommodate commercial crops. The settlement of a dispute in 1773 reveals the following basic principles for dealing with such crops.[22] (1) Only trees above a certain size were to be included in the redistribution. This assured the original holder that his initial investment of labor would not come to nothing because of a redistribution (how long he could continue to use the land on which these trees were planted is unclear). (2) Before land was turned over to the new cultivator, all trees were to be cut by the original cultivator. (3) If there was mutual benefit to not cutting trees, they could remain for an additional year. This judgment was left to the individuals involved. (4) However, if there was not agreement: "when the redistribution period is exceeded, the land must be cleared within two months and if there is a dispute, the trees become the (new) landholder's [unless there is prior mutual agreement]."

Clearly the institutional support for some long-term agricultural investments was present; however, other facets of the settlement clearly restricted cultivator initiative. Residential lands (*yashiki-chi*) involved not only the land on which houses were built, but also certain dry field lands. Some enterprising cultivators converted dry field into paddy. The same dispute settlement just noted specifically instructed that these lands be re-converted to dry field. The issue for villagers here was not simply one of keeping a particular category of land sacrosanct. More important was the problem raised by the need to supply water for paddy in regions where supplies were limited. Where water supply was uncertain, as was the case in the Yoshikawa area, an upstream resident who took water for his newly converted residential land was usually depriving those downstream of their ration of water. The same issue was involved in *privately* converting dry field and mountain land to paddy.[23] Such restrictions were frequently in place throughout Japan and are not the specific product of warichi practices. That some conversions of this sort were accommodated is attested to by the presence of paddy in warichi sections that were otherwise dry field.[24] These fields appear to have remained in the dry field allotment because they were generally considered to have the same value as the dry fields they replaced; that is to say, they were considered inferior or, at best, average paddy.

In the Yoshikawa area, like many other warichi regions in Echigo, all land was in principle included in the redistribution; nonetheless, certain lands were excludable. We have seen one example above, in the case of lacquer trees smaller than a given size. Residential lands of 35 *bu* (somewhat more than 140 square yards) for each participating household were to be excluded. This included the families of dependent cultivators (*nago*) as well as independent farmers. In measuring this land, the area around the house was measured, excluding paths, up to the main road. This area was then subtracted from 35 bu. If there was extra land, and it was not possible to partition it off to another holder, then that amount of land was subtracted from the registrant's access to superior paddy—a very sharp disincentive to expand one's garden. On the other hand, if there was not enough land contiguous to the house itself, compensating acreage was to be provided from another, superior dry field section of the village and the cultivator was to receive a bonus allotment of 20 percent of the area of the detached holdings—presumably as compensation for the inconvenience of having to work land a distance from the residence. Village headmans' land and that of district chiefs (*ōkimoiri*) were also partially excludable as remuneration for their office work (these lands were partially tax exempt).[25] With these limited exceptions, however, all land was subject to redistribution during a general warichi.[26]

Such a comprehensive system of corporate land tenures probably engendered much more conflict within villages than we can ever document. The process of measuring and grading land could take several weeks; and, despite the fact that farmers in each village knew the characteristics of the village arable land in great detail, there must certainly have been quibbling over what land to include in which category, how big each was, and whether the division of each section of the village into fields yielded comparable land areas for each share of land. In spite of this potential for conflict, I have yet to discover a single documented case of purely intravillage conflict over warichi procedures or outcomes. Certainly participants had the option of appealing an intravillage settlement to district or other officials, but they appear not to have done so. All dispute cases I have found to date involve a primary litigant who is either a nonresident landlord or someone else viewed as an outsider by many villagers.[27]

Why do we lack records of intravillage disputes? We can begin with a process of elimination. First, we can rule out communal harmony. When nonresident shareholders brought lawsuits, they often found allies among the resident shareholders.[28] Clearly, when someone else was prepared to take the lead, others were waiting to take advantage of the opportunity.

Why wait for an outside leader? Several social and political factors may have played an important role. First, although old, landed wealth had lost much of its grip on smaller shareholders since the early seventeenth century, hierarchical relationships within villages were still quite strong. Even when parvenus had challenged old wealth for a share of political power, that did not necessarily expand the base of political rights substantially nor did it mean that the lesser shareholders gained a base for autonomous political action. Many were still beholden to their wealthier counterparts in some way. In a society as stratified as Japan's, intravillage politicking could involve significant threats to one's livelihood, and these kinds of pressures should not be forgotten as we consider why we lack evidence of intravillage disputes.

Wealth may also have played a role in a very different way as well. At each stage of an investigation, villagers had to bear the expenses of the investigating officials' visits. Furthermore, in many parts of Echigo, at least

after the early eighteenth century, it was common for shareholders to provide gifts to district officials (*kimōiri*, and such), county-based officials of
the domain (*daikan*), and so on. These gifts, in addition to basic meals and
lodging, had to be provided to any official who visited a village; and the
gifts were quite rigidly scaled to the rank of the official. When villagers
requested an inspection to lower taxes due to poor harvests, these gifts had
to be made. When officials were called to inspect the village to arbitrate or
mediate a dispute, such gifts had to be presented.[29]

These gifts represented a significant expenditure, and the way of dividing contributions among villagers tended to penalize those who brought
the suit or requested an inspection. The largest share was born by the plain-
tiff, with the balance borne by the other shareholders. As is true today
when justice is most readily available to those who can pay for it, early
modern Echigo shareholders had to be able to afford the costs of carrying a
dispute outside the village. These costs were substantial; even the division
of that financial burden sometimes became a cause for dispute or further
complicated an ongoing case![30]

Dispute records that involve nonresident shareholders nonetheless
reveal some additional significant characteristics of Echigo warichi. In one
instance, it is clear that a single, intermediate-level village official (*kumigashira*) was able to stop a request for a new redistribution. The village
headman (*shōya*) deferred to his objections. In another instance, the failure of another kumigashira to sign off on a request hindered, but did not
stop, one Tomizaeimon from pressing on with a direct appeal to a district
official (kimōiri). Many would have lacked the *chutzpah* to carry on with
this enterprise.[31] Under the circumstances, we can conclude that in order
to press for a warichi (either as an emergency or when one had not been
implemented for some time), one had to have the unanimous consent of
all village officials (almost coterminous with the wealthiest shareholders).
In addition, the dispute resolutions I have examined suggest that where a
tradition of redistribution existed, outside authority was prone to support
its continuance—even when that involved supporting the claims of nonresident shareholders against a united village officialdom. One such case
suggests there may even have been a penchant to extend the practice
beyond paddy and dry field to marginal lands that in most of Japan would
have been treated as common land (*iriai*).

Why would a system of corporate landholding and periodic reallocation of access to fields work for so long and in such diverse socioeconomic
and political environments as seventeenth century agrarian and contemporary Japan? Why would farmers, engaged in a risky business to begin
with, compound their uncertainties by allowing a lottery to determine

which fields they tilled? By way of summary of Echigo warichi, the following observations seem pertinent.

First, mechanisms existed through which this particular "harvest of chance" could be ameliorated. If parcels allocated for individuals were unsuitable for some reason, they could be exchanged privately.

Second, the system made provision to protect investments with long-term return horizons, including homes and commercial crops. Those constraints on innovative agriculture which were present came from other sources such as irrigation needs in areas where water supplies were limited and had to be rationed, like Yoshikawa.

Third, while it was seldom a major active force in shaping warichi, supravillage society's inertia reinforced the legitimacy of local practice and the influence of village elites who had a preponderant influence on how the system operated. It was representatives of those elites who acted as leaders of village factions in shaping redistributional patterns. Outside influence was not always benign; but when outside authorities did become involved, it was to adjudicate disputes in the context of local village custom and widespread ideas of equity, not to impose external "foreign" ideas.

Fourth, the system provided—and in a few cases still provides—real benefits for participants. Whatever benefits villagers perceived—insurance, welfare, or the like—were significant enough to offset the need occasionally to swallow one's pride and accept compromises that were not always to one's liking. Interviews with recent warichi participants further suggest that people commonly felt that if things worked out poorly for them this time, they would have a good claim for compensatory treatment next time, a claim that was likely to be respected. Reinforcing the idea that there was real value provided is the malleability of objectives evidenced over time, from insurance to welfare and other functions—especially after the end of the Shogunate, when the system had to be maintained in the face of new and inimical land tax/property regimes.[32]

A final issue, quite different in nature, also should be addressed briefly in the context of the longevity of this system of corporate tenures. Some might argue that the absence of chronic warfare such as that which characterized Western Europe during the early modern era contributed to both the longevity of corporate tenures and their ecological stability by limiting pressure on the land. Charles Tilly, for example, argues that such warfare provided the stimulus for increased centralization and state intrusion into local affairs.[33] Yet in early modern Japan between 1590, when Hideyoshi subdued the last of his domestic enemies, and the 1860s, when the anti-Shogunal forces took up arms, there were only four major domestic battles and two foreign conflicts. All of these ended by 1637.[34]

That the absence of war may have reduced the sense of urgency felt by domain and Shogunal administrators cannot be entirely denied, but that did not mean an absence of red ink in administrative budgets and of pressure to increase revenues. Japan's ruling classes did not let peace interfere with profligate spending. On the one hand, costs spiraled as upper-level samurai pursued increasingly luxurious consumption patterns. On the other hand, the real purchasing power of government and samurai incomes declined as economic growth and diversification resulted in a secular decline in the value of the rice and soybeans that comprised the principal forms of tax payment the daimyos received and in which the salaries of their samurai retainers were paid. The ways in which rulers attempted to deal with these crises tell us something about where they found expedient approaches to deal with financial exigencies.

In the face of floods of red ink, domain and Shogunal administrators attempted to raise land taxes, exhorted villagers to be more frugal, and accused villages of cheating on their taxes. Yet problems of maintaining knowledge of agricultural affairs among administrators, the technological limitations of transportation and land measurement, the administrative effort necessary to enforce a more efficient system of land taxation, and the marginal costs of improving land taxation through more accurate land surveys and ownership records and the like were either greater than the capacity of daimyo and Shogunal administrators could bear or not worth overcoming the opposition from villagers that was endemic.[35] When all such measures and more failed, they turned to debt cancellation and reduction of the salaries they paid samurai retainers. The latter tactics had the virtues of being expedient and inexpensive in terms of administrative time and effort. For farmers, these policies meant that the key long-term pressures they placed on the land were those of (1) paying a relatively stable rate of taxation, and (2) providing for their families. At no point was there an effort to convert land taxes to cash payments, in large part because the spread of a cash economy into the villages was viewed as a threat to the maintenance of a large, revenue-producing rural population—an ideological constraint reinforced by Confucian teachings that was absent in Western Europe.

PRELIMINARY CONJECTURES
ON ECOLOGICAL CONSEQUENCES OF WARICHI

What ecological consequences were apparent in areas where warichi was practiced? While future research may reveal a very different picture, to date

I have discovered no evidence that suggests that this practice led to widespread free rider problems on arable lands subject to redistribution. While we might expect a "tragedy of the commons" to be a logical outcome that leads to the destruction of corporate control, none seems to develop and these systems endured for several centuries in sizable areas of Japan. This remained true even as population increased and the economy diversified and grew during the early modern and modern eras.

Two factors may account for the lack of degradation of fields. First, the potential sources of degradation in most warichi areas were limited, and crop varieties that placed a heavy drain on soil nutrients were not involved. In rice agriculture the major nutrients are delivered to plants via irrigation water, rather than from the soil directly. The rice plants themselves neither depend on the soil for most nutrients nor do they leech them from the soil. Thus, a key issue in rice agriculture was assuring an adequate supply of irrigation water and its regular, predictable distribution. Irrigation, of course, was not a matter that could be handled by one family alone. Throughout Japanese history, the need to cooperate with other villagers, villagers in nearby communities, and with higher administrative authorities imposed a variety of rigorous constraints on cultivators everywhere. The need for a regular supply of water, the need to cooperate in creating and sharing that supply, and the ability of others to impose sanctions on those who violated irrigation cooperative dictates, all placed substantial constraints on those who sought to escape their responsibilities to the broader community.

Dry field crops commonly planted, either as a second crop on paddy or on fields reserved for dry crops, also tended to require little fertilizer: wheat, barley, millet, barnyard millet, soybeans, giant white radish (*daikon*), red beans (*azuki*), mulberry, arrowroot, lacquer trees, and the like. In the case of some vegetables, fertilizer could boost yields, but failure to provide it led quickly to harvests of lower value and volume. These also tended to be supplemental crops produced on limited acreage rather than basic crops produced on most of a farmer's lands, even when they had commercial value.

The key problem in rice paddies lay in maintenance of a good bed. Even with a well-controlled supply of water into a paddy, the irrigation gates, paddy ridges, and beds had to be in good repair to assure that one's allotted supply of water would not be wasted and that appropriate amounts would reach all the plants in a field. The essential investments in this endeavor were labor inputs to minimize unwanted drainage and to create an even paddy bed that permitted all plants to get the necessary water. Failure to do either resulted in significant and immediately detectable declines in yield. In other words, the failure to invest in field maintenance naturally led to substantial loss of income for the farmer. Second, although a number of these crops found their way into the expanding regional and national trade networks of the seventeenth to nineteenth centuries, external demands for increased production came gradually, were relatively modest, and give no evidence of encouraging the degradation of fields under warichi.[36] Vegetables were transported to towns and cities for sale; soybeans were processed into tofu and other products; the silk and paper trades expanded; and rice not turned over to officials as taxes was converted to rice wine *(sake)*, all in increased volume over time. Yet given the need for households to supply all of their own basic food needs and the need to pay the majority of land taxes in rice until the 1870s (when the new Meiji government introduced mandatory cash tax payments), there was limited flexibility to abandon production of rice or basic foodstuffs in favor of full commercial farming. The necessary food and tax rice simply could not be purchased on the market. The key pre-Meiji disputes over land use involved agriculturally marginal lands—common lands, woodlands, and the like. Could they be maintained as is or were they better devoted to extending arable land for increasing foodstuffs or a growing (but still minority) share of commercial crops? In the seventeenth century, the tendency had been to use such newly cultivated lands for foodstuffs; by the late eighteenth century, the trend in some regions of Japan, especially those surrounding major metropolitan centers, was to plant more commercially oriented crops. Yet at no point did the pressures from outside a village encourage overexploitation of arable land itself on any wide scale. There was no substantial incentive to overuse the land, and substantial risk in doing so.

Losses from overexploitation might not be of substantial consequence in contexts where "moving on" or locating alternative careers was an option, but an early modern Japanese farmer could not readily pull up stakes and move on to another location or occupation. In the very earliest decades of the era, some such mobility was possible. The century of civil war created such disorder and destruction that a large amount of land was removed from cultivation. During the very late sixteenth and early seventeenth centuries, there were substantial efforts to bring this and other lands under cultivation. These efforts provided opportunities for a number of people to move to new farmsteads or to expand their farm operations, and in some cases for urban and other poor to become full-fledged farmers. But by the late seventeenth century, such opportunities were rapidly declining throughout Japan. Even if one could move to another region, establishing one's self as a farmer in a new community was difficult. Credit depended on having collateral in land. Even agricultural labor markets were not very fluid during the early modern era. Finally, there were no longer significant frontier areas available. At the same time, patterns of urban growth changed. The rapid period of urban growth based on castle town expansion slowed, and emphasis shifted to the growth of smaller towns with somewhat more limited opportunities for new, full-time employment in nonagricultural careers.[37] With limited opportunities to move, disincentives to overexploit farmlands were reinforced, effectively holding free riders to face the ecological or social consequences of their actions.[38]

However, this particular set of incentives and disincentives changed dramatically in the mid–nineteenth century. In the early Meiji era, the new government removed old constraints on domestic trade and introduced a much improved system of transportation; and the state placed land tax obligations directly on the backs of individual cultivators, each of whom was given a formal certificate (*chiken*) of ownership. The new land tax system mandated cash tax payments and made no provision to lower taxes in years of poor harvests.

To what degree this new system pushed cultivators into the marketplace is hotly debated. What is clear is that the new system permitted substitution of cash crops for subsistence crops. Nonetheless, the basic range of crops and farming techniques and patterns remained largely unchanged until the mid–twentieth century.

While this new environment may have contributed to the gradual abandonment of warichi in many areas, other regions (Echigo among them) continued to practice redistribution; I have yet to find evidence that redistribution created significant free rider problems on fields that remained under corporate control. Even under the new land tax system, redistributional practices do not appear to have contributed to ecological degradation.[39]

The new commercial environment of the late nineteenth century even had the opposite effect. Instead of pushing arable land beyond its limits, farmers actually retreated from cultivating the most marginal of arable land, allowing it to revert to forest or scrublands. In part, this pattern of restraint may have resulted from the accumulated wisdom and habits of intensive cultivation developed over many decades. Whatever the explanation, simply enacting a new tax law from above did not change the orientations of those who tilled the land, especially when the great new economic adventures lay in industry and other urban-centered venues.

Viewed from a different perspective, we may see limited degradation of the soil itself was a significant factor enhancing the durability of warichi systems. Had there been significant damage to the land, we would expect to see these redistributional systems self-destruct or at least to see declines in agricultural yields where redistribution was practiced. Yet per hectare yields in warichi regions did not fall with the passage of time, but rose in tandem with those of non-warichi villages.[40]

From the standpoint of understanding the ecological consequences of land rights, the above analysis suggests that the structure of rights in themselves may not be determinant. In considering the ecological viability of this system of corporate tenures and its longevity, we have ventured into discussions of the nature of Japanese agriculture and irrigation, the relations of agriculture to markets, state demands for increased taxes, and the nature of local controls that could be exercised over villagers. All suggest a structure of incentives that made it difficult for farmers to view their relationship to land as one of unrestrained exploiter. The constellation of factors we have examined meant that they could not escape the consequences of abuse of the land. In preventing ecological degradation, the total effect of that cluster of elements weighed more heavily than the system of land tenures itself.

NOTES

1. See David Feeny, Susan Hana, and Arthur F. McEvoy, "Questioning the Assumptions of the 'Tragedy of the Commons' Model of Fisheries," *Land Economics* 72, no. 2 (May 1996): 187, which lists major contributions to this effort.

2. The use of irrigation and the scheduled release of water to different sections of the village at different times did, however, impose some constraints on what could be planted, where, and when. Even these constraints, however, were not absolute. Cooperative segments of rice cropping (in particular, transplanting and harvesting) and the labor obligations of subordinate to superordinate farmers that were associated with them also imposed some constraints on farmers.

3. It is also worth noting that this form of tenure did not simply disappear with the effort of the Meiji government to establish a modern system of private landownership. The impact of this form of tenure can be seen in rare instances even today. Philip C. Brown, "Feudal Remnants and Tenant Power: The Case Of Niigata, Japan, in the Nineteenth and Early Twentieth Centuries," *Peasant Studies* 15, no. 1 (Fall 1987): 1–26.

There was not even an effort through a national system of courts to structure a uniform system of commoner land rights until the nineteenth century. Indeed, resort to adjudication of land disputes, even within a daimyo's jurisdiction, was rare and typically involved disputes between two or more villages over control of land, not definition of individual or corporate landholding rights. The even more rare cases of suits by an individual (several examples are discussed later) typically resulted from purchase of land rights in one village by a nonresident. In this environment, custom, often transmitted only orally, ruled until the late eighteenth century. In several of the cases cited later, domain officials attempted to determine what local custom was and to make their rulings based on that. They did not try to nudge practices toward a form of tenure derived from outside the village.

4. Araki Moriaki and several other historians of Japan have advanced the argument that central authorities did have effective policies to define individual land-holding rights. I strongly disagree with this interpretation. For a brief introduction to the literature on Toyotomi Hideyoshi's purportedly national land surveys, see Philip C. Brown, *Central Authority and Local Autonomy in the Formation of Early Modern Japan: The Case of Kaga Domain* (Stanford, Calif.: Stanford University Press, 1993), Chapters I and III in particular.

5. The Bakufu's attempt to forbid the sale of arable land (1643) was never nationally enforced and was a miserable failure, even within Shogunal domains. It was so widely circumvented through adoptions and other subterfuges that sales were openly permitted once again early in the eighteenth century.

6. See Margaret McKean, "The Japanese Experience with Scarcity: Management of Traditional Common Lands," in *Environmental History: Critical Issues in Comparative Perspective*, ed. Kendall E. Bailes, (Lanham, Md.: University Press of America, 1985), 334–59; and "Management of Traditional Common Lands (*Iriaichi*) in Japan," in Panel on Common Property Resource Management, Board on Science and Technology for International Development, Office of International Affairs, National Research Council, *Proceedings of the Conference on Common Property Resource Management* (Washington, D.C.: National Academy Press, 1986), 533–89.

7. Interviews with several people in Nagaoka City in January–February 1994 revealed several cases where respondents permitted me to see private notebooks of recent reallocations and pro-rata distribution of funds received when land subject to redistribution was purchased by the city for development of recreational facilities.

8. The potential use of warichi as a vehicle to understand Japanese history, village customs, and so on, especially in the modern era, is not widely appreciated. Even in Niigata prefecture, where village-based warichi was widespread, local tradition stresses the complete end of the system with the early Meiji land tax reforms of the 1870s. Even when documents for later warichi are discovered, they (and the implications of them for understanding state-society relations, and so on) are not copied or collected by local history offices. Such cases don't fit the standard pattern, and people may not know how to deal with them. At the national level, even among professional scholars of wide repute, many argue that warichi was an inconsequential, exceptional practice and they ignore it. Thus, local holders or collectors of documents abdicate responsibility for defining the importance of data to more established historians, who in turn are unprepared to appreciate the implications of warichi. As a result, much documentation has been lost, and continues to be lost today, especially that regarding the modern use of warichi.

9. This process was not as simple as it sounds for some cultivated land was common land (iriai) that was contested not only among individual cultivators, but also by the village as an autonomous entity or by the state. Although rural literacy was very high by international standards, many still could not read and had a difficult time defending their claims to "ownership." Rights in land were sufficiently confused and complex that even where there was relatively good documentation the determination of rights was not always clear cut.

10. These conclusions are based on interviews with residents of Kumayama-machi (Okayama prefecture), Nagaoka-shi, Tokamachi-shi, and Yoshikawa-machi (Niigata prefecture) during the fall of 1993 and spring of 1994. The natural assumption that these practices continue in largely rural areas is not correct. Even in the midst of Nagaoka City today, warichi is practiced in some areas; and it was practiced until quite recently in a number of other areas of the city.

11. I wish to include here the practice of using this method to allocate cooperatively reclaimed land among participants, another early explanation for the origins of warichi. See, for example, Nakada Kaoru, Echigo kuni warichi seido (The *Warichi* System in Echigo Province), *Kokka gakkai zasshi* 18, no. 205 (March 1904): 51–76 and 18, no. 206 (April 1904): 27–63. See especially the opening pages of the first part of this article. Uchida Ginzo, *Nihon keizai shi no kenkyū* (Studies in Japanese Economic History) (Tokyo: Dōbunkan, 1921), 256–59, also notes the association between land reclamation and corporate tenures.

12. Land reclamation took place under three different forms of organization. The most well known perhaps are the large multi-village projects that were financed by the Shogunate or daimyo in the seventeenth century. Individuals also engaged in private land reclamation. While much of this activity was rather small scale, by the eighteenth and early nineteenth centuries, some merchants were financing some rather large-scale projects (for example, Zeniya Gohei's investments in reclaiming part of Kahokugata in Kaga domain). Less well known are efforts in which several individuals or an entire village cooperated to reclaim land, sometimes in conjunction with domain-financed projects.

13. Brown, *Central Authority and Local Autonomy*, 35, 97, 202–3, 210, 225.

14. The head of a Nagaoka family spoke proudly to me of the pressure tactics he used to get cooperation on some issues when the chair of the local agricultural committee proved obstinate. Personal interviews, January–February 1994, Nagaoka, Japan.

15. Aono Shunsui, "Echigo ni okeru warichisei" ("The *Warichi* System in Echigo"), *Hiroshima daigaku kyōiku gakubu kiyō, Dai 2 bu* no. 26 (1977), 101.

16. Unfortunately, I do not yet have any insights into why this might be.

17. Some local historians with whom I talked believe that daimyo enacted the system. None of these scholars was able to produce any documentary evidence to support their contention. Even if we were to accept the argument advanced by

many Japanese scholars that Hideyoshi attempted to implement a system of nearly modern private landownership in Echigo and the rest of Japan, we would have to conclude that the effort failed: The very existence of warichi contradicts the intent of any effort to define only a single owner-cultivator for each plot.

18. There are not sufficient records of dispute settlements for me to determine if there was a consistent direction to the outcomes of disputes, even within one domain. Even those that do remain are often unusual in that they involve complaints by nonresident "landlords" rather than purely internal village disputes. This kind of dispute also appears to have been much less common than those between villagers over rights to exploit common land (iriai).

19. Some local scholars have told me that outsiders always had to have a local "stand-in" representative at redistributions or during decision-making meetings; however, to date I have seen no direct evidence in support of this contention.

20. Here I refer to productive value as estimated by the participants. Their assessment of land value usually had little to do with the formal putative yield (kokudaka) of the land that domain authorities used in calculating the taxes due from the village.

21. There is a close similarity between the procedures for allocating access to the common lands from which villagers collected firewood, grasses for fertilizer, and so on, and the warichi mechanism. This similarity raises the interesting question of whether or not there is a relationship between the two systems. Because of a lack of data, however, it is not possible to indicate clearly whether there was a relationship and, if so, what the nature of that relationship was. I suspect that, in general, corporate control of the commons preceded warichi. Two scenarios are possible—one which was propelled by local population growth and the other by changes in land tax administration. In the first instance, population in a region grew and encouraged the expansion of arable land. As arable land expanded, common lands were lost to cultivation. As common "wasteland" became an increasingly scarce resource, villagers would have needed to develop controlled access. Only with the expansion of arable land into marginal land would there have arisen a need to repartition arable land. Second, even if we were to assume that the stimulus to repartition arable land was not the extension of assart and reclamation into very marginal lands but rather the imposition of village responsibility for land taxation, the origin of commons—a medieval development—came during an era in which corporate village tax responsibility was not imposed by domains. Once warichi became established custom in a region, it probably moved even into those areas of reclamation and assart that were large enough to form the basis for new villages (shinmura).

22. "An'ei 2 mi Ozawa Village Sōzaeimon chi heikin negai narabini utsushi, tori-atsukainin kakitsuke" ("Sōzaeimon of Ozawa Village's 1772 Request for Land

Redistribution and Document Copies with Adjudicator's Attachment"), Hoshino-ke monjo, (Yoshikawa chō shi shiryō VI-10, B5-7, 1521, 4447).

23. Procedures existed for changing mountain land to dry field or paddy and dry field to paddy, but village approval had to be granted. Such conversions were commonly treated under the regulations for land reclamation.

24. "Ta-hatake chiwari chō, Hōreki roku mi aki ta-wari, Hōreki nana ushi haru hatake-wari san gatsu" ("Register of Land Redistribution of Paddy and Dry Field for the Autumn 1756 and Spring 1757 Redistributions"), Echigo Kuni Kubiki Kōri Iwade-mura Satō-ke Monjo, (Tokyo: Kokubungaku Kenkyū Shiryōkan, Shiryōkan) #57-A, 8009.

25. For one example of this practice, see Niigata-ken Nōgyō Kyōiku Sentaa, Niigata Kenritsu Kōnōkan Kōtōgakkō, Niigata-ken Nishi Kanbara-gun ni okeru warichi seido no chōsa—nōminteki tochi shoyū no rekishiteki tenkai (Survey of Land Redistribution in Niigata Prefecture, Nishi Kanbara County: The Historical Development of Peasant Land Possession) (Niigata: Niigata Kenritsu Kōnōkan Kōtōgakkō, 1968), 110 ff. Niigata Ken Naimubu, Niigata ken ni okeru warichi seido (The Land Redistribution System of Niigata Prefecture) (Niigata: Niigata Ken Naimubu, 1929), 48–49 ff., discusses more examples. For a discussion of the inter-relationship between warichi and accumulation of land rights by some, see Nōsei Chōsa Kai, Imai-ke no jinushi kōzo (The Structure of the Imai Family Landlordism) (Niigata: Nōsei Chōsa Kai, 1967) Niigata Ken Dai Jinushi Shozo shiryō, dai kyū shū, 103–16, 163–64. For an example of a listing of salary lands, see "Kyōhō 2 (1717) nen Echigo kuni Kariwa kōri Fujii kumi Tsurugi mura sashidashi chō" (1717 Registers from Tsurugi Village, Fujii District of Kariwa County in Echigo Province), Ihara Jun'ei Monjo, Oaza Tsurugi, Kashiwazaki-shi, Niigata prefecture.

26. I want to repeat, however, that there were times when a village which practiced general warichi would conduct a partial redistribution. All villagers recognized it as partial and as an exigency. They understood that there would be a return to a general redistribution at a later time.

27. See, for example, "Kansei jū ushi nen yori Ozawa-mura Tomizaeimon deiri sho ikken" ("Records of the Disputes concerning Tomizaeimon of Ozawa Village from 1798"), VI-10, B3-4, 775, 3701, Yoshikawa Chō Shi Hensanshitsu, Yoshikawa-machi, Niigata prefecture; "An'ei hachi nen chi kabu ikken gansho tome chō" ("Requests concerning the Landholding Incident of 1779"), Ihara Jun'ei Monjo, Oaza Tsurugi, Kashiwazaki-shi, Niigata prefecture.

28. See the various documents related to the petitions of Sozaeimon of Ozawa village in the collection of Yoshikawa Chō Shi Hensanshitsu, Yoshikawa-machi, Niigata prefecture: VI-10 B5-7, 1537, 4463; VI-10 B5-7, 1538, 4464; VI-10 B5-7, 1521, 4447.

29. In the case of Bakufu officials such as the daikan, this practice was associated with a change in the system for financing office expenses. Prior to the Kyōhō Reforms of the 1720s, daikan took office expenses directly from tax receipts before passing the balance on to Edo. During the reforms, the Bakufu insisted that all tax receipts be sent to Edo. Officials there then disbursed fixed allowances for office expenditures. Ostensibly because these allowances were insufficient, representatives from Shogunal offices notified villagers of what gifts were expected. There were standard gifts asked from all villages. For one example of the way villagers divided up such expenses among themselves, see the Tempō 7 "Hamen hikimai narabini on rei muki sho nyūyō wappu chō" ("Expense Register for Gifts to Officials and Tax Reductions"), Tokamachi Shishi Hensan Shitsu, Kawaji-kuyū Monjo C-1-148.

30. See the pledge of Sozaeimon of Ozawa village, An'ei 6.2.12, Hoshino-ke monjo, Yoshikawa Chōshi Hensanshitsu, Yoshikawa chō shi shiryō VI-10, B5-7, 1538, 4464, for one example.

31. Tomizaeimon was indeed a man of considerable initiative. He ultimately made a direct appeal to the Temples and Shrines magistrate of another domain by taking his petition directly to Edo. For this, he was placed under a light form of arrest and was ultimately fined—very light penalties by contrast with the common image, purveyed in historical literature, of imposition of the death penalty. See Note 22 for sources.

32. From the perspective of the less than enthusiastic participants, the attitude might have been that redistributive practices were not such a burden as to be worth fighting to abandon.

33. Charles Tilly, "War Making and State Making as Organized Crime," in *Bringing the State Back in*, ed. Peter B. Evans, Dietrich Rueschemeyer, and Theda Skocpol, (Cambridge, New York, and Melbourne: Cambridge University Press, 1985), 169–91.

34. The domestic confrontations were the Battle of Sekigahara (1600) that brought the Tokugawa family to national domination, the two Osaka campaigns of 1614–15, that eliminated the last remnants of the coalition defeated at Sekigahara, and the Shimabara Revolt of 1637. The two international conflicts were Hideyoshi's two attempts to conquer China by invading Korea in the 1590s.

35. For further exploration of the problems created by the challenges of time, distance, and technology, see Philip C. Brown, "The Mismeasure of Land: Land Surveying in the Tokugawa Period," *Monumenta Nipponica* 42, no. 2 (Summer 1987): 115–55; Philip C. Brown, "Never the Twain Shall Meet: European and Japanese Land Survey Techniques in Tokugawa Japan," *Chinese Science* 9 (1989): 53–79; and Philip C. Brown, "Practical Constraints on Early Tokugawa Land Taxation: Annual Versus Fixed Assessments in Kaga Domain," *Journal of Japanese Studies* 14, no. 2 (Winter 1988): 369–401. Philip C. Brown, in Chapter 3 of *Central*

Authority and Local Autonomy, discusses limitations on the effectiveness of Hideyoshi's supposedly national land survey policy.

36. There were instances in which the effort to extend arable land into upstream fields or to introduce irrigation to previously dry fields resulted in disputes over water for older downstream fields. Disputes over water apparently were not the source of widespread degradation of existing fields. They were often resolved so as to protect older fields. However, extension of cultivation into common lands and their privatization could and did lead to very different outcomes for nonfarm land, where woods, watershed, and erosion control could and did suffer. On these issues, see Margaret McKean, "The Japanese Experience with Scarcity: Management of Traditional Common Lands," in *Environmental History: Critical Issues in Comparative Perspective,* ed. Kendall E. Bailes, (Lanham, Md.: University Press of America, 1985), 334–59; and "Management of Traditional Common Lands *(Iriaichi)* in Japan," in Panel on Common Property Resource Management, Board on Science and Technology for International Development, Office of International Affairs, National Research Council, *Proceedings of the Conference on Common Property Resource Management* (Washington, D.C.: National Academy Press, 1986), 533–89. See also Conrad Totman, *The Origins of Japan's Modern Forests: The Case of Akita* no. 31 (Honolulu: University of Hawaii Press, Asian Studies at Hawaii, 1984).

37. Thomas C. Smith, "Pre-Modern Economic Growth: Japan and the West," *Past and Present* 60 (1973): 127–60.

38. In areas like Yoshikawa, the inability of a farm family to subsist on just a single nonrice cash crop and the need to produce rice for tax payments during the early modern era left farmers heavily dependent on cooperation from the village in the form of providing irrigation water and some cooperation in planting and harvesting. This was typical of most of Japan at this time.

39. Philip C. Brown, "Feudal Remnants and Tenant Power: The Case of Niigata, Japan, in the Nineteenth and Early Twentieth Centuries," *Peasant Studies* 15, no. 1 (Fall 1987): 1–26, explores one prefecture's experience with continued warichi despite the national government's enactment of private landholding in the early 1870s. This and other cases mentioned above clearly indicate the limits of the reach of the state.

40. In both areas, increases in yields were accomplished largely through increased investments of labor. New seed varieties, improved irrigation, and flood control also made major contributions. The classic English-language study is by Thomas C. Smith in *The Agrarian Origins of Modern Japan* (New York: Athenaeum, 1966) and in his "Okura Nagatsune and the Technologists," in *Personality in Japanese History,* ed. Albert M. Craig and Donald H. Shively, (Berkeley: University of California Press, 1970), 127–54. See also Francesca Bray, *The Rice Economies: Technology and Development in Asian Societies* (Oxford and New York: Basil Blackwell, 1986), for a more extended essay on the characteristics of intensified rice agriculture.

A general outline of the changes in agricultural practices described in Japanese agriculturalists' writings is provided by Furushima Toshio, "*Nōgyō no hatten— inasaku o chūshin ni*" ("The Development of Agriculture, with Focus on Rice"), in *Nihon sangyyō shi taikei* ("Outline of the Development of Japan's Early Modern Industries") I, ed. *Chihō shi Kenkyū Kyōgikai*, (Tokyo: Tokyo Daigaku Shuppan Kai, 1961); *Sōron hen* (General Interpretive Essays), 87–131; and Sugimoto Tsutomu, "*Jiseiteki kagaku bunka—jitsugaku no kōryū*" ("A Culture of Autonomous Science: The Flowering of Practical Studies"), in Taikei Nihon shi sōsho 19, Kagaku shi (Outline of Japanese History: Science) (Tokyo: Yamakawa Shuppansha, 1976), 154–61. For more detailed treatment of developments in the Kaga domain and Echigo regions, see the same author's *Nihon nōgyō gijutsu shi* (Development of Agricultural Technology in Japan) (Tokyo: Tokyo Daigaku Shuppan Kai, 1975); *Furushima Toshio chōsaku shū* (The Collected Works of Furushima Toshio) VI, 557–61; and Arashi Keiichi, *Kinsei inasaku gijutsu shi* (A History of Early Modern Rice Cultivation Technology) (Tokyo: Nōbunkyō, 1975) 246–60. Arashi's work seldom mentions changes in agriculture specifically in Satsuma domain but does, throughout his extensive treatment of the impact of new seed varieties on rice cultivation in the warmer regions of Japan, demonstrate that developments which occurred elsewhere in Kyushu also appeared in Satsuma, a region that practiced redistribution.

3

Property Rights on Imperial China's Frontiers

PETER C. PERDUE

P roperty rights approaches have become a powerful tool for analyzing social and economic change (Barzel 1989; Bromley 1991; North and Thomas 1973; North 1977, 1981; Feeny 1989). Several scholars have recently used the model to analyze landed property relations in imperial China (Buoye 1993; Myers and Chang 1976; Myers 1982; Yang 1987). But debates over Chinese property rights long precede these attempts. In this chapter, I criticize some applications to China of the property rights model and offer suggestions for improving its use, especially as connected with environmental change and land use.

Ever since seventeenth-century Jesuit visitors began reporting back to Europe about the Chinese empire, the nature of Chinese property rights in land has been a central focus of debate. French Enlightenment writers argued about the relationship between state and society in imperial China. The Physiocrats, especially Francois Quesnay, argued that the emperor's rights over land were limited by "natural law":

> I have concluded from the reports about China that the Chinese constitution is founded upon wise and irrevocable laws which the emperor enforces and which he carefully observes himself. (Quesnay 1946, cited in Perdue 1987, 1)

They held up China as a model for Europe. They approved of the Chinese view that land was the true basis of all wealth, and that promotion of agricultural production was the primary goal of a well-governed state. Low taxes and secure rights of possession provided incentives for farmers to invest effort, improve productivity, and create agricultural abundance.

Others like Montesquieu, by contrast, saw China as a pure despotism, where the emperor held title to all the land. Because complete state control of land removed incentives for private owners to improve production, China remained backward and poor. Montesquieu systematized the concept of China and other Asian empires as "Oriental despotisms." China, for him, was the negative model for Europe, an image of what absolutist regimes might become if individual rights to land were not protected against an all-powerful state. He promoted individual rights protected by formal constitutional guarantees in order to distinguish the free West from Asia. Marx adopted the Montesquieu view of Asia and incorporated other elements to create his model of the Asiatic Mode of Production, a society unchanging at its base beneath the rise and fall of imperial regimes (Anderson 1979).

The same debates have continued today. Some scholars stress the limited control of the imperial state over landed property and point to its encouragement of productive investment, its support for land contracts, and its encouragement of trade. Others, especially Chinese scholars, continue to promote the despotism view of imperial China as a backward, self-sufficient economy dominated by an oppressive, all-controlling state. The entire imperial era, from the second century B.C. to the collapse of the final Chinese dynasty—the Qing—in A.D. 1911, is seen as an era of "stagnation," during which "the system . . . remain[ed] basically the same for the whole of imperial history" (Yang, citing Pye 1968, 12–16).

These theorists have rejected the orthodox vulgar Marxist interpretation, which viewed the period as one of "feudalism," a socioeconomic formation dominated by private property land rights held by landlords. The imperial state was merely a servant of the landlord class, protecting its interests against rebellion by the exploited peasantry. Feudalism as a social formation contains the seeds of change within it, which sporadically produced "sprouts of capitalism" in either the tenth, sixteenth, or eighteenth century, depending on the analyst. Because private property systems create exploitation and class conflict, they will change, driven by the class conflict, but the Oriental despotic system, which features the "universal serfdom" of all to the state, has no dynamic of change.

All of these analysts were primarily concerned with the link between economic growth and property rights. They seldom considered the environmental consequences of growth. If we ask about the sustainability of socioeconomic structures, old questions about Chinese property rights appear in new guise. We are led to ask not merely whether farmers in imperial China had independent rights to land autonomous from the state and whether they had incentives to improve production, but whether the ultimate consequences were so damaging as to make the continuation of agrarian life impossible. In Marxist analysis, "sustainability" depends only on the resolution of conflict between humans. The relationship of humans to the natural world is not a contradictory one, unlike the class struggle of property owners versus the exploited.

This question has gained new urgency after the dramatic Chinese agrarian reforms of the 1990s. These reforms have produced a massive shift of control over land use to peasant proprietors, freeing them from the many restrictions imposed by the Communist state since 1949. One of the consequences has been extraordinarily rapid economic growth, but the environmental outcome is uncertain. Vaclav Smil argues that the reforms have exacerbated severe environmental strains, which may lead to ecological and economic disaster (Smil 1992, 1993). Some go farther, predicting massive political and social collapse produced by environmental crisis (Goldstone 1992). William Hinton defends the collective property regime that ruled from the 1950s to 1980 as having provided much more effective protection for public goods like the environment than the private property regime now spreading today (Hinton 1983). Lester Ross, by contrast, argues that effective laws for protection of the environment can only take effect after private property rights are secure, and that only during the reform period have genuine limits on environmental destruction been enforced (Ross 1988).

Examining the opposing sides in these historical and contemporary debates, I have a frustrating sense of inconclusiveness. These theories suffer from excessive abstraction from the Chinese physical, economic, and social environment. Their proponents outline global models which ignore variations of time and space. Hence confusion persists. A social history approach begins with sensitivity to local variations and change over time, and with the premise that the environmental consequences of property rights changes can only be profitably analyzed in local contexts. I begin with a critique of some of the prevailing models, then outline some case studies suggesting the value of the social historical approach.

WRONG TURNS IN THE
STUDY OF CHINESE PROPERTY RIGHTS

A Man of Sung decided to help his crops grow. He went into his fields and pulled on each of the sprouts, hoping to make them grow

taller. The next morning he returned and found all of his plants
dead. —Mencius

Grau, mein Freund, ist aller Theorie; doch grün des Lebens teurer
Baum. —Goethe (All theory, my friend, is gray; but the lovely tree
of life is green.)

"To abstract" means, in Latin, to "pull out," or to select the essential
features of an object for analysis. Like the Man of Sung, however, excessive
abstraction risks killing lived experience. Static models, whether cultural
or economic, ignore the contingencies of time and space that determine
development. I should stress that I am not attacking all abstraction in the
following critique, but only those forms of abstraction about imperial
China that misconstrue its development because they ignore processes of
substantial variation over space and time.

Karl Wittfogel's *Oriental Despotism* still remains an important reference
point for proponents of the Chinese despotism model (Wittfogel 1956,
1963). A Sinologist, member of the German Communist party, and
Marxist theoretician in the 1930s, Wittfogel converted to virulent anti-
Communism after his arrival in the U.S. in the 1950s. Arguing that
imperial China was the source of the violent domination by terror that was
responsible for the victory of communism in the Soviet Union and in the
People's Republic of China after 1949, he traced the rule of totalitarian
Communist states back to the "hydraulic state" of ancient China.
Distorting Marx's Asiatic Mode of Production into a simplistic, determin-
istic model, he argued that centralized imperial control over vital irrigation
sources secured the basis for a system of total power, in which there was no
private property because the state held all the land and productive
resources. Officials served as slaves of the emperor, with no intellectual
or territorial bases of autonomy. Villages were self-sufficient units of production, with no exchange relations. There was no historical dynamic of
progress, because there was no class struggle and all were slaves of the state.

Wittfogel's model lacks any empirical grounding. Studies of irrigation
organizations in imperial China have demonstrated that nearly all control
of water resources was local, not centralized. Most of China's agriculture
did not depend on large waterworks, but on natural streams or on tube
wells. The model is technological determinism of the most vulgar sort. Like
Hegel and Marx, Wittfogel excludes Asia from "History" of the Western
type. His argument is a late phase in a longstanding Orientalist project
designed to prove the superiority of the West over Asia.

Yet why does Wittfogel's model retain its appeal? Like the Chinese *budaoweng* doll, every time it is knocked down, it bounces back up in a new guise. The myth of changeless China has many uses. The popular Chinese TV documentary "River Elegy" invoked the same myth of a stagnant China, victimized by an oppressive imperial state controlling waterworks and sealing off the country behind the Great Wall. In this mythical version, only the arrival of the Western powers in the sixteenth century, sailing their ships across the blue ocean, could save China from its millennia of stagnation on the Yellow Earth locked behind the Great Wall. The grandiose sweep of the vision, combined with technological determinism, lent it great popular appeal in China, at the cost of distorting history (Perdue, in Smith 1994).

Yang Tai-shuenn, in a dissertation titled "Property Rights and Constitutional Order in Imperial China," adopts uncritically most of the essential features of the Wittfogel and Marxist Asiatic mode model and applies them to the analysis of property rights in imperial China. (Yang 1987) Invoking Douglass North on the importance of the "constitutional order" underlying the rules which specify transaction costs, he looks for common features of a Chinese constitutional order spanning two millennia of the imperial period (221 B.C–A.D. 1911), and explicitly downplays the significance of historical change or regional variation. Taking the existence of "stagnation" as unproblematic, he deduces the nature of property rights in China from classical philosophical texts, law codes, and cosmological and ideological assertions. He finds that the emperor owned all the land; there was little change over millennia, because the cultural emphasis on filiality, hierarchy, and imperial unity precluded individual rights. State control of property interfered with the efficient allocation of resources, and Confucian officials denigrated the value of trade. Because peasants had no secure property rights, villages remained self-sufficient, with little specialization or cooperative contact.

The model is very recognizable as Asiatic despotism dressed up in the terms of modern "property rights" analysis. As with Hegel, Montesquieu, and Marx, a construction of timeless China is erected in contrast to the dynamic evolution of "freedom" in the West. Globalist and totalistic in its characterization of the two modes of production, it is classically Orientalist: It "others" the West, radically separating it from China and the East. It is also "Occidentalist" in fetishizing the recent Western Europe experience as the norm for all. It is equally unconcerned with empirical research, relying as it does on documents referring to cosmology and norms, and never analyzing real land transactions.

Within China, Occidentalism can become a liberating ideology, as it did in the "River Elegy" television series, because it opens space beyond the strictures of Stalinist vulgar Marxism (Chen 1995); but as a method of social science analysis, it damages our ability to do empirically based cross-cultural comparisons. It is a static cultural analysis that removes two millennia of Chinese history from the reach of the market. The Oriental Despotism model removes China from world history, instead of including China's experience in global processes.[1] In fact, the "sprouts of capitalism" argument that flourished within the old, vulgar Marxist model—despite its crudity—did have the advantage of seeking trends in China parallel to those elsewhere in the early modern world.

Ramon Myers also applies property rights analysis to imperial China, but comes up with completely contrasting conclusions (Myers 1982). He points, first, to the sustained, massive expansion of the Chinese economy from A.D. 1400 to 1800. During this period, the population grew from roughly 65 million to 300 million people, maintaining at least constant per capita income; a rural marketing system developed, embracing 27,000 standard marketing areas linked to a hierarchy of marketing areas reaching up to central metropolises; specialization and exchange of agricultural products allowed rural households to allocate factors of production efficiently to their best uses; and the imperial state enforced and encouraged the development of customary law which undergirded this commercial development. It was the spread of customary law as the dominant allocation system in rural China after the seventeenth century that enabled the lowering of transaction costs and the spread of trade:

> The state combined the role of noninterference or slight modulation of the private sector with very limited authoritarian allocation of resources so as to create a fairly beneficent economic environment for private enterprise. (Myers 1982, 280)

Myers' argument, with its stress on the limited state and the beneficent effects of the state on private enterprise, echoes in more up-to-date language the eighteenth-century Physiocrats. His perspective is based on more solid evidence than the despotic view: To support his argument that contracts were significant and enforceable, he discusses actual transactions. Still, he creates an almost equally abstract, idealized picture of a competitive society filled with free markets, the society where Adam Smith should have been born. His view of China in this work is spatially undifferentiated; and although he focuses on economic change after the sixteenth century, he does not provide an explanation of the dynamic of change. Although he admits that the commercial and population growth of the eighteenth and nineteenth centuries "led to ecological devastation almost ignored by communities and state" (Myers 1982, 279), he regards this devastation as merely a "dysfunction of development," not a critical weakness.

I will return to his discussion of customary law below, but here I will simply point out the parallels in this style of analysis with the Oriental Despotism model. Both applications of the property rights approach can lead to excessively stylized pictures of a complex society, like snapshots of a living organism that fail to capture its dynamic of growth and decline.

A social history approach does not look for essential principles of a social structure in formal legal codes and religio-philosophical texts, but finds them revealed in social practice. Land sales and litigation are the best places to study property rights, not law codes and the principles of filial piety. I would deny that there is one completely consistent set of underlying principles that uniformly characterized Chinese social space. Particular transactions exhibited conflicting values, which required individual judgment of cases.

The Chinese land mass is of continental scale, and regional variation across the empire was quite pronounced. Let us turn to two regional examples of the determination of property rights in land.

CASE STUDIES

Taiwan

Taiwan had been almost uninhabited by Han Chinese until the late sixteenth century (Shepherd 1993). Its aboriginal peoples, who numbered about 100,000 in the seventeenth century, practiced deer hunting; fishing; and low-yield swidden cultivation of rice, taro, yams, and sugar cane. When Chinese merchants began to arrive in the late sixteenth century, trade began between Taiwan and the southeast China coast. The aborigines exchanged mainly deerskins, venison, and herbal medicines for iron, clothing, and salt. Meanwhile the Dutch built a fortress in the south in the 1640s. They failed to extract large revenues from the aborigines, whose productivity was low; but they were much more successful in generating revenue by selling deer hunting licenses to Chinese merchants.

The pirate-adventurer Zheng Chenggong (known to Europeans as Koxinga) drove out the Dutch in 1662 and established a base on the island. He focused primarily on security and revenue collection to protect his military refuge on Taiwan; and until his death in 1681, he promoted land reclamation and immigration to supply his wars against the Manchus. The Qing rulers took over the island in 1683.

The first consideration of the new rulers, likewise, was security. Taiwan was not expected to be highly productive. The new Qing rulers did not encourage immigration or trade, fearing that the island would once again become a base for piracy. They stationed only a small garrison of 10,000 men there. Soon, however, demographic and commercial pressures outstripped official policy. Chinese merchants promoted greatly increased trade in deerskins with the aborigines. Demographic pressures along the southeast coast induced peasants to leave for more abundant lands on Taiwan. By 1750, the combined population of Han and aborigines exceeded 660,000. The Han settlers cleared new lands along the western coast of Taiwan, and fought off aborigines with claims to these lands. Partly to stabilize the land conflicts, the Qing state supported the large rent system, at first introduced by Chinese merchants. This system of property rights divided land rights into two: The large rent owner paid the tax to the state and held title by contract; the small rent owner was the actual worker on the land, who paid a fixed rent to the large rent owner. Both rights could be sold independently or subleased to others. Aboriginal large rent holders given title to unopened deer fields contracted with Han peasant settlers, who took over the small rent rights and cleared these lands for agriculture. The Qing state made special efforts to secure the rights of both parties. It was especially interested in protecting the rights of aboriginal landholders and in preventing conflict between the arriving waves of Han settlers and the native inhabitants. With only a small garrison on the island and with little expectation of revenue, the court's main priority on Taiwan was to keep peace at low cost. The new property system seemed to satisfy the demands of Han settlers, aboriginal inhabitants, and state officials. Aboriginal landholders could receive a fixed income without engaging in cultivation, while their Chinese tenants were assured of secure tenures and incentives to improve productivity. Court policy in the early eighteenth century, in sum, "was to give Han settlers access to tribal land on the condition that they pay rents to aborigine tribes and land taxes to the state" (Shepherd 1993, 257).

Further economic and demographic developments of the eighteenth century, however, put great pressure on the system. The population flow to Taiwan continued at increasing rates, as Fujian province, across the straits, became increasingly crowded. Fujian producers also, as agriculture commercialized, turned to production of sugar cane and tea on the lowlands and sweet potatoes and maize on the highlands, causing the province to become a grain deficit area. Taiwan became a profitable source of grain exports to the mainland. Increasing profits in the grain trade and increasing integration of Taiwan's economy with the mainland greatly raised its revenue potential in the eyes of both the state and Han settlers, but severely damaged the aboriginal economy. The deerskin trade was eliminated by overhunting and replaced by commercial agriculture as the herds were exhausted. The deer population, in effect, suffered from the "fishermen's problem": Deer were an open-access resource, the extraction of which no one could limit (McEvoy 1986). Therefore, they were vulnerable to overhunting when commercial and demographic pressures grew, and the tribal hunters lost their livelihood.

After the destruction of the deer herds, the plains aborigines depended critically on large rent holdings for survival. Han settlers illegally bought tribal lands, and conflict occurred on the frontier between Han settlers and aborigines. Despite state efforts, aborigines fell into debt to Chinese merchants and lost their land. The officials feared that land losses among the aborigines would drive them into the mountains and turn them into the more dangerous wild tribal peoples who staged raids on the plains.

Compared to the non-Han peoples on other Chinese frontiers, the Taiwan aborigines received unusually favorable treatment. There is little evidence of impact of epidemic diseases on Taiwan's native peoples; their population did not decrease. Unlike the native North Americans, or the Mongols of China's northwest frontier, the aboriginal Taiwanese had had sufficient contact with the mainland germ pool to avoid near extinction. The plains aborigines saw the Qing state as their main protector. They enrolled in militia units for self-defense, under official supervision; and these militia units helped the Qing state suppress rebellions by Han immigrants.

Despite economic pressures, the large rent–small rent system persisted, because the state supported it. Qing officials debated the effects on landholding of unrestricted migration to the island. Some argued for keeping the island relatively isolated, allowing immigration only by soldiers and single male settlers, so as to reduce conflict with the aborigines. They attempted to stabilize conflicts over resources and freeze the status quo by restricting immigration and land clearance and by drawing boundaries between aboriginal and Han settler lands. Other officials, however, energetically promoted Han settlement. They argued that single men were much more likely than married couples and families to become involved in feuds and banditry. Their solution to land conflict was to push the Han settlement frontier much farther inland and drive aborigines off the plains. Imperial policy fluctuated under pressure from isolationist and integrationist (or separatist and imperialist) factions during the eighteenth century. In the end, demographic and commercial pressures overrode state policy. Settlers pushed the land frontier farther inland as the Han population increased, driving many aborigines into the mountains. The best the state could do was to protect the land rights of the remaining plains aborigines by shoring up the legal foundations of the large rent system.

The Qing rulers, despite autocratic pretensions, were far from "despotic" in practice: Their garrisons could not prevent movement of large numbers of settlers to an island far offshore. Nor could they stop conflict between aggressive Han settlers and the aborigines they wanted to protect. But they could fight a rearguard action against indiscriminate land takeovers, mainly through the legal guarantees of property rights and tax collection. As a result, the large rent system persisted until 1895, when the Japanese abolished it; and plains aborigines have maintained their presence on the flatlands of Taiwan to this day.

On the other hand, the Qing rulers were not simply "neutral adjudicators" of property conflicts. Their own security and revenue interests in the island affected their decisions about property. Taiwan, at first, was a low revenue region, important only in military terms as a potential base for rebels and pirates. During the eighteenth century, it became much more productive, a major supplier of grain reserves for Fujian and of tax income. Consequently, the state become increasingly interested in preserving stability of land tenure there.

Preservation of aboriginal livelihood also influenced state intervention in the property system. That livelihood depended ultimately on a successful transition from a hunting to a cultivating economy. Thus local ecology was clearly intertwined with the property system. The deer hunting economy of the aborigines eventually was pushed out by commercial grain production on the plains. The "raw" aborigines, those who refused to make the transition, moved to the mountainous uplands to continue their hunting and slash-and-burn cultivation; but the "cooked" plains aborigines adapted to the new intensive agriculture (Chen 1994, 1996).

Was this economy sustainable? "Sustainability" is an ambiguous concept. Mark Elvin has argued that Chinese agriculture has been unsustainable for 3,000 years (Elvin 1993). If "sustainable" means "unchanging," he may be right. But let us define "sustainability" more narrowly as the ability to continue an agricultural system for at least a century without radical shifts in the property rights regime or extensive outside subsidies. In these terms, Taiwan's agriculture was sustainable under Qing rule. It required low investment from the state. The subtropical climate of Taiwan lent itself easily to the production of rice and sugar cane. Maritime links to China's southeast coast attracted considerable mercantile capital. The Qing rulers encouraged this maritime trade, because it enhanced the revenue potential of the island. Taiwan remained a densely populated, highly commercialized center for high-yielding agriculture, very much integrated into the mainland Chinese economy—until the Japanese conquest in 1895, after which it developed agriculture even more rapidly to service Japanese markets. It was one of the last regions to be incorporated in the expanding Chinese rice economy sphere, a process which had begun with clearance of the lower Yangzi marshes in the ninth century A.D.

The Northwest

The security threat from Taiwan had been a temporary result of the decline of the Ming dynasty in the sixteenth century. In the Northwest, however, threats to the core lasted for millennia. The Northwest was China's most open frontier. No major mountain or river barriers separated the region of settled agriculture from the steppe and desert. Pastoral nomadism emerged out of settled agriculture in the Near East by 900 to 800 B.C. Once the nomads adopted the crucial weaponry of the horse, the stirrup, and the bow, they became a constant, and unbeatable, military threat to the states developing in the North China plain (Barfield 1989). These states had several responses. Most conspicuous but least effective was the building of defensive walls. In the second century B.C., the first Qing emperor unified many existing walls into a series of "Long Walls," which stretched across the Northwest frontier and were manned by military garrisons designed for quick response to nomadic attacks.

The concept of a single, unified "Great Wall" lasting for millennia, which has captured the Western and Chinese imagination—becoming along with the panda one of the two major symbols of China today, was in fact a mythical invention of eighteenth-century Western Sinophiles (Waldron 1990). Although defensive walls did sometimes help to repel nomadic attacks, they were often far too expensive and ineffective.

Founding emperors of new dynasties launched aggressive military campaigns into the steppe, but these often ended in disaster. The nomads retreated before the superior Chinese forces, waiting until the infantry troops outstripped their supply lines. Then the nomads wheeled around and struck from ambush, devastating the slow-moving Chinese forces with rapid maneuver and lightning raids. Diplomacy, "using barbarians against barbarians" and the lure of trade, was often more effective. Winning over certain nomadic tribes as allies against others and bribing leaders to refrain from attacks, disguised as the "tribute system," protected the regime until either the Chinese dynasty grew too weak to pay the price, or until a powerful nomadic leader unified the entire steppe frontier.

Over the centuries, despite Chinese efforts, nomadic rulers repeatedly staged attacks on the Northwest frontier and on certain occasions occupied part of the North China plain, or, as in the case of the Mongol dynasty (A.D. 1279–1368), the entire empire.

Only in the mid–eighteenth century could the Manchu rulers of the Qing dynasty finally resolve the Northwest security problem. They used a combination of all the earlier methods plus two essential innovations: solving the logistical problems of steppe warfare, and radically reorganizing property relations in the Northwest. Solving the logistical problem required building a chain of magazine posts from Gansu out to Xinjiang, and setting up a purchasing operation that could move camel loads of grain, clothing, and weaponry thousands of kilometers through steppe and desert out to the core bases in Central Eurasia. Once the Qing could keep a 50,000 man army in the field for up to three years, nomadic holdouts could no longer rely on temporary retreat before they were tracked down and wiped out. Stabilizing the Russian border through treaty negotiations in 1689 and 1727 also deprived the Mongols of a rear area, once the Russians decided it was more in their interest to pursue trade with China than alliance with the Mongols.

Most important for our purposes was the drastic reallocation of property rights pursued by the Qing, a process parallel to, but contrasting with, its concurrent policy decision about Taiwan. For autonomous pastoralists, rights to herds and men were far more important than rights to land. Customary law regulated seasonal movements of herds by each tribe to its pastures, but fluctuations in climate and changing power relations in the steppe often led to conflict. Any tribe which could not defend its pasturelands by warfare faced elimination, or incorporation of its members as slaves into the victor's tribe. Constant warfare between nomadic tribes was the general norm in the steppe. As the Qing rulers consolidated control in North China, they offered Mongolian tribesmen who surrendered to the Qing relief from incessant feuding and conflict. Those who surrendered were given titles of nobility and material rewards, and their pastureland rights were guaranteed and regulated by Qing officials. The Manchus, far more familiar than Han Chinese with steppe politics, also intermarried with the Mongol nobility to draw many of the Eastern Mongols (Khalkha) to their side. The basic process was a surrender of autonomy by the Mongols, handing over insecure but flexible rights to pasturelands to the Qing administration. Fluctuating claims on land, people, and herds were replaced by static, allocated rights to specific regions and territories incorporated within the bureaucratic state.

The Western Mongols, or Zunghars, resisted this process, unifying themselves under a succession of great leaders to confront the expanding Manchu regime. From 1690 to 1697, the Kangxi emperor conducted a series of campaigns against the Zunghar leader, Galdan, which ended with Galdan's death. Kangxi, proud of his victory, nevertheless had not crushed the Zunghar state. Only his grandson the Qianlong emperor, in a second series of campaigns from 1755 to 1760, could finally eliminate independent Zunghar power. He could only do this after overcoming logistical barriers and settling the Russian border question. Then began the great reallocation of property rights: the extermination of the Zunghars and the introduction of Chinese settlers into Central Eurasia.

The emperor ordered the massacre of young, able-bodied male Zunghars who refused to surrender when defeated. The elderly, women, and children were redistributed to surrendered tribes or made slaves and wives of Chinese military officials. By the end of the campaigns, the Zunghar population of roughly 600,000 had been entirely eliminated from their homeland. Wei Yuan, writing in the early nineteenth century, estimated that one-third had died from disease, one-third had fled, and one-third died in battle (Wei Yuan 1984). Zungharia was by the mid–eighteenth century tabula rasa for new social experimentation. The Qing solution was to relieve the overpopulation in Gansu and the poor provinces of Northwest China by encouraging immigration to Xinjiang. Pasturelands and wastelands were converted to cultivated fields. The first settlers were military colonists. Each soldier was given sufficient land to support a family. He owed half his crop to his garrison and kept the rest. The state bore the cost of seed, tools, and irrigation works (Borei 1991; Hua 1995; Millward 1998, 50–52).

The next step was to allow settlement by military families. The soldiers were no longer rotated back to the interior after the end of the campaigns, but remained as permanent settlers on the frontier. The goal was to create self-sufficient settlements, thus preserving a military presence in the newly conquered territory while promoting land settlement. As in the nineteenth-century American West, land settlement was explicitly linked to frontier security (Allen 1991).

Next came the encouragement of civilian migrants. Beginning in the mid–eighteenth century, Gansu provincial officials sent out convoys of peasant settlers, equipped with clothing, agricultural tools, seeds, and cattle. They were to establish settlements in areas already surveyed by the government and found to have sufficient water and good soil. Every year, caravans of officially sponsored immigrants crossed the steppe to the oases around Urumqi, the capital city. By 1800, over 50,000 settlers had moved to the region (Hua 1987; Perdue 1992). Officially sponsored settlers were followed by unofficial migrants, who heard tales of the abundant land on the new frontier. Merchants put up funds to sponsor migrants, who paid off their debts after arrival. Finally, the state encouraged new settlements by Turkic peoples from southern Xinjiang, who had expertise in irrigated oasis agriculture.

When Zungharia had been steppe, low population density and nomadic customary law protected the grasslands from overexploitation. After the Qing conquest, the government, frontier merchants, military colonists, and civilian settlers pushed vigorously for more land clearance, more seeds, more water, and more fertilizer. The result was a much more intensely driven system, with higher population density, higher agricultural yields, and heavy use of irrigation channels. All these measures required heavy government investment.

Contrary to the Oriental Despotism model, the Qing state had an interest in improving agrarian production on both military and civilian lands, so as to promote self-sufficiency on the new frontier. Each of the settlers had a different relationship to the land they cultivated and to the state; but in general, there was a trend toward greater civilian control, as the officials focused more on productivity and less on security. Concerns for incentives to increase both production and revenue replaced the focus on simple sustainability and military defense.

The following report of the provincial treasurer of Gansu is one example:

> I have investigated and found that people's effort varies from dili-
> gent to lazy. They do not treat state land as their own fields; they
> only get the planting over with quickly with loaned seed; they do
> not plow deeply or rotate crops, they use little fertilizer. . . . When
> the crops sprout they do not go to the fields to protect them; or
> they even damage them or cut crops illegally for themselves and
> conceal it. Many abuses occur. Although officials inspect, there are
> 2400 households scattered widely over 160 *li*, and they cannot all
> be watched. If we do not set up a taxation system, then yearly the
> government share will decrease; there will be only the empty name
> of dividing the harvest, and no real military land cultivation. The
> land will get rockier, or have no yield. (*Zhupi* memorials in First
> National Archives, Beijing, "Land Clearance," 1762/5/13 *Gansu
> buzhengshi* Wu Zhaoshi)

This writer goes on to recommend changing from the military colony land system, in which the crop was divided evenly between the cultivators and the state, to a fixed rent system, which turned the military colony lands into private land. This discussion shows that state officials were clearly aware of incentive and supervision costs connected with the military colony system, and they were willing to alter the property rights regime in order to increase agrarian productivity.

Besides altering the property regime, the state also indirectly promoted land development by fostering the growth of trade. Commercial networks penetrated Mongolia and Xinjiang after the conquest. Increased market integration with the interior was promoted by state efforts to create a common currency, build roads, and facilitate trade by suppressing banditry.

As mentioned above, the question of sustainability is mainly a question of cost and time. A state willing to invest substantial resources can keep an agricultural regime going for a long time even in very unfavorable environments. Unlike Taiwan, Xinjiang was always a financial burden. It never became completely self-supporting, because the arid region could not support high-yielding agriculture on its own (Millward 1998). Literati representatives of the well-watered lower Yangzi region, who bore some of the heaviest tax burdens in the empire, recurrently criticized the expense of ruling Xinjiang during the eighteenth and nineteenth centuries; but security considerations led imperial officials to reassert its importance. Considerations of defense against restive Turkish peoples of Xinjiang, Chinese Muslims, and the aggressive Russians overrode considerations of cost. Although officials did try to create incentives to improve productivity, sustainability of the intensive agricultural regime had little significance in itself: It was more important in imperial eyes to keep the fields of Xinjiang open to Han settlement.

Both Taiwan and Xinjiang were frontier regions where landed property relations were radically transformed in the eighteenth century under the combined impact of people, markets, and states. Native peoples were swamped by Han immigrants; swidden and pastoral economies replaced by intensive cultivated fields; and tribal societies put under the domination of an expanding agrarian bureaucratic empire. The interaction of ecological, demographic, and commercial pressures with state interests accounts for much of their similar and different experiences.

COMMON PROPERTY AND CUSTOMARY LAW

Let me more briefly point out the usefulness of the historical approach for two central questions about Chinese land rights: the existence of common property, and the nature of customary law.

Daniel Bromley has argued that the failure to distinguish "common property" from "open-access" property has caused a great deal of confusion

(Bromley 1991). Open-access property is really unowned property, which faces no restrictions on its use. Common property, properly speaking, restricts enjoyment of its benefit stream to a defined group, and lays down restrictions on members of the group. Garrett Hardin's famous "tragedy of the commons" in fact referred to open-access property; but really existing commons, as in English open field villages for example, in fact restricted usage so as to preserve the resource. In Bromley's view, most "traditional" common-property regimes do preserve their resources. It is their undermining by forces of commercial capitalism that unleashes unrestricted use and ultimate devastation of the resource.

There are many examples of common property in China which support this analysis. Nomadic pasturelands, whose use was regulated by tribal customary law and enforced by constant warfare, can count as at least a sporadically regulated common property resource before the Chinese invasion. After the Chinese conquest, the property rights became much more privatized, intensity of exploitation increased, and overgrazing on the remaining pasturelands became a serious problem. The overexploitation of China's grasslands driven by commercial profit and demographic pressure has become extremely serious today, but the origins lie in the eighteenth-century conquest (National Research Council 1992).

Lineage land provides a second example that needs more investigation. Chinese lineages—groups of families with the same surname claiming descent from a common ancestor—maintained common lands to provide income to maintain the ancestral temples and to finance education of promising members of the lineage. Once again, static analyses lead to contradictory claims. In Yang Tai-shuenn's view, lineage common property is necessary for the protection of village autonomy against the state (117). He sees lineage landholdings as defending against the state abuse of tax/rent power. Japanese scholars, however, see lineage property as the basis of a "despotic" order in which common landholding overrode individual property rights.

Historical analyses, by contrast, show a fluctuating process, where efforts to maintain lineage lands were under siege by forces of commercial profit, population pressure, and free rider problems. Land managers were tempted to sell off lineage lands for individual profit, despite the efforts of both state officials and lineage heads to maintain them in order to shore up the ideology of familial harmony (Twitchett 1959).

Water resources form another large category of common property regimes in China. These include large reservoirs, jointly managed by the peasant producers; small polders, whose dike maintenance was allocated in rotation to the landholders within them; and numerous lakes, which were used for irrigation and fishing, whose bottoms were dredged for clay, and which were enjoyed for their aesthetic qualities by poets and admirers (Morita 1964, Schoppa 1989, Perdue 1990). All of these resources faced the same pressures. Population growth created incentives to clear more land around the lakes, reducing the size of the reservoirs and endangering flood control. The attractions of cash cropping and commercial markets led other investors to attempt to "privatize" the resources by seizing them, defying official prohibitions. Unlike the frontier cases, these resources seldom had significant security implications, but free rider effects were strong: Dike repairs, for example, should have been allocated to all those who benefited from the water supply, but in fact it was often only possible to get the immediately adjacent landowners to carry out repairs. The preservation of these common-property resources was precarious and difficult. Only a historical examination can demonstrate how officials, literati, peasant users, and proto-industrial "entrepreneurs" struggled over their exploitation, with a mixed record of success and failure.

The preservation of these resources concerned not just the immediate fate of a lake or forest; the ability of the Chinese to keep the resource common is an important indicator of the nature of the "public" (*gong*) realm. As Keith Schoppa brilliantly points out in his study of one small lake in southeast China, the fate of this lake parallels in miniature the fate of Chinese society over the long term. Despite the best efforts of poets, literati, proto-ecologists, and officials, the lake—besieged by the demands of peasants for water, of tile makers for clay, and of powerful local elites for tax-free land—disappeared in the twentieth century after a 1,000-year history, like the Chinese empire itself.

Customary Law

Customary law regulated most Chinese land transactions, but official administrative law interacted with it. Thomas Buoye has studied the combined effects of the two legal systems in responding to conflicts over land use in the eighteenth century (Buoye 1993, 2000). He focuses on cases of homicide arising from land disputes, which were "rooted in the tension between the emerging concept of land as commodity and the historical concept of land as patrimony" (Buoye 1993, 33). Customary law allowed most sellers of land to redeem it at the original price. Absolute sales with no redemption rights could be specified in contracts, but they were not the normal contract. In Guangdong province in the eighteenth century, population growth and increased commercialization continually raised land values, causing many sellers to claim redemption rights; but the buyers, interpreting their rights as absolute, often resisted, leading to violent conflicts. The state had to step in to adjudicate these conflicts; and it ended up reinforcing the idea of land as a commodity which could be alienated permanently, thus curtailing redemption rights. An imperial edict of 1756 limited redemption rights to thirty years, but local officials and provincial legal precedents often shortened the period. I have found a similar process at work in Hunan (Perdue 1987).

These examples demonstrate neither a stagnant despotism nor a fully laissez-faire regime, but a state struggling to direct institutional change in response to social and economic pressures. Customary and statutory rights to land moved closer toward absolute private property, but never reached total control. Limits on rights of sale remained, and limited redemption rights still persisted. Also, the changes varied regionally, depending on the balance of demographic, commercial, and security factors. Growing population densities drove up land values but also increased the landless population. The spread of cash cropping and specialization also raised land values in rapidly commercializing regions. Here, the claimants for land could be entrepreneurial landlords seeking profit from landed investment rather than impoverished immigrants. In frontier areas, conflicts also broke out between immigrants from different regions of China and between immigrants and native inhabitants. Amid these conflicts, state officials wrestled with conflicting goals. The ideology of "patrimony"—harmonious relations between official and subject, or landlord and tenant, based on a familial model, where land provided subsistence—was challenged by the spread of commodity relations. The state had both defense and welfare concerns. Military security was paramount in some regions, but relief of the poor was equally important. The two concerns were connected, as large landless groups could foment revolt, while loss of territory caused refugees and disruption. Conversely, territorial expansion provided elbow room for the landless, and settling a mobile population contributed to social order. Hence the Qing state both conducted aggressive military campaigns on an unprecedented scale and built the largest system of relief granaries the world had seen. Both were responses to new trends of population growth, commercialization, and ecological exploitation. Redefining landed property rights was part and parcel of this broader process.

CONCLUSION

There is nothing which so generally strikes the imagination, and engages the affections of mankind, as the right of property; or that sole and despotic dominion which one man claims and exercises over the external things of the world, in total exclusion of the right of any other individual in the universe. (William Blackstone, *Commentaries on the Laws of England,* 1807, 1–2)

To summarize the argument: Proponents of the property rights perspective disagree on many aspects, but they agree about the insufficiency of economic analyses restricted to the variables of supply and demand. Institutional structures that define the use and transfer of property significantly affect economic growth and environmental change. This paradigm marks a great advance in the use of economic theory to illuminate institutional change, but misapplication of the model outside Western Europe has led to misunderstanding. First, misuse of the model has created an implicit binary division between the privileged West, purported to be the first society to develop true private property rights in land, and the backward, despotic East. Second, the theoreticians have neither embedded property rights in the wider social and historical context, nor have they considered sufficiently the environmental effects of development based on property rights. Analysis of specific cases outside the West should contribute to productive application of this perspective.

As Yoram Barzel argues, too many economists and lawyers have assumed that property rights must be an all-or-nothing affair. Either they are absolute and unlimited, or private property rights do not exist. In real life, transactions are costly, and "property rights are never fully delineated" (Barzel 1989, 1). Some economists of the property rights school have claimed that only absolute property rights will provide the incentives to drive economic growth and have made misleading policy recommendations accordingly (Bromley 1991, 136). Recent legal studies have shown that absolute property rights of the Blackstone definition characterized only a little more than one century of American legal history. By the early twentieth century, they had been transformed into notions of contingently bundled rights, limited by social consensus (Vandevelde 1980, Grey 1980). Some economists have moved in the same direction. Because of high measurement and enforcement costs, many attributes of a good cannot be captured by one individual, nor transferred absolutely by contract. Many of them have to be left in the public domain, and it is efficient to do so (Barzel 1989, 115).

In this new perspective, Chinese property rights look neither backward nor particularly "Asian." Chinese land contracts transferred limited aspects of rights to land; they were enforceable by the state to a degree, but not completely; and yet they did provide sufficient incentives for agricultural investment and growth. Imperial China's property system was neither identical to the idealized market economy, as Myers would have it, nor utterly divided from it, as Yang argues. It was simply a different arrangement of bundles. You do not need absolute individual property rights to get economic growth—or ecological devastation. If we turn away from bipolar classifications to historically contingent, mixed combinations of particular rights and obligations created by varieties of states and legal institutions, we place less emphasis on the absolute individual and more on the social context, less stress on personal rights and more on the rights of nature and the rights of future generations (or, in other words, a move in Western theory from Locke to Kant (Bromley 1991, 5–7). We recognize that property rights have always been blurred bundles. Looking at the Chinese form sheds light on the Western variant.

NOTE

1. Many of the same points can be made against Eric Jones's discussion of "The European Miracle," although his work is much richer in ecological and economic detail. His later work, *Growth Recurring*, however, does find much more dynamism in the Chinese economy at certain times (Jones 1987, 1988).

BIBLIOGRAPHY

Allen, Douglas W. 1991. "Homesteading and Property Rights; Or, How the West Was Really Won." *Journal of Law and Economics* 34 (April): 1–23.

Anderson, Perry. 1979. *Lineages of the Absolutist State*. London: Verso.

Barfield, Thomas. 1989. *The Perilous Frontier: Nomadic Empires and China*. Cambridge, Mass.: Basil Blackwell.

Barzel, Yoram. 1989. *Economic Analysis of Property Rights*. Cambridge: Cambridge University Press.

Blackstone, William. 1807. *Commentaries on the Laws of England*, Book the Second. Portland, Maine: Thomas B. Wait & Co.

Blaut, James M. 1993. *The Colonizer's Model of the World: Geographic Diffusionism and Eurocentric History*. New York: Guilford Press.

———. 2000. *Eight Eurocentric Historians*. New York: Guilford Press.

Borei, Dorothy. 1991. "Beyond the Great Wall: Agricultural Development in Northern Xinjiang, 1760–1820." In *To Achieve Security and Wealth: The Qing Imperial State and the Economy, 1644–1911*, Jane K. Leonard and John Watt, eds., 21–46. Ithaca: Cornell University Press,

Bromley, Daniel W. 1991. *Environment and Economy: Property Rights and Public Policy*. Cambridge, England: Basil Blackwell.

Buoye, Thomas. 1993. "From Patrimony to Commodity: Changing Concepts of Land and Social Conflict in Guangdong Province during the Qianlong Reign (1736–1795)." *Late Imperial China* 14 (2): 33–59.

Buoye, Thomas M. 2000. *Manslaughter, Markets, and Moral Economy: Violent Disputes over Property Rights in Eighteenth-Century China.* New York: Cambridge University Press.

Chen, Qiukun. 1994. *Qingdai Taiwan Tuzhu Diquan: Guanliao, Handian, yu Anli Sheren di Tudi Bianqian, 1700–1895* (Land Rights in Qing Dynasty Taiwan: Changes in Land Ownership by Han Tenants, Officials, and Anli Aborigines, 1700–1895). Taibei: Zhongyang Yanjiuyuan Jindaishi Yanjiusuo.

Ch'en, Ch'iu-k'un (Chen, Qiukun). 1996. "From Aborigines to Landed Proprietors: Taiwan Aboriginal Land Rights, 1690–1850." In *Remapping China: Fissures in Historical Terrain*, Gail Hershatter et al., eds. Stanford: Stanford University Press.

Chen, Xiaomei. 1995. *Occidentalism: A Theory of Counter-discourse in Post-Mao China.* New York: Oxford University Press.

Committee on Scholarly Communication with the People's Republic of China. 1992. *Grasslands and Grassland Sciences in Northern China.* Washington, D.C.: National Academy Press.

Elvin, Mark. 1993. "Three Thousand Years of Unsustainable Growth: China's Environment from Archaic Times to the Present." *East Asian History* 6.

Feeny, David. 1989. "The Decline of Property Rights in Man in Thailand, 1800–1913." *Journal of Economic History* 49/2/285–96.

Goldstone, Jack A. 1992. "Imminent political conflicts arising from China's environmental crises." *AAAS Occasional Papers* (December): 41–59.

Grey, Thomas C. 1980. "The Disintegration of Property." Chapter 3 in *Nomos 22.*

Harrell, Stevan, ed. 1995. *Cultural Encounters on China's Ethnic Frontiers.* Seattle: University of Washington Press.

Hinton, William. 1983–84. "Report from Fengyang." *Monthly Review* 35 (6): 1–28; 35 (11): 43–45.

Hua Li. 1987. "Qianlong nianjian yimin chuguan yu Qing qianqi Tianshan Beilu nongye di fazhan" (Migration of people beyond the Wall in early Qianlong and the development of agriculture in Northern Tianshan in the early Qing). *Xibeishidi* 4:119–31.

———. 1995. *Qingdai Xinjiang Nongye Fazhanshi* (A History of Agricultural Development in Xinjiang). Heilongjiang: Heilongjiang Jiaoyu Chubanshe.

Jones, Eric L. 1987. *The European Miracle: Environments, economies, and geopolitics in the history of Europe and Asia.* Cambridge: Cambridge University Press.

———. 1988. *Growth Recurring: Economic Change in World History.* New York: Oxford University Press.

Landes, David. 1998. *The Wealth and Poverty of Nations: Why Some Are So Rich and Some So Poor*. New York: Norton.

McEvoy, Arthur F. 1986. *The Fisherman's Problem: Ecology and Law in the California Fisheries, 1850–1980*. Cambridge: Cambridge University Press.

Millward, James A. 1998. *Beyond the Pass: Commerce, Ethnicity, and the Qing Empire in Xinjiang*. Stanford: Stanford University Press.

Morita, Akira. 1964. "Guangdong' shô 'Nanhai xian Sangyuanwei' no jisui" (Water Control in the Guangdong Nanhai country Sangyuan polder). *Tôyô Gakuhô* 47 (2): 65–88.

Myers, Ramon H. 1982. "Customary Law, Markets, and Resource Transactions in Late Imperial China." In *Explorations in the New Economic History*, Roger L. Ransom, Richard Sutch, and Gary M. Walton, eds, 273–98. New York: Academic Press.

Myers, Ramon and Fu-mei Chen Chang. 1976. "Customary Law and the Economic Growth of China." *Ch'ing-shih Wen-t'i* 3/5.3/10.

North, Douglass C. 1977. "Markets and Other Allocation Systems in History: The Challenge of Karl Polanyi." *Journal of European Economic History* 6 (3): 703–17.

———. 1981. *Structure and Change in Economic History*. New York: Norton.

North, Douglass C. and Robert Paul Thomas. 1973. *The Rise of the Western World: A New Economic History*. Cambridge: Cambridge University Press.

Perdue, Peter C. 1987. *Exhausting the Earth: State and Peasant in Hunan, 1500–1850*. Cambridge, Mass.: Harvard University Press.

———. 1990. "Lakes of Empire: Man and Water in Chinese History." *Modern China* 16, no. 1 (January): 119–29.

———. 1992. "Land Settlement on China's Northwest Frontier." Delivered at Annual Meeting of American Historical Association, December.

———. 1994. "Technological Determinism in Agrarian Societies." In *Does Technology Drive History? The Dilemma of Technological Determinism*, Merritt Roe Smith and Leo Marx, eds. Cambridge: MIT Press, 169–200.

Pye, Lucian. 1968. *The Spirit of Chinese Politics: A Psychocultural Study of the Authority Crisis in Political Development*. Cambridge: MIT Press.

Quesnay, Francois. 1946. *Le Despotisme de la Chine*. Trans. Lewis A. Maverick under the title *China, A Model for Europe*. San Antonio, Texas: Paul Anderson Co.

Ross, Lester. 1988. *Environmental Policy in China*. Bloomington: Indiana University Press.

Schoppa, R. Keith. 1989. *Xiang Lake: Nine Centuries of Chinese Life*. New Haven: Yale University Press.

Shepherd, John Robert. 1993. *Statecraft and Political Economy on the Taiwan Frontier, 1600–1800*. Palo Alto, Calif.: Stanford University Press.

Smil, Vaclav. 1992. "Environmental Change as a Source of Conflict and Economic Loss in China." *AAAS Occasional Papers*. December.

———. 1993. *China's Environmental Crisis: An Inquiry into the Limits of National Development*. Armonk, N.Y.: M. E. Sharpe.

Twitchett, Denis C. 1959. "The Fan Clan's Charitable Estate, 1050–1760," In *Confucianism in Action*, Arthur F. Wright and David Nivison, eds., 97–133. Stanford: Stanford University Press.

Vandevelde, Kenneth J. 1980. "The New Property of the Nineteenth Century: The Development of the Modern Concept of Property." *Buffalo Law Review*.

Waldron, Arthur. 1990. *The Great Wall of China: From History to Myth*. Cambridge: Cambridge University Press.

Wei Yuan. 1984. *Shengwuji* (Record of Sacred Military Victories). Beijing: Zhonghua Shuju.

Wittfogel, Karl A. 1956. "Hydraulic Civilization." In *Man's Role in Changing the Face of the Earth*, William L. Thomas et al., eds. Chicago: University of Chicago Press.

Wittfogel, Karl A. 1963. *Oriental Despotism*. New Haven: Yale University Press.

Yang Tai-Shuenn. 1987. "Property Rights and Constitutional Order in Imperial China." Ph.D. dissertation, Indiana University.

4

Land as Law: Negotiating the Meaning of Property in Indonesia

ANNA TSING

> "How much more can they take from us? We have nothing left for them to steal."—Indonesian villager interviewed by anthropologist Emily Harwell in 1998 about destructive fires initiated by corporate oil palm plantations. (personal communication)

Some things seem too terrible to tell. Yet watching while History quietly forgets them seems even more terrible. How could the International Monetary Fund (IMF), in 1998, recommend—that is, command—the Indonesian government to increase its commitment to turning its remaining tropical rainforests into oil palm plantations by inviting more firms to participate, when in 1997 this very plantation sector was responsible for one of the biggest, best publicized environmental disasters in recent Southeast Asian history? The issue here is not just the destruction of the forest, but the handing over of land rights to plantation concessions where people with a deep sense of rights to the forest already live. Who blinded the IMF, not only to the environment, but to struggles over the meaning of property?

In these times of attention to environmental crisis, scholars have some kind of obligation to tell their readers (who with rare luck might include educable international policy makers) about property rights. Yet how best to do so? If we take the perspective of the oil palm plantation owners, we would talk about state property rules asserting themselves in frontier areas, replacing outdated and unworkable customary rights. If we take the perspective of the forest dwellers, the plantations are invaders, destroying their livelihoods and homes and running roughshod over their well-defined and certainly not outdated land and resource rights. Besides, both state and customary property rights are continually changing in mutual confrontation and dialogue. In this context, one must write of the replacement of customary property with state property with care: On the one hand, it is important to show how power works; on the other, one must avoid ignoring or erasing those who are arguing for or practicing alternatives, finding loopholes, making trouble for corporate plans, or finding places to stay out of the way. The plantations need not be privileged by assuming their unscathed triumph. I hesitate, then, to write a history of the penetration of the frontier by modern property rights. "Modern" tells us nothing about what these property rights are really like. Besides, property rights are not *things* but kinds of social relationships, and terms like "penetration" and "expansion" tell us nothing about social relationships. Instead, it seems more respectful, more critically aware, and more hopeful for building a livable future to write of the *instability* of even the most powerful property claims and regimes, to show their cultural-political specificities and limitations, and to admit the importance of the debates, struggles, and negotiations through which they influence human and environmental histories.

In this chapter, I discuss changing and contested understandings of property in Indonesia, with an emphasis on those ideas about customary property rights that have since the nineteenth century focused discussion about the rights of rural communities. In the context of the current corporate invasion of the forest, my goal is to show the conceptual resources that both empower and limit discussion of property rights alternatives. In the context of this volume, my goal is to raise questions and open perspectives on the instability of property as a category. A history of property is always a history of shifting contests over meaning and power in which the textualization and enforcement of particular property concepts are only tentatively confirmed. To study this instability is to acknowledge cultural and political legacies yet admit that one does not yet know the outcome— or even the outline—of the unfolding story.

FIRES

In the fall of 1997, Indonesian rainforests burst into fire. The smoke rose all over Southeast Asia, and with it reports of rural drought, displacement, and hunger. When the smoke blocked international air traffic and smothered cities, the world noticed. The Indonesian government, embarrassed, pulled out its familiar refrain: The fires were set by peasants burning the forest for their "slash-and-burn" farms. But this time, the world wasn't buying this story. Environmental organizations traced the fires to corporate projects of clearing the forest to plant oil palm and pulp and paper plantations. Satellite imagery confirmed their findings. In one amazing moment, the Indonesian minister of the environment announced that he knew the companies who were doing the burning and would publicize their locations and identities. Although the minister was forced to apologize, a breach in government bureaucracy was established; and environmental advocates, both in Indonesia and internationally, took heart and pressed their criticisms.

By the end of 1997, Indonesia's financial crisis displaced the forest fires in both national and international news. Yet some fires were still burning. And the slower pace of on-the-ground investigations suggested what environmental justice advocates most feared: In at least some areas, plantation corporations had set fires, intending to burn out already existing smallholder agriculture and village landholdings—that is, to confirm in the strongest way the corporation's property rights for would-be plantations. Meanwhile, in the heat of the dispute, local residents also set fire to plantations—and sometimes to each other's land.

Plantation corporations obtain concessions in forests controlled by the state. Indeed, in theory, all forests in Indonesia are owned by the state. Areas classified as forests, however, include towns, permanent farms, swiddens, orchards, villages, peasant agroforestry, enriched harvesting and hunting territories, and much more. Multiple parties claim rights, of varied kinds, to land and resources. The heritage of local claims is both older and more practical than the claims of the state; most forest dwellers are not recent settlers. If plantation corporations resorted to fire to burn out local residents, it was certainly in recognition of the shaky grounds of their own land claims. Their own weakness within the complex nexus of property rights and claims pushed them toward the most drastic solution: fire.

Settling land claims, once and for all, has become popular as a strategy in some international policy circles as a remedy for environmental destruction. Here, it worked in the opposite way: The property settlement was the destruction. But I should rather say, the *attempt* at property settlement, for these fire-expedited land claims may or may not continue to hold sway. Force doesn't settle the situation; it just frames new kinds of resistance and negotiation, albeit on unequal terms. It seems unlikely that the multiplicity of land and resource claims in the once-and-perhaps-yet-future forest will go away. In order to speak more clearly about this multiplicity of claims, I need to say something about property itself.

PROPERTY

Property is a social relationship between nonowners and owners, in which nonowners are expected to respect the rights of owners to their claimed objects. Yet property is more commonly presented as an attribute of the owned objects themselves. Property works by creating an aura around objects, a taboo. The owned object itself is supposed to radiate this fear-inspiring aura, warding off nonowners, and forcing them to feel terror and abjection should they attempt to enjoy the things that belong to others. The trinkets at the store glitter and draw the eye, but you cannot take them. This aura takes an enormous amount of work to make and maintain; and for this work, laws, ethics, customs, teachings, fences, "friendly" suspicion, bureaucratic and judicial procedures, and, of course, the threat of police or military force are called into service.

The aura of property—that is, the ability of objects to seem "owned" all by themselves—has been greatly strengthened by the great codification and administration projects of the nineteenth and twentieth centuries in which property laws and procedures became a definitional commitment of colonial and national states. Of course, most of the property conventions of these sweeping colonial and national projects were much older; and even new practices grew from older roots. But in the seeming alignment of parallel state visions of expansion and regularization—the same aligned visions that filled world maps with neatly adjoining territories—it came to seem possible that the whole world would be filled up with state-controlled and properly documented property. By the late twentieth century, national and international administrators began to hope that particular conventions of property—in such forms as reverence for the law, fear of the national police, cultural knowledge of the "no trespassing" sign, and religious devotion to the registered deed—might reach around the globe.

At the same time, however, the late twentieth century was a time of enormous instability and creativity in negotiating what would count as property. Consider just a few of the still-current negotiations that affect forested land as property: The *environmental movement* worldwide has contested what property owners should be allowed to do on their forested land; meanwhile, alternate forms of property are continually being imagined, ranging from trees with rights in themselves to semipublic and semiprivate reserves to community forests. The *indigenous rights movement* has also shaken up conventions for land and resource rights, demanding consideration for indigenous land claims that fall outside nationally codified property conventions. *Corporate aims and organization* have shifted to reckon with these, as well as other kinds of, challenges. Corporate practices make new kinds of property that respond to emergent conventions for intellectual and genetic property; international trade agreements; national deregulation; and the shifting conditions of global competition, subcontracting, off-shore processing, and finance. *International meetings and agreements* also influence states in their remaking of property laws and procedures; thus, experimental environmental laws with implications for property have multiplied in many countries. In this climate of renegotiation and change, administrators cannot just mop up recalcitrant corners into an evolutionary narrative of property. It is unclear at any given moment what forms of property will succeed in making forest history.

Meanwhile, it has been an enormous temptation for social scientists and social advocates to join projects of global codification, to contribute to understanding and managing the whole globe as a single, regularized system. Yet can we record this global synthesis without giving up our analysis to participate in the administrative visions that will the global synthesis into existence? Much of the research of the Human Dimensions of Global Environmental Change community responds to the call for globally regularized social categories. To discuss property rights at all within this science-and-policy-oriented context is an important intervention, and not easy. The study of property rights has the potential to call attention to social inequalities, regional idiosyncrasies, and political struggles: topics too often ignored in global studies of the environment. How can we best do this?

In contrast to an administrative vision which assumes property regularization as it makes it more possible, I would argue for a strategy that draws attention to the cultural specificity and incompleteness of the regularization process. In turn, this requires that we consider the alternatives to the regionally most powerful forms of property, and that in particular we study the definitional struggles through which both powerful forms and their alternatives become established. Only through these negotiations of the definitions of conventions of owning, owned objects, and people capable of ownership do particular forms of property gain hegemony. This chapter looks at alternative meanings of property and strategies of property making in Indonesian rainforests. At first glance, the terms seem rather stable: Since colonial times, state, private, and customary property have been the major alternative venues for claiming land. Yet I will show that the meanings of these categories and their relationship to each other has shifted dramatically in varied administrative projects.

My analysis is focused on the changing meanings of one kind of property: that defined by *adat* or customary law. The relationship between adat law property and state property—a relationship always overshadowed by the possibility of an idealized "modern European" kind of individual private property—has been key to rural administration and exploitation since the nineteenth century. In contrast to its much naturalized interlocutor, modern European law, adat law has become well established as an object of debate and disagreement. Thus, an investigation of shifts in the meaning of adat law illuminates shifts in the whole set of state-customary-private relationships on which Indonesian thinking about property has grown.

ADAT LAW

The word *adat* has its origin in Arabic; but it has become naturalized, in a variety of cognate forms, in many Indonesian languages.[1] Most commonly, the term refers to the ways things ought to be done, such as the organization of ceremonies and life cycle events, the settlement of disputes, and the delegation of authority. The term is most commonly translated into English as "custom."

In contrast, adat law, *hukum adat* in Indonesian, translates a Dutch term coined to refer to customary law in the colonial Netherland East Indies: *adatrecht*. Dutch adat law scholars based their research on ethnic-regional Indonesian adat and believed that their task was to make indigenous Indonesian customs more legible and usable in colonial courts. For this, they attempted to separate out "adat that has legal consequence."[2] And as much as their work is indigenously framed, adat law is necessarily a hybrid product, formed within colonial inequalities in the encounter between Dutch ideas of "legal consequence" and particular kinds of Indonesian adat.

Dutch colonial policy based native governance on adat law. In post-colonial Indonesia, adat law has continued to play a role, not only as it enters a substantial body of legal policy but also as it has become the subject of legal scholarship, political philosophy, government administration, and social justice advocacy. In these contexts, the colonial hybridity of adat law continues to shape its uses; at the same time, however, adat law has been transformed many times over. Furthermore, adat—and adat law with it—continues to mean very different things in different areas of Indonesia, and particularly in the varied rural areas in which adat continues to be important in daily life. In some parts of Indonesia, including some rural areas, adat is quite unimportant. In the Javanese countryside, which forms the basis of so much Indonesian national thinking about the "rural," adat is reasonably irrelevant as the basis of local law or dispute settlement.[3] In other areas, most disputes are brought to adat settlements. Yet there is enormous regional and ethnic variation in what adat means and for what it is used. In some places, for example, adat as ceremony is alive and strong, but not adat as criminal or property law; in other areas, the converse holds.

A further ambiguity is introduced in the commonly used subject of adat: the *masyarakat adat* or "adat society." A significant number of national thinkers imagine adat as the philosophical basis of Indonesian national society; to them, the whole nation would be an "adat society." However, the term is commonly used less inclusively, referring to all "traditional" rural people; or, more recently, only those who are ethnically marked as different from national norms; or, alternatively, those who are simultaneously rural, ethnically marked, and politically marginal to the nation. One important use of the term in the last ten years has been as a translation of the internationally circulating English term "indigenous people." Because Indonesia is not a European settler society, the word "indigenous" does not particularize the problems of marginalized "tribal" populations; the officially recognized alternative has been *masyarakat adat*. In this sense, but retaining all its ambiguities, the term shows up not only in laws and administrative policies but also in rural advocacy and public discussion of the environment and democracy.

For a key concept to be so hard to pin down is not unusual; consider "freedom" or, despite the intent of so much law and policy, "property" itself. Rather than consider this a problem for scholarship, I suggest we see these ambiguities as an opening to understand the liveliness of adat law and the ways it is used and transformed in "definitional struggles." Certainly, the question "What counts as adat law?" is debated and negotiated at every level of adat law's use. Villagers worry through not only the appropriate adat but also the appropriate context and social arrangements for even asking these questions. Furthermore, because adat never exists alone as a form of authority, villagers may claim the legitimacy of explicitly non-adat forms of state power and national law. It is possible, for example, to register land as private property even where adat law property is the general rule. Where adat law is used as a part of local judgments, people are always thinking about how it is being expanded, reduced, or used in eclectic or syncretic combinations with non-adat-like principles and procedures. Meanwhile, regional officials have considerable say in defining in what senses adat law will or will not be used by judges at the regency and provincial level; and they are likely to make powerful pronouncements about which ethnic groups in their areas do and do not have significant adat law. Finally, nationally operating lawyers, judges, scholars, administrators, and policy makers, as well as their international interlocutors, continually argue about the nature of adat law and its proper relationship to the larger body of national law and government administration.

Here I will focus on this national level of debate and negotiation, although not because the other levels are unimportant.[4] To focus on national negotiations allows me to work with "Indonesia" as a unit of analysis; and while it certainly is not the only relevant unit for thinking about property and the environment, it is particularly important for the two principal contexts in which I am writing this chapter. It is the national lawyers, activists, and policy makers who have something to say about corporate forest plantations; and it is the national bureaucrats who are listened to in international scholarship on property laws and conventions. Thus, first, I am interested in the national resources available for rural advocates working against those corporate invasions into the forest that displace long-term forest residents. At some level, this kind of advocacy will fail or succeed only within the conditions and struggles of particular rural areas, yet it requires national resources to be effective against the national and international policy-making elites who support plantation invasions. What are the legal, rhetorical, and policy tools that seem legitimate within the national context? A first step to understanding the constraints and possibilities of the debate is an appreciation of the cultural histories of the categories available for use, including adat law. Second, I am interested in national debates because they intervene most directly in histories of property law that take "property" as a stable object within, and sometimes across, nations. If we pay attention to the shifts and ambiguities that characterize property in law- and policy making, we are forced to abandon the idea that we know in advance of our analysis what property is as an object of study. Instead of global codifications, we might center "definitional struggles" in our analyses of the history of property.

My attention to national debates means I focus on adat law rather than actual on-the-ground adat practices in particular places. Debate about the national position of rural communities is already inside the concept of adat law. Adat law carries with it two ghostly opponents—real enough, but bigger and more insidiously definitional than their practical threats. On the one hand, adat law is advocacy for "local" control, where local is defined against a centralized, transcendent state without commitments of people and place. "Local" can be defined as big as the nation or as small as a village faction; through adat law, it becomes formulated as a point of engagement that forms an ordered alternative to a disengaged state.[5] On the other hand, adat law is defined as "tradition" against the imagined modernity and cosmopolitan legitimacy of European-origin law. Adat law property is "traditional" and "communal" and even "public" in distinction to European-origin law's private property. In this dichotomy, the state is not the opponent but the mediator, capable of protecting "public" and "communal" interests against voracious private greed. The presence of these overlapping double dichotomies, through which adat law is defined and redefined, accounts for the importance of adat law advocacy which attempts to put adat law safely inside the state at the same time as it opposes a whole history of state policies. Indeed, it is the flexibility that this double dichotomy gives to thinking about adat law that makes it such a useful tool for rural administrative policy as well as advocacy. The double dichotomy also means that a history of debates about adat law is always also a history of the state and private property. As the meanings of adat law shift, so do those of the state and private property, and their relationship.

The complexity of the conceptual frames for defining adat law owes something to the fact that each element was acquired at a different historical moment, in a different agenda for constructing property and administration. Two of these agendas are foundational in defining contemporary possibilities for imagining state, private, and adat law property: the late colonial period and the early nationalist period. From the late nineteenth century through the early twentieth century, adat law became part of a colonial definitional complex in which "natives" were differentiated from "Europeans" as "tradition" is to "modernity." Adat law property looked communal, timeless, and concrete in contrast to the imagined individuality, dynamism, and generalizing expansiveness of European-derived private property. Colonial rule in the form of the state was expected to mediate and guarantee the native/European difference, guarding each side from the other.

After national independence was declared, the ways property and administration were imagined shifted sharply. No longer was there to be a divided domain, part native and part European; the new nation would be unified in its culture and politics. In this climate, instead of being enshrined as a principle of difference, adat law became a principle of national unity. Instead of being a lens for the concreteness of village rules and lives, adat law became a flexible national philosophy. Rather than being a vulnerable domain to be protected by the state, adat law was charged with maintaining the harmonious balance between nation and state, community and leadership, public good and bureaucracy. This new national importance worked in contradictory ways to empower adat law; adat law became more difficult to grasp materially and concretely as it became more clearly charged with spiritual authority.

Both these agendas continue to have an important influence on the ways state, private, and adat law domains can be imagined in contemporary projects of making property, law, and government. In order to show the very different ways they contribute to the projects of the present, I need to trace the logic each agenda introduced in more detail.

COLONIAL DIFFERENCE

"He who turns from the law of the Netherlands to the law of the Dutch East Indies enters a new world." Thus begins a famous treatise of the Dutch adat law scholar, van Vollenhoven (1981, 1). Indeed, adat law came to mark the difference between the Netherlands and their "new world," the East Indies. This was a colonial difference, that is, one in which the condition of autonomy was subordination. Adat law was continually measured against a European legal standard. Furthermore, this condition of autonomy could only be maintained under the watchful eye of colonial rule, which protected both segregation and subordination.

Dutch colonial pluralism received its inspiration from sixteenth- and seventeenth-century Dutch commercial arrangements with administration in their trading territories.[6] The Dutch East India Company segregated its settlers and provided separate regulations for non-Europeans living in the regions they controlled. Yet the company's legal system was aimed mainly at the coastal settlements under its control and rarely reached the rural hinterland. When the Netherlands took over the territory as a colonial possession at the end of the eighteenth century, there was no colonywide administrative standard. It seems important to note that law in the Netherlands was not fully codified until 1838 (Sonius 1981, lviii). It was nineteenth-century codifications that unified racial and legal categories in the Netherland East Indies as well.

Governor-General Daendals, serving between 1808 and 1811, helped define colonial legal process by setting up native courts in Java, for Javanese, and Dutch courts, for Europeans. However, only British imaginings of a territorially hegemonic state could support legal interventions in both city and countryside. It was the brief British rule of Java (1811–1814) under Sir Thomas Raffles that made the significant change. The importance of a British contribution is particularly surprising because the British are known for a rather different legal approach in their Southeast Asian colonies: Where the Dutch established legal pluralism based on racial and cultural difference, the English made their own law sovereign even as they made a place for "native" accommodations. But perhaps it should not be surprising that pluralism, whose adherents were so often at odds with supporters of direct state administrative claims, could be established on the back of such claims.[7] The state Raffles imagined was spread territorially across the countryside, and its spread gave it the power of its own finances and political rights. Basing his claims on "native" understandings, Raffles investigated Javanese land tenure and "discovered" that all land was the property of the state. He also found that the village was the basic unit of

administration and that the village headman was the appropriate representative of the village as well as the appropriate agent of the government.
Tellingly, these same facts of native custom had earlier been discovered by
the British in India; certainly, it was convenient to extend the same administrative framework to Java.

These were productive interventions for the returned authority of the
Netherlands. In 1815, a Netherlands-Indies Constitutional Regulation
continued Raffles' scheme, in which village land and administration
formed the basis of the native judicial system; the Dutch also reintroduced
native courts, but now with the territorial imagination to make them
significant. In 1836, legislation confirmed that the native population
should be left under the government of their own headmen. In 1848, a
General Regulation classified all the inhabitants of the archipelago into
"Europeans" and "natives" and extended the dual court system across the
colony.[8] Legal pluralism was made more complicated by the Agrarian Law
of 1870, which divided land racially—not by the racial classification of
its owners or users, but by "European" and "native" land types, each with
their separate laws.[9] "European" land was land that could be claimed by
European ownership concepts; "native" lands were those governed by adat.
"Native" lands could be leased but not sold. The 1870 Agrarian Law
responded to pressure to guarantee secure private property rights for
European entrepreneurs; in the process, adat law property rights were also
confirmed. This kind of linkage, in which arguments for native autonomy
were never divorced from intensified state control and European commercial demands, frames the history of colonial adat law.[10]

Colonial endorsement of legal pluralism aimed to allow the application of local standards of justice and ownership. Yet colonial
administration consisted of a back-and-forth movement between colonial
military intervention and imagined self rule. A brief glance at a particular
area illustrates this dynamic better than does a colonywide perspective.
Franz von Benda-Beckmann (1979) descries the establishment of colonial
justice in West Sumatra as an uneven movement between colonial intrusions and invasions, on the one hand, and endorsements of adat, on the
other. Dutch concern with the region intensified after 1819, when adat
leaders approached the Dutch for military help against the fervently
Muslim Padri, who were trying to displace adat authorities. In 1821 the
Dutch made a treaty with adat leaders, confirming their sovereignty as they
sent in colonial troops.[11] In 1825 the Dutch began levying a market tax;
that same year, native courts were first set up in the Minangkabau Padang
Highlands. In 1833 local autonomy was affirmed with the decree "that the
law should be applied in accordance with the existing customs in each

district" (Benda-Beckmann 1979, 122); Dutch military action in the region continued until 1837. In 1847 forced cultivation of coffee was introduced. Adat leaders were responsible for the fulfillment of village quotas. Then in 1875 a change in regulations abolished the jurisdiction of the village government, leaving the adat leadership to flourish without official recognition. The lower courts, however, were expected to base their decisions on adat law. A differentiated system of adat and adat law developed, in which one kind of adat served village needs while a differently put together legal instrument, adat law, was used by colonial courts (Benda-Beckmann 1979, 117–18; Benda-Beckmann 1984, 17).[12] Only in 1935 was the village structure of adat leadership officially resuscitated; it lasted until the end of colonial rule.

Colonial administrators fought over the proper role of adat: Some argued that it should form the basis for administration of native areas, while others argued for its abolition in unified legal-political rule (Burns 1989). Policies shifted with these debates. In 1871, for example, colonial rules stated that European private law is "the standard and measure of law," "not only for Europeans but also for the indigenous population" (van Vollenhoven 1981, 26). It was within such standards and measures that adat law, even for its proponents, came to be a principle of difference. Adat law would always be defined by what it was not: European law.[13] Indeed, it was this negatively measured difference that was turned into a sympathetic science by the adat law scholars of the late nineteenth and early twentieth century.

Van Vollenhoven turned the study of adat law into a branch of scholarship and, in the process, built an influential model for colonial policy. For van Vollenhoven and the adat law scholars who followed him, adat was not just the name for a legal system; it opened up a whole world of exotic conceptions, cosmologies, subjectivities, and ways of life. The division of legal jurisdictions marked this division of worlds. Thus, one view:

> We can translate the word *hadat* only with the greatest of difficulty, for the thing itself is not to be found among ourselves. . . . We can only grasp and interpret it through the conception of God. Seen in this context the notion has a double meaning. Firstly that of divine cosmic order and harmony, and secondly that of life and actions in agreement with this order (Scharer 1963, 74–75).

Van Vollenhoven thought it would be relatively "easy to distinguish the adat with legal consequences, and to set them apart from adats without legal consequences." (1981, 6) Later scholars of adat have not agreed about the ease of separating out legally relevant aspects of adat, and they have blamed the Dutch policies associated with van Vollenhoven's influence for creating an artificial distinction between adat and adat law (for example, Geertz 1983). However, this was not intended as a way of forcing adat into a European model. It did seem necessary to formulate an adat law that could seem legitimate, because of its parallels with European law, within colonial debates (Benda-Beckmann and Benda-Beckmann 1984, 152). But the point was not to codify adat law to make it resemble European law; the point was to understand its difference—as oral tradition, as a system of forming communities, as a set of principles of social action.

Furthermore, for the Dutch adat law scholars, differences proliferated within the native system, marking separations between regions, ethnic groups, and villages. Some adat groups were organized by varied kinship principles; some were organized by territory or by some combination of kinship and territory and voluntary corporate association.[14] Adat was an art of differences not just between Europeans and natives, but among natives all the way down. James Boon's description of V. E. Korn's work in Bali is probably apt for a number of colonial adat law scholars:

> Korn's massive *Het Adatrecht van Bali* (1932) was an exemplary product of the 'new and typically Dutch' form of science. Seven-hundred pages are packed with most of the social rules and varying customary usages known in Bali. The tome divides everything according to Western legal divisions. . . . Yet the prevailing theme is not standardization, but local variation. Korn did not try to force a Western legal apparatus onto a more subtle Balinese ritual and social life. . . .[H]e tried to plot the way to preserve the rich varia-tions of Balinese culture. (Boon 1977, 52–53)

In the process, Boon argues, Korn was so involved with local difference that he made every village seem an autonomous republic, a culture of its own; but his exaggerations worked "to defend all locales from being reduced to average cases" (1977, 53).

To what extent was colonial adat scholarship a defense of "locales," if not of the peoples who lived in them? Van Vollenhoven was adamant that adat law gave native communities jural rights, including the "right of avail" *(beschikkingsrecht)*, the right to use and administer land and resources for the benefit of their members and the exclusion of outsiders (Holleman 1981, xlvi–xlvii). Yet, as I have been arguing, to the colonial adat law scholars, this right inspired a plea to the colonial government, not a mobilization for polit-ical independence. Colonial justice guaranteed adat law. And in this posture of dependence, adat law could only be the communal, spiritual, primitive Other of European law, entrepreneurship, and private property. All this, however, changed with Indonesia's independence: Where adat law once stood for proliferating differentiations, it became the spirit of unity.

NATIONAL UNITY

Indonesian nationalists denounced the colonial legislation of racial differ-ence as well as its internal divisions, which, they argued, divided and conquered the colony's subjects. Sentiment against the plural legal system, which enshrined adat law as difference, was strong. The Constitution of 1945, however, contained a provision that reaffirmed the validity of colo-nial law, unless it was contrary to the Constitution, until new laws could be written (Gautama and Hornick 1974, 182).[15] The next two decades were enlivened by active debate on the building of a new legal system—and the role of adat within it (Lev 1965).

Many young republicans saw no role for adat law in building the new nation. They wanted a modern nation and felt that adat law was unsuited to the challenges of the modern world. In particular, they argued that adat law was too uncertain to become a strong national law. In contrast, some lawmakers saw a limited but important role for adat. For example, promi-nent adat law scholar Supomo, who promoted the Indonesianization of the state, argued that sectors of national law involving the family and inheri-tance should be based on adat; in other sectors, European-derived laws should be applied. Commercial transactions, he argued, required coopera-tion with international standards, but family matters were more closely associated with community religious beliefs (Gautama and Hornick 1974, 183). Finally, some lawmakers thought that adat law could be the founda-tion of a distinctive and dynamic national law (Koesnoe 1971, 35). This last group was encouraged by the wording of a pronouncement of the Provisional People's Congress in 1960, which declared that adat was to be the basis of Indonesian national law:

> . . .[T]he Principles for developing the national law have to corre-spond with the political direction of the state and must be based on adat law which does not hamper the promotion of a just and prosperous society. (MPRS 11/1960 in Hooker 1978b, 27)

Unfortunately for proponents of adat law, "the promotion of a just and prosperous society," which could contravene adat, came increasingly to be identified with adherence to Eurocentric ideals of modernization and development. The People's Congress support of adat here could be read as a pious prologue that leaves little room for any specific adat law provisions.

It was in this climate of nation-building compromises that adat law began to be seen by its proponents as a unified national heritage. Gone completely were the studies of more and more finely differentiated rules and practices. Instead, nationalist adat law scholars argued that adat law offered a common community sensibility and a set of general but vague and flexible moral guidelines. Adat law scholar Mohammed Koesnoe describes the new view succinctly: "Adat law provides the principles only, and as such does not dwell on detailed prescriptions" (1971, B17).

> As law, Adat law provides a framework of norms for behavior and conduct regarding social relations. This framework, understandably, does not provide details, but indicates bare outlines called "asas-asas" (principles). The details are left to the discretion of Adat functionaries when administering the practical aspects of daily life. (Koesnoe 1971, B14)

This is a far cry from colonial adat studies: Details become principles; difference becomes unity; stasis becomes flexibility; structure becomes agency. Adat law could even help guide the developing national interest in "revolutionary law"—law that is dynamically built and rebuilt in relation to the Constitution and its national commitments.[16] Because adat law encodes national moral sentiment, it provides a frame for nation building and a check against the resurrection of a culturally inappropriate and disengaged bureaucratic state. Adat law in this sense is not archaic; it helps shape the national future. "'Adat' is the path of life of the Indonesian people welling up from its sense of ethics," writes Koesnoe (1971, B8).[17]

In the process of depicting adat as national ethics, Koesnoe also seems to echo the communitarian and perhaps orientalizing characterizations of colonial scholars, reminding his audiences of the definitional status of the ideally individualized and secularized European standard.

> The principle of totality in Adat law contains in itself certain conditions requiring every act and deed to be executed in such a manner that the harmony between the community and the universe (including the unseen world) be preserved. (1971, B21)

The context for such familiar generalizations, however, has changed from that of colonial administration. Koesnoe's statements may be utopian or nostalgic, as Clifford Geertz (1983) charges,[18] but they do not constitute rules for exclusion. Like European affectations of humanism or democracy, they attempt to create a sufficiently broad and inclusive moral background for all well-meaning citizens to be able to participate in national ideals. Their overgeneralizing quality is the key to their nationalism.

For Koesnoe and other nationalist adat law scholars, adat law does not create barriers and limitations but forms a ground for growth and new incorporations. One of the adat law interpretations in which Koesnoe breaks most clearly from the Dutch colonial scholars (with whom, indeed, he had close and respectful contact) is his understanding of "interracial law" as an example of the flexibility of adat law. For the Dutch colonial scholars, the emergence of interracial law revealed the inevitable problems of disparate cultures in contact. Dutch colonial scholars believed that intergroup conflict did not arise in the holistic, segregated precolonial world of adat. The arrival of European standards of difference led to conflicts—and proved the stability, boundedness, and incompatibility of the native system (Hooker 1978b, 200–204). In contrast, Koesnoe argues that the negotiation of intergroup conflicts shows the adaptability of adat law, its ability to meet new needs for new kinds of actors.

> Adat law, even as law based on communal principles, as a [consequence] of its supple and dynamic character, does not refuse to acknowledge new legal needs originating from individualist or other kinds of legal institutions. (1971: B36)

The problems and possibilities of the nationalist advocacy of adat law for national guidance are seen in a key piece of legislation for landed property rights issues: the Basic Agrarian Law of 1960. This was landmark legislation for national law and political culture in general. It was the first national law to abolish colonial pluralism, as it set up a single land law for the nation; there would no longer be "native" and "European" kinds of land. This was a major step in the nationalist project of unification. Further, the Basic Agrarian Law (BAL) affirmed that adat law was the law of the land—but with some overriding considerations. Even with these considerations, this gave a sense of success to nationalist promoters of adat law; and it laid a basis for future campaigns on behalf of adat law rights. At the same time, the BAL ignored, and even abolished, the specific provisos of most local adat systems in regard to land claims as it established a national law based on Dutch principles of landownership and disposal. These features are important enough to deserve some further specification.[19]

The BAL repealed the colonial Agrarian Act of 1870, which created dual systems of tenures, to set the founding stone for a unified Indonesian law. "All Indonesian citizens shall have an equal opportunity to acquire rights in land," says Article 9.[20] Like the colonial act, the BAL gives the state power to control all decisions involving land and natural resources. But the rhetoric has changed. "All of the earth, water, and air, including the natural wealth within it in the territory of the Republic of Indonesia has been given by God, and as the earth, water, and air of the Indonesian nation, it represents national wealth" (Article 1). "[I]n exercising its jurisdiction over these matters the State acts not as an 'owner,' but as a representative of the Indonesian people, to whom it is said the land, etc. has been given by God. Thus the Basic Agrarian Law abandons the feudal concept of 'domain' and introduces a theory of socialist responsibility" (Gautama and Hornick 1974, 81).

Article 5 declares that adat law is the law for all Indonesia. However, adat law must not be contrary to the national interest, the BAL itself—or to several other things. "The Agrarian Law that holds for the earth, water, and air is Adat law, as long as it does not come into conflict with national priorities and the state, which has its base in national unity, with Indonesian socialism, as well as with legislation included in this law, with other legislation, and while heeding the basic principles of religious law" (Article 5). National priorities, the state, Indonesian socialism, all legislation included here or otherwise, religious law: These are some rather severe limitations for adat law. "[T]he national government is always free, on behalf of the national interest, to intervene and dispose of the village's community land in some way other than that determined by the village" (Gautama and Hornick 1974, 81).

> The *hak ulayat* [the village "right of avail" over land cultivated and claimed by its members] and similar rights of adat law communities, so far as they still exist in fact, must be exercised in such a way as to accord with national and state interests, based on national unity, and so as not to contradict laws and other regulations which are of higher order. (Article 3)

The BAL sets up a variety of kinds of ownership and use rights, including categories ranging from rights of cultivation to rights to build, rights to clear land, and rights to harvest forest products. The most important right defined, however, is the right of ownership *(hak milik)*, modeled after the Dutch *eigendom*. Individual property rights are not unknown in Indonesian adat systems; but promoters of adat law have been particularly concerned that in stressing individual ownership, the law allows many adat law use rights and distribution principles to fall by the wayside. For example, the law allows and expects individuals to register lineage or village land as individual property and do with it as they wish during their lifetimes. Lineage and village rights of disposal are thus corroded. According to ethnographer Benda-Beckmann, for the Minangkabau of West Sumatra:

> It is obvious that a conversion of *adat* rights into *hak milik* rights
> would be the doom for the *adat pusako* [matrilineal adat], and this
> is fully realized by the villagers and lineage elders. In spite of fre-
> quent exhortations by the Government, nobody has had his or her
> *kaum's* land registered [according to the principles of the Basic
> Agrarian Law], for one is "afraid that the land will become *hak
> milik* and then be inherited by the children [and not the matrilin-
> eage members]." (1979, 321)

According to adat law scholar Hooker, "The [Basic Agrarian] Act may be
seen . . . as both a limitation on specific adat property rights and as an affir-
mation of adat general principles relating to land" (1978a, 26).

This ambivalence of the law, indeed, opens it to varied interpretations.
Some see the BAL as a defeat for adat law; others see it as a victory; still
others see it as the beginning of an unfulfilled promise. European adat law
scholars tend to see the law as limiting the possibilities for the practice of
adat law. Hooker, for example, introduces it as follows: "[T]here is legislation which limits adat rights (e.g., the Basic Agrarian Law of 1960). . . ."
(1978a, 3) Like a number of other European adat law scholars, including
Benda-Beckmann, Hooker sees the main potential for the continuance
of adat-based practices in the nonenforcement of the law.

Hooker continues the sentence I quoted: ". . . but the legislation itself
is not fully operable for administrative reasons. Consequently, the adat persists, that is, it is *descriptively* valid although formally limited" (ibid.). In
contrast, Indonesian nationalist adat law scholars tend to see the law as a
national triumph for adat-law ideals. Here is Koesnoe: "In [the Basic
Agrarian Law], Adat law is even recognized as the law applicable to problems of land, and Adat law institutions are ruled to be the institutions
which are to be followed in the respective statutes" (1971, B36). Even in
its combinations with European-derived property conceptions, Koesnoe
argues, adat law is being extended as the living law of the land.[21]

These interpretations worry through the principles of the BAL; other
readers have looked instead for the implications of the law for the unfolding future of legal practices involving land and property rights. Two kinds
of legal-practice readings are significant here. In the most common reading,
lawyers, legislators, and policy makers conclude that adat law has little relevance in the everyday practice of making law and policy. Since adat law
appears as the basis for, but not the practice of, property making, they read
the law as tucking adat into a few odd corners: Adat law may be something
to study in law school as history or philosophy; or it may be something to
investigate as custom in rural villages they know little about; but it need

not concern them as middle class professionals and bureaucrats in their cosmopolitan legal, commercial, and political affairs. A second reading, however, puts some of these urban professionals back in touch with rural concerns: The law is read as a promise to the people that has not yet been fulfilled. This was the reading of the social justice advocates of the national environmental movement of the 1980s and 1990s. These activists wanted to speak out for the rights of rural people affected by the environmental destruction caused by state-supported private entrepreneurship, with its transfer of land and resources from village people to national and international elites. For them, the BAL stands as a cornerstone of possibility for enforcing land rights for rural communities. They have argued that these rights have not been respected by government policies and private entrepreneurs. However, they have suggested, there is still something potentially good about the national plan, as seen in the BAL's endorsement of national responsibility and the rights of adat communities.

Both of these interpretive stances emerged within the cultural politics of the era of state building between the 1970s and 1990s called the New Order. The New Order state contrasted sharply with the earlier nationalist period. The state made its constituency the middle class urban professionals, bureaucrats, and entrepreneurs who were willing to commit themselves to a nation tied to international commerce and domestic order. There was to be no more nationalist mobilization connecting city and countryside in common causes; rural people were to be watched and managed, not included in nation making. In metropolitan concerns, adat law was irrelevant; but it could be used in the depoliticization and ritualization of rural life.

This was a repressive regime in which most social movements, such as those organized around the demands of labor, ethnicity, region, religion, gender, freedom of expression, or student idealism, were banned. Yet somehow the environmental movement blossomed in the 1980s, evading the ban on political life by its ties to the "neutrality" of science, technology, and international agreements. The national environmental movement drew attention back to social and environmental problems in the countryside, if through the words of urban activists. In this process, activists rediscovered adat and adat law: the best tools they could find to defend the rights of rural communities.

This was a form of adat law that was different from both colonial and nationalist agendas: It protected national minorities, not colonial native majorities; it reached out to national and international notions of justice, rather than into colonially bounded local knowledge; and it provided concrete rights, not just nationalist guiding philosophies. This adat law drew significantly on the foundational agendas I have described, but it shaped the framing distinctions between state, private, and adat law property in relation to the terms of a new law- and administration-making dream. In order to see how this project was imagined, I begin with the New Order context and the dominant administrative project in which adat was irrelevant to the nation except as rural social control.

BUILDING THE STATE

Indonesia's first president, Sukarno, enjoyed mobilizing the country, and particularly the Javanese countryside, through nationalist causes that brought people together under his leadership. All this nationalist mobilizing, however, came to a crashing end in 1965 when an attempted coup inspired an army takeover of the country and the purging of all those suspected of association with the Communist party. After the mass killing of some half a million people, the countryside became very quiet. General Suharto's New Order regime was free to turn its energy to attracting international investment, enriching domestic elites, and building the appropriate material and administrative infrastructure for investment through the proudly authoritarian program the government called "development."

As legal scholar Daniel Lev explains, one of the more enthusiastic constituencies for the activities of the new regime was professional lawyers (Lev 1992). Lawyers had suffered under the last few years of the Sukarno presidency, not only because of the failing national economy but also because their privileges had been arbitrarily limited and their abilities abused by Sukarno and his associates. In contrast, the New Order brought a booming economy, an expanding professional class, and a vast new need for commercial contracts and other legal services. Furthermore, lawyers were excited about the possibilities in the new regime for building the rule of law, in contrast to the patrimonial privileges they felt characterized the Sukarno era. These lawyers were trained in the European system; they had the greatest respect for European-derived law because of the clarity of its codifications, the confidence of its standing, and the professional expertise of its authority. To them, adat law seemed the plaything of traditional elites, allowing the manipulative flexibility of rank; the nationalist promoters of adat law were elite Javanese trying to protect their traditional privileges. They found adat law irrelevant in the international world of commerce and Western culture that Indonesian New Order "development" allowed them to embrace.

Particularly at the outset, lawyers imagined themselves in common cause with lawmakers and administrators in building a rule-governed, bureaucratic state that would be more effective, modern, and fair than any traditional authority. Lev explains, however, that as the New Order state developed and expanded, some lawyers also positioned themselves as critics (1992). Using their commitment to law against the state rather than for it, they defended dissidents, argued for regularized criminal procedures, and began to think about human rights. One of their most significant innovations was the creation of Legal Aid Institutes to defend the rights of the poor. In all of these critical activities, a commitment to the possibilities for justice within an adherence to law—that is, European-derived, standardized national law—was the framework from which their opposition to arbitrary and repressive state actions could take shape. Yet, when those lawyers working with Legal Aid Institutes began taking on cases involving marginal, rural communities, they could not help running back into adat law, since this was the only significant national framework for giving people in marginal, rural communities any rights at all. Some of these lawyers became important proponents for adat law rights: But this is a story that I postpone until fleshing out the context of the fate of adat law in the New Order.

Within the busy developments of Indonesian national cities, adat law came to seem irrelevant. International legal scholars wrote essays and monographs about the Indonesian legal system without mentioning adat law at all, except as ancient history (for example, Thoolen 1987). However, adat law had not really withered away; it had only disappeared within the realm of internationally attuned national politics. Two sites for the continuing development of thinking about adat law were, first, law school scholarship and, second, the bureaucratic apparatus in charge of the ongoing management of rural social life.

As adat law remained a subject of study in law schools, it inspired textbooks, essays, professional seminars, and continuing discussion among interested lawyers. The textbooks codified a genealogy of thinking about adat law, beginning with Dutch scholars van Vollenhoven and ter Haar, and running through nationalist scholars such as Supomo, Djojodiguno, and Koesnoe. (See, for example, Hadikusumah 1980; and Sudiyat 1978.) This genealogy made the nationalist thinkers appear to be updating and modernizing earlier colonial discoveries. It also made it possible to further update the nationalist line by showing its patriotic relevance within the New Order. In keeping with New Order politics, adat law scholars argued—although to increasingly smaller audiences—that adat law was a useful basis for inspiring "development" (Abdurrahman 1978), maintaining national Panca Sila thinking (Hadikusumah 1980),[22] and guiding the making of national law (Badan Pembinaan Hukum Nasional 1976). They carefully picked out all the national laws in which adat law was recognized in any way. They introduced anthropological theories to bring science to the study of adat law (for example, Soleman 1987). Occasionally, they described kinds of adat law to be found around the country (for example, Bushar Muhammad 1981). But, in general, this teaching literature did not stress empirical details about particular areas, but rather philosophical principles and historical trajectories of law and scholarly thinking. Its goal was to keep adat law a national issue, even if at a low level of public attention.

Meanwhile, a great deal of empirical research was being done on adat law in particular regions; but this was research of a very specific form: research that aimed for a nationally regularized inventory of regional laws and customs. The Department of Justice sponsored research on adat law, both in the interests of inventory as a goal in itself and to aid judges in regency-level courts in their decisions. The Department of Education and Culture also gathered material on adat law as part of an inventory of all rural culture and custom across the country. (Mahadi 1988 lists regional adat law studies from these as well as other sources.) These studies shared a number of common frames and assumptions. Assigned nationally and organized at the provincial level, research aimed to create a definitive record of regional adat law. Standard questions and outlines were used to achieve this record. Teams of researchers asked these questions of village and district authorities and sometimes offered survey questions to less important villagers. They compiled their results in standardized form for easy comparison with other research results.

The results are, of course, amazingly uniform.[23] Even the more sophisticated reports are limited by their outline structure to answering the assigned questions. Sometimes the researchers learned enough that they were tempted to become advocates for the local people they were studying. The team sent to study "the traditional patterns of control, ownership, and use of land in East Kalimantan" (Proyek Inventarisasi dan Pembinaan Nilai-Nilai Budaya Kalimantan Barat 1990–91) found that the precolonial state was a "constitutional monarchy" with an adat law constitution (29); they found that villagers were suffering from the loss of the forest (14–15); they found that villagers had a traditional "right of avail" over this fast-disappearing forest (39); and, most dangerously, they found that village demands for compensation against the government transmigration project that had stolen their forest were entirely reasonable, not only in accordance with their adat law, but in relation to government policy (133). However, this comparatively critical conclusion probably had little effect because the report's purpose was to "prepare data" (3) for the General Directorate of Culture in Jakarta, where it was intended to sit beside data in identical outlines from across the country to inspire a sense of completeness. The "traditional patterns of control, ownership, and use of land" project as a whole was launched to manage a frictionless interface between adat law and national law by gathering data; the reports in general were expected to speak of internal differences among villagers as they accommodate themselves to the contradictions between adat law and national law (for example, Manan 1989; Dakung 1989). The somewhat uppity conclusions of the East Kalimantan report may easily have gone unnoticed within these national codifications.

Furthermore, the whole set of reports on land tenure, with its potentially unsettling conclusions, is buried in a series of investigations of other aspects of rural life. The East Kalimantan land tenure report is the third part of an inventory project from the fourth national five-year plan, beginning in 1984, which was to specialize in the following topics: "1. The meaning of symbols and function of decorations of bride and bridegroom in the implantation of cultural values. 2. Foods, their shape, variation, and function as well as their presentation. 3. Traditional patterns of control, ownership, and use of land. 4. The proper ordering of behavior between families and society. 5. The growth of social settlement in riverine areas" (Proyek Inventarisasi 1990–91, viii).

It seems quite important that land tenure was considered of less concern than wedding decorations and the presentation of food. A number of scholars of New Order culture and politics, including John Pemberton (1994), have argued that the New Order government promotes local ceremonialism, in forms such as weddings, as a depoliticization of the countryside. The government-supported versions of village ceremonies that Pemberton describes in Java are missing all elements of tension and popular self-expression; instead, ritual order supports political obedience. In a related vein, Carol Warren describes the New Order compartmentalization and "aestheticization" of adat on Bali, as officials attempt to separate adat from religion, on the one hand, and official village authority, on the other (1993, 296–97). Adat reemerges nationally within these kinds of programs as the name for a local ritual order subordinated to national management. The Department of Education and Culture's inventory project of regional adat law appears as an instance of this very kind of ritualization of rural life, in which adat law, appropriately codified and managed at the national level, ideally offers customs without rights.

As Pemberton points out, the New Order administrative agenda is reminiscent in many ways of the colonial era, with its emphasis on political order and ceremonially enclosed autonomy. In terms of the codification of adat as law and custom, however, there are some distinctive transformations of the colonial project. National unity always frames the New Order collection; difference itself is uninteresting, and variation must fit within a prearranged national whole. In adat's role as variation on a national theme, there is no tension involving the possibilities for adat to actually rule; the kind of adat that can be collected in these national codification projects is that which is already inside the outlines and questions generated by a bureaucratic national consciousness. New Order adat is domesticated inside the nation; variation is an attraction for tourism and the raw material for development management. Yet the very centrality of this kind of variation to New Order images of national unity makes the regime vulnerable to regional unrest: thus, the more reason that regionalisms needed to be monitored and controlled by central authorities.

It is only in this climate of metropolitan attention to middle class development and international commerce, on the one hand, and of political silence and ritualization in the countryside, on the other, that a major dispossession of the land and resource rights of rural people could be simply planned and silently executed. In 1967, at the beginning of the New Order, a new law was passed concerning Indonesia's forests, giving the state full control over their disposal and exploitation. The government wanted control over the forests at that point for two reasons: income from logging and sites for transmigrants. Both of these projects involved displacing forest residents; the law recognized these residents mainly to keep them out of the way. By then there was little question of adat law as national law; adat is mentioned only to refer to marginal "traditional communities" (*masyarakat adat*). Traditional communities are allowed to continue to use the forest as long as their uses do not interfere with national plans (Article 17). But, already viewed as future forest vandals, they are advised to stop destroying the forest so that it will remain fit for national priorities (Safitri 1995).[24]

Beginning in the 1970s, logging companies gained concessions over the richest sectors of Indonesia's rainforests, and transmigration sites claimed other sectors for settler agriculture. Local forest residents were resettled or merely swept out of the way. By the 1980s, the situation had sparked major protests nationally and internationally. Those protests, indeed, turned the tide of national discussion of adat law property and the state.

SEEKING JUSTICE

In the late 1970s, urban Indonesian nature lovers and green consumers started to form environmental clubs and organizations. Drawing on the emerging prestige and legitimacy of environmental causes worldwide, they quickly gained in popularity. As the government came under pressure internationally to take part in conferences and agreements concerning the environment, government officials drew on the growing expertise of national environmentalists; and a cordial national atmosphere emerged for environmental concerns. By 1978, the environment had been added to ministry-level assignments, at first jointly with population. The presence of sympathetic officials at a high level encouraged the burgeoning environmental organizations, whose ranks swelled with engineers, journalists, and other urban professionals.

As the organizations grew, they differentiated: Some were technical, some educational, and so on. Nature lovers, at first concerned with preserving natural beauty, became increasingly caught up in the social and political problems that marked environmental degradation in rural areas. Where at first most assumed that rural people were part of the problem of degrading nature, their interaction with village people convinced them that government and corporate policies that marginalized villagers and stole their resources were much more serious environmental problems. Soon enough, a vibrant wing of the environmental movement had grown up in which environmental issues were diagnosed as social and political issues. Idealistic students flocked to this social justice wing of the environmental movement. Since most politically critical activities were banned, environmentalism was one of the few available areas for thinking about social justice; and the energy of the movement grew from its incorporation of suppressed thinking about human rights, class and ethnic discrimination, and other forbidden causes. In the 1980s and early 1990s, when politics critical of the state was still mainly hidden, the environmental movement—protected by a few technocrat engineers and government ministers—was one of the most important venues for social justice mobilizing and the expansion of national democracy.

In this environmental guise, ideas about social justice, nationalism, and democracy also expanded. Not only did activists direct attention to the class-divided Javanese countryside, the classical site of Sukarno-era populism, they also highlighted injustices practiced against marginal ethnic groups in the non-Javanese Outer Islands of Indonesia, such as Kalimantan, Sulawesi, and Irian Jaya. Beginning in the 1980s, they turned attention to the indigenous residents of the forests whose lands were being stolen by timber companies and transmigration projects. It was in this advocacy that they returned to the idea of adat communities and adat law rights.

Why shouldn't villagers be forcibly relocated from—or impoverished within—their lands? The most obvious answer to this question within the arena of national discussion was adat law rights. Adat law had a continuing legacy of legitimacy in national thinking. The activists of the 1980s were removed enough from colonialism to avoid its taint. Furthermore, the

New Order metropolitan culture of law, which had excluded adat law, made adat law available for those areas excluded from this metropolitan culture: marginal, "tribal" groups. No one confused adat law and the denigration of the Indonesian majority anymore; adat was a characteristic of traditional peoples in the remote countryside.

Other possibilities were available for the welfare of forest-area villagers. Government policy in many cases required compensation to be given for loss of crops when land was taken or destroyed for state or corporate projects. Many environmental activists, however, did not think that compensation for crops was enough—even on those rare occasions on which the nominal sums of cash were paid. The cash was quickly spent and provided no substitute for the means to livelihood not only over a lifetime but over generations. In this position, Indonesian activists found common cause with international environmentalists, who increasingly stressed the importance of land and resource rights for the rural people who protect the forest environment. The international indigenous rights movement joined environmentalists in calling for the recognition of customary land and resource rights. Thus, for example, the World Rainforests Movement's *Forest People's Charter* articulates the issue as follows:

> Above all, forest peoples are demanding secure control of the lands that they depend on. . . . Forest people's lands should be defined in accordance with local and customary systems of ownership and use. Where appropriate, land should be held communally and be inalienable (Colchester 1991, 261).

Some Indonesian environmental activists also argued for the importance of preserving local cultures in saving the forests. Internationally, too, social activists and conservationists were arguing that traditional local cultures had a good record of maintaining tropical forests. There was considerable debate on the question of the importance of traditional cultures in forest preservation (for example, Redford 1992); but in the context of the comparison between tribal cultures and the development projects associated with corporate entrepreneurship and government administration, it was hard to disagree that preserving tribal cultures worked better to safeguard forests than destroying both cultures and forests. Some northern environmentalists became so involved in thinking about this contrast that they romanticized traditional cultures; in considering Indonesian cultures, they exoticized adat as a sacred orientation to nature. The worst kind of romantic excess can be seen, for example, in this rhetoric from an Australian film about the Penan of Malaysian Borneo:

[The Penan] believe that the forest, the earth, the rivers, the stones, every living thing has a soul and an existence of its own. They call this belief "adat," which is the balance and harmony each person keeps with all things. Nature is the Creator, and they are the caretakers of the forest. If they neglect their "adat," then trouble will come (Kendall and Tait 1988, 1–2).

When Indonesian activists use adat law rights as a tool for advocacy for forest residents, they make alliances with northern environmentalists with concerns such as these. At the same time, Indonesian activists rarely romanticize adat law in this same way. Indonesian activists often hold romantic ideas about rural people and nature; but adat law, embedded in a legacy of legal thinking in Indonesia, is a realistic legal and political tool for them, not a window on exotic life ways. In this sense, national activists took a further step away from colonial discourse on adat; at the same time, they draw on the legalistic distortions colonial adat law made possible.

In this spirit then, national Indonesian activists began to call for the protection of the adat law rights of forest dwellers as a major advance both for social justice and for environmental protection.[25] One influential environmental journal articulated the issue as follows:

The indigenous people of Indonesia are national citizens and possess the right to live a normal and dignified life with a right to a clean and healthy environment. [These people] still respect and live by adat law. . . . There is a clear correlation between the impact of breaking traditional rights and the decline in the quality of the environment (WALHI [Indonesian Environmental Forum] 1990, 16).

A number of successes followed environmentalists' campaigns on behalf of forest people. The World Bank, which had been funding government transmigration projects that moved Javanese and Balinese settlers to the Outer Islands, agreed to discontinue this funding and to look more closely into government policies in regard to marginal people. The World Bank commissioned research on alternative legal options in relation to Indonesia's forests and their residents.[26] Meanwhile, other international organizations, such as the Ford Foundation, became interested in these issues. The Indonesian nongovernmental organizations that advocated for forest residents and worked to imagine alternatives received international funding for research, education, and advocacy on issues such as community-based forest management. Meanwhile, the corporate timber context had changed by the mid-1980s, as domestic logging companies gained increasing control of forest concessions. It was difficult for activists to put pressure directly on the timber companies, most of which had tight ties to the regime. However, there were small victories, as particular regional officials made decisions in favor of villagers (for example, Tsing 1995); and there were symbolic successes, as when one village leader won the prestigious international Goldman Environmental Prize for his efforts to save village adat forests from timber company destruction.[27]

The terms of engagement changed again, however, in the early 1990s. Under environmentalists' pressure, the government had noticed the extensive tracts of degraded forest in the Outer Islands, and attention turned to a particularly entrepreneurial idea for reforestation: corporate tree plantations. Corporate tree plantations offered few of the environmental benefits of natural rainforests; however, they satisfied international demands for "forests" at the same time as they generated corporate profits. In this spirit, the regime put its political backing behind these plantations, refitting its transmigration program to provide plantation labor and providing financial support from the national reforestation fund. While corporations were receiving national welfare, however, the lands and resources of forest-area residents were being expropriated even more finally than they had been for logging. Plantations sometimes measured off their territories right through the fields and yards of local residents.[28] Furthermore, since plantations were to be located on degraded forest, impatient corporations logged mature rainforest in order to create degraded sites for their plantations, thus further reducing the remaining rainforest area claimed and used by rural residents.

National activists objected. In an important case, the Indonesian Environmental Forum sued the Indorayon Company over its Sumatran pulp plantations, winning the right to sue on behalf of the environment (Tim WALHI dan YLBHI 1993). Local residents whose adat land was taken for eucalyptus plantations entered the suit, but the unsympathetic court combined versions of adat law and European-derived law in ways that were the least helpful to these claimants. Indorayon won on all points, but the suit made legal history in being heard at all; and in this capacity it continues to inspire activists.

In suits like this one, indeed, critical lawyers had entered the fray, supporting the national status of adat law rights to land and resources for forest-area residents against government and corporate expropriations. One of the most articulate and active of these lawyers has been Sandra Moniaga, originally an activist with the Indonesian Environmental Forum; then the cofounder of a Kalimantan-based nongovernmental organization, the Institute for Dayakology; and most recently the cofounder of a Jakarta-based human rights organization, Elsam. Her work has been particularly concerned with the legal rights of forest-area residents. In this capacity, she has argued for the importance of strengthening legal recognition of adat law. (See, for example, Moniaga 1993; 1994.) In contrast to the Basic Forestry Law of 1967, which is generally interpreted as giving all rights over forests to the state, she advocates a return to the spirit of the Basic Agrarian Law of 1960—with its recognition of adat law rights—as well as the Constitution—which promises a national commitment to the welfare of the people.

> [The Constitution] provides no basis for ignoring or abolishing *adat* property rights. Rather, it is, among other things, a constitutional mandate to recognize the *adat* property rights of indigenous forest dwellers so that they will be able to use their unique knowledge and experience to promote better land and forest management, and thereby benefit all Indonesian people. (Moniaga 1993, 143)

In her work, the drive for the recognition of adat rights is self-consciously a negotiation of the meaning of property more generally. Thus, she argues that the BAL promises the national community adat law "rights of avail" over all the nation's natural resources. Rather than giving the state rights to the lands of marginal adat communities, this requires a rethinking of the social justice of private property itself.

> In other words, the Indonesian people as a whole possess a kind of *hak ulayat* ["right of avail"] to all land, water, and forest resources within the nation. This interpretation is tenable and just only if it is understood to apply to all natural resources in Indonesia, including those that the government concedes to be private. (Moniaga 1993, 140)

Moniaga's arguments consistently ask lawmakers and policy makers to be reflective about the frameworks and assumptions that drive them to endorse unjust laws.[29] Instead of technical adherence to policy as it stands, she asks for a national discussion of the unfulfilled promise of the laws for a renegotiated national democracy. To argue for recognition of adat law rights is, for her, also a commitment to rethink the relationships of rural communities, private property, and state policy.

Moniaga has been effective in stimulating national and international discussion. Ford Foundation officers, interested in good relations with the government, said she had gone too far (Seymour and Rutherford 1993, 184); but their interest in the matters she raises has been clearly stimulated by her thinking. World Bank lawyers protested that, despite all that New Order adat law codification, they did not know whether and where adat law actually existed (Evers 1995, 14); but they have been forced to discuss the matter. Open-minded government bureaucrats began to rethink policy options to preserve corporate and bureaucratic precedence but give at least something to rural people (for example, Wangsadidjaja and Ismanto 1993). In the 1990s, new laws were passed mandating the protection of "vulnerable populations"—not yet ensuring land and resource rights, but making a step toward recognition of the problem. (The 1992 law concerning "Population Development and the Development of Happy and Prosperous Families" is discussed in Zerner 1992.) As popular debate continues to grow, all of this may yet make a difference.

The New Order saw its last days in May 1998. Activists working for social and environmental justice were in the forefront of those who helped change the regime and took responsibility for beginning to build something new. What legal and political arrangements will emerge is not yet clear. The first years of the new regime saw a rising tide of discussion of the role of adat in national life. In March 1999, a national congress of "adat peoples" was held, which brought together representatives from a variety of groups from across the country. The congress stimulated further debate about the definition and significance of adat. Meanwhile, too, new attempts to reform forestry law and regulations to recognize adat forests have been made. Adat-oriented protest in the countryside has increased. Discussions of adat property rights for forest dwellers is an issue that is unlikely to go away.

THE INSTABILITY OF PROPERTY

The success or failure of attempts to revive the national status of adat law land rights for forest-dwelling communities will rest not only on the national climate of discussion and policy making but also on the circumstances of particular regions and communities, and on the possibilities for what might even count as "adat law rights" for them. If activists are to succeed in empowering communities with adat law rights, it will be because of delicate and particularized negotiations about the kinds of national and international support engaged community members want for their demands and claims. No regularized national formula—such as that used in the New Order inventory projects—will be of much use. Activists will

have to confront a host of varied problems in translating community practices and dreams into a rhetoric that national supporters can recognize.
Thus, for example, in many areas local residents have clear ideas about the
social relations that tie community members to forest places and resources;
but these may not be stated in terms of boundaries, rules of exclusion, or
authoritative settlement policies. These kinds of relationships to land and
resources—which might include narratives of forest use and settlement,
histories of forest enhancement, or networklike and overlapping territorial
claims—must not be shuffled away as "open access" property but instead
used as the beginning of negotiated restatements of community rights.

This process has begun in the attempts of activists to work with community members in establishing their land and resource rights. In some
areas, community leaders have learned new vocabularies of rights and
needs with which to advocate for their villages in the shadow of government and timber company forest claims (for example, Tsing 1998; Li 1997).
In some, the rhetoric of "social forestry" has helped villagers make adat
rights demands (Rumansara and Rumwaropen 1993). In others, mapping
projects involving community elders as well as national and sometimes
international advocates delineate community boundaries that might stand
a chance in national policy decisions (for example, Fox 1990; Peluso 1995;
Moniaga 1993). These kinds of experiments will need to be multiplied
without losing their particularities.

Because adat means something very different in different areas, the
ways activists use their own national rhetorics of adat law to connect
villagers with national and international supporters will have to vary
considerably. One axis of variation that has already shown itself to be significant, for example, involves the relationships that have been established
among adat, religion, and local administration in the constitution of "local
community" in particular areas. Colonial adat scholars worked hard to
separate adat law and religion as separate domains, but their efforts were
not always very successful. Indeed, the Acehnese, studied by colonial
scholar-administrator Snouck Hurgronje in a pioneering effort to segregate
adat law and Islam, have, despite his efforts, continued to regard the two as
seamlessly intertwined (Siegel 1969). In contrast, the distinction between
adat and Islam has long been a vexed problem for the Minangkabau, as
described by Benda-Beckmann (1979) as well as many other scholars.
Furthermore, in many Christian areas of Indonesia, a stark distinction is
maintained between adat and religion. Volkman (1985) describes the distinction the Toraja have made between *aluk*, "traditional religion," on the
one hand, and *adat*, secular "traditional custom," on the other; this distinction allows Christian Toraja to practice adat without religious heresy.

In this spirit, too, Christian missionaries in Kalimantan worked to create a secular sense of adat for the Kenyah that allowed a continued "traditional" practice without the contamination of pagan cosmology (Whittier 1978).

Benda-Beckmann and Benda-Beckmann insightfully argue that in order to appreciate local understandings of either the unity of or the distinction between adat and religion, analysts must consider the relationship of each to local government administration, and their common historical roles in the founding of what have come to count as "local communities" (1988). Thus, they observe that Christian Ambonese seem more similar to Minangkabau in the distinctions they make between adat and religion than either does to Muslim Ambonese, for whom adat and religion are combined; to compare these groups, they look at the development of political organization in each area and the founding of village hierarchies of authority involving adat, religion, and government. This approach is useful to appreciate the distinctive alliances rural people have been able to make with environmental activists in defense of adat institutions. Thus, the Benda-Beckmanns themselves describe one alliance that relies heavily on the conflation of adat and local government: the environmentalist endorsement of conservation-oriented *sasi* prohibitions on harvesting land and marine products in the Moluccas (Benda-Beckmann, Benda-Beckmann, and Brouwer 1995). While these prohibitions draw from precolonial adat practices, they were most distinctively crafted as a form of colonial social control, under the rhetoric of adat law. Local administrations used sasi, across lines of Muslim-Christian difference, to regulate the village economy. If a revitalized sasi became popular with the New Order Ministry of Environment, it is in part because of its long association with rural social administration (Zerner 1994).

In contrast, one might consider environmentalist alliances that rely heavily on religion in defense of adat institutions. In Bali, adat, religion, and local governance continue to be tightly interwoven despite attempts to separate them (Warren 1993). In this context, anthropologist Stephen Lansing (1991) was able to work with irrigation temple priests to defend adat-based irrigation systems from the Ministry of Agriculture's attempts to modernize and regularize the irrigated landscape. Using computer modeling, Lansing showed the usefulness of irrigation temples, and he helped to coordinate a successful campaign for the recognition of traditional irrigation. While the computers were important, the success of their alliance with priestly knowledge depended on international and national support for religious and spiritual autonomy.

A third contrast is provided by environmentalist alliances based on the technical abilities of rural people to understand and manage their environment. This is an entirely secular alliance, and it can flourish where adat has become a secular matter. Among the Christian Kenyah of East Kalimantan, community elders were able to work together with non-government organizations and scholars to map the land use areas and boundaries of their communities (Sirait et al. 1994; Zerner 1992; Peluso 1995). Their maps, made with Geographical Positioning System (GPS) receivers and Geographic Information Systems (GIS) computer programs as well as Kenyah knowledge of the landscape, were considerably more accurate than anything available to the regional government. With the authority of both local adat and national-international expertise, they were able to play a role in making claims for adat law property rights. As in the case of Moluccan sasi, religion was not a definitional issue. Among the Kenyah, unlike the Balinese, adat has become secular. But in contrast to the alliance around sasi, this alliance bypassed local government officials to privilege customary elders. Among the Kenyah, government administration and adat law are far from synonymous; and thus the alliance was able to work against regional state policies for a legal and political alternative. As in the Balinese case, however, the use of prestigious modern technology was necessary, in working against the state, to make adat appear "realistic" in the modern world and not archaic.

Each of these cases draws on a distinct sense of what adat law might have to offer in the alliance between environmentalists and rural people. As each becomes an influential model for defending adat law property and resource management, it is important to hold the cases apart, to recognize and remember the creative agency involved on both the part of villagers and activists. This creative agency is necessary in formulating the kind of "adat" that might be a useful local empowerment as well as a possible source of national engagement and international support in each case. Yet creativity is much maligned; indeed, it has become the source of the biggest fears and hesitations of national activists and policy makers concerning the revitalization of adat law rights. The policy makers warn activists against the revitalization of adat, because, they say, local people are always making it up to fit current circumstances.[30] The more technocratically inclined environmentalists join them, finding adat law rights irrelevant to the solid, unshifting facts they want about the environment.

Why is adat law creativity such a terrible thing? For its critics, adat law must be timeless, static, and traditional—that is, utterly powerless in the contemporary world—to be anything at all. In this, they draw on the heritage of colonial discourse, in which adat law by definition must mark the traditional Other that has been surpassed by history. Furthermore, adat law is surely discredited in their eyes once it forms itself in alliance with national and international supporters; adat law, to be authentic, must be locally limited. From this perspective, the only agents of creativity should be themselves: the Western-educated, powerful agents of professional expertise. If rural people would only lie still, the experts would surely make the best policy decisions for them. Rural creativity is stepping out of line.

In contrast, I have been arguing that adat law property, like other forms of property, is constantly changing its meaning and social significance within struggles over the organization of land and resource administration. Activists necessarily change the local meanings of adat practices in order to work with villagers to bring adat into the national arena of discussion and debate. This is not necessarily a positive development; but, handled with sensitivity to both local and national concerns, it is about as hopeful a strategy as I can think of at this time for empowering forest-area rural communities and bringing rural people into national attempts to rework and expand democracy.

Consider the alternative: In 1997, in a forest-area village I visited in South Kalimantan, corporate plantations were already drawing their surveying lines through villager's fallowing swiddens, orchards, and fields. "Indonesia owns this land, not you," surveyors said to villagers who complained, reminding everyone of the regime's support for the plantations. The local response was panic; and those people who were able were selling forest resources as quickly as they could, before migrants, government officials, and corporate or individual thieves stole them all. Meanwhile, the regional police, working with appointed village officials, had decided to sell plots of land as private property to migrants and entrepreneurs. They merely measured off plots—never mind that these were other people's land claims—posted a sign, and sold them, pocketing the cash. Everyone knew about adat land and resource claims, but no one knew what to do with them. Violence reigned; local people were afraid and depressed. My best friend in the village chided me, after I had distributed my gifts from the United States: "Why didn't you bring a bomb so we could blow this place up?" A few months later, metaphorical bombs started going off: fires, drought, and financial panic and collapse.[31] In this desperate situation, to speak only of the inevitable encroachment of private property and the state, while warning against rural creativity, seems wrong.

What scholarship can do is modest. Here I have argued that property is by its nature an unstable social relationship, changing within social and political struggles and debates. Property owners expect property to be stable, especially landed property: We pass laws about it; we record it in deeds; we put up fences around it and will it to stay in place. On rainforest frontiers, impatient entrepreneurs want property to settle down, to put itself properly in their hands. Scholars can help these entrepreneurs by predicting the coming neatness of the situation, as the state asserts its support for "modern" entrepreneurial cultural forms. Yet I have argued that instability better characterizes the history of property rights in Indonesia—in national metropolises as well as rainforest peripheries. It is not only that local practices involving property are unpredictable (a subject I have not been able to touch on here), but that concepts of property at every level—local, national, international—are continually shifting. The possibility for shifting meanings is not a curse: It is the reason why concerned citizens bother fighting for social and environmental justice. It is also the reason why scholarship on the history of property tells us something about the richness and complexity and open-endedness of the world.

ACKNOWLEDGMENTS

My interest in this topic was conceived in the interdisciplinary workshops convened by John Richards in the early 1990s to discuss "landed property and the environment." I owe all the seminar participants, and particularly Professor Richards, a debt for their lively and engaged discussion, even as it sometimes stimulated my feisty rejoinders. This essay was first drafted to address a rather different audience—a 1993 conference of scholars of Southeast Asia convened by Renato Rosaldo to discuss "cultural citizenship"—and I am also grateful to the participants of that conference for their reactions and suggestions. Parts of this essay then entered talks I gave at Harvard University and at the University of Georgia in 1994. A slow process of editing drafts ensued. I am particularly thankful to Celia Lowe and Emily Harwell for their perceptive comments. Sara Berry and William Twinning kindly read a late draft.

NOTES

1. For example, van Vollenhoven lists *adat* as Malay, Javanese, and Achenese, *ngadat* as Javanese, and *odot* as Gayonese (1981, 4).

2. The phrase "adat that has legal consequence" is Snouck Hurgonje's (1893, 1:357). Snouck Hurgonje is credited with coining the term *adatrecht*; van Vollenhoven's adaptation of the idea (for example, Holleman 1981) brought the term into the center of public discussion of colonial rule.

3. Nancy Florida, personal communication.

4. I refer readers to several nicely researched ethnographies and regional histories of adat law and property rights. For studies of the regional development of

notions of adat as property and access rights, see F. Benda-Beckmann 1979; Benda-Beckmann and Benda-Beckmann 1994; Zerner 1994; and Peluso 1996. For studies of how particular kinds of adat law are used and abused in the national context, see K. Benda-Beckmann 1984; Vargas 1985; Tim WALHI dan YLBHI 1993, Warren 1993; and Zerner forthcoming.

5. In this conceptual framework for adat law, it joins other nationally disseminated adat concepts formed in opposition to state generalizations: adat territories (defined against state mappings); adat ceremonies (defined against state or "foreign" religious ritual); and adat leadership (defined against state functionaries).

6. Useful histories of colonial commitment to adat law in the Dutch East Indies can be found in Hooker 1978a; Hooker 1978b; Gautama and Hornick 1974; and Holleman 1981. I draw my information in the following few paragraphs from these sources.

7. Burns (1989) describes the early twentieth-century hostilities between supporters of legal pluralism, on the one hand, and of unified law under direct state domains, on the other.

8. In 1854, the Constitution recognized three population groups: Europeans, Natives, and Foreign Orientals, each with their own legal procedures (Benda-Beckmann 1979, 124).

9. The act also reconfirms the ownership of all land by the state. The state is free to alienate some lands to European entrepreneurs, on Dutch principles of ownership; native lands are not to be alienated to foreigners, but the state claims ultimate rights.

10. Meanwhile, the colonial administration created an increasingly direct jurisdiction over criminal cases. A common police court was established in 1914, and a common Penal Code was introduced in 1918 (Hooker 1978b, 189). Plural law became civil law. There were also various historical shifts in the colonial legitimacy of Islamic courts.

11. The treaty stated: "The time-honored customs and traditions of the land and the relationships between the Native Heads and their subordinates shall be completely safeguarded. In no case shall they be violated, *insofar as they are not contrary to the regulations stipulated above*" (emphasis added). "Safeguarding" comes with its limitations. Benda-Beckmann explains the italicized phrase: "The regulations referred to concerned the military presence of the Dutch in the highlands and the obligation of the Minangkabau to provide the Dutch with coolies" (1979, 121–22).

12. Keebet von Benda-Beckmann (1984) shows how the adat law used by West Sumatran state courts in postcolonial contemporary Indonesia differs from the adat used by Minangkabau village authorities in many ways, including the training and position of experts, the kinds of admissible evidence, the appropriate procedures as well as the role of procedures in decision making, and the kind of final decision

expected from the process. These differences between court and village decision making have their roots in the colonial situations discussed here.

13. Thus Gautama and Hornick (1974:, 122–24) offer the following principles of adat law: (1) No distinction between real rights and personal rights; (2) No distinction between movable and immovable property; (3) No distinction between public and private law; and (4) No distinction between civil and criminal delicts. The principles are intended to explain adat law for lawyers and legal scholars; no insult is intended. But it is difficult to explain colonially inspired adat law except as not-European law.

14. Van Vollenhoven divided the East Indies into nineteen adat law areas, and these were distinguished further internally by ethnic areas (Holleman 1981, 44–53). Burns (1989) argues that van Vollenhoven aimed to form a classificatory scheme with the power of Linnean biological classification or historical linguistics; in this spirit, Burns writes, van Vollenhoven understood regional differences as variations on a deep structure of pan-Indonesian commitment to balance. Differences were important, then, not just because they had been empirically discovered, but because they formed a node in a master system in which all difference might ideally sometime be encoded.

15. At first, this provision was interpreted as a way of keeping Dutch regulations in place. In the early 1960s, however, the provision was reinterpreted to stress that colonial statutes had to meet the standards of the Indonesian Constitution in order to be applied. Courts were asked to examine the constitutionality of every colonial law they invoked (Gautama and Hornick 1974, 184–88). This was the "revolutionary approach" discussed further in the next note.

16. In the early 1960s, there was considerable excitement among nationalist lawyers and legislators for a "revolutionary approach" in which the validity of laws would be reevaluated according to the spirit of the Constitution of 1945 (Gautama and Hornick 1974, 183–88). For a short period, laws were modified and justified by the courts in relation to such principles as "revolutionary independence" and "revolutionary socialism" (Hooker 1978a, 47–48). This approach remained powerful until the end of the Sukarno era, when nationalist mass politics were squashed and the standards of the bureaucratic state were reasserted in Suharto's New Order. Lev (1965) offers a critical assessment of the damage done to the legal profession during the Sukarno era.

17. Clifford Geertz objects to the use of the English word "ethics" in this translation and chooses "propriety," which he thinks better captures the sensibility of adat (1983, 210). I have chosen the English included in Koesnoe's bilingual text precisely because it does address the audience of nationalists and their international supporters I believe Koesnoe was trying to reach. For more on Geertz's perspective, see the next note.

18. Geertz describes Koesnoe's work as follows: "the best, most reflective, and most sustained of the postwar discussions [of adat], only somewhat marred by a

rather utopian view of village life, the nostalgia, perhaps, of the urban intellectual for an 'organic' society that never was." He adds, dismissively, "nationalism being what nationalism is, [it is] accompanied by a certain idealization, the romantic apologetics of the culturally defensive" (1983, 209). Geertz's goal is to characterize the legal sensibility of adat as practiced in particular rural communities; and for this job the nationalist making of adat law into a tool of nation building that might check neocolonial state making does not seem adequate. For my purposes here, in contrast, the question of just what nationalism "is" seems more compelling than it does to Geertz; it is worth a closer look at what nationalist scholars and jurists were making of adat law.

19. Quotations from the Basic Agrarian Law in the following paragaphs are taken from the following sources: Gautama and Hornick 1974, 78–90; Abdurrahman 1994; Abdurrahman 1978; Hooker 1978a, 26. Indonesian sources are put into English in my translation.

20. The law also addressed land reform: It regulates absentee ownership and limits the size of landholdings. But the regulations are vague and unspecified. As Hurst explains, "excessive" holdings are not permitted, but "excessive" is not defined (1990, 10).

21. Abdurrahman (1994) gathers the opinions of a number of jurists and legal scholars concerning the role of adat in the Basic Agrarian Law.

22. Panca Sila are five principles that were promoted to the status of a national oath of loyalty during the New Order. Hadikusuman (1980, 120–28) argues that each of the five principles is derived from adat law.

23. In the crudest reports, the standardized lists come close to parody. Answers to questions on the outline which no one answered in the research are left blank, with question numbers intact, in the final report. Adat law, measured against the standard questions, often appears in the negative—as when, in the report on adat law in a village in South Kalimantan sponsored by the Justice Department, the section on commercial transactions is full of findings such as "13. Here no one has ever sold or bought a ship or a boat" (Direktorat Jenderal Pembinaan Badan Peradilan Umum 1983, 36).

24. Zerner (1990) discusses the framework of the Basic Forestry Law in relation to the legal options it creates for forest residents, as well as the national economy. His optimistic yet critical assessment of the possibilities, created in part through attention to international precedents, has been an important inspiration for Indonesian social activists attempting to forge better options within existing laws. The research of Nancy Peluso (1990; 1992) as well as Charles Barber (1989) on the history of social forestry policy have similarly offered critical insights.

25. There are also many national environmental activists who do not want adat property rights to be recognized. These range from environmental activists who do not see social justice issues as central to environmental problems to those who,

recognizing social inequalities, think that the adat law will not help create a more just situation. For example, Myrna Safitri reviews national laws regarding the access of local populations to forest resources and finds that more rights are given to residents who approach the situation without adat law than to those who are recognized as adat communities (1995). She suggests that local residents forget about adat law and organize themselves as government-recognized cooperatives, foundations, and other forms that can draw upon European-derived law for their rights. Many of those activists and researchers who have worked most closely with forest-area residents, however, see adat law rights as more easily translatable in relation to local understandings and practices than cooperatives and foundations; advocacy for adat law, then, seems both more realistic and more just. See, for example, Mering Ngo (1996) for one adat law advocate's view.

26. See, for example, Zerner 1992; Evers 1995.

27. Other case studies of the conflict between forest-area villagers and timber companies, corporate plantations, and transmigration projects include: Vargas 1985; Tjitradjaja 1993; Fried in press; Tim WALHI dan YLBHI 1993.

28. This was the situation during my 1997 fieldwork in forest villages in South Kalimantan.

29. The translation and publication for an Indonesian audience of international conventions concerning indigenous rights has been one important facet of Moniaga's work in this regard. See, for example, Djuweng and Moniaga n.d.

30. Some readers of the Basic Agrarian Law note that the law demands that adat law "rights of avail" must "exist in fact" in order to be recognized; "once it has disappeared it cannot be revived" (Evers 1995, 20)

31. In 2000, the village was still reeling from these assaults.

BIBLIOGRAPHY

Abdurrahman. 1978. *Kedudukan Hukum Adat Dalam Rangka Pembangunan Nasional* (The Position of Adat Law in the Framework of National Development). Bandung, Indonesia: Alumni.

————. 1994. *Kedudukan Hukum Adat Dalam Perundang-undangan Agraria Indonesia* (The Position of Adat Law in Indonesian Agrarian Legislation). Jakarta: Penerbit Akademia Pressindo.

Badan Pembinaan Hukum Nasional. 1976. *Seminar Hukum Adat dan Pembinaan Hukum Nasional* (Seminar on Adat Law and the Making of National Law). Yogyakarta, Indonesia: Binacipta.

Barber, Charles. 1989. *The State, the Environment, and Development: The Genesis and Transformation of Social Forestry Policy in New Order Indonesia.* Ph.D. dissertation, University of California, Berkeley.

Benda-Beckmann, Franz von. 1979. *Property in Social Continuity: Continuity and Change in the Maintenance of Property Relationships through Time in Minangkabau, West Sumatra*. The Hague: Martinus Nijhoff.

Benda-Beckmann, Keebet von. 1984. *The Broken Stairways to Consensus: Village Justice and State Courts in Minangkabau*. Dordrecht, Netherlands: Foris Publications.

Benda-Beckmann, Keebet von, and Franz von Benda-Beckmann. 1984. "Transformation and Change in Minangkabau," in *The Broken Stairways to Consensus*. Dordrecht, Netherlands: Foris Publications, 149–81.

Benda-Beckmann, Franz von, and Keebet von Benda-Beckmann. 1988. "Adat and Religion in Minangkabau and Ambon," in *Time Past, Time Present, Time Future*, Henri Claessen and David Moyer, eds. Dordrecht, Netherlands: Foris Publications, 195–212.

———. 1994. "Property, Politics, and Conflict: Ambon and Minangkabau Compared." *Law and Society Review* 28 (3): 589–607.

Benda-Beckmann, Franz von, Keebet von Benda-Beckmann, and Arie Brouer. 1995. "Changing 'Indigenous Environmental Law' in the Central Moluccas: Communal Regulation and Privatization of Sasi." *Ekonesia* 2:1–38.

Boon, James. 1977.*The Anthropological Romance of Bali, 1597–1972*. New York: Cambridge University Press.

Burns, Peter. 1989. "The Myth of Adat." *Journal of Legal Pluralism* 28:1–127.

Bushar, Muhammad. 1981. *Pokok-Pokok Hukum Adat* (Fundamentals of Adat Law). Jakarta: Pradnya Paramita.

Colchester, Marcus. 1991. "Toward a Forest People's Charter." *IWGIA Yearbook 1990*. Copenhagen: IWGIA, 257–64.

Dakung, Sugiarto. 1989. *Pola Penguasan Pemilikan dan Pengunaan Tanah Secara Trradisional Daerah Sulawesi Selatan* (Traditional Patterns of Control, Ownership, and Use of Land in South Sulawesi). Jakarta: Departemen Pendidikan dan Kebudayaan.

Direktorat Jenderal Pembinaan Badan Peradilan Umum. 1983. *Masalah-masalah Hukum Perdata Adat di Desa Warukin, Kecamatan Tanta, Kabupaten DATI II Tabalong, Daerah Hukum Pengadilan Negeri Tanjung, Wilayah Hukum Pengadilan Tinggi Banjarmasin* (Problems of Adat Civil Law in Warukin Village in Tanta District, Tabalong Regency, Tanjung Jurisdict, Banjarmasin Greater Regional Jurisdiction). Jakarta: Departemen Kehakiman.

Djuweng, Stepanus, and Sandra Moniaga. n.d. *Konvensi ILO 169: Menganai Bangsa Pribumi dan Masyarakat Adat di Negara-negara Merdeka* (ILO Convention 169: Concerning Indigenous and Traditional Peoples in Democratic Countries). Jakarta: Elsam.

Evers, Pieter J. 1995. "Preliminary Policy and Legal Questions about Recognizing Traditional Land in Indonesia." *Ekonesia* 3:1–23.

Fox, Jefferson. 1990. "Diagnostic Tools for Social Forestry," in *Keepers of the Forest: Land Management Alternatives in Southeast Asia*, ed. Mark Poffenberger. West Hartford, Conn.: Kumarian Press, 119–33.

Fried, Stephanie. In press. "Fighting for Their Lives: Bentian Dayak Authors and the Indonesian Development Discourse," in *Culture and the Question of Rights in Southeast Asian Environments: Forests, Coasts, and Seas*, ed. Charles Zerner. Durham, N.C.: Duke University Press.

Gautama, Sudargo, and Robert N. Hornick. 1974. *An Introduction to Indonesian Law: Unity in Diversity*. Bandung, Indonesia: Alumni.

Geertz, Clifford. 1983. "Local Knowledge: Fact and Law in Comparative Perspective," in *Local Knowledge*. New York: Basic Books, 167–234.

Hadikusumah, Hilman. 1980. *Pokok-Pokok Pengertian Hukum Adat* (Fundamentals for Understanding Adat Law). Bandung, Indonesia: Alumni.

Holleman, J. F., ed. 1981. *Van Vollenhoven on Indonesian Adat Law: Selections from Het Adatrecht van Nederlandsche-Indie*. The Hague: Martinus Nijhoff.

Hooker, M. B. 1978a. *Adat Law in Modern Indonesia*. Kuala Lumpur: Oxford University Press.

———. 1978b. *A Concise Legal History of South-East Asia*. Oxford: Clarendon Press.

Hurst, Philip. 1990. *Rainforest Politics: Ecological Destruction in South-East Asia*. London: Zed Press.

Kendall, Jenny, and Paul Tait. 1988. *Blowpipes and Bulldozers*. New South Wales: Gaia Films.

Koesnoe, Mohammed. 1971. *An Introduction into Indonesian Adat Law*. Nijmegan, Netherlands: Publicaties over Adatrecht van de Katholieke Universiteit te Nijmegen 3.

Lansing, Stephen. 1991. *Priests and Programmers: Technologies of Power in the Engineered Landscapes of Bali*. Princeton, N.J.: Princeton University Press.

Lev, Daniel S. 1965. "The Lady and the Banyan Tree: Civil-Law Change in Indonesia." *The American Journal of Comparative Law* 14:282–307.

———. 1992. *Lawyers as Outsiders: Advocates versus the State in Indonesia*. SOAS Law Department Working Paper no. 2. London: University of London, School of Oriental and African Studies.

Li, Tania. 1997. "Constituting Tribal Space: Indigenous Identities and Resource Politics in Indonesia." Paper presented at the Environmental Politics Seminar, Institute of International Studies, University of California, Berkeley, October.

Mahadi. 1988. *Monografi Hukum Adat* (Monograph on Adat Law). Yogyakarta, Indonesia: Binacipta.

Manan, Fadjria Novari. 1989. *Pola Penguasaan Pemilikan dan Penggunaan Tanah Secara Tradisional Daerah Sumatera Utara* (Traditional Patterns of Control,

Ownership, and Use of Land in North Sumatra.) Jakarta: Departemen Pendidikan dan Kebudayaan.

Moniaga, Sandra. 1993. "Toward Community-Based Forestry and Recognition of *Adat* Property Rights in the Outer Islands of Indonesia," in *Legal Frameworks for Forest Management in Asia: Case Studies of Community/State Relations*, ed. Jefferson Fox.. Occasional Paper no. 16, 131–50. Honolulu: East-West Center Program on Environment.

———. 1994. "The Systematic Destruction of the Indigenous System of Various Adat Communities throughout Indonesia," in *Seminar on the Human Dimensions of Environmentally Sound Development*, ed. Arimbi H. P. Jakarta: WALHI, 31–36.

Ngo, Mering T. H. G. 1996. "A New Perspective on Property Rights: An Example from the Kayan of Kalimantan," in *Borneo in Transition: People, Forests, Conservation, and Development*, Christine Padoch and Nancy Peluso, eds. Kuala Lumpur: Oxford University Press.

Peluso, Nancy. 1990. "A History of State Forest Management in Java," in *Keepers of the Forest: Land Management Alternatives in Southeast Asia*, ed. Mark Poffenberger. West Hartford, Conn.: Kumarian Press, 27–55.

———. 1992. *Rich Forests, Poor People: Resource Control and Resistance in Java.* Berkeley: University of California Press.

———. 1995. "Whose Woods Are These? Counter-Mapping Forest Territories in Kalimantan, Indonesia." *Antipode* 27 (4): 383–406.

———. 1996. "Fruit Trees and Family Trees in an Anthropogenic Forest: Property Rights, Ethics of Access, and Environmental Change in Indonesia." *Comparative Studies in Society and History.*38 (3): 510–49.

Pemberton, John. 1994. *On the Subject of "Java."* Ithaca, N.Y.: Cornell University Press.

Proyek Inventarisasi dan Pembinaan Nilai-Nilai Budaya Kalimantan Barat. 1990–91. *Pola Penguasaan, Pemilikan, dan Penggunaan Tanah Secara Tradisional Daerah Kalimantan Timur* (Traditional Patterns of Control, Ownership, and Use of Land in East Kalimantan.) Jakarta: Departemen Pendidikan dan Kebudayaan.

Redford, Kent. 1992. "The Ecologically Noble Savage." *Cultural Survival Quarterly* 15 (1): 46–48.

Rumansara, Augustinus, and Decky Rumwaropen. 1993. "The Parieri Land Dispute: A Case Study from Biak," in *Legal Frameworks for Forest Management in Asia: Case Studies of Community/State Relations*, ed. Jefferson Fox. Occasional Paper no. 16, 161–69. Honolulu: East-West Center Program on Environment.

Safitri, Myrna. 1995. "Hak dan Akses Masyarakat Lokal Pada Sumberdaya Hutan: Kajian Peraturan Perundang-Undangan Indonesia (Rights and Access of

Local People to Forest Resources: A Study of the Regulations of Indonesian Legislation)." *Ekonesia* 3:43–59.

Scharer, Hans. 1963. *Ngaju Religion*, translated by Rodney Needham. The Hague: Martinus Nijhoff.

Seymour, Frances J., and Danilyn Rutherford. 1993. "Contractual Agreements for Community-Based Social Forestry Programs in Asia," in *Legal Frameworks for Forest Management in Asia: Case Studies of Community/State Relations*, ed. Jefferson Fox. Occasional Paper no. 16, 173–87. Honolulu: East-West Center Program on Environment.

Siegel, James. 1969. *The Rope of God*. Berkeley: University of California Press.

Sirait, Martua, Sukirno Prasodjo, Nancy Podger, Alex Flavelle, and Jefferson Fox. 1994. "Mapping Customary Land in East Kalimantan, Indonesia: A Tool for Forest Management." *Ambio* 23 (7): 416–17.

Snouck Hurgronje, C. 1893. *De Atjehers* (The Acehnese). 2 vols. Leiden, Netherlands: E. J. Brill.

Soleman, Taneko. 1987. *Hukum Adat: Suata Pangantar Awal dan Prediksi Masa Mendatang* (Adat Law: An Initial Introduction and Predictions for the Coming Age). Bandung, Indonesia: PT. Eresco.

Sonius, H. W. J. 1981. "Introduction," in *Van Vollenhoven on Indonesian Adat Law: Selections from Het Adatrecht van Nederlandsche-Indie*, ed. J. F. Holleman, xxix–lxvii. The Hague: Martinus Nijhoff.

Soesangobeng, H. 1988. "Perkembangan konsepsi tanah dalam masyarakat desa: 25 tahun U.U.P.A (The Development of Conceptions about Land in Village Society: 25 Years of the Basic Agrarian Law)." *Kabar Seberang* 19–20:59–83.

Sudiyat, Iman. 1978. *Asas-Asas Hukum Adat: Bekal Pengantar* (Principles of Adat Law: Sources for an Introduction). Yogyakarta, Indonesia: Liberty.

Thoolen, Hans, ed. 1987. *Indonesia and the Rule of Law: Twenty Years of "New Order" Government*. London: Frances Pinter.

Tjitradjaja, Iwan. 1993. "Differential Access to Resources and Conflict Resolution in a Forest Concession in Irian Jaya," in *Legal Frameworks for Forest Management in Asia: Case Studies of Community/State Relations*, ed. Jefferson Fox, Occasional Paper no. 16, 151–60. Honolulu: East-West Center Program on Environment.

Tsing, Anna. 1995. "From the Village to the Capital: A Successful Environmental Alliance." Report prepared for WALHI (the Indonesian Environmental Forum).

———. 1998. "Becoming a Tribal Elder, and Other Green Development Fantasies," in *Transforming the Indonesian Uplands*, ed. Tania Li. London: Harwood Academic Press.

van Vollenhoven, Cornelis. 1981. *Het Adatrecht van Nederlandsche-Indie*, selections translated by J. F. Holleman, in *Van Vollenhoven on Indonesian Adat Law*, ed. J. F. Holleman. The Hague: Martinus Nijhoff.

Vargas, Donna. 1985. *The Interface of Customary and National Land Law in East Kalimantan, Indonesia*. Ph.D. dissertation, Yale University.

Volkman, Toby. 1985. *Feasts of Honor: Ritual and Change in the Toraja Highlands*. Urbana: University of Illinois Press.

WALHI (Indonesian Environmental Forum). 1990. "Who is Violating Whose Laws?" *Environesia* 4 (2): 7, 10–11, 16.

Tim WALHI dan YLBHI. 1993. *Perjalanan Secarik Kertas: Suatu Tinjauan Terhadap Pengembangan Industri Pulp dan Kertas di Indonesia* (The Travels of a Piece of Paper: A Consideration of the Development of the Pulp and Paper Industry in Indonesia). Jakarta: Wahana Lingkungan Hidup Indonesia (WALHI).

Wansadidjaja, Sopari, and Agus Djoko Ismanto. 1993. "The Legal Case for Social Forestry in the Production Forests of Indonesia," in *Legal Frameworks for Forest Management in Asia: Case Studies of Community/State Relations*, ed. Jefferson Fox. Occasional Paper no. 16, 115–30. Honolulu: East-West Center Program on Environment.

Warren, Carol. 1993. *Adat and Dinas: Balinese Communities in the Indonesian State*. Kuala Lumpur: Oxford University Press.

Whittier, Herbert. 1978. "Changing Concepts of Adat and Cosmology among the Kenyah Dayak of Borneo," *Sarawak Museum Journal* 26 (47): 103–13.

Zerner, Charles. 1990. *Legal Options for the Indonesian Forestry Sector*. UTF/INS/065/INS/Forestry Studies, Field Document no. VI-4. Jakarta: Directorate General of Forest Utilization, Ministry of Forestry, Government of Indonesia, Food and Agriculture Organization of the United Nations.

———. 1992. "Indigenous Forest-Dwelling Communities in Indonesia's Outer Islands: Livelihood, Rights, and Environmental Management Institutions in the Era of Industrial Forest Exploitation." Report commissioned by the World Bank in preparation for the Forestry Sector Review.

———. 1994. "Through a Green Lens: The Construction of Customary Environmental Law and Community in Indonesia's Maluku Islands." *Law and Society Review* 28 (5): 1079–122.

———. In press. "Sounding the Makassar Strait: The Political Economy of Authority in an Indonesian Marine Environment," in *Culture and the Question of Rights in Southeast Asian Environments: Forests, Coasts, Seas*, ed. Charles Zerner. Durham, N.C.: Duke University Press.

5

Land Tenure, Traditions of Thought about Land, and Their Environmental Implications in Tanzania

JAMES GIBLIN

THE NEGLECT OF HISTORY IN RECENT TANZANIAN DEBATES ABOUT LAND

Over the past decade, conflicts over land and their environmental consequences have become increasingly important subjects of political debate in Tanzania. During that period, they have gained much of the urgency which land issues have long possessed in Tanzania's northern neighbor, Kenya. In Kenya, European land alienation, widespread landlessness and soil degradation in the colonial period, and an ambitious policy of individualized land registration and land grabbing by politically well connected elites in the postcolonial era have caused unceasing conflict over land. In Tanzania, by contrast, land matters have until recently been much less important in national political life, largely because government discouragement of agrarian capitalism and much lower population densities have spared most Tanzanians the prospect of landlessness.

Since the early 1980s, however, land matters have become much more controversial—partly because of the nearly chaotic situation in Dar es Salaam, Tanzania's center of government, commerce, academia, and media. The dramatic increase of Dar's population from 350,000 in 1967 to 1,370,000 in 1988, coupled with the absence throughout most of the city of registration and supervision over allocation and use of land, has left 70 percent of the city's inhabitants without title to the parcels on which they live and work.[1] These "squatters" include much of the professional middle class and wealthy elite as well as the poor. Thus apprehension ripples through all ranks of Dar's population whenever the government undertakes well-publicized exercises in eviction and land clearance, as it did during the summer of 1996 to free land for construction and road-widening projects. At the same time, unregulated land use is believed to cause various environmental problems, including the beachfront erosion which has accompanied the construction of villas and hotels along the shore, and also the flooding of low-lying areas which appears to be increasing because construction impedes drainage.

Yet, while the urban situation shapes the views of the journalists, parliamentarians, and scholars who carry on public discussion of land matters, it is the question of rural land which more immediately affects the farmers and pastoralists who constitute 80 percent of Tanzania's population. In recent years, Tanzania has witnessed several controversies over the transfer of rural lands, including the government allocation of the Loliondo portion of the Serengeti National Park as a private hunting ground, and the acquisition of some 120,000 acres in Hanang District by "private businessmen and public officials hiding under" a parastatal wheat-growing scheme.[2] A much more widespread rural land problem, however, resulted from the vast villagization movement of the early 1970s—when the Tanzanian government resettled some 5 million people, or more than one-third of its rural population, in 8,300 *ujamaa* villages. By the late 1970s, virtually the entire rural population of Tanzania lived in these villages. Yet, despite the scale of this initiative, the government never created a legal basis for the transfer of rights in land which would inevitably accompany large-scale resettlement.[3] Hence by the early 1980s, as commitment to villagization weakened in the government and among the villagers themselves, complex claims and counterclaims surfaced. They pitted the prior owners of the land on which ujamaa settlements had been established, who now demanded either compensation or the return of land, against villagers who sought to make secure their rights in the land which they had occupied since villagization in the 1970s.

Between 1986 and 1992, the government tried to forestall claims to compensation by denying that pre-villagization occupants continued to enjoy rights in the land which had been taken for ujamaa settlements. However, the government's key instrument in this effort, the Regulation of Land Tenure (Established Villages) Act of 1992, was declared unconstitutional in 1994 by the Court of Appeal. In extinguishing the "customary" land rights which formed the basis of claims for compensation, declared the court, the act was abolishing property rights.[4] This failure to find a legislative solution to land disputes arising out of villagization shifted attention back to the findings of a Commission of Inquiry into Land Matters which, having been appointed by President Ali Hassan Mwinyi in 1991, had issued its *Report* only days before passage of the 1992 act.

In its *Report*, the commission, a body of academicians and civil servants, concluded that modes of land use should be "environmentally friendly," and that to achieve this end, control of land should be vested in local communities in accordance with "customary law." The commission's *Report* characterizes "customary law" as a flexible, evolving body of precedents which can become the source of "Tanzanian common law using local customs and practices."[5] Among the most important features of customary law, according to the commission, is that it places control of land in the hands of entire "communities" rather than individuals, and makes "security of tenure dependent on use and occupation." These qualities, asserted the commission, give "village communities" protection against large-scale alienation and enable them to attain "food self-sufficiency and production of surpluses for domestic and export markets."[6] Subsequently, a number of the commission's recommendations became part of the National Land Policy, which was issued by the Ministry of Lands, Housing, and Urban Development in 1995. This new policy is intended to "ensure that existing rights in land especially customary rights of small holders . . . are recognized, clarified, and secured in law," and to "protect land resources from degradation."[7]

In arriving at their recommendations, both the commission and the Ministry of Lands adhere to the longstanding definition of customary tenure as the "deemed rights of occupancy" which were recognized in a 1928 amendment to the Land Ordinance of 1923, the British colonial basis of Tanzanian land law. These "deemed rights of occupancy" were defined by the 1928 amendment as "the title of a native or a native community lawfully using or occupying land in accordance with native law and custom."[8] As they did when considering other aspects of "native law and custom," here the British were speaking of what they assumed to be precolonial practices and institutions that had survived at the village level into the twentieth century. Thus both the commission *Report* and the National Land Policy, like earlier commentaries on Tanzanian land law,[9] take "customary" tenure to be a system which, though it has been interpreted and elaborated by colonial and postcolonial courts,[10] derives essentially from precolonial practices. Indeed, the National Land Policy explicitly makes this assumption in stating that the precolonial system "was continued" under colonial rule.[11] Yet, despite their belief that customary tenure has precolonial origins, neither the commission nor the Ministry of

Lands—and in this respect their documents resemble a large body of writing about African land tenure—inquired about its precolonial history.

HOW THE COLONIAL ORIGINS OF KNOWLEDGE ABOUT LAND TENURE IMPEDE HISTORICAL INQUIRY

Opening up the neglected precolonial history of land tenure and its environmental effects in East Africa is the purpose of this study. It does so by taking from one region of Tanzania—the northeastern lowlands—precolonial evidence of a kind that is virtually never used in studies of African land tenure. This approach takes us into seldom-explored territory, for, like the National Land Policy and the Presidential Commission's *Report,* scholarly literature on African land tenure rarely pays attention to precolonial history and usually confines consideration of environmental consequences to the problem of soil conservation.[12] Moreover, discussions of customary tenure usually do not consider conflict and struggle over land in precolonial situations. This remains true even though a recent body of highly nuanced writing on land matters, led by the work of Sara Berry, has emphasized the significance of multiple competing claims to land, and has suggested that the existence of such multiple claims can be traced back into the precolonial past.[13] Yet, despite increased interest in the multiplicity of claims to land, the literature retains a strong tendency to downplay the likelihood of conflict and expropriation. Indeed, even works which discuss sharing of land rights between rulers and the ruled almost never raise the possibility that powerful persons might deprive the weak of their crops, their land, and the improvements which they had made in it.[14]

At least three factors help account for the tendency to emphasize reciprocity and reconciliation of competing claims, rather than conflict. First, many studies assume that precolonial access to land was derived primarily through kinship groups in which affinity could be expected to minimize conflict. Second, evidence from precolonial societies about tensions and debate within communities and households, or between spouses and between generations, over various forms of property, including bridewealth and livestock as well as land, is exceedingly scarce. Consequently, much of what we say about the customary practices of the precolonial past is based on information collected in the colonial period

The production of this colonial knowledge was heavily influenced, moreover, by a third factor which encouraged writers to minimize the significance of conflict over precolonial property rights. This was the colonial-period discourse over African communalism which, as Martin Chanock has shown, developed in opposition to notions of individual rights, and was influenced by the political interests of both Europeans and Africans. Chanock argues that ideas of communal custom facilitated segregation and preservation of settler privilege by consigning Africans to a separate legal sphere of "communal rights," where they could not obtain the right to individual freehold enjoyed by European settlers.[15] Within the structure of British administration by indirect rule, moreover, ideas of customary communal rights seemed to offer appointed colonial chiefs an important source of authority: Administrators hoped that chiefs could assume the power of granting access to, and mediating disputes over, communally held land.[16] (As we shall see later, however, this argument blurs the distinction which arose in some cases between intention and reality; for even though administrators wished to devolve authority in land matters onto their chieftain subordinates, sometimes chiefs exercised relatively little control over land use and allocation.) Chanock also shows that the idea of communalism was embraced not only by European administrators and their appointed chiefs, but also by European critics of empire and by African opponents of settler privilege. "Discussion of land rights," argues Chanock, "had, realistically, to be in terms of groups. The land, as Africans emphasized over and over again was *ours*, not yours. . . . As liberal anthropologists built their versions of customary systems of tenure in this context, they too emphasized those features which would defend African land holdings—the rights of the group and the inalienability of rights."[17]

While the circumstances influencing the production of colonial knowledge are becoming better understood, scholars confronted by the scarcity of documentary and oral evidence from the precolonial period continue to rely heavily upon ethnographic knowledge generated in the colonial period. At the same time, ideas about the evolutionary tendencies of social institutions such as tenure systems which underlay colonial legal thinking have also percolated into recent literature on African land tenure.[18] Tenure systems in Africa are characterized as undergoing processes of "natural" or "spontaneous" evolution toward individualization.[19] Thus ideas of evolution stand in place of knowledge about the social processes which bring about change in tenure systems. They reveal nothing, however, about how social relationships affect conflict over land, how land matters are debated, and how ideas about land change as people debate land matters and assimilate new ideas from external sources.

Unfortunately, the fragmentary evidence discussed in the following sections also yields a frustratingly incomplete understanding of precolonial land tenure, particularly in the area of thought and discourse about land. Moreover, it does not allow us to explore numerous issues which are crucial to the comparative study of land tenure, such as eminent domain, reversionary rights, and administrative jurisdiction.[20] Nevertheless, it does help us to appreciate that precolonial systems of land tenure grew out of social conflict, and that their effects on the environment went far beyond the condition of soils.

REGIONAL AND ETHNOGRAPHIC CONTEXTS

The following sections address three broad questions about precolonial control of land. They inquire first about the nature of late precolonial rights in land, about how claims to land were asserted, and how control of land was transferred. Second, they ask about the degree to which custom guaranteed security of tenure in a society which was becoming more sharply differentiated as external forces exerted increasingly stronger control over political and economic institutions. Finally, they ask how changes in land tenure affected the disease environment.

They do so by focusing on the farming villages of lowlands northeastern Tanzania, an area of about 80,000 square kilometers.[21] The region excludes both the major mountain range of the Tanzanian northeast—the Usambara Mountains—and also the port cities of the coast such as Dar es Salaam. Thus it deliberately puts aside the portions of the region where large-scale land alienation, parcelization, and individualization of landholding have occurred, in order to concentrate on areas where customary practices are most likely to have persisted throughout the twentieth century. In addition, this chapter also leaves aside consideration of land tenure in pastoral communities and for that reason does not discuss the Maasai, the pastoralists who constitute an important minority of northeastern Tanzania's rural population.

The farmers of the northeastern lowlands inhabit an undulating, heavily wooded plain which rises gradually from the coastline to an altitude of about 1,000 meters about 100 miles west of the coast, where it meets several ranges of low mountains. In the lowlands, a pattern of scarce, irregular rains, which average about 750 to 1,000 mm annually and which fall mainly during two brief rainy seasons, forces farmers to search for areas of above-average soil moisture. To the north of the lowlands are the Usambara Mountains near the Tanzania-Kenya border, which reach elevations above 2,000 meters. Abundant precipitation exceeding 2,000 mm annually and a cool climate allow extraordinarily diverse flora to flourish in the Usambaras.[22] Along the western edge of the lowlands run several ranges—the mountains of Nguu, Ukaguru, and Uluguru—which, although they rarely rise above 1,500 meters in elevation, separate the wooded lowlands to their east from the great arid plateau of central Tanzania to their west. The eastern slopes of these ranges are well watered and favorable for farming, but their western sides are much drier and agriculturally marginal.

Although they spoke a number of different languages, the precolonial farming peoples of northeastern Tanzania shared essentially the same culture. Despite their linguistic diversity, many facets of culture—including farming practices, mud-and-wattle building styles, and other aspects of material life, art and oral literature, healing, cosmology and veneration of ancestors, gender relations, and conceptions of kinship and descent—were all quite similar throughout the region. In the nineteenth century, the major contrasts in the region were between the Usambara Mountains and the rest of rural northeastern Tanzania on the one hand, and between the rural hinterland and the cosmopolitan Swahili towns of the coast on the other hand. Not only was the climate more propitious and the diversity of vegetation more profuse in Usambara than in the lowlands and lower mountains, but as early as the eighteenth century Usambara had developed a powerful centralized monarchy, while the rest of the region retained highly localized forms of political authority. Indeed, throughout the wooded lowlands and minor mountain ranges, political authority rarely extended beyond the bounds of a few small villages. Yet, despite the difference of scale in political organization, the late-precolonial societies of both Usambara and the lowlands were quite distinct from the Swahili towns—where the lives of urban elites revolved around coral-rag mosques and residences, where Bombay merchants controlled a highly commercialized economy which looked outward to the Persian Gulf and India, and where Omani Arab rulers from Zanzibar exerted the dominant political influence.

Given the combination of considerable cultural similarity throughout the northeastern lowlands and the influence which the discourse about African custom and communalism exerted in Tanzania during the 1920s and 1930s, it is not surprising that ethnographic writings from this region are quite consistent when they touch (and indeed they touch only very briefly) on customary land tenure. Most often they say that land was controlled by matrilineal clans or matrilineages, and that decisions about land were made by clan heads and elders.[23] Less often, twentieth-century written accounts say that land rights derived from occupation and use of land. Representative of this approach is an administrative report written in the 1920s, which held that among the Zigua people, "after being used by one individual for a period of no great dimension [land] reverts to the community for new distribution."[24]

More rarely, twentieth-century accounts say that precolonial chiefs controlled and distributed land. Writing of communities along the Pangani River in the 1930s, for example, a British administrator asserted that "land is the property of the Zumbe [Chief]."[25] Another administrative report of the 1930s argued that in Zaramo villages near Dar es Salaam, a precolonial village chief "allocated land over which his people had right of use . . . which right could not be taken from him or his heirs provided they made full use of the land."[26] A similar view was expressed by a Swahili writer of the early colonial period, who commented that precolonial chiefs had enjoyed "authority over land and fields."[27] The most extensive colonial-period study of land tenure in northeastern Tanzania tried to account for the fact that in Usambara, chieftain control of land seemed to coexist with landholding by lineages and individuals. It suggested that land tenure was undergoing an evolution from collective, tribal rights to a system which combined ownership by families with individual landholding.[28]

The following sections will also try to account for evidence which speaks of control of land by occupants, lineages, and chiefs. They will do so, however, not by arguing that these forms of tenure represented stages of an evolutionary process, but rather by suggesting that statements about different kinds of land rights reflect varied aspects of the political authority, social relations, and ideology which shaped land tenure. I will contend that precolonial land tenure was shaped by struggles between chiefs and subjects who wished to defend heritable land rights. The balance between chiefs and commoners could be shifted by changing historical circumstances, however; and in the late nineteenth century the expansion of slave trading and other forms of long-distance commerce stimulated by external merchant capital placed enormous power in the hands of chiefs. Thus we turn next to control of land by chiefs.

Land Rights and Late Precolonial Chiefs

When the Europeans who would leave the earliest written testimony about land tenure in northeastern Tanzania entered the region in the 1870s and 1880s, they found social and political circumstances that had been dramatically transformed over the preceding four decades. Far from encountering timeless tribal societies where customary practices had remained unchanged over many generations, they arrived in an era of profound social change.[29] The root cause of change was the expansion of long-distance commerce, for, beginning in the 1820s and 1830s, Indian merchants living on the island entrepot of Zanzibar underwrote the development of an export-producing plantation economy on Zanzibar and mainland trading ventures which supplied slave labor to the plantation sector. Bombay merchants conducted trade in ivory and cloth between India and East Africa, provided credit to the Omani Arabs who governed Zanzibar and opened clove plantations, and financed long-distance trading ventures which supplied slaves and ivory to Zanzibar from a vast hinterland.

These developments brought momentous changes throughout northeastern Tanzania. In Usambara, a long-stable kingdom dissolved into protracted civil war as rival pretenders to the throne, having gained weapons and wealth from coastal traders, used them to pursue their political ambitions. In the stateless societies throughout the rest of the region, a new generation of ruthless and often youthful leaders arose. By cooperating with slave- and ivory-seeking traders from the coast, these leaders gained firearms and the wealth which they needed to attract followers. They were then able to control districts of perhaps twenty to thirty villages. To be sure, their authority remained small in scale, but its growth nevertheless brought significant change to regions whose villages had formerly been autonomous. Eventually a hierarchy of chiefs developed as the major chiefs imposed their authority over minor village heads who became their clients. To both the subordinate village chiefs and commoners who accepted their authority, the major chiefs offered protection and the benefits of their patronage. At the same time, however, the major chiefs became a terrible menace to all communities which did not enjoy the protection of a major patron, because they sought slaves who could be traded to the coast. For a time the chiefs also menaced the trading caravans which passed through the Tanzanian northeast as they made their way between the coast and distant interior regions, but eventually they found that their interests were better served by imposing a system of regularized toll payments upon passing caravans.

It was the second generation of these trading chieftains whom Europeans found when they began to establish a presence in the region during the 1870s and 1880s. Both Christian missionaries and the commercial agents of the German East Africa Company needed the cooperation of local leaders if they were to succeed in founding permanent stations.[30] Cooperative chiefs could assist them in procuring labor and provisions, could serve as military allies and trading partners, and, as the Europeans soon learned, could provide land. To gain these advantages, precolonial European settlers tried—the missionaries with much greater success than the German East Africa Company agents—to integrate themselves into the chieftain hierarchy at a middle level as subordinates of dominant chiefs and as patrons of less powerful village heads. In so doing, they followed the lead of merchants from the coast who had long formed similar relationships with political leaders of the interior. Assimilated into the region's political structure, they learned much about prevailing social relations; and as settlers who needed land, they learned quickly about prevailing modes of land tenure.

The French Catholic missionaries of the Spiritan (Holy Ghost) Order, who, after building the first Christian mission in mainland Tanzania at the coastal town of Bagamoyo in 1868, subsequently established a string of hinterland mission stations, left the most detailed accounts of precolonial European activity in the region. The Spiritans obtained their initial parcel of land at Bagamoyo, along with permission to work elsewhere on the mainland, from the Sultan of Zanzibar, who claimed control of northeastern Tanzania. They founded their first inland mission at Mhonda in the southern Nguu Mountains in 1877, after the Spiritan Anton Horner made a reconnaissance and selected a site in a country of "numerous villages and immense herds of cattle." Horner won the assurance of several village leaders that the Spiritans would be allowed to build wherever they wished, but the missionaries did not encounter the region's dominant chief until a second party of Spiritans returned to Mhonda without Horner. Upon their arrival they were given a sheep as a token of welcome from "the major chief of the whole country," who lived some distance away. On the following day, wrote Horner,

> in the presence of the inhabitants of Mhonda, the principal chiefs of the country and notables of the surrounding area, [the major chief] officially bequeathed to them full ownership of the terrain which I myself had chosen. He added, "If this parcel is not sufficient, you may also farm on the other side of the river." The parcel is very large, fertile and quite near the village and the Kulula River.[31]

Two aspects of this transaction are notable. First, by choosing to arrange a public ceremony attended by both commoners and subordinate village leaders, the dominant chief transformed the act of handing over land into a demonstration of his authority over a village where he did not reside. Second, it is almost certain that he transferred control over land which was already occupied. Areas near watercourses are the preferred locations for farming because their soils are exceptionally moist. It is most unlikely that a large riverside parcel in a heavily populated neighborhood would have been left uncultivated.

The Spiritans next sought land at Mandera in the Wami River Valley, midway between Bagamoyo and Mhonda.[32] Once again they had to negotiate with both a major regional chief, Kolwa, and one of his subordinate village leaders, Kingaru. When the Spiritans began to show interest in building a station at his village in 1881, Kingaru went to great lengths to establish a close relationship with them, journeying to Bagamoyo to invite the missionaries to his village and providing the first European settlers at Mandera with housing and abundant provisions. He knew that a missionary presence in his village would mean increased opportunities for trade with the coast and greater availability of imports. Yet, even though Kingaru was plainly eager to have a mission station in his village, his superior, Kolwa, now interposed himself between Kingaru and the Spiritans, reaffirming his primacy over village leaders such as Kingaru by ordering Kingaru to provide land to the missionaries. The extent of Kolwa's rights in land was not beyond dispute, however. In 1883, some village heads who were growing increasingly resentful of missionary interference implicitly challenged Kolwa's authority by threatening to revoke his grant of land to the Spiritans. Other chiefs, anxious to ensure that the missionaries remained at Mandera, opposed this threat by arguing that they could not countermand Kolwa's order to provide the missionaries with land. Although in the end the chiefs allowed the Spiritans to stay at Mandera, their deliberations showed that the power of a district chief to allocate land outside his home village could be questioned.

The Spiritans learned that they had to respect the authority of both Kingaru and Kolwa in matters of land. When they sought to expand their concession in 1883, they were careful not only to consult with Kingaru, but also to make gifts of cash and cloth to Kolwa. A short time later, wishing to acquire riverine plots on which they might experiment with coffee and vanilla, they addressed their request to both Kingaru and Kolwa.

The acquisition of this riverside parcel suggests that at Mandera, just as at Mhonda, the Spiritans depended upon cooperative chiefs to appropriate already-occupied land. The fields which the missionaries acquired stretched 20 to 30 meters wide for a distance of some 4 kilometers along the Wami River. As the Spiritans recognized, these were prime soils in this well-populated neighborhood; the missionaries thought that they were the best place to experiment with difficult cultigens such as coffee and vanilla. It is inconceivable that such a large expanse of riverine land in close proximity to several villages would have been left idle in the rain-poor lowlands of the Tanzanian northeast. Nor is it likely that the missionaries were occupying vacant land when they later established a settlement of Christian Africans "only a few hundred meters" from a village, or when they began farming in a "large and fertile valley [near a village] . . . which has been entirely conceded to us."[33] Neighboring farmers would surely not have left such a valley idle, particularly because the stream which ran through it was the best source of water in the area (the Wami was about thirty-five minutes' walk distant). Instead, it is much more likely that the Spiritans at Mandera followed the precedent set at Mhonda and allowed Kingaru and Kolwa to evict farmers from their fields. Not wishing to draw attention to this practice in their publications, however, they gave the impression that they had found abundant arable land to which there were no competing claims. The Spiritan pastor at Mandera, Cado Picarda, embellished this image when, overlooking the work which went into the clearing and improvement of farmland as well as the advantages gained from possession of moist soils which could be planted twice annually, he suggested that farmers chose their fields in an almost whimsical manner. "Because the natives are not numerous," he wrote, "each one chooses the plot which seems best to him and when he is tired of this field, he simply chooses another."[34]

The Spiritans once again sought the assistance of local chiefs in obtaining land when they opened another mission at Tununguo in the Ruvu River Valley south of the Uluguru Mountains in 1884.[35] Here again they dealt both with a subordinate village chief, who in this case was Kunzagira, and his patron, whom they knew as "Mwinyi Mkuu," meaning "chief" or literally "chief owner." After presenting numerous gifts to Mwinyi Mkuu as well as his subordinate village heads, the Spiritans won the chief's permission to build a station. Initially, Mwinyi Mkuu tried to persuade the missionaries to build on the north side of the river; but, finding it more heavily occupied than the south bank (during this period of intense slave dealing, villagers found the north bank safer because slave raiders usually approached Tununguo from the south), the missionaries proposed to build across the river. The Spiritans may have preferred the south bank because building there would mean fewer evictions and less animosity among villagers whom they hoped to evangelize. Their negotiations were interrupted by Bumboma, a trader from the coast who represented himself as the agent of Said Bargash, the Omani Sultan of Zanzibar. Bumboma disputed Mwinyi Mkuu's right to concede land on the south bank of the Ruvu, saying that he himself controlled the area in the name of the Sultan. He had acquired power in the area, learned the Spiritans, by assuming the debts of the village chief, an act which also gave him control over the chief's dependents and property.

Thus the missionaries found their progress halted by a three-cornered dispute over land involving not only a village head and a district chief, but also a trading representative of the Sultan of Zanzibar. All three of them based their claims to control of the land on the fact that they extended patronage to the people living on the disputed land. Yet a patron-client relationship helped resolve the conflict, for when Bumboma realized that he was obstructing missionary activities which had been sanctioned by his own patron, the Sultan, he withdrew his claims to the south bank and ordered villagers off the land which the Spiritans wanted. "Seeing that natives had farms on the parcel which had been conceded to us," commented a Spiritan report, "and that we were unsuccessful in removing them, he [Bumboma] ordered them in the name of Said Bargash to clear off as quickly as possible. This order was decisive."[36]

The Spiritans once again sought chieftain assistance in removing cultivators from their land when they decided to shift the site of their station. Having obtained Mwinyi Mkuu's consent, they took possession of fields already under cultivation. Yet neither Mwinyi Mkuu nor the village chief Kunzagira would allow the Europeans to occupy their own prime riverine plots. Nevertheless, it is clear that the Spiritans were able to acquire attractive parcels of land when chiefs were willing to expel cultivators. Like their confreres at Mhonda and Mandera, the Spiritans at Tununguo found a complex pattern of land control which allowed patrons to override rights in the land that their clients had acquired through inheritance and occupation. In the region's chieftain hierarchy, however, even the village leaders who were the dominant local patrons had to concede control over land to their own patrons, the major chiefs. The situation encountered by the Spiritans at Tununguo was further complicated by the intrusion of a representative of the Sultan who also established ties with local clients. Nevertheless, just as they did at Mhonda and Mandera, the Spiritans obtained land at Tununguo by using their trade connections to become patrons of village leaders like Kunzagira while submitting to the patronly authority of the major chief Mwinyi Mkuu.

The Spiritans were not the only missionaries who found themselves negotiating through a complex hierarchy of patronage when they sought to obtain land. In 1888, when Johann Jakob Greiner of the Evangelical Mission Society established a station at Kisarawe, just inland from Dar es Salaam, he reached an agreement with the residents and leader of the neighboring village to acquire a parcel, only to find that the dominant chief of the area considered it to be under his control. Greiner obtained the land only after the chief and his subordinates, having met privately to settle their differences, decided that Greiner would be required to pay Rs. 60 for the land. Yet, Greiner did not obtain unencumbered ownership with this payment, for thereafter the villagers expected the missionary to become their new patron and to provide them with food and cloth. "They now pointed out that since they were in the care of the missionaries, yea, that they considered them to be their 'new' parents, surely they would not be sent away hungry!"[37]

By comparison with the Spiritan and Evangelical missionaries, the other precolonial Europeans in the northeastern lowlands, the agents of the German East Africa Company, were much less well integrated into the regional power structure. Primarily interested in turning a profit and far less concerned than the missionaries with gaining political and spiritual influence, company officials would only grudgingly acknowledge the suzerainty of major chiefs and would not act as patrons. For that reason, they had much greater difficulty than the Spiritans in obtaining land.

An early company station was established inland from Bagamoyo at Dunda in 1885 by Eugen Krenzler.[38] Krenzler readily won the assent of Maulidi, the village leader at Dunda, when he proposed building a station there; but the dominant regional chief, Pasi Songera, opposed a German presence in his country. Yet, even though Pasi Songera called an assembly of village heads in an effort to expel Krenzler, the company agent obtained a concession of land from Maulidi. Krenzler understood his agreement with Maulidi as a simple cash purchase of Maulidi's village and about 50 acres. In his view, the deal was concluded when Maulidi distributed to his villagers the Rs. 50 which Krenzler had paid. By contrast, however, Maulidi evidently saw the matter as a transfer of his allegiance from one patron, Pasi Songera, to a new patron, Krenzler. For no sooner than he had accepted Krenzler's payment, Maulidi declared his intention to remain at Dunda with his villagers under Krenzler's protection. Krenzler was stricken with malaria shortly thereafter and abandoned Dunda, leaving unresolved the conflict between the company, which thought that it had obtained freehold tenure, and villagers, who thought that they were granting access to land in return for entitlement to reside and farm under the new patron's protection.

Another German East Africa Company station was located at Lewa in the Pangani River Valley, where the company wished to establish a tobacco plantation. Its founder, Friedrich Schroeder, encountered great difficulty in obtaining land and labor until he met with chiefs of the district, including not only the heads of villages around Lewa but also "Mfa," a district chief whom Schroeder credited with controlling numerous villages.[39] Although Schroeder provided gifts to the village chiefs, he recognized the superior status of Mfa by providing him with a treaty which promised the friendship of the company. Probably Mfa believed that the company now intended to enter into a trading alliance with him, for the longstanding practice of merchants from the coast had been to recognize powerful district leaders as their local agents. With gifts and treaty in hand, Mfa and his subordinate chiefs agreed that they would provide labor for the company's plantation; and indeed more than 100 villagers appeared the very next day ready to begin wage labor. Because the supply of local labor to the plantation remained strong through the following weeks, Schroeder not only abandoned plans to import workers from Zanzibar, but also decided to expand the plantation. When his plans became known to his workers, however, they immediately left the plantation. Schroeder inquired in local villages and learned that his neighbors feared that the expansion of the plantation would deprive them of farm fields and woods. He then offered to purchase farms adjoining the plantation for money and food stocks; but their owners refused, telling him that he could gain rights to their land not through purchase but only by becoming their patron.[40] "You are the master," they told Schroeder. "You may wish to take our land by your authority, but we are not willing to sell it." Schroeder was able to attract villagers back into plantation work only by abandoning his plans for expansion.

The experience of Krenzler and Schroeder shows that rights in land were determined not only by use and inheritance, but also by the structure of authority created by patronage and political power. Like the missionaries, they found that access to both land and labor depended above all upon their relationship with major chiefs. Yet they also found that the chiefs could be challenged by subordinates, for just as the residents of Mandera questioned the right of Kolwa to allocate land to missionaries, so too villagers at Dunda and Lewa refused to abide by the decisions of *their* dominant chiefs. Villagers at Dunda switched their allegiance to the company, while at Lewa villagers withdrew their labor in protest against imminent dispossession. Yet, although the villagers questioned chieftain authority and were unwilling to alienate their land through sale, they stood ready to surrender rights in land to powerful individuals (including Krenzler and Schroeder) in exchange for the reciprocal right to claim the protection and benefits of patronage.

Land, Politics, and the Ideology of Patriarchal Kinship

As we have seen, documentary sources indicate that late-precolonial political leaders were capable of evictions and allocation of land. But what of the matrilineages and clan elders to whom ethnographic accounts often attribute control of land? Neither in the present nor, so far as historical evidence can tell us, in the past have individuals who share a clan identity acted as corporate bodies. Thus it might appear that ideas of clan control of land is merely an artifact of the general discourse of African communalism which, as Chanock tells us, prevailed throughout colonial eastern and southern Africa. Yet missionary and administrative ethnographers of the colonial period were not simply inventing concepts of clan control in conformity with this discourse when they spoke, as they often did, of matri-clan and matrilineage land rights in northeastern Tanzania. They were also drawing upon widespread oral traditions which attribute control of land to clans and lineages.

One body of traditions, those which describe the founding of clans, reveals a close association between conceptions of kinship and territoriality. They help explain why a clan identity is believed to bring with it the right to claim land in a certain territory. They also explain why villagers in the northeastern lowlands often describe their country as being divided into many small clan territories.

Another genre of traditions, which relate the exploits of late precolonial chiefs, shows why kinship identities rooted in shared claims to land played an important role in conflicts between precolonial chiefs and commoners. They suggest that clans and matrilineages entered into disputes over land not as corporate bodies, but rather as ideological constructs which were manipulated to justify claims to land. They also suggest that the "clan heads" mentioned in ethnographic accounts were actually the same chiefs and village leaders whom we have already encountered. As we shall see, traditions of chiefs show that these leaders sought to legitimize control over subjects and land by creating a sense of shared kinship and common clan identity, while at the same time commoners and clients were employing constructed ideas of shared clan identities to resist their leaders' claims to land.

Stories about the founding of matrilineal descent groups are a major source of orally transmitted knowledge about the precolonial northeastern lowlands. These traditions describe the founding of small territories which in the Handeni portion of the northeastern lowlands are called *si*.[41] The individuals who inherit the names of these si consider the founders to be their ancestors. The founders of a si usually include a male leader as well as several females who are considered the founders of matrilineages. The traditions show that the founders establish claim to si territories by becoming the first people to occupy them permanently. Sometimes the stories say that the founders encountered hunting and gathering peoples when they first entered their si, but such encounters only serve to emphasize that the founders were its first permanent, cultivating occupants. Occupation of the si by the founders is the basis of the right to land in the si territory, which all bearers of the si name believe they have inherited from their ancestors.

Although these stories establish the primacy of claims to land through occupation and farming, a si territory is usually much larger than the space settled and cultivated by its residents. The confines of a si territory, which usually include not only villages and farms but also unoccupied woodland beyond villages, are carefully demarcated in the founders' stories. The traditions trace the movements of si founders around the periphery of the territory as they sleep in caves or at other landmarks, which become known as the markers of si boundaries. The fact that the landmarks and boundaries are invariably located in uninhabited areas outside villages makes quarrels about the precise boundaries of si unlikely. It also means that descent is intertwined not only with shared claims to farmland, but also with shared concern about woodlands and pasture which are not farmed. Thus traditions of the si founders inspire a sense of joint responsibility for unoccupied lands. This was a crucial aspect of the relationship between precolonial land tenure and environmental conditions, for, as we shall see below, management of unoccupied woodlands beyond the boundaries of villages played a vital part in maintaining a healthy disease environment.

Yet if the stories of si founders affirm rights in land obtained through occupation, they also show that such rights could be disputed and overridden by powerful leaders. Conflicts over land frequently lead in these traditions to the division of a si territory or to the establishment of a new si. The victors in struggles for land are sometimes individuals who have been successful in gaining power. Thus even though the stories appear to establish indisputable rights to land, they also speak of conflicts over land which may be resolved through the exercise of power. The conflicts in these stories probably reflect situations which developed frequently in the precolonial farming communities of the northeastern lowlands; for even though the region's scattered population lived in widely dispersed neighborhoods, farmers tended to congregate in areas which possessed comparatively moist soils and surface water. Because even in these areas productive farmland was not abundant, however, conflicts over the best plots must have been frequent.

The stories of si founders are the source of ideas about "clan territories" and clan control of land in northeastern Tanzania. Yet it must be emphasized that the persons who share a si name do not constitute corporate groups. Indeed, although most persons in Handeni have at least a sketchy knowledge of the traditions which link their names to particular territories, many people have only an exceedingly vague notion of the location of their si. Few individuals live in the si territory whose name they bear, and in modern Handeni there are no dominant matrilineages which actually control the territory after which they are named. Indeed, there is no evidence that territories were controlled by corporate clans in the precolonial past, nor any likelihood that descent groups which were exogamous could have done so. An additional factor which worked against the corporate cohesiveness of any descent group is the fact that an individual inherits si names from both father and mother. Therefore, individuals did not inhabit a world of clearly bounded, corporate descent groups, but instead experienced a lifetime of choice and negotiation with different groups of kin over rights, duties, and obligations. Likewise, stories of si founders did not establish an individual's rights to land in the place where the person would actually live. Instead, they created a broader association between space and descent, making claims to land part of the wider rights and obligations of kinship.

More than any other factor, these shared claims to space allowed the bearers of a common si name to imagine themselves as a community. Not only do the bearers of a si name not live together, but they have no word which unambiguously designates all the persons who share claims to land in a particular si. The closest term for such a group in the Zigua language is *lukolo*, but this word has a variety of meanings. Other words for kinship groups explicitly evoke ideas of shared space. For example, the Zigua word *mwango*, which might be rendered in English as "household" or "lineage," literally means "door" or "entrance," and refers to a group which is assumed to occupy one house. Similarly, the word *mzi* or *mji*, which is sometimes used to denote a group of kin, literally refers to the space inhabited by a group. Thus ideas of shared claims to space are a crucial aspect of the indigenous "imagined communities," which would become known in ethnography as clans and lineages.[42]

Concepts of kinship grounded in shared claims to land shaped the thought, language, and political alliances involved in conflicts over land. Chiefs and commoners, patrons and clients all turned to notions of si communities—and to the concepts of rights in land which lay behind them—when they made claims to land. In so doing, they activated si identities. Conflict over land made individuals think and act as members of a particular si community.

Chiefs sought to legitimize their authority over land and people by claiming that they were members of a particular si community. Frequently they sought recognition by their subjects as leaders of si communities. They might do this by suggesting that they themselves had descended through a long-forgotten line from certain si founders.[43] A chief might also do this by encouraging his subjects to participate in *matambiko*, or ancestor propitiation, which he would lead at the burial place of his own ancestors. By attending these matambiko, subjects signified their acceptance of the chief's ability to mediate with the powerful ancestors who brought rain. Thus by persuading his subjects that *his* ancestors were also *their* ancestors, a chief was able to claim a dominant role in a community. That this role included control of land is signified by the use of the term ngoto, which in various portions of northeastern Tanzania means both "sheep" and also a small payment made in return for the right to use land.[44] Hence rendering ngoto could mean either furnishing a sheep, the most common item of sacrifice at matambiko, or making a small payment of grain to an individual who had provided land. These associated meanings of ngoto suggest that providing the sacrificial sheep which a patron used when venerating si founders was one of the ways in which clients acknowledged his authority over land.

Reflective of the importance of kinship ideology in political relations were the terms by which chiefs and commoners spoke of each other. A chieftain patron was called "father" or "uncle" by his subordinates, while a patron referred to his clients as "children." "All those living in a village are called 'children,'" explained the Spiritan Cado Picarda in 1886, "and the chief is considered their father."[45] Chiefs used concepts of kinship and descent from si ancestors to justify their control of land. At Tununguo, for example, the chief Mwinyi Mkuu claimed rights to land by saying that formerly it had been owned by his maternal uncles. Like Mwinyi Mkuu, many chiefs took possession of the most fertile land in their settlements by invoking their status as senior kinsmen. Oral traditions of precolonial chiefs explain their power over land in the idiom of kinship, saying that they ruled territory which had originally been settled by the ancestors of their mothers and other matrilineal kin.[46]

Yet if the idiom of kinship justified the exercise of power by leaders, it also gave subjects and clients grounds for making claims on the protection and assistance of their patronly "fathers" and "uncles." Thus if a "father" or "uncle" were to expropriate the fields of his "children," as clearly happened when the Spiritans established their missions, he would be obliged to provide other land for his dispossessed subordinates, for no senior kinsman could brazenly disregard the welfare of his juniors and hope to retain their respect.

An example of the ways in which the rights to land affirmed by si membership could enter into conflict between chiefs and commoners comes from Magamba, a village of the central Handeni District.[47] From about 1850 until 1884, Magamba was ruled by Mani, who—like other important chiefs of his generation—traded with coastal merchants, extracted tolls from passing caravans, hunted for ivory, and raided for slaves. Traditions from Magamba relate that although Mani originally came from a different part of Handeni, he gained control of the relatively fertile and well-watered valleys around the village after becoming wealthy and powerful. For this reason, Mani was regarded by many villagers at Magamba not as a senior kinsman, but rather as an alien conqueror. On these grounds they refused to allow his burial in their si territory. In the face of this posthumous rejection of his claims to rights in the si territory around Magamba, Mani's son, who had succeeded him as chief, was forced to bury him some distance outside the village.

After succeeding his father, Mani's son Sonyo increased his authority by persuading the villagers of Magamba to make their matambiko at Mani's grave. At least two factors helped persuade the villagers to accept Sonyo as their senior kinsman despite their animosity toward his father. First, their acceptance of a common si identity strengthened their claim on Sonyo's patronly resources. Second, by forging a closer relationship with Sonyo, free commoners gained assurance that he would not allocate the best fields to his own slaves, who were numerous. For if Sonyo wished to gain legitimacy by being recognized as the senior kinsman of his subjects, he could not exclude his own kin from the best land.

As the Magamba episode demonstrates, the idiom of kinship both legitimized authority and imposed reciprocal obligations on patrons as well as clients. It gave clients reason to expect their patrons to act as benevolent fathers and uncles, and gave patrons the authority to override the rights of their subordinates in a variety of spheres. For example, a male client might be forced to surrender authority over his own children and spouses to his patron. At the height of the slave trade in the 1880s, a powerful leader might agree to prevent the enslavement of a weak or indebted household head's wives and children only at the price of his submission to servile clientage. Then, having placed the household head in a subordinate condition, he would thereafter treat the man's wives and children as his own dependents.[48]

Situations such as this show not only that the ideology of kinship sanctioned the primacy of a patron's authority in many aspects of his male clients' existence, but also that it placed women in an especially vulnerable position. Women were more vulnerable to enslavement or pawning than were men because kinship granted them few rights of their own. Women obtained rights through their relations with men; and their security depended on the fortunes of their fathers, uncles, and husbands.[49] Although women could, like men, inherit land from fathers and uncles, married women often relinquished rights to land in their natal settlements and became dependent on husbands for land when they moved into their husbands' households.[50] Should their husbands die or become hopelessly indebted, women could well lose rights in land and might even become pawns or slaves. Thus just as a woman might unexpectedly find herself, solely as the consequence of change in a man's status, transformed from the wife of an independent household head into the servile client of a chief, so too the security of her rights in land depended upon the circumstances of her husband and male kin.

Land Tenure and Control of the Disease Environment

The ideology and daily conflicts which shaped precolonial land tenure in northeastern Tanzania also influenced changes in the region's disease environment. The most important environmental problem throughout Tanzania's northeastern lowlands over the past 100 years has been the spread of livestock diseases which are carried by insect vectors.[51] Trypanosomiasis (better known as a human disease called sleeping sickness) and theileriosis (more commonly known as East Coast Fever) have eliminated cattle from large portions of the northeastern lowlands. Because these infections are found in many parts of Sub-Saharan Africa, they have been studied intensively by epidemiologists, immunologists, and parasitologists; yet there is still no universally accepted explanation for why they become epidemic. Nevertheless, it is clear that land use plays a crucial part in their epidemiology.

Both infections are caused by blood parasites which insects carry from immune wildlife to domesticated livestock. Trypanosomiasis is spread by tsetse fly, while East Coast Fever is transmitted by ticks. The insect vectors ingest the parasites when they take blood meals from undomesticated mammals (or from infected livestock), and inoculate the next mammal on which they feed. Human land use can affect the transmission of these infections in two ways. First, by hunting and clearing land, agriculturists can keep wildlife away from livestock, so that the insect vectors (which have little mobility) cannot carry infections from the immune undomesticated hosts to susceptible domesticated animals. Second, agriculturists can reduce insect populations (or even eradicate them altogether from some localities) by destroying the habitats in which they thrive. Fortunately, both tsetse flies and ticks require quite specific conditions. Tsetse flies, which cannot tolerate direct sunlight and high temperatures for long periods, need shady, moist, cool habitats. Ticks thrive best in a moist micro-environment created by long grasses in which they climb from the soil to a height where they can easily attach themselves to animals. Thus farmers and cattle keepers can control tsetse flies and ticks by burning and clearing the bush and grasses which they infest. Precolonial farmers were not likely to eradicate all tsetse flies and ticks, but they could reduce their numbers so that cattle were exposed to infection only occasionally. Cattle which avoided intense, deadly levels of infection and instead experienced only intermittent exposure could build immunological resistance against infection.

Late-precolonial communities of the northeastern lowlands created vector-free oases in which they could keep cattle herds. Indeed, these infections were less important as obstacles to precolonial cattle keeping than was the scarcity of water and moist soils. In the areas of the north-eastern woodlands where farmers found sufficient water sources and arable soils to support relatively dense populations, they practiced burning and clearing to create a healthy, vector-free parkland. Late precolonial European visitors remarked on the pleasing appearance of wooded park-lands near villages, where, because underbrush and rank grasses had been burned away, newly sprouted grasses created a brilliant green carpet at the beginning of each rainy season. Thus surrounding the villages and farm fields of each densely populated neighborhood was a carefully tended park-land. European visitors found the oases of concentrated settlement along watercourses (particularly along the major rivers such as the Pangani and Wami), in mountain valleys, and beneath the isolated hills which were watersheds. Away from these centers of farming, however, in areas where there was insufficient soil moisture, agriculturists could not settle perma-nently and could not control insects and wildlife. Consequently, these uninhabited areas were quite dangerous to cattle.

While precolonial farming communities possessed the ability to main-tain disease-free environments for cattle, whether they were successful in doing so depended upon the nature of their social and political relation-ships. In late-precolonial villages, control of the disease environment depended upon patron-client relations which, while allowing leaders to accumulate power and wealth, also imposed upon them the obligation to serve as patrons. Chieftain patrons used their power to attract client farm-ers into their settlements, enforce stipulations that farming land be kept cleared, organize work parties which tended farmland and peripheral park-land with fire and hoe, and regulate competition for the best soils. Yet, control of the disease environment in a drought-prone environment also required that political leaders serve as patrons for, in order to keep farmers at home during droughts and crop failures so that they could continue tending the land, chiefs had to provide subsistence.

Late-precolonial chiefs were able to extend patronage because they used power to accumulate wealth. From their subjects they extracted trib-ute and labor service, which could be converted through trade into currency and cattle. When drought and crop failures struck, the chieftain patrons used their reserves of wealth to procure subsistence for their sub-jects, enabling them to continue the work of environmental control. Patron-client relations became the foundation of demographic and envi-ronmental stability not only because chiefs had the power to accumulate wealth, but also because commoners demanded that their leaders fulfill their patronal responsibilities. Thus the ideology of mutual responsibility which governed relations between patrons and clients, and which influenced the allocation of land as well as other resources, was the basis of precolonial control over the environment.

Control over trypanosomiasis and theileriosis broke down in the early colonial period. German veterinary records and oral accounts from Handeni agree that these infections first inflicted heavy losses on cattle holdings in 1907–1908. They became lethal at this time because transmission of the infections, which had been interrupted by rinderpest, resumed among cattle that no longer possessed immunological resistance. Rinderpest—a cattle infection from Eurasia which in the 1890s cut a horrific swath through eastern and southern Africa, causing the deaths of perhaps 90 percent of cattle in many areas—interrupted disease transmission because along with killing most cattle, it also devastated many undomesticated species which were reservoirs of trypanosomal and theilerial infection. Thus when wildlife and cattle populations began to recover (herders were able to restock by purchasing cattle from areas which had not been stricken by rinderpest), infection spread with lethal effect among cattle which had not developed immunity through intermittent exposure to the trypanosomes and theileria.

Post-rinderpest loss of immunity was not the only cause of the trypanosomiasis and theileriosis epizootics, however. In late-precolonial societies where patronage maintained demographic stability, agriculturists could have helped their cattle to regain immunity by clearing and burning bush and grasses to reduce vector populations. By 1907, however, the northeastern lowlands had experienced more than a decade of demographic catastrophe. In many areas, a series of famines beginning in 1894–1895 had reduced the population by one-half. Famine caused great loss of population because the dislocation of long-distance trade in the first years of colonial rule, together with a series of violent military campaigns intended to destroy the independent power of chiefs, had left political authorities unable to fulfill their patronal obligations. Thus when droughts and crop failures occurred after 1894, the commoners who once would have relied on the patronage of chiefs now left their villages in great numbers in desperate search of food. As these destitute commoners abandoned their farms, villages and formerly cultivated fields became overgrown by the bush and grasses which harbor tsetse flies and ticks. At the same time, the wildlife species, such as buffalo, antelope, and bush pig, which are the reservoir of trypanosomiasis and theileriosis moved closer to pastures and the remaining farms. Under these conditions, cattle were exposed to infections so intense that they died rather than gaining immunological resistance.

The cattle disease environment would continue to deteriorate through the 1940s. Further devastating famines occurred in 1916–1918, 1925, and 1932–1935. In each instance, famine caused depletion of the farming population and further spread of disease vectors throughout areas which had once been healthy for cattle. The worst of the interwar famines occurred in the mid-1930s. In its wake, the British colonial government, fearing that the upsurge of cattle trypanosomiasis would lead to outbreaks of human sleeping sickness (administrators were particularly worried about the many thousands of migrant laborers who walked through the region each year), commissioned studies of cattle disease in Handeni District. Researchers identified post-famine decline of human population and encroachment of uncontrolled bush and grasses as the primary causes of epizootics. Thus the destruction of both chieftain authority and relations of reciprocal obligation between patrons and clients left farmers without the means of surviving episodes of crop failure in their homes. Forced to migrate, destitute farmers abandoned their farms to bush, insects, and wildlife, and left remaining villagers with no means of protecting their cattle against vector-borne infections.

Was Land Tenure a Factor in the Breakdown of Environmental Control?

Although as a cause of cattle epizootics land tenure was less important than famine, demographic decline, and the disappearance of patronage, the decreasing influence of political authority over land during the colonial period (1889–1961) contributed to the breakdown of control over these infections. Indeed, the surprising outcome of the period when German and British regimes imposed a colonial state on Tanzania was that political authority lost control over land in many rural communities. This happened even though the German state, by an Imperial Ordinance of 1895, declared that all land for which there was no written proof of ownership would henceforth be Crown Land. It also happened even though the British— despite pledging to "respect the rights . . . of the native population" when they assumed control of Tanganyika as a League of Nations Mandate after the First World War—declared through their Land Ordinance of 1923 that, whether occupied or not, all land would henceforth be under the control of the governor.[52] Of course, it is true that the enormous power over land which these ordinances vested in the colonial state was used in some places to achieve arbitrary expropriations of land, especially in the highland and urban areas which attracted Europeans.[53] Such expropriations created intense resentment and made colonial land policy one of the primary targets of nationalist protest during the 1950s. Indeed, it was British expropriation of land on Mount Meru which would lead to one of the most famous episodes in the nationalist struggle: hearings at the United Nations over African land rights in 1952.[54]

In the northeastern lowlands, however, the colonial government rarely became involved in land disputes. Only in the Usambaras and the sisal plantation zone of the lower Pangani Valley did it alienate large tracts as forest reserves and European plantations. Otherwise, colonial administrators tended to devolve issues of land use and land rights to appointed chiefs. Yet, despite the authority which appointed chiefs were granted by the colonial state, they had much less influence than their precolonial predecessors in matters of land. For while they drew stipends from the colonial government, administered local courts, and held the power to enforce colonial tax and compulsory labor demands, the appointed chiefs were in a weaker position than the precolonial leaders who had used patronage and armed force to induce their subjects' submission.

A mark of the difference between chiefs of the precolonial and colonial periods is that whereas precolonial leaders had been able to override the authority of household heads when claiming control of their dependents and land, colonial chiefs were often limited to adjudicating disputes between household heads. Whereas a precolonial chief had been able to seize the land of subjects, colonial chiefs who heard land cases in their courts were much less likely to impose their will on influential villagers. Knowing that complaints from villagers sometimes persuaded the British to depose office holders, colonial chiefs were unwilling to antagonize the wealthier and more influential men in their villages. Nowhere was this more true than at Magamba, the Handeni village where the powerful precolonial chief Sonyo was succceeded in the early 1920s by Kasukwa, an appointee whose subjects were constantly trying to undermine his position. Moreover, the decisions of chiefs were not infrequently influenced by bribery. Thus disputes over land, which must have been common in the pre–Second World War colonial period when famine and the collapse of patronage caused great dislocation, increasingly became matters to be settled by household heads without the intervention of political authorities.

Another mark of the decreased power of colonial chiefs is that they were unable to affect land use. In theory, colonial law gave appointed chiefs broad powers to implement an array of regulations governing land use. Chiefs could enforce compulsory cultivation of certain crops, require that villagers destroy insect-harboring bush, authorize the destruction of dangerous wildlife, punish farmers who failed to do weeding or who allowed their fields to become overgrown, prohibit the setting of fires in areas where they were deemed harmful, regulate the movement of livestock, and compel cattle dipping and other measures which were intended to reduce livestock infections. In reality, however, chiefs rarely succeeded in enforcing such measures. Farmers, who were struggling to survive despite colonial taxation in shrinking, famine-stricken communities, regarded most of these regulations as burdensome and ineffective, and resisted them vigorously.[55] Deeply frustrated, colonial administrators reacted to the failure of policies intended to maintain food self-sufficiency, prevent depletion of soil fertility, and reduce cattle disease by blaming the appointed chiefs.

As the chiefs lost their power to regulate land use, individual farmers gained greater autonomy. Although increased autonomy was undoubtedly prized by household heads, its impact on environmental management was in many ways damaging. Farmers were no longer under pressure to cultivate contiguous plots in accordance with a pattern which had formerly facilitated the task of keeping crop pests and wildlife out of farm fields. Nor were farmers forced by chiefs to keep their fields carefully tended. Consequently, wildlife could hide in untended fields by day and emerge at night to ravage grain crops in adjoining fields. As the pressure to enter communal work parties decreased, both the peripheral parklands around villages and the paths between settlements became overgrown, leading to the encroachment of wildlife and a dramatic increase of lion attacks on humans and cattle.[56] The memory of the pre–Second World War days when lions had roamed through villages and cattle keeping had become virtually impossible would in the early 1980s lead older farmers in Handeni District to conclude that they needed strong political leaders who, like the famous chiefs of the late-precolonial era, could force villagers to work together and farm contiguous fields.[57]

In Handeni, the most telling example of the appointed chiefs' powerlessness to shape land use was their inability to deal with abandoned European plantations. Before the First World War, Handeni had attracted a few settlers who tried to grow rubber on a dozen small estates, the largest of which was about 1,100 hectares. They fled as the British occupied Tanganyika during the war, however, leaving most of their estates abandoned and overgrown with bush throughout the interwar period. As epidemiological investigators would learn in the late 1930s, these untended plantations became dangerously infested with tsetse and ticks. Moreover, the abandoned plantations were all the more dangerous to cattle because settlers had been careful to make sure that their estates enclosed scarce sources of surface water. Consequently, livestock owners frequently had to take their cattle to watering holes on these abandoned parcels, even though it meant exposing them to heavy infestations of disease-bearing insects. However, neither neighboring villagers nor their chiefs could do anything about the problem because the government, having classified the estates as alienated enemy property, prohibited Africans from occupying them.[58]

Just as chiefs could not deal with the danger posed by abandoned plantations, so too they were unable to respond to requests for land by merchants who wished to undertake commercial farming. During the German period, Indian businessmen replaced the precolonial chiefs as the dominant figures in trade and established networks of village shops where they sold cloth and other consumer goods while also purchasing crops. During the interwar years, these merchants became interested in hiring African agricultural labor to grow crops both for export and for the growing urban markets of the coastal cities. Had they been successful, these merchants would have become a source of wages, which would have enabled villagers to purchase food and remain in their homes during droughts. Thus had the Indian merchant community expanded its activities, employment on its farms might have substituted for the declining patronage of chiefs. However, the British administration, fearing that land alienation and accumulation by Indians would create a rural proletariat, refused to allow purchases of land by Indians.[59] Here again, the political structure of colonial rule prevented chiefs and communities from responding to their problems by modifying property rights.

CONCLUSION: RECOVERING THE MISSING ELEMENT IN ANALYSIS OF AFRICAN LAND TENURE— TRADITIONS OF THOUGHT ABOUT LAND

We have now seen that recent tensions over land have increased interest in making customary tenure the basis of reformed land law in Tanzania; that one of the concerns underlying the interest in customary tenure is the fear that unregulated allocation and use of land are causing the degradation of both urban and rural environments; and that, while the reports and policy statements which articulate this approach assume that custom derives from precolonial practices, these documents pay little attention to the history of land tenure. We have also discussed the relationship between environmental change and land tenure during precolonial and colonial periods in the northeastern lowlands of Tanzania. Thus we are now prepared to ask how the historical study of these matters can help to achieve the goal of the Presidental Commission on Land Matters—an equitable and "environmentally friendly" tenure system.

The lesson which emerges most clearly from our historical evidence is that land tenure cannot be understood apart from the social relations, institutions, and traditions of thought in which it is embedded.[60] Moreover, East African experience since the late-precolonial period has also shown that the reason why land tenure reform fails to achieve anticipated results is precisely because means of controlling land are inseparable from this wider social context. East African history has also shown that the influence of land tenure reform on environmental and agrarian change cannot be distinguished clearly from the influence made by numerous other economic, social, and political factors. These conclusions emerge not only from study of Tanzanian developments of the late nineteenth and early twentieth centuries, but also from more recent experience in Kenya.

Unlike Tanzania, Kenya has long been committed to individualized tenure and registration of holdings. These policies were instituted during the Mau-Mau Rebellion of the 1950s by colonial officials who hoped that consolidation and registration of land held under individual tenure would hasten the emergence of a stable and politically quiescent peasantry. Since that time, land administrators have continued to work with the same ideas about the benefits of individualized tenure which colonial officials formulated in the 1950s. These benefits, they have assumed, would include consolidation of fragmented holdings, reduction of time-wasting disputes over land, improved access to credit for farmers able to use land as collateral, incentive to produce perennial cash crops, and a market in alienable land. This last development, they have expected, would facilitate the transfer of land into the hands of more efficient farmers, while also converting a portion of the agrarian population into a landless pool of labor which could be hired by freeholders. Administrators have also assumed that individualized and registered tenure would produce environmental benefits by giving farmers increased incentive to arrest soil erosion through terracing and other means.

Nevertheless, the results of land reform have not been what administrators anticipated. Recent studies have shown that individualization has been accompanied by frequent unregistered land transactions and the multiplication of claims to land. These trends have not, however, increased women's access to land. Nor has individualized titling substantially improved freeholders' chances of obtaining credit. Moreover, while some districts have witnessed increased output of perennial exportable crops such as coffee and improved soil conservation, it is not clear that land reform has been a major factor in this development.[61]

This point is made particularly well in a remarkable recent study of Machakos, a district which, although drought-prone, "has sustained agricultural intensification, improved conservation and increased output through several decades of population growth in excess of 3% per annum." Although the authors of this study cite security of tenure as a crucial factor in encouraging improvement and conservation of land by the Kamba farmers of Machakos, they also show that these developments did not await tenure reform. "Land titling," they say, "was not a prior condition of agricultural development because Akamba traditional law already protected individual investment." Indeed, rather than emphasizing tenure reform in their explanation of the progress made in Machakos, the authors place much heavier weight on increased access to knowledge and technology, wider market opportunities, and the formation of institutions which raise capital and organize trade.[62]

Thus recent Kenyan experience with land reform shows two things: First, its effects cannot be predicted with precision, because the decisions people make about land are influenced both by a multiplicity of claims made on it and by a variety of meanings and values attached to it. Second, the agrarian and environmental conditions which policy makers wish to modify through tenure reform may be less strongly affected by land tenure than by various other economic and political circumstances. These same points can also be drawn from the late-precolonial and early colonial history of land tenure in northeastern Tanzania. Here again we see that while access to productive land was obviously critical, at the same time precolonial farmers balanced various considerations when making decisions about land. In particular, they weighed the disadvantages of surrendering claims to land against the advantages of obtaining the patronage of powerful political leaders and traders. At the same time, they also put into the balance the importance of clan identities which—when activated by asserting rights in land—could produce solidarity in defense of political and property rights, but which also could be weakened by alienation of land. In precolonial Tanzania, moreover, just as in Kenya more recently, systems of land tenure seem to have had less impact on agricultural productivity and environmental conditions than other, broader economic and political circumstances. During the final precolonial decades in northeastern Tanzania, control of labor was the crucial variable. Precolonial chiefdoms produced crop surpluses and maintained a stable disease environment because their leaders, by taking advantage of increasing trade and connections with mercantile capital, extended their patronage and authority widely, thereby gaining the ability to coordinate the labor of dependents.

Many of the authors who have contributed to the recent literature on African land tenure are fully cognizant of these matters.[63] Frequently they take pains to show that the consequences of land tenure are not easily distinguishable from those of other factors, and that land tenure must be understood within its social and cultural context. Thus while Berry, to take the most prominent example, argues that land is inseparable from social identity and that decisions about land often reflect a landholder's desire to maintain membership in a social network which provides economic and political resources, she also contends that the critical problem for African farmers is not access to land, but rather access to labor.[64] In her 1993 book, moreover, Berry made an important improvement on earlier discussions of land and social identity by placing greater stress on the frequently conflictual nature of relationships involving land.[65]

Nevertheless, historical inquiry needs to be pushed a step further if we are to address the problem with which policy makers in the Tanzanian government have been grappling—that is, how customary tenure can be adapted to produce an equitable and "environmentally friendly" tenure system. The next step should follow in the direction already taken by Berry when, in her 1993 discussion of land matters, she criticized Chanock for focusing on the discourse about property rights found in the writings of government officials and anthropologists, rather than on "records of actual transactions and disputes."[66] Historical inquiry could go one step further, however, by examining how in the course of such transactions and disputes people give voice to their own discourse about land. In other words, the dimension of African land tenure which is still missing from the literature is the tradition of thought in which disputants formulate and debate ideas, articulate conceptions of rights, attach notions of obligation to authority, defend the rights of the powerless, and resist the encroachment of outsiders. Obviously the recovery of such a tradition from precolonial sources is extremely difficult, though the evidence from late-precolonial Tanzania which we have used here suggests that the task is not impossible.

Indeed, while scholars have sometimes wondered whether so-called customary tenure has any connection with the precolonial past,[67] perhaps the most enduring aspect of precolonial land tenure is a tradition of thought about rights in land, and about the responsibilities that inhere in control of land. There are many indications that such a tradition remains vigorous in Tanzania, and has adapted to a wide variety of social and economic circumstances. Farmers still subscribe to the principle that each person has a right to the land needed to obtain subsistence; they still adhere to the belief that the occupation and improvement of land bestows rights; and they continue to accept the idea that political authorities may indeed be justified in overriding the rights of the occupants of land, but only if they provide compensating benefits. These attitudes continue to govern the inheritance of land from mothers, fathers, and mothers' brothers, just as they did in the late-precolonial period. They still inspire the belief that a just division of land through inheritance is one which takes account of the needs of all heirs.

Many signs show the persistence and adaptability of these attitudes. In the late 1930s, to take one example, a colonial official heard speakers of the Digo language expressing the notion that a farmer obtains rights in land by improving it: "Wadigo," he wrote, "say that all land belongs to God. Grass belongs to the occupier of the land, who must have marks on the land such as coconut and mango trees as proof of his occupancy. An Mdigo claims grass to be his property because after clearing the land of all the big forest trees the grass grows as the result of his labours."[68] The persistence of old attitudes in new contexts can also be seen, to take another example, in a disagreement which developed in the early 1950s, when European settlers were clearing land for new sisal plantations. The settlers perceived themselves to be hiring wage-earning workers to clear land which had already been allocated to the settlers by the colonial government. The workers, however, had an entirely different view. They believed that in the act of clearing the land they were establishing their ownership of it. In their view, the money which they received from the settlers was not wages, but was instead payment for land which they were selling.[69] One final example of the persistence, despite changing circumstances, of customary views about land comes from the period of ujamaa villagization in the early 1970s. At this time, the Tanzanian government forcibly resettled much of the dispersed rural population in larger, centralized villages. In Handeni District, where government tactics were particularly heavy handed, farmers initially resisted resettlement though eventually most villagers, bowing to police and military intimidation, moved into new settlements. Thus with great reluctance they accepted government authority over land, but they believed that in so doing they were becoming the clients of a government which was henceforth obliged to assist them. Consequently, resettled farmers tended to see government famine relief (for resettlement took place in years of severe food shortages) not as provisions which they must earn, but rather as a form of government patronage to which resettlement had entitled them.[70]

These twentieth-century examples, like our precolonial evidence from northeastern Tanzania, remind us that when we assume in rather impoverished fashion that precolonial or indigenous land tenure, if not a communal system, must be based on either chiefship or clans, we fall into the trap of thinking about precolonial Africa in an essentialist and reductionist way.

For this kind of simplistic equivalence overlooks the rich complexity and dynamism with which "traditional" thought and social institutions have achieved great variation, adaptation, and transformation.

Nevertheless, while enduring conceptions about rights in land, just allocation of land, and the obligations which stem from possession of land remain alive in farming communities, they do not always govern decisions about land. Instead, when courts assume the power of adjudicating disputes about land, they may base their decisions on very different considerations which may not be understood by disputants and observers.[71] This severing of the connection between a tradition of thought about land and administration of land has helped place agrarian communities, which have found that communal tenure provided no defense against the state, in a condition of "rightlessness."[72] Thus the restoration of the connection between indigenous thought and land law is imperative, argues a thoughtful study of Tanzanian customary law, if this condition of rightlessness is to be eradicated. "[Court-administered] customary land law," says Ringo Willy Tenga, has

> little that is inherently "traditional," [or] "indigenous." . . . It is backed by the whole institutionalized coercive agencies of the post-colonial state and is as much a part of the legal system as the penal code.[73]

"If the post-colonial state aims at building a democratic society," he contends, "legal processes that are based on widely accepted norms (for example, mediation and negotiation) must be at the foundation of dispute processing."[74]

If customary tenure were indeed to become the basis of a more equitable Tanzanian land law, as the Presidential Commission on Land Matters intended, it is the tradition of thought about land to which Tenga refers, rather than essentialist notions of the customary such as those associated with clan- and lineage-based tenure, that would have to be recovered and made the basis of land law. At this juncture, however, we may draw one final lesson from recent Kenyan experience. The recent study of Machakos District to which we have referred, like some commentary on land problems in Tanzania, identifies gender inequity in matters of land as a persistent and fundamental problem.[75] It suggests, however, that the factor already identified as having critical importance in the development of Machakos—access by both men and women to education and wider economic opportunity—must play a decisive role in allowing women to win equal access to land.[76] If they are to adapt their tradition of thought about land rights to ensure equitable access to land by women, both men and women need the education and experience which provide increased awareness of the benefits of change.

Yet here again, just as the Machakos case shows that the state must play a vital, if only indirect, role in establishing the preconditions for progress through the provision of education and economic infrastructure, so too in Tanzania the extent to which the state encourages the extension of women's rights and defends the rights of agrarian communities and poor urban people when they are threatened by powerful economic interests will be critical as economic liberalization increases Tanzania's integration into global capitalist markets. However, precisely because the widening of women's rights and the maintenance of sustainable agrarian and environmental conditions necessitate state action, a tradition of thought which links the legitimacy of authority with rights and obligations remains an indispensable means of defense against political and economic power, just as it did in the late-precolonial context. Indeed, in East Africa, where rural populations have had little participation in national political life and no opportunity to develop autonomous political institutions, their traditions of thought about the limits and obligations of authority are one of the few foundations on which popular resistance to the concentration of power and resources in the hands of business and bureaucratic elites can be organized.[77]

Indeed, the history of land tenure in northeastern Tanzania suggests that, in itself, reform of land law will not be sufficient to protect the land rights of the powerless and promote "environmentally friendly" land use. Precolonial history shows that in the past—just as in the present—land rights have had to be actively defended against both external and domestic forces. In late-precolonial societies, commoners preserved access to land and other resources by using an idiom of kinship to articulate concepts of mutual obligation. In this manner they engaged in constant struggle with powerful members of their communities over the definition of obligations and the distribution of resources. Out of this struggle developed a system of patronage which—by allowing accumulation, encouraging redistribution of wealth, and curbing the environmentally *unfriendly* autonomy of individual farmers—maintained population stability and allowed uninterrupted control of the vegetation, wildlife, and insects which affected the disease environment. Similarly, in postcolonial Tanzania the creation of a just and environmentally beneficial system of land control will be achieved not merely in land courts and villages, but through broad-based, national struggle. It will require continued striving for democratization of political institutions not only in the arena of party politics, but also through the activities of various popular organizations including churches, mosques, women's associations, and farmers' cooperatives. The history of land tenure suggests, in other words, that advocating devolution of control of land to "village communities" on the basis of customary tenure must not become a retreat from struggles over control of the state.

NOTES

1. J. M. Lusugga Kironde, "Access to Land by the Urban Poor in Tanzania: Some Findings from Dar es Salaam," *Environment and Urbanization* 7, no. 1 (1995): 78. See also Joe Lugalla, *Crisis, Urbanization, and Urban Poverty in Tanzania: A Study of Urban Poverty and Survival Politics* (Lanham, Md.: University Press of America, 1995), Chapter 3.

2. Sengondo Mvungi and Harrison Mwakyembe, "Populism and Invented Traditions: The New Land Tenure Act of 1992 and its Implications on Customary Land Rights in Tanzania," *Afrika Spectrum* 29, no. 3 (1994): 334.

3. Mvungi and Mwakyembe, 333; Simon Coldham, "Land Tenure Reform in Tanzania: Legal Problems and Perspectives," *Journal of Modern African Studies* 33, no. 2 (1995): 229.

4. Coldham, 236–41; Mvungi and Mwakyembe, 333–34; Issa G. Shivji, "A Legal Quagmire: Tanzania's Regulation of Land Tenure (Establishment of Villages) Act, 1992," Pastoral Land Tenure Series no. 5 (London: International Institute for Environment and Development, Drylands Programme, 1994).

5. United Republic of Tanzania, *Report of the Presidential Commission of Inquiry into Land Matters* I (Uppsala: Ministry of Lands, Housing, and Urban Development in cooperation with the Scandinavian Institute of African Studies, 1994) 193–94; on the evolution of "customary law," see also pp. 121 and 157.

6. *Report of the Presidential Commission*, especially pp. 141–43, 153–54, and 193.

7. Ministry of Lands, Housing, and Urban Development, "National Land Policy" (Dar es Salaam, June 1995), 5. I am indebted to Mr. Ignas Kaduma for valuable discussions of this policy. The National Land Policy and the findings of the Presidential Commission are compared in Kjell J. Havnevik, "Pressing Land Tenure Issues in Tanzania in Light of Experiences from Other Sub-Saharan African Countries," *Forum for Development Studies* no. 2 (1995): 267–84.

8. *Report of the Presidential Commission*, 11. Also, R. W. James, *Land Tenure and Policy in Tanzania* (Nairobi: East African Literature Bureau, 1971), 18–19. Indeed, the 1995 National Land Policy makes explicit its aim of preserving the essence of the colonial tenure system, for like the 1923 Land Ordinance it holds that "all land in Tanzania is public land," and also states that "rights of occupancy . . . will continue to be the only recognized types of land tenure." National Land Policy, 9 and 3.

9. For example, James, Land Tenure, 61ff.

10. See R. W. James and G. M. Fimbo, Customary Land Law of Tanzania: A Source Book (Nairobi: East African Literature Bureau, 1973).

11. National Land Policy, 6.

12. Thomas J. Bassett, "Introduction: The Land Question and Agricultural Transformation in Sub-Saharan Africa," in Thomas J. Bassett and Donald E. Crummey, eds., Land in African Agrarian Systems (Madison: University of Wisconsin Press, 1993), 3–31; Parker Shipton and Mitzi Goheen, "Understanding African Land-Holding: Power, Wealth, and Meaning" (Introduction to special issue titled "Rights Over Land: Categories and Controversies"), Africa 62, no. 3 (1992): 307–25. One highly schematic attempt to survey precolonial Tanzanian land tenure is Andrew B. Lyall, "The Social Origins of Property and Contract: A Study of East Africa before 1918" (Ph.D. thesis, University of London, 1980).

13. Sara Berry, No Condition Is Permanent: The Social Dynamics of Agrarian Change in Sub-Saharan Africa (Madison: University of Wisconsin Press, 1993), 132–33.

14. H. W. O. Okoth-Ogendo goes so far as to say that "the outright disposal of land to persons external to a given unit of production is therefore alien to African land law": H. W. O. Okoth-Ogendo, "Some Issues of Theory in the Study of Tenure Relations in African Agriculture," Africa 59, no. 1 (1989): 11.

15. Martin Chanock, "A Peculiar Sharpness: An Essay on Property in the History of Customary Law in Colonial Africa," Journal of African History 32 (1991): 65–88; Martin Chanock, "Paradigms, Policies, and Property: A Review of the Customary Law of Land Tenure," in Kristin Mann and Richard Roberts, eds., Law in Colonial Africa (Portsmouth, N.H., and London: Heinemann and James Currey, 1991), 61–84; Martin Chanock, Law, Custom, and Social Order: The Colonial Experience in Malawi and Zambia (Cambridge, England: Cambridge University Press, 1985), 232–33. Chanock builds on a very important earlier contribution by Elizabeth Colson, "The Impact of the Colonial Period on the Definition of Land Rights," in Louis Gann and Peter Duignan, eds., Colonialism in Africa 3; Victor Turner, ed., Profiles of Change: African Society and Colonial Rule (Cambridge, England: Cambridge University Press, 1971), 193–215, especially p. 196.

16. Chanock, "Paradigms, Policies, and Property," 64.

17. Chanock, "Paradigms, Policies, and Property," 66–67.

18. Chanock, "Paradigms, Policies, and Property," 63; Chanock, "A Peculiar Sharpness," 69–70; Chanock, Law, Custom, and Social Order, 25–31.

19. "Customary land tenure systems evolve naturally. . . .": Arild Angelsen and Odd-Helge Fjeldstad, "Land Reforms and Land Degradation in Tanzania: Alternative Economic Approaches" (Bergen, Norway: Chr. Michelsen Institute, Working Paper 1995:3, 1995), 17; "Customary tenure systems experience spontaneous simplification and individualization. . . .": John W. Bruce and Shem E. Migot-Adholla, eds., Searching for Land Tenure Security in Africa (Dubuque, Iowa:

Kendall/Hunt, 1993), 4; "There is a spontaneous individualization of land rights over time. . . .": Shem Migot-Adholla, Peter Hazell, Benoit Blarel, and Frank Place, "Indigenous Land Rights Systems in Sub-Saharan Africa: A Constraint on Productivity?" *World Bank Economic Review* 5, no. 1 (1991): 155.

20. For bringing these issues to my attention, and for numerous other comments and suggestions, I am grateful to Professor Sally Falk Moore.

21. This includes Bagamoyo, Kibaha, and Kisarawe districts in Coast Region, Morogoro District in Morogoro Region, and the entire Dar es Salaam and Tanga regions.

22. For a recent discussion of the Usambara environment, see Christopher Conte, "Nature Reorganized: Ecological History in the Plateau Forests of the West Usambara Mountains, 1850–1935," in Gregory Maddox, James L. Giblin, and Isaria N. Kimambo, eds., *Custodians of the Land: Ecology and Culture in the History of Tanzania* (London: James Currey, 1996), 96–121.

23. T. O. Beidelman, *The Matrilineal Peoples of Eastern Tanzania* (London: International African Institute, 1967), xiii, 17, 23, 24, 28–29, 30–31, 35, 40–41, 51, 56, 59, 67–68. Clan control of land is also mentioned in Erich Schultz-Ewerth and Leonhard Adam, eds., *Das Eingeborenenrecht* 1 (Stuttgart, 1929); Bernhard Ankermann, *Ostafrika,* 229; E. C. Baker, *Report on the Social and Economic Conditions in the Tanga Province* (Dar es Salaam: Government Printer, 1934), 141–42; A. S. Armstrong, "Land Tenure in Nguru, Morogoro District," Tanzania National Archives (hereafter TNA), Morogoro District Book 1, (1939). The most detailed argument for matrilineage control of land in northeastern Tanzania was made in a study of Uluguru by Young and Fosbrooke, who asserted that the basis of lineage unity was "habitation within a clearly defined area of land, which was regarded as the property of a particular lineage. In some cases the local community consisted almost entirely of lineage members, together with their spouses and their children (51)." The only detailed data to support this assertion, however, came from a single hamlet of thirty-seven houses (49). Moreover, this hamlet was located in an area where, unlike most of Uluguru, farmers were beginning to prosper in the 1950s by growing vegetables for the Dar es Salaam market. Thus rather than proving that communities were generally made up of members of the same lineage, their evidence more likely shows that some entrepreneurial growers of cash crops were able to persuade their sons and sons-in-law to live with them. Indeed, Young and Fosbrooke also provide evidence that lineage members were widely dispersed (57, 61, 64, 76): Roland Young and Henry Fosbrooke, *Smoke in the Hills: Political Tension in the Morogoro District of Tanganyika* (Evanston, Ill.: Northwestern University Press, 1960).

24. TNA, "Native Land Tenure," Pangani District Book II (n.d.). Also, Ankermann, *Ostafrika,* 229; Armstrong, "Land Tenure in Nguru"; Dr. Reuss, "Answers to Questions Sent Regarding Jurisprudence among the Natives in the German Colonies" (trans. by C. C. Dundas) TNA, Early Secretariat File 2587.

25. Baker, *Report on the Social and Economic Conditions*, 144.

26. H. H. McCleery, "An Inquiry into Conditions under which Natives are Occupying Land on the Outskirts of Dar es Salaam Township," TNA, Dar es Salaam Extra Province District Book I, (1939).

27. Mtoro bin Mwinyi Bakari, *The Customs of the Swahili: The Desturi za Waswahili*, edited by J. W. T. Allen (Berkeley: University of California Press, 1981), 151. Also, Reuss, "Answers," 8–9.

28. E. B. Dobson, "Land Tenure of the Wasambaa," *Tanganyika Notes and Records* 10 (1940): 1–27.

29. Events described in the following paragraphs are covered more fully in James L. Giblin, *The Politics of Environmental Control in Northeastern Tanzania, 1840–1940* (Philadelphia: University of Pennsylvania Press, 1993), Chapter 3.

30. The missionary practice of obtaining land from African leaders has led one historian to suggest that in so doing missionaries "helped to establish the idea of private land rights": Juhani Koponen, *Development for Exploitation: German Colonial Policies in Mainland Tanzania, 1884–1914* (Helsinki and Hamburg: Finnish Historical Society and Lit Verlag, 1995), 581.

31. Anton Horner, "De Bagamoyo à Mhonda," *Les Missions Catholiques* (hereafter LMC) 10 (1878): 202.

32. The following discussion of Mandera is based upon the unpublished Mandera Mission Journal, 1881–1883 (especially entries of October 30, 1881; January 21, 1882; February 9, 1883; and July 29–30, 1883); Cado Picarda, "Autour de Mandera," LMC 28 (1886): 236 and 356; "Rapport d'ensemble sur la Mission de Mandera," *Annales Apostoliques de la Congrégation du Saint-Esprit et du Saint Coeur de Marie* (Apostolic Annals of the Congregation of the Holy Spirit and the Sacred Heart of Mary) no. 1 (January 1886): 15; Alexandre Le Roy, "Lettre," *Annales de l'Oeuvre de la Sainte Enfance* (Annals of the Work of the Holy Child) 34 (1883): 312.

33. Picarda, "Autour de Mandera," 356.

34. Picarda, "Autour de Mandera," 236.

35. The following discussion of Tununguo is based on unpublished Tununguo Mission Journal, entry of July 20, 1905; and also Francois Coulbois, "Une tournée dans le vicariat apostolique de Zanguebar, Oct.-Nov. 1884 (A Tour in the Apostolic Vicariate of Zanzibar," LMC 17 (1885): 523–24 and 536–38.

36. François Coulbois, "Une tournée," 538.

37. S. Von Sicard, *The Lutheran Church on the Coast of Tanzania, 1887–1914* (Uppsala: Gleerup, 1970), 102–103 and 122 (quote from 122).

38. Eugen Krenzler, *Ein Jahr in Ostafrika* (A Year in East Africa) (Ulm, 1888), 81–100.

39. The discussion of Lewa is based on Friedrich Schroeder, "Einiges über Arbeiterverhältnisse in Usambara," *Deutsche Kolonialzeitung* no. 28 (1888): 220–22.

40. This is one example of the "uneasiness"''' stirred by alienation of land by the German East Africa Company: Koponen, *Development for Exploitation*, 189.

41. The si traditions are discussed more fully in Giblin, *The Politics of Environmental Control*, 73–78. See also three works by Thomas O. Beidelman: *Moral Imagination in Kaguru Modes of Thought* (Bloomington, Indiana University Press, 1986), 70 and Chapters 5 and 10; "Kaguru Oral Literature: Discussion (Tanzania)" *Anthropos* 74 (1979): 497–529; and "Kaguru Descent Groups (East-Central Tanzania)" *Anthropos* 66 (1971): 373–96.

42. A recent study of central Kenya by Jack Glazier finds a similar relationship between land and the construction of kinship identities. "Through the manifold effects of population pressure, land scarcity, capitalist penetration and offical edict," he says, "descent ideology has found new expression in the incorporation of lineages, in the enhancement of their geneological depth, and in their new and continuing associations with particular segments of land. All of this is presented in the idiom of tradition. . . . [D]escent-based groups can be constituted on non-descent criteria, but, once established, those groups enjoin their membership to comport themselves like clanmates. . . ." Jack Glazier, *Land and the Uses of Tradition among the Mbeere of Kenya* (Lanham, Md.: University Press of America, 1985), 273.

43. The discovery of forgotten si connections often seemed plausible because individuals would never know everyone with whom they shared a si name. Thus no one would be surprised to learn of a previously unknown genealogical tie. The chiefs' propensity for discovering genealogical connections is demonstrated by chieftain traditions collected by the British colonial administration, which invariably depicted chiefs appointed by British officials as the descendants of the founders of the si territory which they were chosen to administer.

44. Young and Fosbrooke, 64–69 and 187; Walter H. Kisbey, *Zigua-English Dictionary* (London: Society for Promoting Christian Knowledge, 1906), 38.

45. Picarda, "Autour de Mandera," 297.

46. For example, see Giblin, *The Politics of Environmental Control*, 53–54.

47. The following discussion of Magamba is based on Giblin, *The Politics of Environmental Control*, 53, 76–77, 96.

48. Giblin, *The Politics of Environmental Control*, 79–80.

49. The argument that a woman's status and rights were mediated by her relationships with men is developed by Elizabeth Schmidt, *Peasants, Traders, and Wives: Shona Women in the History of Zimbabwe, 1870–1939* (London and Portsmouth, N.H.: Heinemann, 1992), Chapter 1; and Marcia Wright, *Strategies of Slaves and Women: Life-Stories from East/Central Africa* (New York and London: Lilian Barber Press and James Currey, 1993), see especially p. 25.

50. For patterns of inheritance, see Steven Feierman, *The Shambaa Kingdom: A History*, (Madison: University of Wisconsin Press, 1974), 33; Baker, *Report on the Social and Economic Conditions*, 142; Godfrey Dale, "An Account of the Principal

Customs and Habits of the Natives Inhabiting the Bondei Country," *Journal of the Anthropological Institute* 25 (1896): 208, 230.

51. See James Giblin, *The Politics of Environmental Control*, 29–34 and Chapters 8 and 10; "Trypanosomiasis Control in African History: An Evaded Issue?" *Journal of African History* 31 (1990): 59–80; "East Coast Fever in Socio-Historical Context: A Case Study from Tanzania," *International Journal of African Historical Studies* 23, no. 3 (1990): 401–21; "Integrating the History of Land Use into Epidemiology: Settler Agriculture as a Cause of Disease in Zimbabwe," Working Papers in African Studies no. 176, African Studies Center, Boston University (1994).

52. James, *Land Tenure*, 14–18.

53. A particularly egregious example of expropriation by the British administration of African-occupied land for European settlers in the Uluguru Mountains is described in C. Louise Sweet, "Inventing Crime: British Colonial Land Policy in Tanganyika," in Colin Sumner, ed., *Crime, Justice, and Underdevelopment* (London: Heinemann, 1982), 76.

54. See Thomas Spear, *Mountain Farmers* (Berkeley: University of California Press, 1997).

55. See Giblin, 147–50.

56. Giblin, 168–74.

57. Giblin, 116–120, 182–83.

58. Giblin, 173.

59. Giblin, 151.

60. Of course, this point is not new. See, for example, Max Gluckman, *The Ideas of Barotse Jurisprudence* (New Haven, 1965), 78–79 and passim; Sally Falk Moore, *Social Facts and Fabrications: "Customary" Law on Kilimanjaro, 1880–1980* (Cambridge, England: Cambridge University Press, 1986), 51; and H. W. O. Okoth-Ogendo, *Tenants of the Crown: Evolution of Agrarian Law and Institutions in Kenya* (Nairobi: African Centre for Technology Studies, 1991), 17–19.

61. The anticipated and actual results of land reform in Kenya are discussed in a large body of literature, including Sara Berry, *No Condition Is Permanent*, 125–129; Migot-Adholla, Hazell, Blarel, and Place, 164ff; Angelique Haugerud, "Land Tenure and Agrarian Change in Kenya," *Africa* 59, no. 1 (1989): 61–90; Parker Shipton, "The Kenyan Land Tenure Reform: Misunderstandings in the Public Creation of Private Property," in R. E. Downs and S. P. Reyna, eds., *Land and Society in Contemporary Africa* (Hanover and London: University Press of New England, 1988), 91–135; Parker Shipton, "Debts and Trespasses: Land, Mortgages, and the Ancestors in Western Kenya," *Africa* 62, no. 3 (1992): 357–88; Anne Fleuret, "Some Consequences of Tenure and Agrarian Reform in Taita, Kenya," in Downs and Reyna, eds., *Land and Society in Contemporary Africa*, 136–58; Fiona Mackenzie, "Land and Territory: The Interface between Two Systems of Land Tenure, Murang'a District, Kenya," *Africa* 59, no. 1 (1989): 91–109; Karuti

Kanyinga, "Struggles of Access to Land: The Land Question, Accumulation, and Changing Politics in Kenya" (University of Nairobi, Institute for Development Studies, Working Paper no. 504, January 1996). Diana Hunt, "The Social and Economic Impacts of Individual Land Titling in Mbeere, Eastern Kenya" (University of Nairobi, Institute for Development Studies, Working Paper no. 505, February 8, 1996). A recent volume which also deemphasizes the significance of tenure reform in promoting conservation, and instead argues that "traditional or customary land use practices already embody ecological principles which should be recognized by the law," is edited by Calestous Juma and J. B. Ojwang, *In Land We Trust: Environment, Private Property, and Constitutional Change* (Nairobi and London: Initiatives Publishers and Zed, 1996), quote from Calestous Juma, "Introduction," 4.

62. Mary Tiffen, Michael Mortimore, and Francis Gichuki, *More People, Less Erosion: Environmental Recovery in Kenya* (Chichester, England; and New York: John Wiley and Sons, 1994). This last point is made on pp. 277–78; quotes are from pp. 276 and 23.

63. A recent survey of the land tenure literature comments that "overlapping and interlocking rights in land are part of whatever a people deem their social fabric . . . this fact has long been considered the essence of African tenures": Parker Shipton, "Land and Culture in Tropical Africa: Soils, Symbols, and the Metaphysics of the Mundane," *Annual Review of Anthropology* 23 (1994): 347–77 (quote from 349).

64. Berry, *No Condition Is Permanent*, Chapter 5. See also Sara Berry, "Concentration without Privatization? Some Consequences of Changing Patterns of Rural Land Control in Africa," in R. E. Downs and S. P. Reyna, eds., *Land and Society in Contemporary Africa* (Hanover and London: University Press of New England, 1988), 53–75; Sara Berry, "Access, Control, and Use of Resources in African Agriculture: An Introduction" *Africa* 59, no. 1 (1989): 1–5; Okoth-Ogendo, "Some Issues of Theory," 6–17.

65. For earlier treatments, see Berry, "Concentration without Privatization?" 53–75; Berry, "Access, Control, and Use of Resources," 1–5; Okoth-Ogendo, "Some Issues of Theory," 6–17.

66. Berry, *No Condition is Permanent*, 103.

67. Elizabeth Wily, "The Political Economy of African Land Tenure: A Case Study from Tanzania" (Ph.D. dissertation, University of East Anglia, 1988), 42–43.

68. TNA 4/651//I, III, District Commissioner (Tanga) to Provincial Commissioner (Tanga), 3/10/1938.

69. Melekia Mlawa (Ilembula, July 20, 1992). Similar evidence was reported by Rayah Feldman, "Custom and Capitalism: Changes in the Basis of Land Tenure in Ismani, Tanzania," *Journal of Development Studies* 10, nos. 3–4 (1974): 314.

70. Giblin, *The Politics of Environmental Control*, 179; and Michaela Von

Freyhold, *Ujamaa Villages in Tanzania: Analysis of a Social Experiment* (New York: Monthly Review Press, 1979), 79, 127, 130, 147, 153, 155.

71. Jan Kees Van Donge, "The Arbitrary State in the Uluguru Mountains: Legal Arenas and Land Disputes in Tanzania," *Journal of Modern African Studies* 31, no. 3 (1993): 431–48; and "Legal Insecurity and Land Conflicts in Mgeta, Uluguru Mountains, Tanzania," *Africa* 63, no. 2 (1993): 197–217. In a different way, Sally Falk Moore's study of Kilimanjaro also shows courts take land matters out of their social context: Moore, *Social Facts and Fabrications*, 169–70.

72. Chanock, "Paradigms, Policies, and Property," 82. In a similar vein, Feldman describes the "weakness of customary law": Feldman, 315. This "weakness" is also discussed by Mvungi and Mwakyembe, 327–38, especially 329–30.

73. Ringo Willy Tenga, "Custom and Law with Reference to the Tanganyika Legal System" (J.S.D. dissertation, Cornell University, 1985), 266.

74. Tenga, 288.

75. The Presidential Commission has been criticized for its failure to address adequately gender inequity in matters of land: Deborah F. Bryceson, "Gender Relations in Rural Tanzania: Power Politics or Cultural Consensus?" in Colin Creighton and C.K. Omari, eds., *Gender, Family, and Household in Tanzania* (Avebury, England: Aldershot and Brookfield, 1985), 60–61. Similar but broader criticisms of the commission's proposals have been advanced by Angelsen and Fjeldstad, who argue that they would likely lead to "misuse and malpractice," (35), and by Tim Kelsall, "African Development: Where to from Here?" *Africa* 65, no. 2 (1995): 306–307.

76. Tiffen, Mortimore, and Gichuki, 152.

77. This issue has been taken up in the context of a wider discussion of law in Tanzania by Issa G. Shivji, "The Rule of Law and *Ujamaa* in the Ideological Formation of Tanzania," *Social and Legal Studies* 4 (1995): 147–74.

6

The Coevolution of Property Rights Regimes for Land, Man, and Forests in Thailand, 1790–1990

DAVID FEENY

In Thailand during the nineteenth and twentieth centuries, there was a remarkable coevolution of property rights in land, man, and forests. At the same time, the Thai polity changed very substantially. Steps to create a modern nation-state based on unitary territorial administration were undertaken. In the early and mid–nineteenth century, Thailand was a land-abundant, labor-scarce economy. Property rights in farmland and forests were only loosely defined while there was a well-developed system of property rights in man. By the early twentieth century, a much more formal and detailed system of property rights in land had been created, the system of property rights in man had been dismantled, the fundamental system of governance had been changed from personal to territorial, a more elaborate system of state property rights in forests had been established, and the area under cultivation had grown substantially.

The chapter will focus on the coevolution of these changes in systems of property rights (coevolution in the Hawaiian case is described in Roumasset and La Croix 1988; Binswanger, Deininger, and Feder 1993 describe evolutionary paths for property rights regimes for land; Otsuka, Chuma, and Hayami 1992 describe institutional arrangements for agricultural labor and land). First, some background material on property rights will be reviewed. Second, evidence on the evolution of each system of property rights will be reviewed. Third, the relationships among the evolving systems of property rights will be considered. Fourth, the importance of these relationships will be assessed by examining counterfactual paths of evolution. Finally, conclusions will be drawn.

NATURE OF PROPERTY RIGHTS IN LAND

In describing any economic system, it is important to describe resource endowments, preferences, technologies, and institutions (Feeny 1987). An important class of institutional arrangements is property rights. In general, "property as a social institution implies a system of relations between individuals. . . . It involves rights, duties, powers, privileges, forbearance, etc., of certain kinds." (Hallowell 1943, 119; for a discussion on the historical evolution of the concept of property, see Schlatter 1951). Property rights are then a bundle of characteristics.

Within this framework, it is important to define the specific concept of property rights for each resource. Providing a definition is more difficult than one might think. For instance for the case of property rights in land, there are a number of important and often overlapping features. Among these are exclusivity, transferability, and alienability (Alchian and Demsetz 1973; Barzel 1989; De Alessi 1980; Demsetz 1967; Feder and Feeny 1991, 1993; Feder and Noronha 1987; Hallowell 1943; North 1981, 1990, 1994; Pejovich 1972; Scott 1983; Scott and Coustalin 1995; and Umbeck 1977). In addition, elements of time, space, use, and enforcement mechanisms are involved. Property rights define the uses which are legitimately viewed as being exclusive and who has these exclusive rights. Uses of land may include hunting, gathering, grazing, cultivation, the mining of minerals, the use of trees, and even the right to destroy the resource. Land rights may further specify the conditions under which the transfer of rights may be effected and the parties to whom such a transfer may be made. Transfer can include bequests. Rights also have a temporal dimension including the present and future. Security of tenure, flexibility in the specification of the rights and duties of tenure, and the extent (by use) to which use rights are divisible are also relevant dimensions of property rights. The institutional arrangements include mechanisms for defining and enforcing rights. These include not only formal procedures but also social custom and the legitimacy and recognition of rights (Hallowell 1943; Taylor 1988). Enforcement depends on a constellation of supporting arrangements and mechanisms including courts, police, financial institutions, the legal profession, land surveys, record keeping systems, and titling agencies in addition to the social legitimacy of property rights in land.

TAXONOMY OF FAMILIES
OF PROPERTY RIGHTS IN LAND

As the discussion above indicates, there is great variety in the nature of property rights in land. It is, however, initially useful to classify land rights into one of four basic categories: (1) none (or open access), (2) communal property, (3) private property, and (4) state (or crown) property (Bromley 1986; Demsetz 1967; Feeny et al. 1990; Feeny 1994; Feeny et al. 1996). Under open access, rights are left unassigned. The lack of any exclusivity implies the lack of an incentive to conserve, and therefore often results in degradation for scarce resources. Under communal property, exclusive rights are assigned to a group of individuals (Bromley and Chapagain 1984; Feeny et al. 1990; National Research Council 1986). Under state property, management of the land is under the authority of the public sector. In private property, an individual is assigned the rights.

GENERALIZATIONS ABOUT PROPERTY RIGHTS IN MAN

The economic history literature on pre-industrial Europe and the Americas provides important generalizations about the origins and evolution of property rights in man. First, property rights in humans are associated with land-abundant, labor-scarce economies (Boyd 1991; Boserup 1965: 72–75; Domar 1970; Domar and Machina 1984; Engerman 1973, 1992; Millward 1984; North and Thomas 1973; Patterson 1977). Labor scarcity creates rents; the scarcity of labor makes it relatively valuable. Property rights in humans provide a mechanism for elites to appropriate part of the high value of human labor.

In circumstances of abundant land and scarce labor, labor markets typically are thin— little labor is supplied to the market and employers cannot rely on being able to hire workers. Thin labor markets pose difficulties for the recruitment and retention of labor, again providing incentives to create and maintain human property rights. Human property rights also provide a means with which to coerce migration and settlement in particular locations. Debt can also serve as a means to compel labor input. Thus human property rights may emerge in economies characterized by low population density—low density is a necessary, but not a sufficient, condition for human property rights.

Second, the choice of slavery versus serfdom depends upon the characteristics of the economy. Slavery is more likely to emerge when a well-developed market economy exists, property rights in humans are more readily enforceable, and there is an economic activity for which the cost of supervision is not prohibitively expensive and for which there may be economies of scale.

Serfdom is more likely to emerge in situations in which markets for products and labor are poorly developed. This seems to imply that the cost of negotiating the consumption bundle for the lord is high, thus enhancing the use of taxes paid in factor services (corvée). A system of payment of factor services may be especially attractive when one party has superior information about the production technology, favoring direction by the lord (Fenoaltea 1975a, 1975b, 1976, 1984, 1988).

Finally, Engerman (1973, 1992), Eltis (1987), Eltis and Walvin (1981), Fogel and Engerman (1974: 29–37), Drescher (1977), and North (1987) stress the importance of political factors in accounting for the abolition of property rights in humans. Gradual emancipation was the rule, swift abolition the exception (Klein 1993). Antislavery movements in the nineteenth century were in part a consequence of the rise of a free labor ideology that argued, on both moral and economic-efficiency grounds, for the removal of various forms of serfdom and slavery (Engerman 1992).

These generalizations based on experience in Europe and the Americas are not entirely consistent with evidence from other settings. As Klein (1993) points out, slavery is observed in economies which are not characterized by well-developed markets. In a number of African societies, the category of slave was used for non-indigenous persons such as war captives. Nonetheless the generalizations are useful, and the Thai case to be discussed below is in large part consistent with their broad interpretation. Corvée and slavery were found in an economy characterized by an abundance of land and scarcity of labor. Their abolition was largely influenced by political rather than strictly economic motives. The two major forms of property rights in man, however, experienced parallel evolutions over the nineteenth century; slavery did not persist as the economy became more commercialized.

BRIEF REVIEW OF HOW SYSTEMS OF PROPERTY RIGHTS IN LAND EVOLVED IN THAILAND, 1790–1990[1]

In the late eighteenth and early nineteenth century in Thailand, in theory all land belonged to the king. In practice there was a system of private usufruct land rights (see Feeny 1982, 1988a, 1988c, 1989, 1993; see also

Table 6.1
Nineteenth- and Twentieth-Century Trends in the Terms of Trade,
Thailand

PERIOD	RATE OF CHANGE (PERCENT PER YEAR)[a]
1865–1867 to 1912	1.41/1.55
1912 to 1925	−3.39/−1.92
1925 to 1939	1.03/1.18
1865–1867 to 1939	0.47/0.85
1865–1867 to 1940	1.52/1.95

Note: a. Export price of rice was divided by import price of white and grey shirting,
respectively.
Source: Feeny (1982), 17 and 131.

Table 6.2
Growth of Agricultural Exports and Manufactured Goods Imports,
Thailand

PERIOD	RATE OF CHANGE (PERCENT PER YEAR)		
	QUANTITY OF RICE EXPORTS	VALUE OF RICE EXPORTS	VALUE OF COTTON GOODS IMPORTS
1864 to 1910	4.43	5.64	4.36
1910 to 1925	1.78	4.14	6.10
1925 to 1940	−0.85	−3.80	−3.19
1864 to 1940	2.84	3.41	3.16

Source: Feeny (1982), 127–30.

Table 6.3

Rates of Change in Thailand's Factor Prices: Land and Wages

RATE OF CHANGE IN REAL LAND PRICES (PERCENT PER YEAR)		
PERIOD	LAND PRICE DEFLATED BY PRICE OF RICE	LAND PRICE DEFLATED BY PRICE OF MANUFACTURED GOODS[a]
1915 to 1925	–0.31	–1.09/–0.14
1925 to 1940	2.58	4.17/4.55
1915 to 1940	1.41	2.03/2.65

Note: a. Deflated by price of white and grey shirting, respectively.
Source: Feeny (1982), 20 and 33.

Rate of Change in Real Wages (percent per year)

PERIOD	REAL WAGE IN:		
	KG PRICE	KG WHITE SHIFTING	KG GREY SHIFTING
1864–1901	–0.71	n.a	n.a.
1865–1901	n.a.	0.49	1.34
1901–1921	–0.47	–2.24	–2.70
1921–1938	1.95	4.01	4.37
1864–1914	–0.60	n.a.	n.a.
1865–1914	n.a.	–0.06	0.10
1914–1938	1.15	1.78	2.58

Note: n.a. not available.
Source: Feeny (1982), 31 and 134.

Engel 1978; Feder, Tongroj, Yongyuth, and Chira 1988b; Kemp 1981; Stifel 1976; Thomson, Feeny, and Oakerson 1992; Yano 1968).[2] By the time of the early Bangkok period (1782 to the present), individuals were allowed to use the land for cultivation, sell it, and pass it on to their heirs as long as they paid taxes on the land and did not leave it fallow for longer than three consecutive years (although it is unlikely that there was a precise definition of idle). Land was not in general used as collateral; instead there was a well-developed system of property rights in humans, who served as collateral. Favorable terms of trade for rice exports (Table 6.1) underwrote the increasing commercialization of rice production and exporting of rice (Table 6.2).[3] In general, land values appreciated (Table 6.3), even though for much of the late nineteenth- and early twentieth-century period the area cultivated per person in fact increased. In contrast there was little trend in real wages (Table 6.3) over much of the mid–nineteenth- to mid–twentieth-century period (nominal and real wage data are presented in Feeny 1982, 132, 134). In particular, real wages declined during the mid–nineteenth- to early twentieth-century period during which the profound changes in property rights systems took place.

The agricultural terms of trade appreciated as international trading opportunities were opened up and transportation costs declined. The result was a rice export boom which induced a rapid expansion in the area under cultivation. The frontier in Thailand has been on the move for most of the period since the late eighteenth century. As land became more valuable and frontier areas were brought under cultivation, land disputes became endemic. The Thai government responded with a series of procedural and administrative changes. Initial responses focused on regularizing administrative procedures and prescribing the use of standardized printed forms. A major new law on land rights was enacted in 1892. Although it provided a more comprehensive framework and more standardization of procedures for documenting landownership rights, the lack of adequate surveys and record keeping continued to inhibit the precise documentation of rights; land disputes continued. In 1896 the government responded by initiating a cadastral survey in an area in which important government officials were also landowners, and in 1901 created a formal system of land titling based on the Torrens system.[4] Cadastral surveys covering most of the commercialized areas in the Central Plain followed.[5] Surveys were not, however, vigorously pursued in most other regions or in upland areas. Thai legislation continued to evolve. The result has been a compromise between the traditional practice of allowing citizens to bring unoccupied forest land under cultivation as private property and the requirements of a cadastral survey–based land titling system.

Table 6.4
**Major Changes in the Thai System of Property Rights in Land,
1800–1982**

PERIOD	INSTITUTIONAL
Early nineteenth century	Usufruct rights, existing system
1811	Survey of landholdings, title deeds based on taxation of land
1836	Removal of tax exemption on rice lands held by nobles
1851–1868	Issue title deeds based on paddy land tax receipts
1861	Edict clarifying private property rights with provision for monarch's right of eminent domain
1867–1868	Title deeds issued based on the area harvested
1882–1883	Title deeds issued based on the area owned
1880s	Standardized forms and procedures prescribed in an effort to reduce land disputes
1892	Comprehensive land law enacted with provision for title deeds and use of land as collateral
1901	Torrens system of land registration instituted and cadastral surveys conducted
1936	1901 law amended to allow for ownership based on registration with the department of claims on unsurveyed lands
1954	New land law enacted providing for variety of documents and levels of security of land rights
1972	Start of use of unrectified aerial photomaps to speed the issuance of certificates of utilization
1982	Increasing the rate of issuance of title deeds made a priority

Sources: Chatthip (1977), 1–3; Feeny (1988c), 285–86; Feeny (1993), 92; Terwiel (1983a), 103–107; Thomson, Feeny, and Oakerson (1992), 146; and Williamson (1983).

These compromises provide for four major levels in the security and documentation of land rights and are embodied in the 1954 legislation which provides the basis for the current system in Thailand. First, occupation certificates are issued by village headmen and commune leaders, and allow the holder to temporarily exclude others from using land as long as it is being developed. Second, reserve licenses issued by district officers also give rights for temporary occupation subject to utilization. Third, exploitation testimonials (again issued by district officers) confirm that utilization of previously reserved land has taken place and confer rights that are transferable and inheritable. Finally, full title deeds determined by cadastral survey and providing for the recording of land transactions are issued by officials in the provincial capital. Greater security in land rights thus comes at the expense of higher transaction cost (both formal and informal). (Under existing law, rights to titled land which is left idle for more than ten consecutive years may be cancelled; for land held under exploitation testimonial, the period is more than five consecutive years.)

In recent decades, the incomplete realization of the private property rights system in land in Thailand, especially in upland areas, has created disincentives that have hindered efforts to intensify cultivation in the face of a rapidly shrinking land frontier. Recent World Bank and other reports (Anan 1987; Anant et al. 1988; Dhira and Suthawan 1988; Kunstadter et al. 1978) have pointed to situations in which socially profitable investments in land development are being underexploited and instead cultivators continue to rely on extensive cultivation systems (such as swidden or slash-and-burn agriculture). The reason for the lack of intensification is often not that farmers are unaware of the higher rates of return on more intensive land development but that they lack the means to obtain secure property rights.

The lack of provision of adequate documentation of private property rights in land in Thailand affects more than the choice between swidden cultivation and more permanent forms of settlement. In many areas outside of the Central Plain, the degree of documentation of land rights is insufficient for land to be used legally as collateral on loans. Although the risk of eviction in these areas is generally low (unlike the hill areas described above), the lack of full documentation means that farmers in these permanently settled areas have restricted access to credit. Typically they are able to obtain less credit and at more unfavorable terms (Siamwalla et al. 1990). Feder et al. (see Feder and Tongroj 1987; Feder 1987; Feder, Tongroj, Yongyuth, and Chira 1988a, 1988b; and Yongyuth and Feder 1988; see also Tongroj 1990) demonstrate that farmers with adequate documentation of property rights farm more intensively, use more capital inputs, and achieve both higher output and productivity. The estimates by Feder et al. also indicate that the private and social benefits of the provision of more fully documented rights exceed the costs.

In response, the Thai government has accelerated the provision of cadastral surveys in areas in which titling was not previously available. The evolution of property rights in land is summarized in Table 6.4.

The current system of land rights in Thailand then was developed in response to the increased benefits of defining property rights in land induced by the commercialization of agriculture and appreciation in the agricultural terms of trade. Government officials, as landowners, shared in the gains from titling and were therefore willing to provide the institutional changes being demanded, especially in localities in which they owned lands. Their motives also reflected the desire to provide mechanisms to resolve land disputes and reduce the incidence of disputes. In addition, the development of land registration and titling systems gave the Thai government a means with which to enforce its decision to prohibit the ownership of land by foreigners (Gehan 1987). Restrictions on land alienation were designed, in part, to avoid disputes that would have given foreign powers an excuse to interfere in local administration. The development and documentation of property rights in land also served the development of territorial government in Thailand. (Sources that discuss the transformation of the Thai system of governance from one based on control of people to a territorial system include Brown 1993; Peluso, Vandergeest, and Potter 1995; Thongchai 1994; Vandergeest and Peluso 1995; and Wilson 1993. Murashima 1988 discusses the related issue of the creation of state ideology.)

PROPERTY RIGHTS IN MAN[6]

Concomitant with the creation of private property rights in crop land, there was a gradual dismantling of property rights in humans in the form of corvée and slavery. Over the period from the mid–nineteenth century to 1913, slavery and corvée were abolished.

The control of manpower had long been viewed as the key to power in Thai society (Akin 1969, 1975; Brummelhuis 1983; Chatchai 1982; Cruikshank 1975; Evers, Korff, and Pas-Ong 1987; Feeny 1982, 1993; Hong Lysa 1984; Sharp and Hanks 1978; Terwiel 1983a, 1983b, 1984; Turton 1980; Wilson 1970, 1993; Wyatt 1968, 1969, 1984, 1986). Thai society comprised five major categories: the monarch, members of the royal family, the nobility, commoners, and slaves. Officials or nobles, the *nai*,

Table 6.5
Corvée Obligations circa 1800

Phrai luang	Obligation to monarch of 6 months per year or 18–24 baht
Phrai som	Obligation to nai (a noble) 2 months/year; obligation to monarch, 1 month per year or fee of 6 baht
Phrai suai	Obligation payable in kind
Slaves	Obligation of 8 days per year or 1.5 baht

Note: Corvée obligations were owed by all males ages 20–60 or until they had three sons at least 20 years of age.
Sources: Akin (1969), 90–96; Chatchai Panananon (1982), 142; Feeny (1993), 89; Terwiel (1983b), 124–25.

were directly responsible for the control of commoners, the *phrai* (Table 6.5). Phrai owed labor services or in-kind payments to the king and nobles.

Although the law recognized seven categories of slaves, there were two more basic categories: war captives and debt slaves (Table 6.6). Human beings were a traditional booty of war in mainland Southeast Asia; usually war captives were settled as whole communities, often under the direction and ownership of officials who had played a role in the successful military operations that led to the capture of the slaves. Although prisoner-of-war slaves were mobile at the time of capture, the Thai practice of creating "slave" communities tended to make them immobile once settled.

Changes in the system of property rights in man (Tables 6.7 and 6.8) took place within an evolving economy, domestic polity, and external conditions. The growing importance of international trade broadened and deepened product and factor markets. In particular, the immigration of Chinese labor helped to create a broad and reliable market for labor (Table 6.9). Growing commercialization facilitated the substitution of monetary for in-kind payments for taxes. Increasingly, the government could reliably turn to the labor market for wage workers for the construction of public works. This shift also undercut the nobility's control of labor and was part

Table 6.6
Existing System of Slavery, circa 1800

SEVEN CATEGORIES OF SLAVES

1. Slaves in which owner had full title.
2. Children born of slaves in master's household.
3. Slaves received as gifts from their parents or inherited.
4. Slaves received as gifts.
5. Slaves rescued from peril or legal penalties.
6. Slaves supported in times of famine.
7. Slaves acquired through capture in war.

TWO MORE BASIC CATEGORIES:

    A. War captives
    B. Debt slaves
       1. Non-redeemable, sold for full fixed price
       2. Redeemable, sold for less than full fixed price; work for master
       3. Redeemable, interest-bearing; work independently

FULL-FIXED PRICE FOR SLAVES FROM AYUTHIA PERIOD

    Adult male: 218.75 baht
    Adult female: 187.50 baht

Sources: Akin (1969), 90–96; Chatchai Panananon (1982), 142; Feeny (1993), 90; and Terwiel (1983b), 124–25.

of the creation of a centralized territorial system of administration (Bunnag 1968, 1977). In addition, the monarch also had important humanitarian motives for abolishing slavery.

The decline of warfare with neighboring states as they became colonized cut off the traditional source of war captive slaves. The colonial threat to Thai sovereignty also underscored the importance of the abolition of slavery.

Changes in the systems of corvée and slavery were implemented gradually. The central edict in the abolition of slavery was proclaimed in 1874. Gradual abolition of slavery blunted the opposition of slave owners, who

Table 6.7

Chronology of Major Changes in Property Rights in Man,
1767–1914: Corvée

Period	Institutional change
1773	Initiate practice of tattooing free men beginning of each reign
1805	Three-Seals laws, codification of laws from Ayuthia period and edicts from Thonburi period and First Reign
1782–1809 (First Reign)	Corvée obligation for Phrai luang lowered from 6 months to 4 months per year or 6 baht per month
1810 (Second Reign)	Corvée obligation for Phrai luang lowered from 4 months to 3 months per year
1870s	Evidence that Phrai luang paid 9–12 baht per year for exemption
1897–1898	Exemption fee lowered to 6 baht per year
1899	Replace corvée with head tax
1900–1910	Replace corvée with a system of conscription; edicts in 1902, 1905
1901	Decree establishing wage payment of 0.5 baht per day for corvée labor unless on local public works
1906	Decree prohibiting corvée during growing season
1909	Decree limiting corvée, paid or unpaid, to maximum of 15 days per year

Sources: Akin (1969), 96–100; Battye (1974), 19, 429, 459; Chatchai Panananon (1982), 134–37, 301; Feeny (1982), 85–98; Feeny (1993), 94; Terwiel (1983a), 214; Terwiel (1983b), 124–30; Wyatt (1984), 155, 210.

were for the most part members of powerful bureaucratic families or the royal family. Concomitant developments in the system of property rights in land created an alternative asset that could supplant people as the major form of collateral in formal credit markets. Legal provisions for personal bankruptcy were also created.

Table 6.8

Chronology of Major Changes in Property Rights in Man, 1767–1914: Slavery

Period	Institutional change
1805	Rama I sets prices for redemption of war captive slaves Adult male: 64 baht Adult female: 56 baht
Mid-19th	Guesstimates that ¼ to ⅓ of population are slaves
1868	Edict requiring consent of wife before she or her children could be sold into slavery by husband
1874	Edict prescribing declining prices for slaves born after October 1868, who are freed at age 21 and cannot sell themselves once they reach age 21; and proclaiming grandchildren of slaves free at birth
1884	Proclamation to eastern provinces ordering children of slaves to be set free, reducing legal value of slaves, and forbidding freed slaves from selling themselves
1890	Law freeing children of redeemable slaves at age 21
1897	Law, no one born after December 16, 1897, can be sold or sell oneself into slavery
1900	Earlier decrees extended to the North
1905	Act to abolish slavery, forbid sales, and cut slave prices by 4 baht per month
1908	Trading in slaves made a criminal offense under 1908 Penal Code
1911–12	Extend geographic coverage of previous legislation
1913	Extend geographic coverage of previous legislation
1915	Abolition to be completed in the provinces

Sources: Chatchai Panananon (1982), 54, 262, 301; Chatthip and Suthy (1977), 57; Feeny (1982), 85–98; Feeny (1993), 96; Terwiel (1983b), 132; Terwiel (1984), 32; Turton (1980), 284; Wilson (1962), 106.

A variety of motivations were important in the dismantling of human property rights in Thailand during the nineteenth century. The commercialization of agriculture and the large influx of Chinese immigrant workers contributed to the development of a reliable market for labor. The rice export boom decreased the attractiveness of institutional arrangements that inhibited labor mobility. In addition to these economic efficiency motives for the abolition of corvée and slavery, there were important domestic and international political motives. The control of manpower had been an important source of power for bureaucratic families in Thailand. As part of the intra-elite struggle between the monarch and nobles for power in Thailand, it was in the interest of the monarch to dismantle the human property rights system in order to reduce the relative power of the nobility. Reduction in the reliance on corvée and shifts to revenue farming, the poll tax, and a conscription were an integral part of the creation of a territorial system of administration (patterned after the one used by the British in India).

There were also important international political motivations for the abolition of slavery. Starting in 1855, Thailand had signed treaties granting extraterritoriality to the Western powers. In order to retain independence in the presence of the very real threat of being colonized, Thailand had to adopt reforms viewed by the Western powers as being legitimate and modern (Hall 1968; Wyatt 1984). In particular to remove extraterritoriality provisions, it was necessary that Thailand abolish slavery. Missionaries in Thailand had long objected to the Thai practice of slavery (Bradley 1981).

FORESTS[7]

In contrast to the creation of private property rights in crop land, the commercialization of forestry was associated with the creation of state property rights in forest lands. De jure state property was often, however, de facto open access. Illegal logging and the expansion of the area under cultivation in response to market opportunities and population growth led to rapid deforestation.

Traditionally in Thailand, forest lands were de jure state property but de facto open access. Local rulers, however, enforced property rights on high-value tree species such as teak (and other valuable forest products). The temporary closure of teak forests in neighboring upper Burma in 1885 led to the entry of foreign logging firms in the teak forests of northern Thailand. Timber stocks were depleted rapidly. At the time northern

Table 6.9

Indirect Evidence on the Development of a Wage Labor Market in
Thailand, 1825–1942

YEAR	PERCENTAGE OF CHINESE IN TOTAL POPULATION	PERIOD	AVERAGE ANNUAL SURPLUS OF ARRIVALS FROM CHINA (ARRIVALS FROM CHINA MINUS DEPARTURES TO CHINA, IN THOUSANDS)
1825	4.8		
1850	5.8		
1860	6.2		
1870	6.6		
1880	7.0	1882–1892	7.1
1890	7.5	1893–1905	14.9
1900	8.3	1906–1917	15.0
1910	9.5		
1917	9.8		
1922	10.5	1918–1931	35.7
1927	11.7		
1932	12.2	1932–1945	6.6
1937	11.8		
1942	11.7		

Source: Skinner (1957), 61, 79, 173, 183.

Thailand was only loosely integrated in the Bangkok-based Thai kingdom
and was ruled by local Lao princes. In return for fees, the local rulers
granted permission for foreign firms to exploit teak forests. At times permission to exploit the same forest was granted to more than one firm,
leading to disputes.

The Bangkok government feared that such disputes would be used as
an excuse for colonial intervention. Thai authorities were aware of the fact
that a dispute over a fine levied by the Burmese on the Bombay-Burmah
Trading Corporation for underreporting teak extractions was the incident
that led to the Third Anglo-Burma War in 1885 and annexation of upper

Table 6.10
Evolution of Thai Forest and Conservation Policy

Period	Institutional change
1885	Closure of upper Burma teak forests; increased exploitation of Thai teak
1896	Creation of Thai Royal Forestry Department
1897	Forest Protection Act and Teak Trees Protection Act, regulation of commercial exploitation of commercial teak
1900	Wildlife Elephant Preservation Act, early example of wildlife preservation legislation
1913–14	Decree establishing reserved (teak and yang) and unreserved species of trees
1936–37	Forest Reservation Act, designation of reserved and protected forests
1941	Forest Act of 1941 (revised in 1948 and 1951)
1947	Forest Industry Organization created
1948	Target of retaining 50% land area in forest proposed by Food and Agriculture Organization (later incorporated into 1962–1966 First Five-Year Plan)
1952	No new leases for exploitation of forests issued to foreign firms
1960	Forest Act of 1960
1960	Wild Animals Reservation and Protection Act of 1960
1961	National Park Act
1964	Major legislation on wildlife preservation
1964	National Reserved Forest Act, enhanced authority to protect forests and watersheds
1977	Ban on exports of logs
1977	Target for proportion of land area to be covered by forests revised to 37%
1985	Target for proportion of land area to be covered by forests revised to 40% (15% of total for watershed and national parks; 25% for economic forests)
1989	Commercial logging ban proclaimed after a series of floods and mudslides in January
1991	40% forest area target incorporated in Seventh Five-Year Plan (1991–1996); conserved forest area target raised from 15% to 25%, economic forest target set at 16%
1992	Conserved forest target area revised to 28%

Sources: Anat et al. (1988), 158–61; Feeny (1988a), 123–27; Kamon and Thomas (1990), 169–77; Sadoff (1992).

Table 6.11
Estimates of the Forest Area and Rates of Change in the Forest Area of Thailand

Year	Percentage of total area in forest	Area in forest (thousands of ha.)	Source and comments
1913	75	38,514	Graham (1924, 347); includes forests, marsh, and jungle
1930	70	35,946.4	Thailand, Ministry of Commerce (1930, 35)
1938	72		Poffenberger (1990, 8)
1947	63		Tsujii (1973, 29); taken from Ministry of Agriculture data
1949	69	32,600	Donner (1978, 71); area in forests and pasture
1955	63	32,129	Sukhum (1955, 8).
1956	58	30,288.3	Pendleton (1962, 134); area in forests and pasture
1959	58	30,010	Chalermrath (1972, 20); official estimate
1961	56	29,000	Donner (1978, 133); estimate from aerial photography survey
1961	52		Chalermrath (1972, 24); estimate of forestry official
1963	53	27,100	Asian Development Bank (1969, 475); estimate based on Food and Agriculture Organization world forest inventory
1965	53	27,300	Donner (1978, 22); author indicates that this estimate, which is based on a land use survey, is probably an overestimate
1965	<40		Chalermrath (1972, 24); estimate of forestry official
1966	51	26,500	Krit (1966, 5)
1969–70	52	26,900	Land Development Department estimates based on aerial photography
1970	39–49	20,000–25,000	Donner (1978, 134); author's estimate

Table 6.11 (continued)
Estimates of the Forest Area and Rates of Change in the Forest Area of Thailand

Year	Percentage of total area in forest	Area in forest (thousands of ha.)	Source and comments
1970	30		Tsujii (1973, 29); estimate of forestry expert
1973	43		Hirsch (1990, 168)
1974	37	19,040	Thailand, National Economic and Social Development Board (NESDB) (1977, 149);
1975	41	21,068	estimate based on satellite imagery
1978	25	13,018	World Bank estimate based on satellite imagery
1980	<30		Wilson (1983, 133); estimate based on satellite imagery
1982	31		Thailand, NESDB (1981, 7)
1985	29		Hirsch (1990, 168)
1990	25		Sadoff (1992, 7)
1991	27		Lynch and Talbott (1995, 12); World Resources Institute estimate
1991	34		Lynch and Talbott (1995, 10); Royal Forestry Department estimate
1992	<27		Lynch and Talbott (1995, 10); Department of Land Development estimate
1992	18		Sadoff (1992, 10); official estimate

Sources: Feeny (1988c), 118–19; Hirsch (1990); Lynch and Talbott (1995); Poffenberger (1990); and Sadoff (1992).

Table 6.11 (continued)
Estimates of the Forest Area and Rates of Change in the Forest Area
of Thailand

PERIOD	AVERAGE ANNUAL RATE OF CHANGE IN FOREST AREA (PERCENT)
1930–1974	−1.43
1930–1975	−1.18
1930–1992[a]	−1.52
1930–1992[b]	−2.17
1974–1992[a]	−1.75
1974–1992[b]	−3.94
1975–1992[a]	−2.43
1975–1992[b]	−4.73

Notes: Calculations marked with *a* assume that the area under forest cover in 1992
is 13,865 thousand ha. or 27% of the total area; calculations marked with *b* instead
assume the 1992 area is 9,243 thousand ha., 18% of the total area. The total area
in Thailand is 51,352,000 ha. (Donner 1978, 907). Data given in Table 6.11 represent a compilation of estimates of the area under forest cover from a wide variety
of sources with varying degrees of accuracy. Official estimates are taken from various government publications and may embody both the best evidence available
and politically motivated interpretations of that evidence. The same can be said of
a number of unofficial estimates. There has been considerable regional variation in
the extent of forest cover and rate of deforestation.
Sources: Feeny (1988c), 118–19; Hirsch (1990); Lynch and Talbott (1995);
Poffenberger (1990); and Sadoff (1992).

Burma in 1886 (Riggs 1966, 62; Steinberg et al. 1971, 175–76). The
Bangkok government intervened in northern Thailand in 1874 by
appointing a commissioner to handle disputes between logging firms and
the local Lao princes (Brown 1988, 111; see also Anat et al. 1988, 158–61;
Riggs 1966, 138; Vandergeest and Peluso 1995). As the level of logging
activity and associated disputes increased in the 1880s and 1890s, the government retained H. A. Slade of the Imperial Forest Service in Burma as a
consultant. His report in 1896 recommended that the forest ownership be
transferred to the central government and that a forestry department be

created (Brown 1988, 114). In 1896 the Thai government created the Royal Forestry Department to regularize the exploitation of teak and shift control of teak forests from local rulers to the central government, and appointed Slade as its first director-general. Colonial Indian civil servants were hired as foreign advisers to help create the Thai forestry department. (The influence of British forestry policy in India on Thai policy was further strengthened when a number of Thai foresters were trained in India.) These British civil servants argued that Thai decision makers had insufficient vision and unduly short time horizons and that as a result private property rights in forest lands were not a viable option. Thus they argued for the creation of state property as the device most capable of fostering adequate conservation of forest resources. With the passage of the Forest Protection Act of 1897, the focus was entirely on the commercial exploitation of teak in which state property rights were declared. By 1899 the government had gained ownership control of all natural forests. A relatively small number of leases for teak were granted to large, foreign timber firms. In a sense by granting long-term leases to these firms, the Thai government gave these firms the incentive to enforce the central government's property rights in forest lands. (Similarly, Lohmann 1991 [14] argues that Royal Forestry Department [RFD] grants of forest lands to private eucalyptus plantations are a mechanism through which the RFD can assert its property rights at the expense of de facto village owners.) Traditional wood cutting and forest clearing were, however, left largely unaffected. Private ownership was allowed for plantations—mainly for rubber, fruit, and oil seed trees.

The recommendation to create state property rights in forests was accepted by elites in the Bangkok regime in part because it served their interest in centralizing control and because it was at least somewhat consistent with traditional concepts of property rights in trees. It is also possible that state property rights were adopted because many of the forest dwellers (who might be viewed as having some legitimate claim to property rights) were not ethnic Thai, often did not practice settled agriculture (instead were swidden cultivators), and were mobile (thus probably were less loyal to the central Thai regime in Bangkok). In more recent times, the RFD has found it convenient to blame swidden cultivators for the degradation of forest resources in Thailand (Kunstadter et al. 1978). The fact that these "hill tribesmen" had relatively little political power made it much easier for Thai regimes to enforce their claim to property rights in trees.

Over time Thai forest policy evolved from a narrow focus on the commercial exploitation of teak to a broader focus on commercial forestry in general. More recently concerns over the preservation of watersheds, water quality, and wildlife have been incorporated into official policy. Thailand has an extensive system of national parks. (It is estimated that Thailand is home to 174 species of endangered animals [Sadoff 1992, 24.]). The evolution of Thai forest policy is described briefly in Table 6.10. Evidence on the area under forest cover is summarized in Table 6.11.

RELATIONSHIPS AMONG EVOLVING SYSTEMS OF PROPERTY RIGHTS

Free land over which secure private property rights could be established, the "freeing" of people with the concomitant reductions in restrictions on labor mobility, and de facto open access to forest lands interacted to underwrite rapid increases in area under cultivation and the accompanying rapid declines in forest area. Evolution in the systems of property rights for crop land, forests, and people all responded to similar pressures for change resulting from increases in the size and scope both of product and factor markets. The development of these markets was supported by investments in infrastructure carried out by the centralizing regime in Bangkok. (The rapid expansion of the highway network in the post-World War II period, especially during the 1960s and 1970s, helped to underwrite rapid deforestation and conversion of land from forest to agricultural use, especially in the Northeast; see Cropper, Griffiths, and Mani 1999.) Changes in property rights were, however, not solely determined by the forces of commercialization and international trade. Both domestic and international political motives were important. The configuration of evolution of the property rights systems is described briefly in Table 6.12.

The "freeing" of man and establishment of private property rights in crop land were consistent with the "requirements" of a market, export-oriented economy. In a sense the "outlier" in the set of changes in property rights systems was the creation of de jure state property rights in forests. Private property rights in crop land, along with the freeing of man, created a situation in which economic agents had powerful incentives to convert land from low-value to high-value uses. (Market prices did not, of course, transmit information to agents on either positive or negative externalities and thus these externalities, which become increasingly important over time, were largely ignored in resource allocation decisions.) For the most part, the conversion of forest land to crop land can be seen in this context. De jure state property rights in forests should have importantly altered the private incentives for land clearing. In practice, however, state property rights were enforced mainly for a few highly valuable commercial species. Forest lands were traditionally viewed as open-access resources,

Table 6.12

Actual Historical Configuration of Systems of Property Rights, 1790 and 1915 Compared

PERIOD, CIRCA 1790		LAND/FOREST RIGHTS				HUMAN PROPERTY RIGHTS	
		Open access	Communal	Private	State	Corvée/ slave	Free
Crop land	In use			De facto	De jure		
	Not in use	De facto			De jure		
Forests	High value				De facto De jure		
	Other	De facto			De jure		
People						De jure	

PERIOD, CIRCA 1915		LAND/FOREST RIGHTS				HUMAN PROPERTY RIGHTS	
		Open access	Communal	Private	State	Corvée/ slave	Free
Crop land	In use			De jure			
	Not in use	De facto			De jure		
Forests	High value				De facto De jure		
	Other	De facto			De jure		
People							De jure

legitimately available to anyone who invested their labor resources in clearing the land (Hafner 1973; Kunstadter et al. 1978). The declaration of state property rights in forests was, in general, not viewed as legitimate. The lack of social legitimacy inhibited the enforceability of the declaration of state property rights in forest lands that might have reduced the extent of socially inappropriate deforestation. Under the traditional system, rights to forest resources were established by exploitation and, in general, were not accompanied by any documentary verification. Under the new system, rights were instead defined by bureaucratic procedures and accompanied by a written record of their legality. In addition to deforestation through land clearing for agricultural purposes, widespread illegal and extralegal logging (often accompanied by extralegal payments to forestry officials who in turn knowingly tolerated the logging) contributed further to deforestation.

In recent decades the expansion of the highway network subsidized the forestry industry. Commercial loggers would then remove the large, valuable trees. Agricultural settlers would then follow and complete the clearing of the land. Although much of this conversion may well have represented a transfer of land use from lower to higher value use, even when externalities are taken into account the lack of enforcement and enforceability of state property rights in forests meant that logging and land clearing also took place on steep slopes and ridge tops vulnerable to degradation. The lack of enforcement and enforceability also meant that little attention was paid to the conservation of water resources and the preservation of wildlife.

For much of the period from the late nineteenth century until quite recently, it is likely that deforestation for the most part represented a conversion from low- to high-value land use. As population density downstream has increased, forest resources have become more scarce, and forest habitats have disappeared, the social efficiency of deforestation has, however, declined. Viewed from the perspective of the 1990s, it was natural to point to the inefficiency of state property rights in forests in Thailand. From the point of view of policy makers during earlier periods when forest resources were still abundant, however, the efficiency implications of state property rights were more benign.

In addition to these economic efficiency arguments, there were additional motives with respect to state building and national security. The creation of de facto open access in forest lands underwrote the settlement of border frontier areas by ethnic Thai more likely to be loyal to the Bangkok regime and displacement of ethnic minorities who were viewed as less loyal. (A similar argument is made by Allen 1991 concerning the design of the homesteading system in the United States.) Thus, there were also national security motives for the choice of property rights regime for forest lands. By populating border areas, the Thai government could establish and enforce its claims to territorial sovereignty.

How different would Thai economic history have been over the last two centuries if a different configuration of property rights systems had been created? The brief preceding discussion (and more detailed discussions) argues that given the forces shaping the demands for institutional change and the factors shaping the provision of institutional change (for a presentation of the underlying framework, see Feeny 1988b), the evolutions which occurred for each individual system of property rights make "sense." The evolutions which occurred, however, were not preordained; alternatives were possible and some in fact were seriously considered.

One approach to assessing the importance of the particular configuration of systems of property rights is to perform a counterfactual analysis as a thought experiment. In a sense such counterfactuals have limited usefulness. This type of counterfactual deviates quite substantially from the actual historical record. Thus, even within a carefully specified quantitative analytical framework, the results of such a counterfactual would not be highly reliable. In this context the counterfactual analysis will be conducted in an even cruder fashion, relying on an implicit qualitative framework instead of an explicit quantitative one. It remains to be seen whether the results have sufficient merit to justify the approach.

Counterfactual 1

Counterfactual analysis involves an attempt to answer a "what if" question. What then is a plausible alternative to what actually happened? As alluded to in the preceding discussion, one alternative would have been the creation of de jure private property rights in forests. How different would changes in land use have been if instead of declaring state property rights in forests the Thai government had created private property rights in forest lands? This counterfactual will be labeled as Counterfactual 1 and is summarized in Table 6.13.

Table 6.13
Counterfactual 1 Configuration of Systems of Property Rights:
Private Property Rights in Land and Forests/Free Humans

PERIOD, CIRCA 1990		LAND/FOREST RIGHTS				HUMAN PROPERTY RIGHTS	
		Open access	Communal	Private	State	Corvée/ slave	Free
Crop land	In use			De jure			
	Not in use			De jure			
Forests	High value			De jure			
	Other			De jure			
People							De jure

Changes in any system of property rights have implications both for efficiency and distribution. The consequences for each depend importantly on the precise nature of the property rights system created. For the first counterfactual, it may be useful to create an alternative that is at least somewhat plausible. Following this approach, the Thai government might have treated forest lands in the late nineteenth century much as they treated crop lands. Thus, the act of exploitation of a tract of forest lands would probably have been sufficient to establish private ownership rights. If in 1897 the government had created private instead of state property rights, it is likely that the original legislation would have included a mechanism for assigning rights in teak and other highly valuable species. Perhaps private rights would have been assigned to local Lao leaders (although this would have been inconsistent with the political motives of officials in Bangkok). Alternatively, private rights may have been auctioned off. (Traditionally, temporary rights to harvest fish or birds' nests in particular localities had often been awarded by auction; more generally, tax farming privileges—the right to collect a certain tax in a specific locality— had often been awarded by auction.) Given the nature of forest lands in general and the dispersed nature of teak in particular, private owners would have experienced difficulties in enforcing their rights. Thus for highly valued species, it is unclear that the outcomes under private property rights would have differed importantly from those under state property rights. It is less than obvious that the state would have expended sufficient resources to enforce private property rights on behalf of private owners.

Alternatively in the actual historical case, one could interpret unofficially sanctioned illegal cutting as de facto usufruct private property. Seen in this light, perhaps there would have been a difference for high-value commercial species between the actual state property system and the counterfactual private property rights system. While the actual state property rights system was a de facto usufruct private system, the counterfactual system that defined rights in the stock rather than just the flow may have given more incentive for the long-run development of forest resources. The difference between defining rights in the flow (harvest of trees) versus stock (the forest itself) would probably have been negligible in the late nineteenth century. More recently, however, as valuable timber has become scarce, this difference might have become meaningful.

For less valuable species and the conversion of forest lands to crop lands, it is likely that, in one sense, a system of private property rights established through exploitation would have produced outcomes very similar to those in the actual case characterized by de facto open access forest lands. There may, however, have been important differences. First, if private property rights in forest lands had been declared, it is likely that the state would have been drawn extensively into the settlement of land disputes, much in the same manner that it was administratively drawn into disputes over farm lands. Second, the creation of private property rights in land would have provided a mechanism through which private forest land could have been used as collateral to gain access to formal credit markets that have, as economic change has occurred, become more important. Thus although initially private property rights in forest lands might have operated in much the same way as state property rights did, over time with private property rights there may have been more scope for the development of long-run incentives for the management of forests and creation of more elaborate and enforceable private property rights in forests. Private instead of state property rights might realistically have produced at least somewhat different outcomes.

Thus, from an efficiency point of view, the creation of private property rights in forest lands might have had little effect on the outcome. Alternatively, there might have been modest effects through the creation of greater security and enforceability in forest land rights. From a distributional point of view, however, the consequences of creating private property rights in forests might well have been quite important. The assignment of the rights to forests by auction or regularization and legalization of the capture of forest lands by exploitation might have broadened the distribution of benefits from forestry relative to the actual situation in which the economic rents from the initial exploitation of forest resources were captured by a small group of officials and their patrons in the forest industry. In the actual case the benefits from the exploitation of agricultural lands were widely shared. Perhaps private property rights in forests would have produced similar distributional outcomes.

Counterfactual 2

In practice, Thailand has relied upon de jure private and state property rights and has made little formal use of communal property rights systems. In many ways this is quite understandable. Historically Thailand, like much of mainland Southeast Asia, was characterized by an abundance of land and scarcity of labor. Before widespread commercialization and more recently rapid growth in population, there was an abundance of most natural resources including agricultural land and forests. When land and forest resources were highly abundant, the benefit of defining property rights for these resources (other than enforcing exclusivity for usufruct purposes) was close to zero. Thus, for the most part, the development of elaborate and costly systems of property rights in land and forests was not worthwhile.

This was also true at the local level. Given the traditional abundance of local forest resources, villagers did not, in general, need to regulate the use of such resources by members of the community. Thus, in general, there were few historical precedents for the development of communal property rights systems. Cultural endowments that accepted highly individualistic behavior probably also served to raise the transaction costs of organizing collective action in Thailand.

There are, of course, a few prominent exceptions to these generalizations. In northern Thailand, characterized by mountains and small river valleys, there were communal irrigation systems. Villagers would work cooperatively each year to construct a temporary weir to divert water onto fields. Traditional institutional arrangements included provisions for the election of an irrigation chief with the authority to tax farmers who received irrigation water and fine those who failed to pay their taxes. Rotating credit societies and peer monitoring of loans by members of groups (typically groups comprise between eight and fifteen members; Siamwalla et al. 1990, 281, 291–93) provide additional evidence that cooperative collective action is feasible when mutual benefits are sufficiently attractive.

Recently a number of commentators on forestry and rural policy in Thailand have advocated the enhancement of local government authority (to produce local public goods and to enhance the management of land, forest, water, and other resources) and the creation of enabling legislation for formal communal property rights (see, for instance, Chusak 1996; Hafner and Yaowalak 1990; Kamon and Thomas 1990, 180–86; Lohmann 1995; Lynch and Talbott 1995). More specifically, there have been proposals advocating the creation of formal communal property rights systems for community forests and village woodlots (Sadoff 1992, 16–17; Mehl 1991; Sukhum 1955). The motives for these suggestions appear to include efficiency (give authority to those with local knowledge and a stake in successful management) and equity (allow local residents to capture the returns).

Would it have been possible to have created some form of communal property rights in forests? Would it have been useful or feasible to have created these institutional arrangements at an earlier date?

As in the case of Counterfactual 1, there are a variety of specifications that could be adopted for the alternative policy. Following the logic of Counterfactual 1, it may be useful to assume that property rights in high-value species would have been treated separately; for purposes of the counterfactual, let us assume that state property rights would have been declared, as in the actual case. Further, let us assume that communal property rights would have been available only for small tracts of forest

Table 6.14
Counterfactual 2 Configuration of Systems of Property Rights: Private Rights in Land/State and Communal Rights in Forests/Free Humans

PERIOD, CIRCA 1990		LAND/FOREST RIGHTS				HUMAN PROPERTY RIGHTS	
		Open access	Communal	Private	State	Corvée/ slave	Free
Crop land	In use			De jure			
	Not in use			De jure			
Forests	High value				De jure		
	Other		De jure				
People							De jure

lands located close to villages. Communal property rights would then have represented a means for the community to exclude others from clearing the forest and to organize and regulate subsistence and small-scale commercial use of the local forest by members of the community. (See Table 6.14.)

It is likely that given the abundance of forests in the late nineteenth and early twentieth centuries, few villages would have judged the benefits of declaring and enforcing communal property rights in local forests sufficient to have offset the cost (even if the government would have been cooperative in formally recognizing such rights). In the post–World War II period, and especially more recently (deforestation was very rapid during the 1970s), the creation of communal rights may well have seemed worthwhile to many villages, especially those outside of the Central Plain.

One can further speculate that the existence and use of this alternative institutional arrangement might have served social efficiency goals to the extent that villagers chose to preserve as community forests environmentally sensitive areas (ridge tops and steep slopes) that were, in general, less attractive as potential farm land. Communal rights would have also broadened the distribution of benefits of forestry relative to the actual case. As in Counterfactual 1, outcomes might have differed modestly both in terms of efficiency and equity.

Counterfactual 3

In the actual case, both domestic and international political motives reinforced the incentives for the monarch to dismantle the system of property rights in man. It is then natural to ask about the relative roles of these two motives. How different would the coevolution of property rights regimes have been if the case for the abolition of slavery due to foreign pressure and the threats to Thai sovereignty had not been so urgent? Although such a counterfactual is not particularly plausible, it is nonetheless useful to consider it.

De facto Thailand served as a buffer zone between the British (Burma and Malaya) and French (Laos, Cambodia, and Vietnam) Southeast Asian colonial empires. How different would the situation in Thailand have been if the Bowring Treaty of 1855 had been signed by both the United Kingdom and France and had guaranteed the sovereignty of Thailand? In this counterfactual it is assumed that the expansion of the world trading system would have gone on as it did in the actual case. The key difference in Counterfactual 3 then is the absence of a direct threat to Thai sovereignty and therefore the lack of an international political incentive to dismantle slavery.

Given the economic pressures to create an institutional framework within which Thais could exploit the new opportunities for international trade and given the domestic political incentive of the monarch to remove the control of manpower from his rivals among the nobility, it is likely that Thailand would still have been interested in creating a unified, territorially based form of governance. Thus it is likely that the monarch would have taken steps to dismantle slavery and corvée. (Economies of scale in rice production are, in general, quite modest—especially for the earlier period before mechanical technologies for rice cultivation were available.) The key difference would have been the timetable for change. With the removal of the imperialist threat to sovereignty, the dismantling of the system of property rights in man might have been more gradual. Formal legislation might have been delayed. In addition, without the threat to sovereignty, the need to bring "outer" provinces under the control of the Bangkok regime would have been less urgent. Therefore, the imposition of centralization might also have been more gradual. Furthermore in the case of forest resources, the Bangkok regime might have been less concerned with removing the control of timber from local leaders. The form of state property rights in trees might have been less centralized than in the actual case. Nonetheless, the overall coevolution of the property rights regimes would likely have occurred in much the same fashion as it did in the actual case but more gradually.

Counterfactual 4

Counterfactuals 1 and 2 were, perhaps, at least somewhat plausible. Like Counterfactual 3, the fourth counterfactual is not (see Table 6.15). It is

Table 6.15
Counterfactual 4 Configuration of Systems of Property Rights:
State Property Rights in All Resources

Period, circa 1915		Land/forest rights				Human property rights	
		Open access	Communal	Private	State	Corvée/ slave	Free
Crop land	In use				De jure		
	Not in use				De jure		
Forests	High value				De jure		
	Other				De jure		
People						De jure	

chosen not because it might have happened, but instead in order to illustrate the importance of the configuration of systems of property rights.
(Because of its implausibility, the date for Counterfactual 4 in Table 6.15 is
circa 1915 rather than a more recent period.)

What would have happened if Thailand had retained some form of the
system of property rights in humans and the feudal-like system of administration? What if restrictions on labor mobility had been retained? In one
sense this counterfactual considerably distorts the actual history. Some of
the reforms of the mid- and late nineteenth century have been interpreted
as a formalization of practices that were already fairly common (Wilson
1990). Nonetheless it may be useful to speculate on what would have happened if labor had not been free to move to exploit the new commercial
opportunities in agriculture and forestry.

How then would production for market have been organized? Perhaps
it would have been directed by nai who would have used corvée obligations
to produce output for sale in the market. Under these circumstances, the
retention of state property rights in crop and forest lands not in use with
private usufruct rights on lands in use, a continuation of earlier property
rights regimes for crop and forest lands, might have been a viable alternative. It is, of course, likely that rice and log production would have
experienced much more modest rates of output growth than in the actual
case. Corvée (and slave) laborers typically do not have the same pecuniary
incentives as "free" wage labor and owner-operated firms and farms. Indeed
it is likely that the outcomes may have been less efficient than in the actual
case and further that the benefits would have been less widely shared.

These speculations are not unlike conclusions reached by Domar (1970). Domar examined the political economic basis for serfdom and slavery. He argued that systems of human property rights were often constructed in economies characterized by abundant land and scarce labor as a means by which elites could capture the scarcity rents due to labor. Domar argued that free land, free peasants, and nonworking landowners would not all exist simultaneously.

In Thailand for the case of crop land, the outcome was that for the most part free land and free peasants prevailed and the benefits were widely distributed. Elites participated in the rice export boom as landowners, owners of rice mills, and government officials but were not able to extract most of the rents.

For the case of forests, the state declared its property rights—land was not "free." In interaction with "free peasants" and the commercial incentives to exploit both forests and crop lands, the result was that the benefits from the initial exploitation of forests were narrowly shared while the benefits of subsequent land clearing and conversion to agricultural use were more widely shared.

CONCLUSION

Not only do property rights systems in particular resources matter, but the overall configuration of property rights systems matters as well. In Thailand given both the market and demographic incentives for increasing the area under cultivation, large-scale deforestation was likely. The incentives to expand the area under cultivation were importantly enhanced both by the creation of private property rights in agricultural land and by the dismantling of the system of property rights in man. The declaration of state property rights in forests was, in this context, problematic. Given the longstanding traditional uses of forests, the unilateral declaration by the state was, in general, not viewed as legitimate. Given the inherent nature of forest resources, enforcement of the state's property rights was problematic. De facto, most forest resources were open access and subject to all the distorting effects of rule of capture. The configuration of property rights gave few incentives for conserving forest resources that might provide for water and soil conservation or the preservation of habitat. Instead the configuration of property rights systems created incentives to accelerate the race to capture rents and convert forest lands from open access (everybody's property) to private agricultural land for which legal and social recognition and enforcement mechanisms were available.

NOTES

An earlier version of the paper was presented at the August 17–21, 1994, seminar of the Comparative Property Rights Project in Stowe, Vermont. Helpful comments from participants in that meeting, in particular John Richards and Peter Perdue, are acknowledged. The paper was also presented at the Fifty-fourth Annual Meeting of the Economic History Association, Cincinnati, Ohio, October 7–9, 1994. The helpful comments of Stanley Engerman, Sumner La Croix, Alan Olmstead, Elinor Ostrom, and Vernon Ruttan are also acknowledged.

1. This section draws heavily on Thomson, Feeny, and Oakerson (1992) and Feder and Feeny (1991, 1993).

2. Anat et al. 1988 (59) report that at the beginning of the Ayuthia period (1350–1767) all land belonged to the king and private landholding was a privilege. By the end of the Ayuthia period, landownership became absolute and rights were alienable. Documents to certify land rights were not, however, issued.

3. For a fuller discussion of the quality of the quantitative evidence on Thai economic history, see Feeny (1982) and Ingram (1971). In the post–World War II period, there has, in general, been an increase in the quality of the data. Nonetheless discrepancies among sources persist, in part because of underlying difficulties in obtaining accurate information and in part because different agencies and authors have incentives to present estimates favorable to their interests. For the nineteenth and early-to-mid–twentieth-century period, there is reason to believe that while the absolute figures are sometimes less than accurate the data do a reasonable job of capturing accurately the trends.

4. The Torrens system for cadastral surveys and land registration was developed and elaborated in Australia (and New Zealand) in the period from 1857 to 1874 (Kain and Baigent 1992, 317–18) and brought to Thailand by British officials (who had conducted cadastral surveys in India) hired by the Thai government to establish its Royal Survey Department. The Torrens system included title deeds based on a cadastral survey and a central place for record keeping.

5. The Torrens systems of land titling with central provincial land record offices and cadastral surveys was formally adopted in 1901. From 1901 to 1909, eleven land record offices were established. By 1909–10, 539,069 title deeds had been issued in the Central Plain (637,001 for the whole kingdom), and the area surveyed was 1,605,000 ha. (1,671,000 ha for the whole kingdom). The work was carried out by Australian and European experts (mainly on loan from the Indian Civil Service) who, in addition to conducting the survey work, also provided training to the Thai staff.

6. This section draws heavily on Feeny (1989) and (1993).

7. This section draws heavily on Feeny (1988a).

BIBLIOGRAPHY

Akin Rabibhadana. 1969. "The Organization of Thai Society in the Early Bangkok Period, 1782–1873." Cornell University Asia Program Data Paper no. 74.
———. 1975. "Clientship and Class Structure in the Early Bangkok Period." In *Change and Persistence in Thai Society: Essays in Honor of Lauriston Sharp*, ed. G. William Skinner and A. Thomas Kirsch. Ithaca, N.Y.: Cornell University Press, 93–124.

Alchian, Armen A., and Harold Demsetz. 1973. "The Property Rights Paradigm." *Journal of Economic History* 33, no. 1 (March): 16–27.

Allen, Douglas W. 1991. "Homesteading and Property Rights; Or, 'How the West Was Really Won.'" *Journal of Law & Economics* 34, no. 4 (April): 1–23.

Anan Ganjanapan. 1987. "Conflicting Patterns of Land Tenure among Ethnic Groups in the Highlands of Northern Thailand: The Impact of State and Market Intervention." In Proceedings of the International Conference on Thai Studies, Vol. 3, Part Two. Canberra: Australian National University, 503–511.

Anat Arbhabhirama, Dhira Phantumvanit, John Elkington, and Phaitoon Ingkasuwan. 1988. *Thailand: Natural Resources Profile*. Singapore: Oxford University Press.

Asian Development Bank (ADB). 1969. *Asian Agricultural Survey*. Seattle: University of Washington Press.

Barzel, Yoram. 1989. *Economic Analysis of Property Rights*. New York: Cambridge University Press.

Battye, Noel Alfred. 1974. "The Military, Government, and Society in Siam, 1868–1910: Politics and Military Reform during the Reign of King Chulalongkorn." Unpublished Ph.D. dissertation. Ithaca, N.Y.: Cornell University.

Binswanger, Hans P., Klaus Deininger, and Gershon Feder. 1993. "Agricultural Land Relations in the Developing World." *American Journal of Agricultural Economics* 75, no. 5 (December): 1242–48.

Boserup, Ester. 1965. *The Conditions of Agricultural Growth: The Economics of Agrarian Change under Population Pressure*. Chicago: Aldine-Atherton.

Boyd, Michael L. 1991. "The Evolution of Agrarian Institutions: The Case of Medieval and Ottoman Serbia." *Explorations in Economic History* 28, no. 1 (January): 36–53.

Bradley, William L., and Siam Then. 1981. *The Foreign Colony in Bangkok before and after Anna*. Pasadena: William Carey Library.

Bromley, Daniel W. 1986. "Closing Comments at the Conference on Common Property Resource Management." In *Proceedings of the Conference on Common Property Resource Management*, National Research Council. Washington, D.C.: National Academy Press, 593–98.

Bromley, Daniel W., and Devendra P. Chapagain. 1984. "The Village against the Center: Resource Depletion in South Asia." *American Journal of Agricultural Economics* 66 no. 5 (December): 868–73.

Brown, Ian. 1988. *The Élite and the Economy in Siam. C. 1890–1920.* Singapore: Oxford University Press.

———. 1993. "Imperialism, Trade, and Investment in Late Nineteenth and Early Twentieth Centuries." In *The Rise and Fall of Revenue Farming*, John Butcher and Howard Dick, eds., 80–88. New York: St. Martin's Press.

Brummelhuis, Hans ten. 1983. "Control of Land and Control of People: The Case of 'Thai Feudalism'" Universiteit van Amsterdam Antropologishch-Sociologisch Centrum Working Paper no 27.

Bunnag, Tej. 1968. "The Provincial Administration of Siam from 1892 to 1915: A Study of the Creation, the Growth, the Achievement, and the Implications for Modern Siam of the Ministry of Interior under Prince Damrong Rachanuphap." Unpublished Ph.D. thesis. University of Oxford, St. Anthony's College.

———. 1977. *The Provincial Administration of Siam 1892–1915.* Kuala Lumpur: Oxford University Press.

Chalermrath Khambanonda. 1972. Thailand's Public Law and Policy for Conservation and Protection of Land with Special Attention to Forests and Natural Areas. Bangkok: The National Institute of Development Administration.

Chatchai Panananon. 1982. "Siamese 'Slavery': The Institution and its Abolition." Unpublished Ph.D. dissertation. University of Michigan.

Chatthip Nartsupha and Suthy Prasartset, eds. 1977. *Socio-Economic Institutions and Cultural Change in Siam, 1851–1910: A Documentary Survey.* Singapore: Institute of Southeast Asian Studies.

Chusak Wittayapak. 1996. "Forestry without Legal Bases: Thailand's Experience." *Common Property Resource Digest* no. 38 (June).

Cropper, Maureen, Charles Griffiths, and Muthukumara Mani. 1999. "Roads, Population Pressures, and Deforestation in Thailand, 1976–1989." *Land Economics* 75, no. 1 (February).

Cruikshank, R. B. 1975. "Slavery in Nineteenth Century Siam." *Journal of the Siam Society* 63, part 2 (July): 315–33.

De Alessi, Louis. 1980. "The Economics of Property Rights: A Review of the Evidence." *Research in Law and Economics* 2:1–47.

Demsetz, Harold. 1967. "Toward a Theory of Property Rights." *American Economic Review* 57, no. 2 (May): 347–59.

Dhira Phantumvanit and Suthawan Sathirathai. 1988. "Thailand: Degradation and Development in a Resource-Rich Land." *Environment* 30:10–15, 30–36.

Domar, Evsey D. 1970. "The Causes of Slavery or Serfdom: A Hypothesis." *Journal of Economic History* 30, no. 1 (March): 18–32.

Domar, Evsey D., and Mark J. Machina. 1984. "On the Profitability of Russian Serfdom." *Journal of Economic History* 44, no. 4 (December): 919–55.

Donner, Wolf. 1978. *The Five Faces of Thailand: An Economic Geography.* New York: St. Martin's Press.

Drescher, Seymour. 1977. "Capitalism and the Decline of Slavery: The British Case in Comparative Perspective." In *Comparative Perspectives on Slavery in New World Plantation Societies,* Vera Rubin and Arthur Tuden, eds. New York: The New York Academy of Sciences, Annals of the New York Academy of Sciences 292, 132–42.

Eltis, David. 1987. *Economic Growth and the Ending of the Transatlantic Slave Trade.* New York: Oxford University Press.

Eltis, David, and James Walvin, eds. 1981. *The Abolition of the Atlantic Slave Trade: Origins and Effects in Europe, Africa, and the Americas.* Madison: University of Wisconsin Press.

Engel, David M. 1978. *Code and Custom in a Thai Provincial Court.* Tucson: University of Arizona Press.

Engerman, Stanley. 1973. "Some Considerations Relating to Property Rights in Man." *Journal of Economic History* 33, no. 1 (March): 43–65.

Engerman, Stanley L. 1992. "Coerced and Free Labor: Property Rights and the Development of the Labor Force." *Explorations in Economic History* 29, no.1 (January): 1–29.

Evers, Hans-Dieter, Ruediger Korff, and Suparb Pas-Ong. 1987. "Trade and State Formation: Siam in the Early Bangkok Period." *Modern Asian Studies* 21 (4): 751–71.

Feder, Gershon. 1987. "Land Ownership Security and Farm Productivity: Evidence from Thailand." *Journal of Development Studies* 24:16–30.

Feder, Gershon, and David Feeny. 1991. "Land Tenure and Property Rights: Theory and Implications for Development Policy." *World Bank Economic Review* 5, no. 1: 135–53.

———. 1993. "The Theory of Land Tenure and Property Rights." In *The Economics of Rural Organization: Theory, Practice, and Policy,* Karla Hoff, Avishay Braverman, and Joseph E. Stiglitz, eds. New York: Oxford University Press, 240–58.

Feder, Gershon, and Raymond Noronha. 1987. "Land Rights Systems and Agricultural Development in Sub-Saharan Africa." *World Bank Research Observer* 2, no. 2 (July): 143–69.

Feder, Gershon, and Tongroj Onchan. 1987. "Land Ownership Security and Farm Investment in Thailand." *American Journal of Agricultural Economics* 69, no. 2 (May): 311–20.

Feder, Gershon, Tongroj Onchan, Yongyuth Chalamwong, and Chira Hongladarom. 1988a. "Land Policies and Farm Performance in Thailand's Forest Reserve Areas." *Economic Development and Cultural Change* 36, no. 3 (April): 483–501.

———. 1988b. *Land Policies and Farm Productivity in Thailand*. Baltimore and London: The Johns Hopkins University Press.

Feeny, David. 1982. *The Political Economy of Productivity: Thai Agricultural Development 1880–1975*. Vancouver: University of British Columbia Press.

———. 1987. "The Exploration of Economic Change: The Contribution of Economic History to Development Economics." In *The Future of Economic History*, ed. Alexander J. Field, 91–119. Boston: Kluwer Nijhoff Publishing.

———. 1988a. "Agricultural Expansion and Forest Depletion in Thailand, 1900–1975." In *World Deforestation in the Twentieth Century*, John F. Richards and Richard P. Tucker, eds., 112–43; 281–87. Durham: Duke University Press.

———. 1988b. "The Demand for and Supply of Institutional Arrangement." In *Rethinking Institutional Analysis and Development: Some Issues, Choices, and Alternatives*, Vincent Ostrom, David Feeny, and Hartmut Picht, eds., 159–209. San Francisco: Institute for Contemporary Studies Press.

———. 1988c. "The Development of Property Rights in Land: A Comparative Study." In *Toward a Political Economy of Development: A Rationalist Perspective*, ed. Robert H. Bates, 272–99. Berkeley: University of California Press.

———. 1989. "The Decline of Property Rights in Man in Thailand, 1800–1913." *Journal of Economic History* 49, no. 2 (June): 285–96.

———. 1993. "The Demise of Corvée and Slavery in Thailand, 1782–1913." In *Breaking the Chains: Slavery, Bondage, and Emancipation in Africa and Asia*, ed. Martin A. Klein, 83–111. Madison: University of Wisconsin Press.

———. 1994. "Frameworks for Understanding Resource Management on the Commons." In *Community Management and Common Property of Coastal Fisheries in Asia and the Pacific: Concepts, Methods, and Experiences*, ed. Robert S. Pomeroy, 20–33. Manila: International Center for Living Aquatic Resources Management Conference Proceedings 45.

Feeny, David, Fikret Berkes, Bonnie J. McCay, and James M. Acheson. 1990. "The Tragedy of the Commons: Twenty-Two Years Later." *Human Ecology* 18, no. 1, 1–19.

Feeny, David, Susan Hanna, and Arthur F. McEvoy. 1996. "Questioning the Assumptions of the 'Tragedy of the Commons' Model of Fisheries." *Land Economics* 72, no. 2 (May): 187–205.

Fenoaltea, Stefano. 1975a. "The Rise and Fall of a Theoretical Model: The Manorial System." *Journal of Economic History* 35, no. 2 (June): 386–409.

———. 1975b. "Authority, Efficiency, and Agricultural Organization in Medieval England and Beyond: A Hypothesis." *Journal of Economic History* 35, no. 4 (December): 693–718.

————. 1976. "Risk, Transactions, Costs, and the Organization of Medieval Agriculture." *Explorations in Economic History* 13, no. 2 (April): 129–51.

————. 1984. "Slavery and Supervision in Comparative Perspective: A Model." *Journal of Economic History* 44, no. 3 (September): 635–88.

Fenoaltea, Stefano. 1988. "Transaction Costs, Whig History, and the Common Fields." *Politics and Society* 16, no. 2–3, 171–240.

Fogel, Robert William, and Stanley L. Engerman. 1974. *Time on the Cross: The Economics of American Negro Slavery* 1. Boston: Little, Brown and Company, Inc.

Gehan Wijeyewardene. 1987. "Notes on Urban Land Tenure in Chiangmai." In Proceedings of the International Conference on Thai Studies 2, 381–89. Canberra: Australian National University.

Graham, W. A. 1924. *Siam*. Third Edition. Two Volumes. London: The De La More Press.

Hafner, James A. 1973. "Man and Environment in Rural Thailand." *Journal of the Siam Society* 61, part 2: 129–38.

————. 1990. "Forces and Policy Issues Affecting Forest Use in Northeast Thailand 1900–1985." In *Keepers of the Forest: Land Management Alternatives in Southeast Asia*, ed. Mark Poffenberger, 69–94. West Hartford: Kumarian Press.

Hafner, James A., and Yaowalak Apichatvullop. 1990. "Migrant Farmers and the Shrinking Forests of Northeast Thailand." In *Keepers of the Forest: Land Management Alternatives in Southeast Asia*, ed. Mark Poffenberger, 187–219. West Hartford: Kumarian Press.

Hall, D. G. E. 1968. *A History of South-East Asia*. Third Edition. New York: St. Martin's Press, Inc.

Hallowell, A. Irving. 1943. "The Nature and Function of Property As a Social Institution." *Journal of Legal and Political Sociology* 1, no. 3–4 (April): 115–38.

Hirsch, Philip. 1990. "Forests, Forest Reserves, and Forest Land in Thailand." *Geographical Journal* 156, no. 2 (July): 166–74.

Hong, Lysa. 1984. *Thailand in the Nineteenth Century: Evolution of the Economy and Society*. Singapore: Institute of Southeast Asian Studies.

Ingram, James C. 1971. *Economic Change in Thailand 1850–1970*. Second Edition. Stanford, Calif.: Stanford University Press.

Kain, Roger J. P. and Elizabeth Baigent. 1992. *The Cadastral Map in Service of the State: A History of Property Mapping*. Chicago: University of Chicago Press.

Kamon Pragtong and David E. Thomas. 1990. "Evolving Management Systems in Thailand." In *Keepers of the Forest: Land Management Alternatives in Southeast Asia*, ed. Mark Poffenberger, 167–86. West Hartford, Conn.: Kumarian Press.

Kemp, Jeremy H. 1981. "Legal and Informal Land Tenures in Thailand." *Modern Asian Studies* 15, part 1 (February): 1–23.

Klein, Martin A. 1993 "Introduction: Modern European Expansion and Traditional Servitude in Africa and Asia." In *Breaking the Chains: Slavery, Bondage, and Emancipation in Africa and Asia,* ed. Martin A. Klein, 3–36. Madison: University of Wisconsin Press.

Krit Samapuddhi. 1966. Forestry Development in Thailand. Bangkok: Royal Forest Department.

Kunstadter, Peter, E.C. Chapman, and Sanga Sabhasri, eds. 1978. *Farmers in the Forest: Economic Development and Marginal Agriculture in Northern Thailand.* Honolulu: University Press of Hawaii.

Lohmann, Larry. 1991. "Peasants, Plantations, and Pulp: The Politics of Eucalyptus in Thailand." *Bulletin of Concerned Asian Scholars* 23, no. 4: 3–18.

———. 1995. "Visitors to the Commons: Approaching Thailand's 'Environmental' Struggles from a Western Starting Point." In *Ecological Resistance Movements: The Global Emergence of Radical and Popular Environmentalism,* ed. Bron Raymond Taylor, 109–26. Albany: State University of New York Press.

Lynch, Owen J., and Kirk Talbott. 1995. *Balancing Acts: Community-Based Forest Management and National Law in Asia and the Pacific.* Washington, D.C.: World Resources Institute.

Mehl, Charles B. 1991. "The Changing Character of Land in Rural Thailand: Possible Common Property Responses to Emerging Land Problems." Paper presented at the Second Annual Meeting of the International Association for the Study of Common Property, University of Manitoba, Winnipeg, September 26–29.

Millward, Robert. 1984. "The Early Stages of European Industrialization: Economic Organization under Serfdom." *Explorations in Economic History* 21, no. 4 (October): 406–28.

Murashima, Eiji. 1988. "The Origin of Modern Official State Ideology in Thailand." *Journal of Southeast Asian Studies* 19, no. 1 (March): 80–96.

National Research Council. 1986. *Proceedings of the Conference on Common Property Resource Management April 21–25, 1985.* Washington, D.C.: National Academy Press.

North, Douglass C. 1981. *Structure and Change in Economic History.* New York: W.W. Norton, Inc.

———. 1987. "Institutions and Economic Growth: An Historical Introduction." Paper prepared for Conference on Knowledge and Institutional Change, University of Minnesota, Nov. 13–15.

———. 1990. *Institutions, Institutional Change, and Economic Performance.* New York: Cambridge University Press.

———. 1994. "Economic Performance through Time." *American Economic Review* 84, no. 3 (June): 359–68.

North, Douglass C., and Robert Paul Thomas. 1973. *The Rise of the Western World: A New Economic History*. London: Cambridge University Press.

Otsuka, Keijiro, Hiroyuki Chuma, and Yujiro Hayami. 1992. "Land and Labor Contracts in Agrarian Economies." *Journal of Economic Literature* 30, no. 4 (December): 1965–2018.

Patterson, Orlando. 1977. "The Structural Origins of Slavery: A Critique of the Nieboer-Domar Hypothesis from a Comparative Perspective." In *Comparative Perspectives on Slavery in New World Plantation Societies*, Vera Rubin and Arthur Tuden, eds., 12–34. New York: The New York Academy of Sciences, Annals of the New York Academy of Sciences 292.

Pejovich, Svetozar. 1972. "Toward an Economic Theory of the Creation and Specification of Property Rights." *Review of Social Economy* 30, no. 3 (September): 309–25.

Peluso, Nancy Lee, Peter Vandergeest, and Lesley Potter. 1995. "Social Aspects of Forestry in Southeast Asia: A Review of Postwar Trends in Scholarly Literature." *Journal of Southeast Asian Studies*, 26, no. 1 (March): 196–218.

Pendleton, Robert L. 1962. *Thailand: Aspects of Landscape and Life*. New York: Duell, Sloan, and Pearce.

Poffenberger, Mark. 1990. "The Evolution of Forest Management Systems in Southeast Asia." In *Keepers of the Forest: Land Management Alternatives in Southeast Asia*, ed. Mark Poffenberger, 7–26. West Hartford: Kumarian Press.

Riggs, Fred W. 1966. *Thailand: The Modernization of a Bureaucratic Polity*. Honolulu: East-West Center Press.

Roumasset, James, and Sumner J. La Croix. 1988. "The Coevolution of Property Rights and Political Order: An Illustration from Nineteenth-Century Hawaii." In *Rethinking Institutional Analysis and Development: Some Issues, Choices, and Alternatives*, Vincent Ostrom, David Feeny, and Hartmut Picht, eds., 315–36. San Francisco: Institute for Contemporary Studies Press.

Sadoff, Claudia W. 1992. "The Effects of Thailand's Logging Ban: A Natural Resource Accounting Approach." Thailand Development Research Institute Foundation, Sectoral Economics Program, Bangkok (June).

Schlatter, Richard. 1951. *Private Property: The History of an Idea*. New Brunswick: Rutgers University Press.

Scott, Anthony. 1983. "Property Rights and Property Wrongs." *Canadian Journal of Economics* 16, no. 4 (November): 555–73.

Scott, Anthony and Georgina Coustalin. 1995. "The Evolution of Water Rights." *Natural Resources Journal* 35, no. 4 (Fall): 821–979.

Sharp, Lauriston, and Lucien M. Hanks. 1978. *Bang Chan: Social History of a Rural Community in Thailand*. Ithaca, N.Y.: Cornell University Press.

Siamwalla, Amar, Chirmsak Pinthong, Nipon Poapongsakorn, Ploenpit Satsanguan, Prayong Nettayarak, Wanrak Mingmaneenakin, and Yuavares

Tubpun. 1990. "The Thai Rural Credit System: Public Subsidies, Private Information, and Segmented Markets." *World Bank Economic Review* 4, no. 3 (September): 271–95.

Skinner, George W. 1957. *Chinese Society in Thailand: An Analytical History.* Ithaca: Cornell University Press.

Steinberg, David Joel, David K. Wyatt, John R. W. Smail, Alexander Woodside, William R. Roff, and David P. Chandler. 1971. *In Search of Southeast Asia: A Modern History.* New York: Praeger Publishers.

Stifel, Laurence D. 1976. "Patterns of Land Ownership in Central Thailand during the Twentieth Century." *Journal of the Siam Society* 64, part 1 (January): 237–74.

Sukhum Thirawat. 1955. Brief Information on Forestry Information in Thailand. Bangkok: Royal Forestry Department.

Taylor, John. 1988. "The Ethical Foundations of the Market." In *Rethinking Institutional Analysis and Development: Issues, Alternatives, and Choices,* Vincent Ostrom, David Feeny, and Hartmut Picht, eds., 377–88. San Francisco: Institute for Contemporary Studies Press.

Terwiel, Barend J. 1983a. *A History of Modern Thailand 1767–1942.* St. Lucia: University of Queensland Press.

———. 1983b. "Bondage and Slavery in Early Nineteenth Century Siam." In *Slavery, Bondage, and Dependency in Southeast Asia,* ed. Anthony Reid, 118–37. St. Lucia: University of Queensland Press.

———. 1984. "Formal Structure and Informal Rules: An Historical Perspective on Hierarchy, Bondage, and Patron-Client Relationship." In *Strategies and Structures in Thai Society,* Hans ten Brummelhuis and Jeremy H. Kemp, eds., 19–38. Amsterdam: Publikatieserie Zuid-en Zuidoost Asie, no. 31, Anthropologisch Sociologisch Centrum, Universiteit van Amsterdam.

Thailand. 1930. Ministry of Commerce and Communications. *Siam: Nature and Industry.* Bangkok.

———. 1977. Office of the Prime Minister. National Economic and Social Development Board. *The Fourth National Economic and Social Development Plan.* Bangkok: National Economic and Social Development Board.

———. 1981. Office of the Prime Minister. National Economic and Social Development Board. *The Fifth National Economic and Social Development Plan (1982–1986).* Bangkok: National Economic and Social Development Board.

Thomson, James T., David H. Feeny, and Ronald J. Oakerson. 1992. "Institutional Dynamics: The Evolution and Dissolution of Common Property Resource Management." In *Making the Commons Work: Theory, Practice, and Policy,* ed. Daniel W. Bromley, 129–60. San Francisco: Institute for Contemporary Studies Press.

Thongchai Winichakul. 1994. *Siam Mapped: A History of the Geo-Body of a Nation.* Honolulu: University of Hawaii Press.

Tongroj Onchan, ed. 1990. *A Land Policy Study*. Bangkok: Thai Development Research Institute Foundation Research Monograph no. 3.

Tsujii, Hiroshi. 1973. "An Econometric Study of Effects of National Policies and the Green Revolution on National Rice Economies and International Trade among Less Developed and Developed Countries: With Special Reference to Thailand, Indonesia, Japan, and the United States." Unpublished Ph.D. thesis. University of Illinois at Urbana-Champaign.

Turton, Andrew. 1980. "Thai Institutions of Slavery." In *Asian and African Systems of Slavery*, ed. James L. Watson, 251–92, 317, 336–39. Oxford: Basil Blackwell.

Umbeck, John F. A. 1977. "The California Gold Rush: A Study of Emerging Property Rights." *Explorations in Economic History* 14, no. 3 (July): 197–226.

Vandergeest, Peter and Nancy Lee Peluso. 1995. "Territorialization and State Power in Thailand." *Theory and Society* 24, 385–426.

Williamson, Ian P. 1983. "Cadastral Survey Techniques in Developing Countries— With Particular Reference to Thailand." Washington, D.C.: World Bank, East Asia and Pacific Projects Department.

Wilson, Constance M. 1970. "State and Society in the Reign of Mongkut, 1851–1868: Thailand on the Eve of Modernization." Unpublished Ph.D. dissertation. Cornell University.

———. 1983. *Thailand: A Handbook of Historical Statistics*. Boston: G. K. Hall and Co.

———. 1990. "Corvée in Thailand: Organization, Structure, and Duties." Paper presented at the Forty-second Annual Meeting of the Association for Asian Studies, Chicago, April 6.

———. 1993. "Revenue Farming, Economic Development, and Government Policy in the Early Bangkok Period, 1832–1892." In *The Rise and Fall of Revenue Farming*, John Butcher and Howard Dick, eds., 142–65. New York: St. Martin's Press.

Wilson, David A. 1962. *Politics in Thailand*. Ithaca, N.Y.: Cornell University Press.

Wyatt, David K. 1968. "Family Politics in Nineteenth Century Thailand." *Journal of Southeast Asian History* 9, no. 2 (September): 208–28.

———. 1969. *The Politics Reform in Thailand: Education in the Reign of King Chulalongkorn*. New Haven, Conn.: Yale University Press.

———. 1984. *Thailand: A Short History*. New Haven, Conn.: Yale University Press.

———. 1986. "Family Politics in Seventeenth- and Eighteenth-Century Siam." In *Papers from a Conference on Thai Studies in Honor of William J. Gedney*, Robert J. Bickner, Thomas J. Hudak, and Patcharin Peyasantiwong, eds., 257–65. Ann Arbor: Michigan Papers on South and Southeast Asia no. 25, University of Michigan.

Yano, Toru. 1968. "Land Tenure in Thailand." *Asian Survey* 8, no. 10 (October): 853–63.

Yongyuth Chalamwong and Gershon Feder. 1988. "The Impact of Landownership Security: Theory and Evidence from Thailand." *World Bank Economic Review* 2, 187–204.

7

Tragedies of Privatization: Land, Liberty, and Environmental Change in Spain and Italy, 1800–1910

JOHN R. MCNEILL

I n nineteenth-century Spain and Italy, liberal ideas often animated state policy. Consequently, in the wake of Napoleonic occupation, feudal property regimes were widely replaced by simpler private property ones. Millions of hectares of state, church, monastic, and village lands were sold to individuals, who enjoyed nearly full freedom as to the disposition of their new lands. Many of these landowners chose to sell off timber from these lands, plant them to cereals, and then eventually resell or abandon them. The impact upon the vegetation, soils, and hydrology of the lands in question was often great and rarely beneficial. This chapter sketches these transitions nationally and more locally in the contexts of a southern Spanish valley (the Alpujarra) and a southern Italian region (Lucania).

THE ARGUMENT

In a 1968 paper that remains influential, ecologist Garrett Hardin elaborated upon observations made by Aristotle twenty-four centuries ago. Aristotle wrote: "What is common to the greatest number gets the least amount of care. Men pay most attention to what is their own; they care less of what is common." (*Politics*, 2.3). Hardin (1968) wrote that in the absence of effective regulation, people pursuing their private interests with common resources inevitably overexploit those resources because restraint, if less than universal, is irrational and self-defeating. Those who restrain themselves suffer as their less scrupulous neighbors deplete resources in their own private interests. This he called the tragedy of the commons, although, as an army of critics has pointed out, his argument applied only to open-access resources, which a commons may or may not be. Such tragedies are indeed routine where regulation of common resources—fisheries, pastures, water, and the like—is weak. A popular remedy for the situation that permits such tragedies is privatization: the elimination of common property and resources in favor of simpler individual ownership. This was the wisdom of Aristotle, and it is the wisdom of most economists and politicians today.

It is not always appropriate wisdom. Privatization of common resources can lead to environmental tragedies too. Where those who own and control a resource have little stake in its continuity, unregulated privatization is no remedy, and can easily permit conditions in which individual rational self-interest and the public interest clash. The nineteenth-century history of Southern Europe provides examples of such tragedies of privatization. The systems that privatization supplanted, while replete with social injustices and economic inefficiencies, inadvertently helped preserve soils and water balances. As Montesquieu wrote twenty-five decades ago, different lands require different laws—including different property laws.

ITALY AND SPAIN IN 1800

Spain and southern Italy before 1800 were what European historians call *ancien régime* societies. Italy was, as Prince Metternich put it, merely a geographical expression, a welter of small dukedoms, principalities, city-states, papal states, and one sizable kingdom that covered the southern third of the peninsula: the Kingdom of Naples. Spain was a unified kingdom, but with strong regional traditions reflected in, among other things, land law and custom. Both Spain and the Kingdom of Naples were hereditary monarchies, dominated by alliances among the nobility, church, and bureaucracy—all of which overlapped. Four-fifths of each population was peasant cultivators and herders. Both societies featured complex patterns of landownership, tenure, and access governed by laws and customs that had accumulated over many centuries, and were often a tangle of inconsistencies. Individuals, families, villages, monasteries, the church, nobility, military orders, and royalty all had various rights and privileges to land, water, trees, animals, and so on. In particular, many villages owned land (or enjoyed recognized access to it) in common. Such arrangements applied most often to pasture and forest. In eighteenth-century Spain, many towns and villages shared pastures, sowed and reaped crops collectively, and periodically reallocated lands, sometimes by lottery. In the Alpujarra, a mountain valley in southeastern Spain, villagers owned high pasture in common. Property rights here in the old Kingdom of Granada derived from conditions at the time the Reconquista reached the Alpujarra (fifteenth–sixteenth centuries). The valley lost most of its population when surviving Muslims fled after a failed revolt in 1571. For centuries thereafter, too few people lived in the villages to take up the lands once cultivated. So the *barrancas,* or high transverse valleys on the slopes of the towering Sierra Nevada, were used as woodland or pasture, held in common by specific villages. Since some patches were better than others, villagers took turns. They allotted access by drawing lots annually.

Advanced thinkers in late eighteenth-century Europe considered such complex arrangements anachronistic and inefficient, which in many ways they were. The interlocking tangle of rights and privileges often made it difficult to realize economies of scale, to make improvements to land, or to buy and sell land, unless one had the power to override law and custom. Vast amounts of land and timber went but little used, while many people went hungry and cold. Reason demanded that such resources be put in the hands of those who would put them to productive use: This was—and is— a key tenet of the gospel of economic efficiency.

Intellectual objections to feudal encumbrances upon land centered in France and Britain, but reigned as well among the *Ilustrados* of Enlightenment Spain and the *Illuminati* in the salons of Naples, one of the leading cities of the Enlightenment. Naples was the first city in the world to fund a chair in political economy (1754), and its occupants and their acolytes cried out against the restrictive laws of the kingdom. Antonio Genovesi, Nicola Fortunato, and Giuseppe Galanti wrote and spoke powerfully on Enlightenment themes. They considered that feudal laws checked population growth, favored pastoralism over cultivation, impeded the accumulation of wealth in the kingdom, and thereby weakened it (Marino 1988, 246–56). A system that did not maximize population and cultivation was worthy of "barbarous Tartary." A free market in land would unshackle the undoubted energies of the King's subjects: "Give men liberty to act in their own way according to their own interests, which together forms the public interest" (Galanti 1786–90, cited in Marino 1988, 255).

Spanish reformers objected with equal vigor to entail, church property, and common property. According to Pedro Rodríguez de Campomanes and

Gaspar Melchior de Jovellanos, the two most prominent Spanish Enlightenment figures, Spain's prosperity and power fell short of its potential because of unwise laws that curtailed market freedom. Of forest lands in particular, Jovellanos wrote: "Allow the owners free and absolute exploitation of their timber and the nation will acquire many fine forests" (Jovellanos 1794, cited in Herr 1989: 74). Spain eventually did as he bade, destroying much of what forest it had.

In Enlightenment thought, laissez-faire economics and simpler landownership contributed fundamentally to liberty; and liberals sought to bring such ideas into practice—as their intellectual heirs do today in Warsaw, Budapest, and Moscow. Liberals received their chance when Napoleonic troops entered Italy in 1796 and Spain in 1808.

THE NEW REGIMES

Italy

Occasional land privatizations took place in Italy, especially in the North, in the eighteenth century. But large-scale privatization of common land in southern Italy began in 1806, under the administration of Napoleon's brother Joseph Bonaparte and Joseph's successor, Joachim Murat. Broad areas of the Kingdom of Naples, especially church lands, were parceled out to new owners between 1806 and 1815.[1] The French restricted timber cutting to protect the interests of their navy, but otherwise seemed determined to put an end to feudal land tenure. The end of French rule and the restoration of the Bourbon monarchy (to what was now the Kingdom of the Two Sicilies) in 1815 interrupted this agenda. New laws, as restrictive as any land laws in Italy, protected noble, public, and ecclesiastic domains from further encroachment until 1860. These laws, although indifferently enforced, added to the tangle of inefficient encumbrances that forestalled the liberal agenda. Instead, herders continued to graze their flocks; peasants kept their access to woodlands for chestnuts, fuelwood, small game, and fish; and nobles and the church kept their big properties, often leaving much land idle. Forest clearance proceeded only slowly in the Kingdom of the Two Sicilies, partly because of this thicket of rights and regulations. Thus the restored ancien régime inadvertently afforded some stability for the ecology of southern Italy.

With the unification of Italy (1849–1870) by northerners much in thrall to liberal ideas, a new and decisive round of privatizations, called *quotizzazioni*, began. Laws of 1863, 1866, and 1867 opened additional public and church lands to sale. The Forest Law of 1877 allowed any clearance for purposes of cultivation, and upheld the freedom of private owners above all other principles. In Italy as a whole, between 1877 and 1910 half of the country's forest land passed into private hands (Nitti 1909–10, 213; on Campania, Montroni 1983). About 3 million hectares of forests were burned or felled between 1860 and 1890 (Sereni 1968, 201–202).

Lucania (or Basilicata), a mostly mountainous region in the instep of the Italian boot, joined the newly unified Italy with vigorous reluctance, called the War of the Brigands (1860–1865). There the new land laws led to the sale of hundreds of thousands of hectares of village and church lands. A handful of alert men got rich in the process, but, ecologically at least, Lucania got much poorer. The quotizzazioni contributed to two ongoing processes in southern Italy: concentration of private property and degradation of landscapes.

Those who passed or implemented the new laws found it easiest to take advantage of them. At Ferruzano, in Calabria (just south of Lucania), communal forest went to eighty-three people, including two brothers of the mayor, two of his brothers-in-law, two nephews, seventeen of his cousins, and several more distant relatives. Many of them, it may safely be supposed, hoped for a quick lira, at whatever cost to landscapes they may never have seen (Clark 1984, 16). High wheat prices until 1881 and tariffs after 1887 made forest clearance a strong temptation to anyone who owned land that could be sown to wheat.

In southern Italy as a whole, and in Lucania especially, the privatizations led to quick lire but also to quick—and durable—ecological changes. Between 1877 and 1900, new landowners cleared about 60 percent of Lucania's forest area. Luigi Savastano visited Lucania in 1893 and remarked: "Anyone crossing Basilicata today will not find the forests that once covered these mountains. The plow and hoe have broken up the land, even above the highest points of 1,200 and 1,300 meters, and along the steepest slopes. Production on these lands is lean and miserable" (Savastano 1893, cited in Sievert 1996). In the Camastra basin, a small zone of highly erodible low hills, forest area shrank from 70 percent to 23 percent of land area (1861–1900). Here, and elsewhere in Lucania, erosion problems increased; landslides (a regular curse in the clayey soils) multiplied; and silt, floods, and intensified malaria menaced the lowlands. The Italian state sold public lands in Lucania for about 30 million lire, but soon spent roughly thirty times that sum on projects to restore hydrological stability to the region (Spera 1903, 14–20; Filangieri 1980, 110–11; Tichy 1962, 66–91).

After four decades of land privatizations, peasants, professors, and some politicians agreed the policy had been a mistake. A petition (undated but circa 1898) signed by 555 agricultural laborers from the Potenza area in central Lucania makes this clear:

> Una delle nostre ricchezze poi erano in passato i boschi che con una smania feroce son venute graduatamente distruggendo . . . e così va via un patrimonio che è esclusivamente popolare. [One of the sources of income in the past were the woods, which have been destroyed with a manic ferocity . . . and thus disappeared a patrimony that was exclusively for the people.][2]

Privatization led not only to the destruction of forests, but also to restrictions on peasant access to remaining woods. Lucanian peasants had grown accustomed to their *usi civici*, or civic rights, to fuelwood, chestnuts, and the special food of Lucanian pigs, acorns. Privatization often meant that these rights were lost, obliging peasants to scour ever smaller public domain for fuelwood and nuts—no small loss for Mediterranean villagers. Many Italian villagers resisted privatizations that restricted their access to forests (and marshes) whence they had long derived a goodly portion of their sustenance (for example, see Clementi 1986). The Potenza peasants' petition went on to link the privatizations and consequent loss of woods to increasing emigration, a connection also made by contemporary scholars (Franzoni 1903, 118; Franciosa 1930, 14; Ahlmann 1925–26, 122). A torrent of Lucanians left their homes between 1880 and 1914, especially mountain folk who had depended more than others on the bounty of communal forests.[3] Lucania's population in 1905 was 66 percent female because so many men had gone to America. One Italian historian goes so far as to say that ecological deterioration, brought on by social and political structures, "expelled" Lucanian emigrants (Colangelo 1977, 16).

This takes matters a bit too far. Emigration arose from many causes, not least a high rate of natural increase in the Lucanian population. But the land alienations of the nineteenth century surely caused incalculable damage to the sustainability of life in the Lucanian mountains. Two parliamentary inquiries into the misery of the *mezzogiorno*, one published in 1902 and the other in 1909–10, concluded that the best possible step was to reconstitute the public domain and undo the privatizations.[4] This view ran counter to the doctrines of the times, and proved politically impossible. They also recommended (also in vain) massive reforestation, 600,000 hectares at a minimum. Lucania has continued to export people throughout the twentieth century. Since the 1950s, it has enjoyed large subsidies from the Italian state, pensions from political parties, and lately funds from the European Union. It remains the poorest part of Italy.

Spain

In Spain in 1800, the nobility owned about half of the land, and the clergy and the municipalities shared almost evenly another third (Gómez Oliver 1983, 21). Liberals found it irksome that a third of the country lay in the hands of often inefficient owners who failed to maximize production. The upheavals surrounding the French Revolution and Napoleonic invasion gave liberals a brief chance to act on their beliefs. Large-scale sale to private individuals of state, church, village, or military orders' lands began in 1798–1813. The immediate impetus came from the need to finance military campaigns: The state needed cash quickly and the prescriptions of Jovellanos promised to provide it. Many sales were conducted under the administration of Joseph Bonaparte, who had exchanged his throne in Naples for another in Madrid; most were undone with the restoration of absolutism in 1814 (Herr 1989, 119–36).

More enduring land privatizations, called *desamortizaciones* in Spain, came in three waves in the nineteenth century and a small ripple in the early twentieth (Rueda Hernanz 1993; Sanz Fernández 1985). Each wave began with the accession to power of a liberal anticlerical government and ended when the government did. The first and least consequential lasted from 1820 to 1822 (González de Molina Navarro 1984; Simón Segura 1973, 65–66). The second, the desamortización de Mendizábal, came in 1836–44; and the third, that of Madoz, followed in 1855–1864—both named for governmental ministers. The first two waves cost the church dearly but had only modest impact on public lands. The desamortización de Madoz, much the largest of the three, put village and communal lands up for sale as well. José Echegaray, the minister of development *(Fomento)* in 1873, expressed the intellectual rationale for these privatizations. In its moral as well as practical objections to common property, it recalled Aristotle:

No son estos los únicos intereses que el Ministerio de Fomento debe proteger y debe en la medida de sus fuerzas desarollar: los usos comunales . . . los aprovechamientos de los pueblos, todos estas prácticas socialistas deben ir desapareciendo, y al disfrute, confuso, irregular, demoledor y primitivo del suelo, bueno es que se substituya por la propriedad individual, germa de todo progreso, garantía de todo orden y correctivo eficacísimo contra este especie de socialismo campesino. (These are not the only interests that the Ministry of Development must protect and develop as much as possible: the communal customs . . . the village exploitations, all these socialist practices must disappear, and for the confused,

irregular, destructive and primitive use of the soil it is well to substitute private property, the germ of all progress, guarantor of all
order, and most efficacious corrective to this variety of peasant
socialism.) (Jiménez Blanco 1986, I, 409)

This sentiment captures the particularly militant laissez-faire spirit
dominant in Spain circa 1850–1880.

In all, the state sold off between 5 million and 10 million hectares
nationally, equivalent to half (or all) of Portugal. According to one calculation, 5.1 million hectares of forest passed into private possession (Sanz
Fernández 1985, 228). More than 600,000 properties changed hands, and
the treasury made more than 11 billion *reales* between 1836 and 1895 from
land sales—a useful tonic for the national debt. A few remaining woodlands were privatized between 1897 and 1924. Sales affected the entire
country, but Andalucía led the way because it had an unusually high proportion of common lands (González de Molina 1996, 23).

All over Spain this led to rapid deforestation, quick and costly plowing of all kinds of soils, and the destruction thereby of millennia of
accumulated natural capital. Between 1860 and 1888, 2 million hectares
were added to Spain's cultivated area. Flash floods and soil erosion threatened and damaged upland and lowland alike. After 1850 Spanish foresters,
many trained in the best German institutions, vocally objected to the privatizations. So did peasants, especially in Andalucía. Neither objection
carried much weight. Every century in Spain has seen ecologically costly
management of forests and soils, but the nineteenth century stands apart
because of the desamortizaciones (Rueda Hernanz 1986; Rueda Hernanz
1993; Bauer Manderscheid 1980, 66–89; Groome 1990; Elorrieta and
Artaza 1948, 91–100; Simón Segura 1973, 263, 273; Cobo, Cruz, and
González de Molina 1992a and 1992b).

As in Italy, land alienations meant great opportunity for the alert and
financially able. Economically shrewd men bought up only lands that
promised good returns on investment. But the socially ambitious regarded
land of any sort as a good investment. Hence many mercantile men bought
up land they could not easily afford, borrowing the purchase price. To pay
their debts, they had to squeeze cash from their lands quickly. This implied
felling all the marketable timber and fuelwood, and renting out as much
land as possible to tenant farmers, sharecroppers, or shepherds. The market
value of timber generally exceeded the annual income derived from forests
by three to five times, so only the patient and unindebted refrained from
logging their new lands (Iglesías Casado 1982, 72). Even those who did
manage to squeeze money from their lands could not always pay their debts,

so many sold out to more prosperous landowners. As in Italy, the Spanish land alienation contributed to the concentration of private property as well as to ecological degradation (Jiménez Blanco 1986, I, 408–16; Artola, Bernal, and Contreras 1978; Gómez Oliver 1983; see also Tedde 1994).

In the Alpujarra, alienated lands belonged primarily to the church and to religious brotherhoods. In the 1836–1844 (Mendizábal) disentailments, the church in the Alpujarra lost only 324 hectares; in all of Granada Province, only 12,000 hectares changed hands (Gómez Oliver 1983, 177). But a greater surge of alienations took place between 1858 and 1864. Of the eleven administrative districts in Granada Province, the Alpujarra ranked third in the area of land privatized: about 7,000 hectares. Of the 156 sales, only three put land into the hands of Alpujarreños. The other 153 purchasers came from outside the valley, mostly from the city of Granada—two to three days' ride away. Many were senators, deputies, or other government figures. Others were already major landowners in the province. One was a professor (Gómez Oliver 1985, 16, 158–64, 171–72, 215–18).

These privatizations in the Alpujarra contributed to a general ecological crisis. Its chief symptoms were loss of woodland and heightened soil erosion. The Alpujarra had enough timber to attract Spanish naval inspectors in the eighteenth century; by 1900 it had virtually none. Runoff, floods, landslides, and erosion all intensified. One short watercourse in the Alpujarra, the Río Chico, was 2 meters wide in 1830 and carried a steady flow capable of powering four flour mills. Its first major (recorded) flood came in 1860, after deforestation in its watershed; and many more followed. By 1908 its bed was 200 meters across and the average current could not power anything. One flour mill was entombed 20 meters deep in gravel, silt, and debris. When in spate, the river drowned crops at Bayacas and chewed away the road linking Orgiva and Albuñol (a locally important route connecting the Alpujarra to the coast). Difficulties of this sort helped drive thousands of sons of the Alpujarra overseas, to French Algeria and to South America, between 1870 and 1914 (McNeill 1992, 304–6, 317–20; Almagro 1932, 1–19; Carandell 1934, 56). Like Lucania, the Alpujarra became a land of emigration. Foreign lands beckoned irresistibly as the Alpujarreños' natal soil washed downstream to the coast and the sea.

PERSPECTIVES

Lest I leave the impression that transitions in property regimes were the sole engine of environmental change in these cases, I must make clear that other forces played important parts as well. Population growth mattered in both instances. Indeed, to some extent legal privatizations merely rerouted what was afoot anyway. Land hunger led to informal occupation of public lands by poor peasants and herders. The land alienations turned public lands over to richer individuals, but privatizations of a sort—squatting—had already occurred on a considerable, if unknowable, scale. The state alienations thus legalized, accelerated, and redirected a process of privatization of church and common lands in train for several decades.

Other fundamental economic changes also contributed to the ecological decay of Lucania and the Alpujarra. The most dramatic was the lead boom in the Sierra de Gádor, just east of the Alpujarra. Lead smelters consumed all available fuel, even grasses, between 1825 and 1860. The tens of thousands of mules used to transport lead to the coast needed oats, much of which came from high, steep, and unstable slopes in the Alpujarra. In a nutshell, the privatizations were one of several factors contributing to these environmental histories (McNeill 1992; Sánchez Picón 1996).

The alienations in Italy and Spain made up a small part of a movement in land tenure that affected much of Europe in the eighteenth and nineteenth centuries. In England, enclosures in the interest of agricultural efficiency quickened in the eighteenth century. Local landowners and the state sought to achieve more rational patterns of land use and to increase national wealth. Cultivated area did indeed expand, at the expense of forest and pasture, and agricultural innovation flourished. All this proved hard on small peasants in the short run (which lasted a couple of generations), but in the long run helped improve food supply to cities and added to national wealth. Elsewhere across the northern European plain, from France to Russia, state-sponsored enclosures and alienations took place throughout the nineteenth century and into the early twentieth. As in England, they provoked fierce resistance from the peasantry but in the long run proved economically rational. Ecologically, in northern Europe these changes generally had much milder consequences than they had in southern Europe. The rugged relief of Mediterranean Europe and the climate, with its winter downpours, meant that forest and pasture played a crucial role in stabilizing hydrology and soils. In the gentler circumstances of northern Europe, deforestation and expansion of arable land did not imply rapid acceleration of soil erosion and an increase in floods. Legislation that made economic sense (if social distress) in one environment made for ecological catastrophe (aggravating social distress) in another. Different lands require different laws, as Montesquieu observed.

NOTES

1. A detailed study for Calabria is Placanica 1979.

2. Archivio Centrale di Stato (Rome), Presidenzia del Consiglio, fondo Zanardelli e La Basilicata, busta 2.

3. Lucanian mountain villages in 1911 had only two-thirds of their 1861 population; in the same years, adjacent lowland population (in Apulia) increased by 64 percent. These data are elaborated from Filangieri 1980, 284–85 and Italy, Istituto Centrale di Statistica 1987, 49.

4. The Zanardelli and Nitti inchieste, undertaken in 1899 and 1908 respectively

BIBLIOGRAPHY

Ahlmann, H. W. 1925–1926. "Etudes de géographie humaine sur l'Italie subtropicale." *Geografiska Annaler* Stockholm, 7:257–322; 8:74–124.

Almagro, José. 1932. *Torrentes y pantanos en Sierra Nevada*. Madrid.

Artola, Miguel, A. M. Bernal, and I. Contreras. 1978. *El latifundio*. Madrid: Servicio de Publicaciones Agrarias.

Bauer Manderscheid, Erich. 1980. *Los montes de España en la historia*. Madrid: Ministerio de Agricultura.

Carandell, Juan. 1934. "El habitat de Sierra Nevada." *Boletín de la sociedad geográfica nacional*. 74:644–99.

Clark, Martin. 1984. *Modern Italy, 1871–1982*. London: Longman.

Clementi, Andreina de. 1986. "Individualismo agrario e mentalità comunitaria in un villaggio del Lazio." *Quaderni Storici*. 21:931–50.

Cobo, F., S. Cruz, and M. González de Molina. 1992a. "Privatización del monte y protesta social: Un aspecto desconocido del movimiento andaluz (1836–1920)." *Revista de Estudios Regionales*. 32:155–86.

———. 1992b. "Privatización del monte y protesta campesina en Andalucía Oriental (1836–1920)." *Agricultura y Sociedad*. 65:253–302.

Colangelo, Angelo. 1977. "Cento anni di emigrazione." In *Basilicata tra passato e presente*, ed. Nino Calice, 11–41. Milan: Teti.

Elorrieta and Artaza, Octavio. 1948. *Economía forestal: Las Tierras incultas y los montes en la política económica de España*. Madrid: Diana.

Filangieri, Angerio. 1980. *Territoria e popolazione nell'Italia meridionale*. Milan: Angeli.

Franciosa, Luchino. 1930. *Basilicata: Rapporti fra proprietà, impresa e mano d'opera nell'agricoltura italiana*. Rome: Istituto Nazionale di Economia Agraria.

Franzoni, Ausonio. 1903. *L'emigrazione in Basilicata*. Brescia: Unione Tipo-Lit Bresciana.

Garrabou, Ramon, and Jesús Sanz, eds. 1985. *Historia agraria de la España contemporánea. II. Expansión y crisis (1850–1900)*. Barcelona: Editorial Crítica.

Gomez Oliver, Miguel. 1983. *La desamortización de Mendizábal en Granada*. Granada: Excellentíssima Diputación Provincial.

———. 1985. *La desamortización de Madoz en la provincia de Granada*. Granada: Centro de Estudios Históricos de Granada y su Reino.

González de Molina Navarro, Manuel. 1984. *La desamortización del trienio liberal en Andalucía*. Ph.D. thesis, University of Granada.

———. 1996. "El medio ambiente en la historia agraria de Andalucía." In *Historia y medio ambiente en el territorio almeriense*, ed. Andrés Sanchez Picon, 15–33.

Groome, Helen. 1990. *Historia de la política forestal en el estado español*. Madrid: Comunidad de Madrid.

Hardin, Garrett. 1968. "The Tragedy of the Commons." *Science* 162: 1243–48.

Herr, Richard. 1989. *Rural Change and Royal Finances in Spain*. Berkeley: University of California Press.

Iglesías Casado, Antonio. 1982. "El papel del estado ante el problema de la erosión." In *La erosión de los suelos de Andalucía*, 69–75, Seville: Junta de Andalucía.

Italy, Istituto Centrale di Statistica. 1987. *Annuario statistico italiano 1987*. Rome: ISTAT.

Jiménez Blanco, José Ignacio. 1986. "La producción agrária de Andalucía Oriental, 1871–1914." 2 vols. Ph.D. thesis, Universidad de Madrid Complutense.

Marino, John A. 1988. *Pastoral Economics in the Kingdom of Naples*. Baltimore: Johns Hopkins University Press.

McNeill, J. R. 1992. *The Mountains of the Mediterranean World: An Environmental History*. Cambridge: Cambridge University Press.

Montroni, Giovanni. 1983. *Società e mercata della terra: la vendita dei terreni della Chiesa in Campania dopo l'unità*. Naples: Guida.

Nitti, F. ed. 1909–10. *Inchiesta parlamentare sulle condizioni dei contadini nelle provincie meridionali e nella Sicilia. V. Basilicata e Calabria*. (Rome: Bertero).

Placanica, Augusto. 1979. *Alle origini dell'egemonia borghese in Calabria: la privatizzazione delle terre ecclesiastiche (1784–1815)*. Salerno: Società Editrice Meridionale.

Rueda Hernanz, Germán. 1986. *La desamortización de Mendizábal y Espartero en España*. Madrid: Catedra.

———. ed. 1993. *La desamortización en la peninsula ibérica*. Madrid: Marcial Pons.

Sánchez Picón, Andrés, ed. 1996. *Historia y medio ambiente en el territorio almeriense*. Almería: Universidad de Almería, Servicio de Publicaciones.

Sanz Fernandez, Jesús. 1985. "La historia contemporánea de los montes públicos españoles, 1812–1930. Notas y reflexiones (I)." In *Historia agraria de la España contemporánea. II. Expansión y crisis (1850–1900)*, ed. Garrabou and Sanz. Barcelona: Editorial Crítica, 193–228.

Sereni, Emilio. 1968. *Capitalismo nelle campagne*. Turin: Einaudi.

Sievert, James. 1996. *The Construction and Destruction of Nature in Italy, 1860–1914*. Ph.D thesis, University of California at Santa Cruz.

Simón Segura, Francisco. 1973. *La desamortización española en el siglo XIX*. Madrid: Instituto de Estudios Fiscales.

Spera, G. 1903. *La Basilicata: Studi e proposte per la sua rigenerazione economica*. Rome: Cooperativo Sociale.

Tedde, Pedro. 1994. "Cambio institucional y cambio económico en la España del siglo XIX." *Revista de Historia Económica*. 12:525–38.

Tichy, Franz. 1962. *Die Wälder der Basilicata und die Entwaldung im 19 jahrhundert*. Heidelberg: Keyserche.

8

Defining Property Rights in Land in Colonial India: Gorakhpur Region in the Indo-Gangetic Plain

MEENA BHARGAVA AND JOHN F. RICHARDS

New notions of power and authority marked the rising influence of the English East India Company in the different regions of the Indian subcontinent from the mid–eighteenth century. The company, previously a mercantile company carrying Indian textiles and spices to Europe, became the territorial ruler of one of the most populous and productive regions of the world. Between 1757 and 1849, few years passed in which the East India Company armies—manned by Indian professional soldiers and commanded by British officers—did not take the field in wars of conquest or subsequent pacification campaigns. Victory over the Sikh regime in the Punjab in the late 1840s put the entire subcontinent under British direct or indirect rule. When completed, about three-quarters of the subcontinent fell under direct British rule; the remainder continued in the hands of Indian rulers who survived annexation and who retained titles and some degree of internal control over their protectorates. In directly ruled areas, company proconsuls displaced defeated Indian rulers and princes. From Calcutta, the governor-general of the East India Company sent out cadres of British civil and military officials to administer each new region added to the company territory.

EFFECTS OF BRITISH RULE
ON PROPERTY RIGHTS IN LAND

The rule of the East India Company began the process of redefining the relationship between the ruler and the ruled "to construct a ritual idiom through and by which British authority was to be represented to the Indians."[1] The company was keen to assert its sovereign authority and be recognized as a legitimate representative of local tradition. In such circumstances, the dilemma of the company was apparent: to preserve the past and yet transform it. To resolve its inner contradictions, the company proposed changes but within the basic framework of continuity. It reformulated and reinvented traditions and customs to suit new symbols of power and authority. In its attempt to change and reform the indigenous institutions and yet sustain them, the company concentrated on measures which would provide rapid changes, but even more sanctify and legitimize its power and authority.[2] It was in this context that the colonial rule brought changes upon diffuse, layered indigenous systems of property rights in land—changes that moved all areas of the subcontinent towards a more uniform property rights regime.[3]

After establishing public order, the most pressing task for the new rulers was to revive agricultural production and to restore collection of state revenues from the land. Indigenous regimes had successfully claimed a substantial surplus share of rural production as a tax on land or land revenue. This tax supplied the bulk of state revenues throughout South Asia. Each region had its own complex system—obscured by a screen of technical terminology in Persian or regional languages—for assessing and collecting the land tax. Colonial officials in newly acquired and pacified territory immediately found themselves puzzling over patterns of land tenure, land management, and assessment and collection of state revenues levied upon that resource. Determining land tenures and assigning tax liabilities from the Mughals, Marathas, or other predecessor regimes was one of the most demanding tasks to fall to colonial administrators and one with significant immediate consequences for those who paid the tax.[4]

Despite distinctive local and regional cultures and polities, however, the new rulers found broad structural similarities in rural society across the subcontinent. Everywhere local notables or landlords acted as rent receivers and tax intermediaries between the state and the peasantry. Most of these *zamindars* were not landlords in the sense of actively managing a manor or estate. Most zamindars confined their management energies and investment funds to a core area consisting of fields under their direct control. There were few estates or manors in the Indian system in which the landlords exercised tight authority over farmers or tied laborers (agricultural laborers). Indian zamindars used what were often substantial resources to fortify their residences and to arm numerous retainers. The zamindars, usually tied by caste and kinship to the dominant peasant cultivators of the locality, were a rural aristocracy. When indigenous states were centralized and powerful, they were subdued and could be displaced; when the state weakened, their local power and resources flourished. For the first decade or two after each annexation, East India Company army units traversed the countryside engaged in small-scale punitive campaigns in which they assaulted and often destroyed the small forts of defiant zamindars. The latter refused to acknowledge or to pay the demanded land tax—the traditional definition of rebellion.

However property claims for aristocratic landlords might be specified, the effective unit of production was the peasant smallholding in which peasant proprietors used plow cultivation to produce food grains and commercial crops. Whether labeled proprietors or tenants, peasant cultivators were decision-taking managers of their fields. (If some Brahmin or Rajput farmers did not actually do the plowing themselves because of caste pollution rules, this did not vitiate their active management role.) By and large, these peasant cultivators decided crops to be sown; draft animals to be obtained and used; how much, when, and where credit was to be obtained; additional labor to be employed; the extent of improvements such as wells to be made to their land; and all other managerial tasks. These were scarcely the tradition-bound, conservative, timid peasants of caricature, but were robust, risk-taking, entrepreneurial folk who managed highly productive smallholdings in a difficult environment. Often, if they needed access to more fields, they leased land as temporary tenants from their fellow cultivators in a neighboring village. If circumstances seemed favorable, they also cleared and plowed new fields in the lands surrounding the village. Given sufficient inducements, they might also migrate as pioneers to open up new lands and settle them.

Throughout the subcontinent, peasant cultivators were organized into some form of local community or village—whether nucleated or scattered settlement patterns—knit together with intricate forms of kinship and caste ties and patron-client relationships. South Asian rural communities were highly stratified. Invariably, wealthier peasant farmers with larger holdings coalesced into an oligarchical elite with one or more headmen officially recognized by the prevailing state. Often these village oligarchs shared membership in one of the dominant castes of the region and were fellow lineage members. Male members of this elite group assumed responsibility for payment of the assessed land tax to the state at specified times and collected shares from all cultivators in the village. Often the burden fell proportionately heavier on weaker fellow cultivators—even if they were members of the same caste. In many villages there was a second tier of peasant cultivators who maintained households in the villages but had less land and status. Members of this stratum may or may not be members of the same subcaste or lineage, but they deferred to the power of the dominant group.

Local peasant communities also maintained pooled fiscal resources for irrigation works or for amenities such as traveling theatre troupes or patronage of local shrines. Management and allocation of grazing lands, village forests, and irrigation resources fell to the local oligarchy in common-property regimes.[5] The headmen and elite members of the community directed community defense and internal dispute settlement in the absence of state intervention. The community also sustained a small body of hereditary village servants and artisan priests, barbers, potters, carpenters, smiths, washermen, tailors, among others. Some form of annual payment or fixed share of the community grain harvest generally remunerated these functionaries. They received small plots of tax-free land and other perquisites.[6]

At the lowest extremity were "untouchable" caste members who supplied domestic and field labor for "clean" caste peasant cultivators in return for a bare subsistence. Upper caste peasants marked the ritually polluting status of "untouchable" and enforced subservience in everyday life by demeaning forms of address and avoidance. They also imposed polluting tasks such as the removal of carrion upon "untouchables." In the South, "untouchable" laborers were so constrained in their freedom of movement by a web of advance payments, housing, and ritual obligations that they were, if not chattel, agrestic serfs. They could evidently be bought and sold until the British refused to employ the powers of the state to enforce these terms in 1843.[7]

Everywhere peasant smallholders meshed with stockbreeding and stockraising communities that maintained varying degrees of mobility in search of pasture for their herds. Graziers, usually identified with specific castes, frequently held time-specified grazing access to village grasslands or to harvested fields on a seasonal basis. Their stockbreeding skills were vital to the maintenance of high-quality draft animals—bullocks and buffalo—essential for Indian plow cultivation.

At the time of colonization, the East India Company officials observed that land was abundant and labor relatively scarce in every region from north to south. Everywhere, in interstitial areas between settlements, could be found uncultivated tracts of forests, woodlands, wetlands, and savannas

that the British termed "waste" or "wastelands." Enterprising pioneer cultivators could occupy, clear, and plow new lands if they could mobilize the
capital and labor to do so. Beyond well-defined zones of peasant settlement
lay a fluctuating frontier line that demarcated less accessible hill regions
inhabited by "tribals" or hunter-gatherers and shifting cultivators. Sometimes
these tribal groups raided plains settlements or moving groups of traders.
More often they were peacefully involved in various types of reciprocal
exchange with sedentary communities in which the products of the forest—
honey, wax, game, medicinal plants—were exchanged for money with which
to purchase salt, metals, guns, or other needed commodities.

Each new region annexed generated voluminous written reports, recommendations, orders, and analyses. Often sharp debates occurred before
final policies were established. Early on, following these debates and their
resolution became a concern for historians of British India and has remained
so to the present. Historians, in common with company administrators,
readily became enmeshed in the coils of detailed questions about land
tenure and land revenue. The enormous official sources blend imperceptibly
into an equally large historical literature, now two or more centuries in
depth, concerned with land policies and issues such as agricultural productivity, labor, dearth and famine, commercialization, and rural social history
under colonial rule. So complex has this historical literature become that
overall structural similarities between regions have been obscured.

All company and, after 1857, imperial officials shared with their supe-
riors at home a belief that any state—and especially a colonial state—had
a profound responsibility to encourage wise land use that would lead to
growth in agricultural production, the primary source of wealth. Armed
with this belief, British officers also shared several firm operating principles:
first, that the state should not normally be a landlord or seek to manage
directly the growing, processing, and trading of agricultural products—
these were for private persons; second, that only stable, well-defined, and
legally enforceable property rights in land kept safe from confiscation or
interference by an arbitrary state would foster productive agriculture and
responsible land management in general; third, efficient markets in land
were essential to discipline ineffectual landowners and to reward capable
landowners (and as a corollary that the state should seize and place on the
market for sale the lands of those proprietors who could not pay the
assessed taxes on their holdings); fourth, that uncultivated "waste" lands
should be brought into cultivation as rapidly as possible; and fifth, that
those proprietors who survived market forces and who paid their taxes
would simultaneously improve production in the land and become staunch
supporters of the regime over the long term. Throughout stormy debates

over such questions as whether large landlords or smallholders should be favored with proprietary rights in land or whether assessments should be fixed in perpetuity or altered periodically, company and later imperial officials never wavered in their devotion to these principles even as they occasionally were forced to compromise them.

Company officials reshaped indigenous property rights in land to meet imperial goals for rural stability and productivity. During the earliest stages of conquest, in Bengal and portions of South India, East India Company officials were not equipped with an overall plan or systematic agrarian policy. Instead they evolved ideas from study of existing property and tax regimes in those regions. Company officials drew upon their operating assumptions, lessons from territories previously assimilated, and intensive study of the institutions of each new territory to establish or "settle" land rights and tax assessments. Land settlement fixed state-backed proprietary rights in land and corresponding obligations for annual land tax payments.

Invariably settlement of the land revenue altered existing indigenous arrangements for control and management of land. Company officials had to decide whether to award these valuable property rights to local aristocrats or tax farmers who would become landlords, to village communities as a collectivity, or to individual peasant cultivators. In so doing, they balanced concerns for political stability and support for the regime with their overall interest in increasing agricultural production and rural prosperity. (Having landlords over larger areas reduced expenses of assessment and collection since the company did not have to deal individually with thousands of villages or tens of thousands of smallholding proprietors in each region.) Those notables and peasants who either acquired or retained state-secured land rights would tend to support the company; those who lost land rights might foment opposition.[8]

Company officials tried to determine the levels of land tax demanded by previous regimes and set a new rate appropriate to the productive capacities of each locality that would encourage investment and improvement of agriculture while returning the revenues demanded by the treasury. They had to decide whether the assessment, once enumerated, would be periodically revised or would be unchanged over long periods of time or even in perpetuity. If revised, would it be necessary to carry out expensive, detailed field-by-field surveys of land to measure changes in cultivated land.

Regional variations

Despite shared principles, land settlement choices made by company officials differed—sometimes dramatically—from one part of India to another. These differences, however, were by and large differences over means rather than ends. For the earliest territory, Bengal, three decades of hesita-tion, false starts, and confusion, as well as a disastrous famine, eventually produced a new land system that came to be called a *zamindari* or landlord system. In 1793 Lord Cornwallis, the governor-general in Calcutta, issued regulations on land called the Permanent Settlement. Cornwallis, formally backed by the company's Board of Directors as well as the British cabinet, awarded secure proprietary rights to large estate owners.[9] Scions of former Mughal officials and tax farmers and heirs to locally prominent rajas and princes of Bengal became large landlords with rights similar to those enjoyed by the large landlords of England. Disarmed and overwhelmed by the power of the company armies, the Bengal zamindars lost their previous military role. Their estates comprised large numbers of villages of peasant cultivators who became tenants paying rent to their landlord. The new landlords enjoyed rights of occupancy and use, sale and lease, mortgage, and inheritance over their estates. They were free to raise or lower the rents of their tenant cultivators. In turn, zamindars assumed an obligation to pay the land tax every year to the state. The assessed figure, expressed in company-issued silver rupees, was based on Mughal figures and could not be raised in the future by the state—hence the term Permanent Settle-ment. Failure to pay the tax could result in confiscation of the estate for arrears and its sale at auction to more capable buyers.

The framers of this scheme hoped to create in Bengal entrepreneurial, reforming landlords similar to those in control of the English countryside who invested energy and funds in improving agriculture. With a fixed tax assessment, profits from increased cultivation would go to the zamindars, who would use them to enhance productivity in the countryside. They also aimed at aligning these zamindars in full political support of the company regime. As an added benefit, the company would not need to employ numerous clerks and officials in order to collect the land tax that could be readily controlled by contact with relatively few zamindars. Furthermore, the unchanging assessment made it unnecessary to do detailed cadastral surveys and keep voluminous records.

Contemporaneously, in South India, a small group of East India Company military officers devised a contrasting approach to the Bengal system. In this approach, dubbed the *ryotwari* system, the state conferred land rights and tax obligations upon individual cultivators (*ryots*), rather than zamindars.[10] The architects of this system were Alexander Read and Thomas Munro, who in the 1790s carried out a land settlement on ryotwari principles in the territory ceded by Tipu Sultan of Mysore after his defeat by Cornwallis. This was a sizable area inhabited by 4–5 million persons. Ryotwari settlement involved sweeping aside the claims of all nonpeasant intermediaries to deal instead with each peasant cultivator in each village. Company officials stipulated to the peasant occupier the land tax due upon the fields in a written document and received in return a written bond assuring payment of the tax when due in installments each year. The taxes fixed would not be permanent, as in the Bengal system, but temporary. In its early stages, this was an annual settlement with revisions of the tax possible each year. In its mature stage, the ryotwari assessments were fixed for thirty years before reassessment by the state occurred.

Essential to this scheme was an official cadastral survey that located, identified, and, as much as practicable, estimated the productivity of individual fields held by each cultivator. The documents issued to each cultivator quickly became certificates of ownership rights over their smallholding. With their agreements in hand, peasant cultivators held guaranteed rights of occupancy and cultivation on payment of the tax. They could bequeath these lands to their heirs; they could sell the rights to the lands; or they could borrow against the value of the land.

During the first decades of the nineteenth century, the prevailing official view turned decisively against the Bengal zamindari system and in favor of some form of ryotwari system that would confer direct proprietary rights on peasant cultivators. In part this reaction stemmed from highly visible flaws in the Bengal system. Those who survived the initial selloff of zamindari estates or bought them up at government auction became rentier landlords with little interest in agricultural improvement. For example, the maharaja of Darbhanga, whose 2,400 square-mile estate was one of the largest zamindari estates surviving under the Bengal Permanent Settlement, invested little, if any, of his Rs. 4 million annual profit from rents on agricultural improvement.[11] Complaints from rack-rented tenants unprotected by anything other than customary rights grew in volume.

New ideological currents stemming from utilitarian thought and the Ricardian theory of unearned land rent put a new perspective on the rentier profits being made by zamindars as cultivation expanded in Bengal. From this theoretical perspective, the state should be recipient of the unearned profits stemming from expanding cultivation, not an idle landlord class. The Madras ryotwari system, in contrast, dealt with peasants who were the true source of energy, managerial acumen, and labor as land managers. The system's success in increasing production under renewable assessments offset the heavy state cost for land surveys and payment of petty officials.[12]

In part, also, the shift toward the ryotwari approach stemmed from growing official appreciation of the economic, political, and even military benefits to be gained from nurturing a strong peasant smallholder society.

The simple virtues of hard-working peasant farmers who were content to work their land without complaint if treated fairly compared favorably with the pretensions and idleness of the Indian landlord class. Peasant families were ideal suppliers of recruits for the colonial armies and could be rewarded with gifts and grants of land after long, loyal service. Peasants did not stint their energies in clearing and expanding cultivation into the wasteland. In addition, if the opportunity presented itself, peasant farmers were ideal pioneer settlers for land clearance in frontier areas.

When, in 1818, the East India Company occupied vast new territories in western India after the final defeat of the Marathas, no serious consideration was given to the Bengal system. Instead the Bombay land settlement assigned tax obligations and property rights on the ryotwari Madras model. Individual peasant cultivators, whose holdings were surveyed and registered by the state, paid land taxes directly.[13] Assessments would be reviewed and changed at thirty-year intervals. Even lands in the ceded and conquered provinces of the Upper Gangetic valley taken from the *nawab* of Awadh in 1801 and 1803 and placed under the administration of Calcutta did not become permanently settled zamindari estates.[14] Instead, in 1819, after an extensive inquiry, Bengal officials decided to settle the land revenue with a single representative for each village community in a laudable attempt to strengthen the tightly knit village communities of that region. In point of fact, this became a de facto peasant system because the lands of all village cultivators were registered and their share of the assessed revenue was recorded by the state. Ryotwari land settlements prevailed in later territorial additions—Sind in 1826, Punjab in 1849, and Berar in 1853—as a matter of course.[15]

Overly optimistic estimates of agricultural productivity, unrealistic notions of unearned rent derived from the utilitarian calculus, and pressure to increase state revenues meant that officials fixed tax demands far too high—especially in ryotwari systems. Remissions and forgiveness for hard-pressed cultivators came reluctantly, if at all. These harsh policies dampened prices, depressed agriculture, and inhibited expansion in the first decades of the nineteenth century. Gradually, however, revenue officials softened their demands and slowly, decade by decade, the tax burden on rural producers diminished.

As the nineteenth century progressed, the new property rights in land imposed by colonial rule revealed similar effects in colonial India. Dominant peasant cultivators were the effective land managers and entrepreneurs who expanded cultivation in every region. Even in Bengal under the Permanent Settlement, an already-existing class of prosperous peasant cultivators or "village landlords" flourished as tenants to absentee zamindars.

These wealthier peasants shifted the burden of increasing rents to poorer cultivators when necessary and acquired new lands by investing in expansion of cultivation at the jungle frontier.[16] By midcentury as urban populations grew and export markets developed for various crops, agricultural prices moved upward. Sedentary cultivation expanded. As landlords and peasant cultivators, encouraged by guarantees of their rights by the state, brought new land under plow, the modern assault on the forests, woodlands, and grasslands of the subcontinent had begun in earnest. Moneylenders lent funds for operating expenses as well as expansion on the security of mortgaged lands. Land sales rose in newly emerging land markets.

DISTRICT CASE STUDY: GORAKHPUR

To illustrate these developments, we now turn to a case study of a single region, that of Gorakhpur in present-day Uttar Pradesh in the Gangetic plain. In 1801, the nawab of the Mughal successor state of Awadh ceded Gorakhpur and several other districts to the East India Company regime in Calcutta to satisfy debts incurred in paying for British military assistance. At the time of its forced cession to the East India Company, the region of Gorakhpur formed a large territorial unit that today covers most of the Azamgarh, Basti, Gonda, and Gorakhpur districts. This region, in 1801, represented diverse characteristics. The region south of the Ghaghra River was well cultivated with soils considered to be of superior quality, and it yielded a high revenue to the state in the form of a tax on agricultural production—or land revenue.[17] However, the area north of the river Ghaghra (present-day Gorakhpur District) was thinly settled and consisted largely of uncultivated "wastelands" and forests.[18] Terai, or the approaches to and the foothills of the Himalayas, formed the northern frontier of Gorakhpur. The East India Company continued the already prevailing forces of economic expansion affecting the region under the Mughal emperors and the nawabs of Awadh.

Acclimatizing and adapting itself to the Mughal patterns and institutions, the company appeared confident and convinced of the success of the Mughal emperors in the realm of extraction of revenue and expansion of cultivation. In its early responses, it even hesitated to subordinate or subdue the Mughal institutions. Nonetheless, anxious to assert its sovereignty and power, the company made numerous but cautious interventions and experiments, wary of alienation should rural India be disturbed. Rural social structure, the company felt, should not only be preserved but also upheld for the ready acceptance and legitimacy of its power. It was within this framework that the company officials restructured and reallocated the landed property rights to continue and extend their efforts at development. The different social classes—whether the zamindars, cultivators, or agricultural laborers—were quick to respond not only to the offers of the state but also to the market forces, leading to growth in cultivation and increased capital investment in land. This reinforced the close relationship between the growth of the economy of Gorakhpur and the landed property rights or vice versa.[19]

The *ashraf* or the notables of the district dominated rural society in Gorakhpur. They generally belonged to castes considered to be upper castes like the Brahmins, Bhumihars, Rajputs, Kshatriyas, Kayasths, and Sayyids. At cession, they held virtually all property rights over settled land and accepted the responsibility of paying the annual land revenue assessment to the state. These landholders avoided direct cultivation themselves, but let out their lands to rent-paying tenant peasant cultivators. The cultivators were largely drawn from castes such as Kurmis, Koris, Ahirs, Chamars, and "Trookia Muslims." Specialized craft castes supplied Gorakhpur with various services and manufactured items.

Members of the trading castes (*vaishya* or *bania*) such as the Agarwals presided over a flourishing and expanding commercial system. The state forced a surplus from every rural village by its annual land revenue demand that had to be paid in currency. The flow of food grains and other commodities was handled by local moneylenders and grain dealers from the trading castes who shipped grain to the town markets and to Gorakhpur itself. These grain dealers in turn advanced funds every season to landholders or to peasant farmers directly in return for a claim on the harvest. Regularly scheduled markets permitted the sale of foodstuffs, textiles, and other necessities and luxuries. Part of Gorakhpur's surplus was exported to Lucknow and part to Patna and Calcutta to the east. There was also a vigorous transit trade north from Gorakhpur to Nepal over the Himalayan trails.[20]

Gorakhpur was a fertile and productive region and showed definite signs of growth and development. The June to October rains were copious and reliable; winter rains were less abundant, but valuable. The Ghagra, Rapti, and lesser and greater Gandaki rivers, fed by the snow pack of the Himalayas, offered year-round water in areas along their courses. Constantly shifting courses left highly fertile alluvial deposits that could be cultivated within a year. Streams and rain-fed ponds served as additional sources of irrigation. Three crops per year were possible with harvests in August-September, November-December, and the spring crops in March-May.

Abundant rainfall encouraged rice and sugar cane as the two staple crops throughout the region. High yields of rice, obtained in both the winter and spring seasons, generally produced a surplus for export to the urban centers of the region and beyond. Sugar cane production expanded steadily in the nineteenth century despite the depredations of herds of wild elephants that fed upon and trampled the crop. Sugar cane met local consumption needs and, after being transformed into a cash crop through processing, was sent to urban markets.

LANDED PROPERTY RIGHTS IN THE EIGHTEENTH CENTURY

As is now generally recognized, landed property rights were extraordinarily complex and layered in every province of Mughal India, and pre-cession Gorakhpur was no exception. The right and obligation to pay the state's assessed land tax, in coin, based on agricultural production was conflated with the right and obligation of occupying peasants to pay rent to superior right holders. Some rights were created and enforced by the state; some by local custom and habit; and some by both agencies. The one unmistakable aspect of the system was the state's urgent interest in encouraging and in fact insisting on active cultivation of the soil by the peasantry.

Those groups holding rights to land and its produce in Gorakhpur consisted of, at the top, ta'alluqdars (lapsed officials) and zamindars with hereditary rights to larger tracts of land; village headmen or muqaddams; rent-paying tenants with rights of occupancy (khudkasht); seasonal rent-paying cultivators (pahikasht); holders of tax-free, charitable subsistence grants of land from the state (madad-i ma'ash); and holders of land clearance or development grants (birt). Let us discuss each of these in turn.

In the latter years of the eighteenth century, a group of powerful officials and local magnates or ta'alluqdars had taken advantage of the weakness of the nawab of Awadh to establish themselves between the gentry and the state. The nawab of Awadh began to grant term revenue contracts (revenue farms) to certain reliable officers over areas in which revenue collection was difficult. These officers became revenue contractors who undertook to deliver payment promptly under the terms of their contract. In order to do so, they began to put severe pressure on refractory zamindars. Many smaller and weaker zamindars began to cede portions of their tax collection rights for a fixed term to the ta'alluqdars in exchange for protection. In some cases this was voluntary; in others the new arrangement was coercive. Weaker zamindars, hard pressed by the nawab of Awadh's revenue collectors, sought refuge with stronger zamindars or with lapsed officials who had seized local power. As time passed, the ta'alluqdars came to regard all their holdings as if they were the original zamindars. The ta'alluqdars were well on their way to becoming a new regional ruling aristocracy with much greater power than the existing rural notables or zamindars.

Throughout Gorakhpur, zamindars held legal proprietary rights over nearly all cultivated lands and vast tracts of uncleared or uncultivated jungle or grassland. Brahmins, Rajputs, Sayyids, and the other ashraf castes, following caste taboos, did not do the cultivating themselves. Instead they hired labor from the cultivating castes and undertook to pay the annual land tax (in seasonal installments) to the collection officers of the state. Each zamindar resided within his stipulated zamindari estate. Many of these zamindars also held larger tracts of land with numerous villages.

The zamindars depended upon the services of village headmen or *muqaddams* to meet their responsibilities. Village headmen, appointed by the state, served as intermediaries. Frequently, village headmen were of the same caste and lineage as the zamindars. The village headmen arranged for payment of the annual land tax from the village fiscal pool to the zamindar and collected this sum in turn from the occupying peasant cultivators of the village. The headman advanced loans (*taqavi*) made available by the zamindar for cultivation. For his services to the state and the zamindar, the village headman held *nankar* or remuneration in the form of tax-free lands or a fixed 2.5 percent of the village land revenue payment.[21] In the scholarly literature, the headmen are sometimes referred to as "village zamindars" to suggest their second function. The village headman could also obtain *malguzari* or zamindari rights. He held zamindari title to his own lands within the village. He could manage the cultivation of these lands himself with hired laborers or he could let the lands out to tenants. That is, he was entitled to the 10 percent *malikana* share from the revenue payments on his own lands that would otherwise have gone to the state.

The primary cultivators who actually held the plow and managed hired laborers in Gorakhpur villages were the *khudkasht* or "self-sustaining" peasants. These cultivators occupied their lands as permanent members of the village community from generation to generation. Usually the greater number of these tenants belonged to the caste and/or lineage of the village headman that held dominant power in the village. As long as they paid their share of the village land tax and village expenses, their occupancy right was secure. They were entitled to the use of the village commons for grazing, building materials, and other benefits. Their house sites were free of taxes, and they had rights in the fruit trees planted by themselves or their family. Khudkasht tenancy rights ordinarily were not alienable. They could not be sold or given to others by the muqaddam or the zamindar without the consent of the khudkasht himself. Khudkasht rights generally passed unchallenged from father to son. If a cultivator died without heirs, the holding reverted to the zamindar.

A second form of tenancy consisted of peasants who took up annual leases for cultivation from the village headman. *Pahikasht* cultivators were usually residents of another village who sought land to cultivate. They held no permanent rights of occupancy and paid rent on the terms agreed when the lease was established.[22]

Complicated they were, but these forms of interlocking proprietorship of land lent themselves to dynamic growth and expansion in eighteenth-century rural society. The zamindars responded vigorously to opportunities for entrepreneurial land clearing and settlement. Village headmen were key entrepreneurial figures in the steady expansion of cultivation in Gorakhpur in the Mughal period. Often muqaddams were appointed to vacant or uncleared village sites and charged with mobilizing tenants to clear and cultivate the land. Caste and lineage affiliations made it relatively easy to organize the colonization of new lands and create new villages in Gorakhpur. New headmen and their rights to newly cleared lands were ratified by the nawab of Awadh and his officers without any hindrance.

The zamindars also adopted an older form of land grant. *Birt* or *birtia* was a device of the Mughal era employed to stimulate land clearance. The Mughal emperors originally conveyed birt grants for favored recipients as a form of maintenance grant (*britti* or *vritti* means subsistence or maintenance). Often these grants were made as an incentive for clearing and cultivating jungle land.[23] The nawabs of Awadh had assumed the royal role and continued the practice of bestowing birt grants. In the latter part of the eighteenth century, zamindars began to offer birt grants themselves to kinsmen, retainers, or worthy recipients of their generosity. Zamindars justified this largesse by their role as representatives of the state, even though they might not have sought formal approval from the nawab of Awadh. Birt concessions provided peasant cultivators with access to uncleared or waste jungle which was not currently paying revenue, but which lay within the nominal jurisdiction of a zamindar. The land to be cleared was actually leased. It was not given outright to the grantee, and the zamindars retained for themselves the possibility of future possession of these reclaimed lands. Zamindars retained the privilege of resuming at their discretion lands they had given out on birt tenure.[24]

Birt holdings were pecuniary in nature, that is, created for cash or to enhance profits. During the lease, birtias (leaseholders) were required to cultivate the lands and to make annual payments to both the zamindar and the state. Each birtia paid the total land revenue assessment (*jama*) for his

lands or villages, from which the zamindar deducted his customary 10 percent allowance, malikana, before paying his total revenues to the state.
After calculation of the costs of cultivation, each birtia was permitted to
retain one-tenth to as much as one-fourth of the surplus or profit from the
sale of crops. The remainder went to the zamindar. Birtias also received a
customary allowance of two *annas* (one-eighth silver rupee) per *bigha* (two-
fifths of an acre) cultivated. They were also entitled to any market taxes
(*sair*) collected by the zamindar in villages within their grant.[25]

Normally, each birtia expected to hold his lands as long as he paid the
revenue and profit shares to the zamindar, and he expected that the zamindar would renew this right. If for some reason the zamindar chose to award
the birt to another person, the resident birtia could then demand from
the zamindar 10 percent allowance, that is, malikana, as compensation. In
other words, a birt grant by the latter years of the eighteenth century had
acquired a form of property right status or quasi-zamindari right in land.

By the end of the century, the birtias, who numbered more than
10,000, constituted a numerous cultivating peasant group in pre-cession
Gorakhpur. During the eighteenth century, the profits of the birtias
increased steadily as prices rose and cultivation intensified. As time passed,
established birtias began to demand more concessions from the zamindars.

PRODUCTION AND LAND RIGHTS AFTER 1801

Understanding, regulating, and then modifying the system of land rights
was the central administrative task for the East India Company officials.
More so than the previous regimes, they sought to simplify and to secure
land rights at every level in order to encourage capital investment in the
land. The new rulers had two aims: to ensure that the state collected the
land revenue more efficiently and exhaustively than the earlier regimes,
and to encourage and shape rural expansion and prosperity by increasing
cultivation. In Gorakhpur, unlike the districts of neighboring Bengal where
the 1793 Permanent Settlement placed an absolute cap on government
land revenue, the Revenue Board remained free to revise revenue assessments at intervals to reflect a changing economy.

An immediate problem for East India Company officials was to define
the rights of the aggrandizing body of ta'alluqdars, the most visible and
powerful local figures in Gorakhpur. They chose not to resort to forceful
removal; instead the power and position of the ta'alluqdars was reduced by
administrative means. Company officials scrutinized all bills or "deeds of
trust" affording ta'alluqdars control over the rights of zamindars. Any

such rights, which were disputed by the zamindars, were declared invalid. Similarly if the deeds or other documents did not detail the period of time and conditions for such transfers they were invalidated. In this tortuous fashion, the ta'alluqdars were reduced to the status of larger zamindars—still powerful, but no longer a political threat.

In the eyes of the East India Company, the most apparent landowners or land proprietors of Gorakhpur (in European terms of ownership) were the zamindars—who held the hereditary right to pay the land revenue (malguzari) for the lands that they possessed. Company officials continued the malguzari rights of the zamindars without any demur, if the zamindars could present the *sanads* (orders of grant) of the Mughal emperors or the nawabs of Awadh as proof of their rights. They could continue to hold lands if they kept up cultivation and paid land revenue regularly to the state. As they had been under the Mughal rule, the zamindar rights continued to be salable, mortgageable, and inheritable. In theory then, a market for zamindari rights had existed before 1801 and could operate freely even under the rule of the East India Company. In practice such a land market was slow to develop.

In theory, if the zamindars failed to meet their annual obligation to collect and remit land revenue to the company, their rights were sold at auction and made available to another, more reliable intermediary. This was certainly the fate of numerous zamindars in Bengal subject to the terms of the Permanent Settlement of 1793. However, in Gorakhpur, the company proved to be much more lenient in its dealings with the zamindars. Even if they could not fulfill their obligations to collect and remit revenue, the zamindars were still protected. They did not lose their proprietorial claim as it existed in 1801. If revenue farmers or birtias or others assumed the revenue-collecting function, the zamindars were still paid their malikana or 10 percent of the revenue and could exercise their claim at any time to resume their responsibilities.

The rights and the status of birtias, that is, whether they were or were not the proprietors entitled to engage for the revenue, posed a dilemma for the company. Company officials at first took a negative view and made settlements with the zamindars, ignoring the birtia demand for direct settlement of land revenue with them. After cession, the company refused to make any new birt grants on the traditional terms. In time they did relent and agreed to look at the claims of existing birtias. Company revenue officers agreed to make direct settlements if the birtias could prove that they held proprietary rights. Occasionally, the company began to negotiate for revenue directly with the birtias if the zamindars fell into heavy arrears or if individual zamindars refused to engage for the revenue. Revenue officers at times even made the plea that the birtias had offered a fair and accept-able jama—higher than what the zamindar would pay.

The company, to ascertain the rights of the birtias, inquired into their documents and reviewed their holdings. Convinced of their legitimacy, it recognized the birtias "as having acquired an actual property in the soil."[26] Direct settlements were made with them except where preexisting agree-ments stipulated that all revenue payments were to be made through the zamindar. After 1835, birt tenures were declared heritable and transferable, and the birtias were considered the zamindars or proprietors of the villages held by them. Thereafter, revenue settlements were made with the birtias, independent of the zamindars. However, the birtias still had to pay into the government treasury a sum that would equal 10 percent of their revenue to be given to their zamindar. By this date birtias had become zamindars, and the East India Company recognized both—the zamindars as well as the bir-tias—as the owners of the land.

The village headmen or the muqaddams initially did not fare so well with the new regime. The muqaddams, while being revenue contractors or revenue collectors for the entire village, also held landholding rights within the village or the area assigned to them for cultivation. The Mughal emperors and subsequently the nawabs of Awadh had given the village headmen lands in lease to encourage expanded cultivation. At the expiry of the lease, the headmen were entitled to retain 7 in 100 bighas of newly cultivated land as their own (*sir*) lands. The remainder became part of the higher zamindar's holdings for revenue purposes.

Even after cession, the functional importance of the muqaddams remained the same. However, the proprietary rights held by muqaddams over their own lands in the village, which were in fact zamindari rights held by title, were not recognized by the East India Company. Instead, the new regime tried to reduce each village headman to the position of a mere intermediary or functionary who collected the village land revenue, made monetary advances (taqavi) to his fellow villagers for cultivation, and managed the village fiscal pool. In return for these official services (*khidmat*), the village headmen continued to be paid a small percentage of the village land revenue which they collected; and for the lands which they cultivated themselves or with hired labor, they were allowed to pay a nom-inal revenue to the state. Under the company, the muqaddams were reduced from higher and more secure status as village zamindars or payers of the state revenue over their own holdings to mere intermediaries between the village and the state. This was the first in a lengthy series of maneuvers by colonial officials designed to convert the village officers to state employees.

The company found the role and the position of the khudkasht culti-vators in the villages initially confusing. Did these cultivators have any recognized rights to the land, and if so, what were they? Were they owners or proprietors? It was clear that the khudkasht cultivators were permanent inhabitants of the village, that they had a number of perquisites such as rights to village commons, and, more often than not, they were linked by ties of caste membership and kinship to the village headmen or the zamindars above them. The khudkasht cultivators did possess the right to alienate their holdings, but in practice this rarely occurred. Social pressures and the need for security held most khudkasht cultivators fast to their vil-lages. That tireless observer, Buchanan-Hamilton, who toured the region in 1810, commented: "In Gorakhpur they (*khudkasht* cultivators) were known as the old tenants . . . who had comfortable abodes, to which they were attached as their birthplaces."[27]

These tightly linked cultivator families constituted the elite (*bhadralok*) of the village community. In 1801 each village possessed exten-sive tracts of uncultivated land which provided a variety of supplementary resources and assets for the community. Khudkasht cultivators and their families had privileged access to the village common lands and resources. They constituted the village community that determined the rules and procedures for making use of these shared resources in each village. For khudkasht cultivators, grazing for their livestock in village grass and shrub wastelands was generally abundant. So also were building materials and wood for implements readily available at only the cost of gathering or extraction. Their habitations and home sites were held free of taxation.

Tree fruits were an especially valuable supplement to household income. Khudkasht cultivators were entitled to the use of the products of fruit-bearing trees on and near their home sites. Tree rights were, however, subject to intricate constraints. The khudkasht cultivators were required to present a portion, determined by custom and the avarice of the zamindar, of the crop to the zamindar. The khudkashts could not cut fruit trees with-out first obtaining the permission of their zamindars. If the trees died or were no longer productive, the khudkashts were obliged to plant fresh trees in their place. (He could, however, make use of the wood of the unpro-ductive fruit trees.) If replanting did not occur, the land on which the khudkasht cultivator's trees stood could be confiscated by the zamindars and new trees planted.[28]

Mango trees and groves (*topes*), presumably because of the value and appeal of the fruit and the verdant appeal of the trees that sheltered the houses of the khudkasht cultivators, were subject to less interference from the zamindars. If a cultivator planted a mango tree or trees, he was entitled to the complete use of its produce and could even cut it down without the zamindar's permission. The cultivator was not required to offer a share of the mango crop to the zamindar. These privileges passed directly to his heirs; but if the cultivating peasant and his family quit the village, the mango trees fell to the possession of the zamindar. Mango trees and groves constituted a distinctive and highly valued form of household property for the khudkasht cultivators of Gorakhpur.[29]

For the East India Company revenue officers, the trickiest question was whether the hereditary occupancy rights of the khudkasht cultivators constituted a form of landownership, or were they indeed tenants who could be removed or replaced by the true owners of the land, that is, the zamindars or village headmen? After considerable inquiry, study, and debate, East India Company officials concluded that khudkasht tenure was both complicated and ambiguous. From one perspective, khudkasht was a form of contracted tenancy. Khudkasht cultivators did engage annually for revenue on their lands with the zamindars. In theory, the latter had the option of either renewing or rejecting the annual engagement upon completion. From another viewpoint, khudkasht tenancy was securely protected by local custom and local society and amounted to hereditary occupancy rights. If the khudkasht cultivators paid the revenue as stipulated, the zamindars were bound not to "molest or oppress them."[30] If the khudkasht cultivator did not pay the revenue because of drought or other calamities, in theory, the zamindar could evict him and bring in someone new. However, the khudkasht cultivator still retained the right to pay his dues and to reclaim his lands even after years had elapsed.

These were extraordinary circumstances; most often rural society regarded the rights of the khudkasht cultivators as hereditary and permanent just as the zamindar's rights were prescriptive and hereditary. If zamindari rights changed, the new zamindar could not arbitrarily eject khudkashts from their holdings, nor could he demand a rent from his new tenants higher than the agreed rate. Only if a tenant paid land revenue at an obviously concessionary rate granted by the previous zamindar could the new owner legitimately raise the land revenue on khudkasht tenants. In lands already brought under cultivation, customary rates quickly emerged for each subdistrict or *pargana*.[31]

In the first decades after cession, East India Company officers in Gorakhpur, in common with those in the other regions seized from the nawab of Awadh, hesitated to make sweeping changes in the prevailing regime of landed property rights. They were confident in deciphering the intricacies of the Mughal and post-Mughal agrarian order. They confirmed those rights that could be verified for zamindars, birtias, muqaddams, and for khudkasht cultivators. Certainly the Mughal and post-Mughal system was successful in extracting revenue for the state and in encouraging the expansion of cultivation north from the river toward the hills in Gorakhpur. During this early period, the critical question was whether the East India Company officers would continue to use Mughal institutions as the settlement frontier moved northward.

THE PUSH TOWARD ECONOMIC DEVELOPMENT

By the 1820s East India Company officials were forced to conclude that multiple proprietorial interests in land did coexist in Gorakhpur. Even with greater understanding they disliked the existing system. Land rights in Gorakhpur remained to them confusing and disputed at every turn. Rather than extend the older property rights pattern, the Board of Revenue struggled throughout the nineteenth century to graft on to the older system new forms of landownership. The board and district officers strove for greater simplicity in proprietary rights for administrative convenience and revenue increases, and to further agricultural expansion and productivity. District collectors in Gorakhpur found themselves under continuing pressure to expand cultivation, increase revenue, and boost the productivity of their respective districts. In effect, they were asked to become land developers for the East India Company.

Collectors faced difficult choices, however, as to which holders of land rights could be counted upon to be effective entrepreneurs. Who would most vigorously respond to government initiatives to press ahead with land clearance and expanded cultivation? By what means could the vast forest and wastelands of Gorakhpur be settled and made to produce revenue?

The zamindars recognized by the East India Company in 1801 were the obvious sources of entrepreneurial energy and capital. District revenue collectors in Gorakhpur pressed zamindars to use their resources to clear, plow, and sow uncultivated lands under their jurisdiction. If peasants already engaged in cultivation for the zamindar could not be attracted to the role of pioneer-settler, others could. The East India Company territories were starting to attract land-seeking migrants from the lands of the nawab of Awadh to the west or from the hill kingdom of Butwal or from Nepal to the north. So concerned was the company to expand the frontier line of cultivation north of the Ghagra that the company revenue officers had little patience for zamindars reluctant to invest in expansion. If the zamindars hesitated to cooperate to clear new lands, East India Company officers turned to other candidates for leadership.

Company revenue officers could bypass the zamindars and enter into three-, five-, or ten-year development contracts with birtias who possessed capital and who were anxious to improve their positions and fortunes. If they succeeded in organizing and financing peasant pioneer settlers, the birtias could exact annual revenue from the new lands the settlers had brought into cultivation. For these new lands, the birtias then paid state revenues at a concessionary rate which rose slowly over the period of engagement. In deference to the rights of the zamindars, they continued to pay 10 percent malikana to the zamindars. Such contracts proved to be a very attractive prospect for many birtias. With a certain amount of initiative, birtias could share in the profits of an expanding agricultural frontier. In the longer interval, energetic birtias could hope to persuade the East India Company to grant them separate zamindari rights over their holdings in Gorakhpur.

The new regime also engaged with the village headmen, who could supply strength, leadership, and capital in mobilizing peasants to clear and cultivate new lands. For this task, however, the rules changed from the Mughal and Nawabi period. Successful pioneering headmen no longer received zamindari rights to 7 of 100 bighas brought under the plow. Instead they were awarded a small percentage of the land revenue collected from new lands—a percentage that would gradually rise over time according to the graduated scale of tax imposed on newly reclaimed lands. Also, they were allowed to cultivate small portions of land on their own for which they could pay nominal revenue. These were the normal perquisites (nankar) of the village headman acting as an intermediary or a functionary. Village headmen were pressured to take on these pioneering responsibilities. If they faltered in the eyes of the state, they could be replaced by other more vigorous candidates and could lose their perquisites.

Failing these options, revenue officers even reached out to individual peasant proprietors and engaged with them for land clearing and cultivation. In these extreme cases, the East India Company assumed the role of a zamindar. The state provided capital (taqavi) funds for seeds, plows, animals, and other expenditures to individual peasant entrepreneurs. These peasant settlers or *raiyats* engaged directly with the state to pay the land revenue on concessionary rates in an annual or multiyear contract. The raiyats were required to pay the malikana, or 10 percent of the land revenue, to the zamindar whose lands they cleared and occupied. Even though the state bypassed the zamindar in this transaction, it still recognized his legal perquisites in this form.

Peasants without land or those with inadequate holdings were quick to respond to the offers of capital and accepted pahikasht status from zamindars, village headmen, birtias, and, at times, the East India Company. These pioneer settlers usually accepted annual leases without any permanent interest in the land. If they were willing to clear and plant wastelands, they paid initially low rents to the birtias, village headmen, or zamindars. The East India Company gave the latter, in turn, concessionaire tax-rate leases over periods of five to ten years.

Land was abundant and people relatively scarce. In Gorakhpur, the abundance of land prompted peasants to opt for pahikasht or annual tenancy leases rather than to seek out khudkasht rights of hereditary occupancy. If they brought in a successful crop in the first year of clearing and cultivation, the revenue paid to the zamindar or birtia was still at a low concessionary rate. But crops in the second, third, and fourth years were subject to rising rental demands. Many pahikasht tenants found it advantageous to take up a series of single-year leases on new lands each year. Pahikasht tenants on annual leases were unencumbered, free to move on, and free of the burden of sharing in the village expenses. In this early period, it became impossible to prevent the peasants from withdrawing their labor and moving from established villages to new sites. Often village headmen, birtias, and established zamindars found themselves in competition for robust tenants who could clear and occupy the land. In the face of labor shortage and abundant land, peasants became more demanding. If the terms offered were not to their liking, they simply moved on and sought a lease with other village headmen, birtias, or zamindars.

For the region of Gorakhpur, the overwhelming priorities of the colonial state were obvious. The strategic, political, and economic interests of the new state dictated this option. The wastelands or the uncultivated lands of the region were to be cleared, settled, and cultivated as rapidly as possible. The East India Company avoided drastic changes in the complex mix of property rights found in Gorakhpur in 1801. Company officers were willing to accept the legitimacy of the basic framework of agrarian rights inherited from the Mughal emperors. Rather than wholesale expulsions or rescissions of rights, the company found that the existing system of property rights in land could be used for this purpose. Zamindars, birtias, village headmen, and peasant cultivators all responded readily to incentives pressed upon them by the colonial state and by the market forces. In this early period, some movement was made toward a radical new form of property rights. In the absence of the zamindars' initiative, the state even went so far as to advance capital and negotiate revenue contracts with individual peasants.

A CENTURY OF MORAL
AND MATERIAL PROGRESS

Expanding cultivation cut deeply into the forests of Gorakhpur. Only gross estimates of the 1801 forested area can be made. The first British attempt at mapping was by Rennell in 1778 and delineated much of the *sarkar* (division of a province) of Gorakhpur, then under the nawab of Awadh, as forest land.[32] An official map of 1835, compiled by East India Company surveyors and cartographers, shows little change in the intervening decades.[33]

As we have observed, the new regime actively encouraged forest clearing and settlement. By 1830, the regime's attention shifted from the more easily accessible and less heavily forested wastelands in Gorakhpur to the more forbidding forest areas. One immediately compelling interest was that of timber and timber concessions. District collectors pressed zamindars to either cut timber themselves or to auction timber rights to European or Indian timber contractors. Rising demand for railway sleepers, for building timbers, and other construction needs encouraged a buoyant market.

The mechanisms by which the East India Company pressed land clearing continued for more remote, more heavily wooded areas. The settlement frontier moved north toward the foothills of the Himalayas every decade. In 1840, concerned that grantees were not given enough time to develop forest lands, the Board of Revenue granted leases for ten years. These leases were rapidly taken up, and the area of settlement and cultivation expanded as the forests contracted.

By 1850, the East India Company land development policies suddenly began to seem too successful. Alarmed by the rapidity with which grants were taken up and forest clearing in Gorakhpur was proceeding, the East India Company suddenly halted all new grants. The colonial state intervened with the zamindars and passed regulations that prohibited further clearing and cutting on forest lands. No new pioneering contracts or grants were to be issued by zamindars or by the state. This was a reversal of a half-century of official policy and a statement of direct state involvement in the district's land management.

In 1868, large portions of the most desirable timber tracts of *sal* were turned over to the newly formed Forest Department under the management of the conservator of forests, NorthWest Provinces. Ten years later, these lands were constituted reserved forests under the Government of India Forest Act of 1878. With additions, the total area of reserved forests in the Gorakhpur District was 110,926 acres or just 3.8 percent of the total area of the district. Additional forest lands under the control of private owners amounted to 178,596 acres to bring the area of officially recognized forests up to 10 percent of the district area.[34]

Most of the remaining private uncultivated lands had been cleared and settled by the end of the century. In addition to the pressures for expanded cultivation, Gorakhpur's sal forests supplied timber to meet the insatiable needs of the new railway system for sleepers and construction timbers. Only village forests and remnant tracts survived in Gorakhpur beyond the government reserves and lands held by a few large landholders. For example, Meer Ahmad Ali Shah, a resident Sufi, or Muslim mystic or saint, owned lands near Ramgarh on which the forest was preserved in order to provide fuel for the perpetual fire that burnt at his hut *(kutya)*.[35]

As the frontier proceeded north, demographic and economic growth followed. Gorakhpur's population rose steadily. A census taken in 1853 enumerated 1.8 million persons. New decennial censuses taken after 1872 showed a steady increase from 2.0 million in that year (generally considered an undercount) to 2.6 million in 1881 and 3.0 million in 1891 and remained steady at that figure in 1901 because of pandemic disease and scarcity in the intervening decade.

Although reliable survey figures for cultivated area are not yet available before midcentury, we can use the change in land revenues as a crude proxy measure. In 1802, the total revenue demanded from the cultivators of the larger Gorakhpur region amounted to approximately a half-million silver rupees. In 1840, the smaller Gorakhpur District's land revenue assessment (demand) was more than Rs. 1.5 million. (This was in a deflationary period as well). The land revenue survey and settlement completed in 1871 revealed that over half the total area or 1.5 million acres were under cultivation in Gorakhpur. By 1900, this figure had risen to 2 million acres (1,966,026 acres) or seven-tenths of the total area.

New crops enhanced rural productivity in nineteenth-century Gorakhpur. Given seed cuttings by the East India Company officials, cultivators avidly seized upon potatoes as a food crop.[36] State encouragement also helped adoption of indigo as a cash crop. There was a new market for indigo as a medium to convey the savings of East India Company officers and company profits to England. European planters leased land, built indigo processing facilities, and made cash advances to cultivators who delivered bundles of harvested plants to be processed. Bengal hemp, highly regarded in European markets, found a growing market for marine supplies and papermaking. Judging the conditions in Gorakhpur to be well suited for the crop, officials eventually obtained high-yielding seeds from wild plants growing in the Himalayan foothills. European technicians demonstrated the proper techniques for cultivating and processing hemp, and conducted experiments to improve production. Simultaneously, however, Gorakhpur lost a longstanding cash crop. The East India Company restricted poppy cultivation in Gorakhpur in favor of the opium-growing districts of Bihar in the east.

The East India Company in Gorakhpur largely succeeded in its political and economic goals. Under the modified Mughal property rights regime, different social classes actively converted wastelands and forests into intensively cultivated and settled lands. Although conservative in its approach to existing institutions, and unwilling to encourage drastic changes in local society, the East India Company officers pushed steadily for expansion and growth in the local economy.

NOTES

1. Bernard Cohn, "Representing Authority in Victorian India," in Bernard Cohn, *An Anthropologist among the Historians and Other Essays*, (New Delhi: Oxford University Press, 1994), 644.

2. Meena Bhargava, *State, Society, and Ecology: Gorakhpur in Transition, 1750–1830*, (New Delhi: Manohar, 1999).

3. See Chapter 1 in this volume, John F. Richards, "Toward a Global System of Property Rights in Land."

4. See Dharma Kumar and Meghnad Desai, eds., *The Cambridge Economic History of India*, (Cambridge, England; New York: Cambridge University Press, 1982), Vol. 2, for a systematic description of the British land revenue system for each of the major regions of the subcontinent.

5. Brian J. Murton, "Land and Class: Cultural, Social, and Biophysical Integration in Interior Tamilnadu in the Late Eighteenth Century," in Robert E. Frykenberg, ed., *Land Tenure and Peasant in South Asia*, (New Delhi: Orient Longman, 1977), 81–99, has the clearest discussion of these issues from a cultural and ecological perspective for Salem District in the 1790s at British annexation.

6. Peter Mayer, "Inventing Village Tradition: The Late 19th Century Origins of the North Indian Jajmani System." *Modern Asian Studies* 27 (1993) 357–95. This system slowly started to break down under colonial rule into arrangements between individual patrons and artisan or ritual specialist clients.

7. For a discussion of this complicated issue, see Gunnel Cederlof, *Bonds Lost: Subordination, Conflict, and Mobilisation in Rural South India, c. 1900–1970* (New Delhi: Manohar, 1997), 34–46; and Haruka Yanagisawa, *A Century of Change: Caste and Irrigated Lands in Tamilnadu, 1860s–1960s* (New Delhi: Manohar, 1996), 32–38.

8. See the discussion of this point in Anand A. Yang, *The Limited Raj: Agrarian Relations in Colonial India, Saran District, 1793–1920* (Berkeley: University of California Press, 1989).

9. See Ratnalekha Ray, "Landlords and Peasants: A Historiographical View of Rural Bengal From Pre-colonial to Colonial Times," *Journal of Peasant Studies* 11 (1984) 236–47, for an overview of the historiography of the Permanent Settlement and its effects. Ratnalekha Ray, *Change in Bengal Agrarian Society, c. 1760–1850* (New Delhi: Manohar, 1979).

10. Burton Stein, *Thomas Munro: The Origins of the Colonial State and His Vision of Empire* (New Delhi; New York: Oxford University Press, 1989). Nilmani Mukherjee, *The Ryotwari System in Madras, 1792–1827* (Calcutta: Firma K. L. Mukhopadhyay, 1962). Dharma Kumar and Meghnad Desai, eds., *The Cambridge Economic History of India* (Cambridge, England; New York: Cambridge University Press, 1982), Vol. 2, 86–177.

11. Stephen Henningham, *A Great Estate and Its Landlords in Colonial India: Darbhanga, 1860–1942* (New Delhi; New York: Oxford University Press, 1990), 61.

12. See, for example, the essay by Eric Stokes, "The Structure of Landholding in Uttar Pradesh, 1860–1948," in Eric Stokes, *The Peasant and the Raj: Studies in Agrarian Society and Peasant Rebellion in Colonial India*, Cambridge South Asian Studies 23, (Cambridge, England; New York: Cambridge University Press, 1978).

13. Dharma Kumar and Meghnad Desai, eds., *The Cambridge Economic History of India*, (Cambridge, England; New York: Cambridge University Press, 1982) Vol. 2, 178–206. Sumit Guha, *The Agrarian Economy of Bombay Deccan, 1818–1941* (New Delhi; New York: Oxford University Press, 1985).

14. Asiya Suddiqi, *Agrarian Change in a Northern Indian State: Uttar Pradesh, 1819–1833* (Oxford: Clarendon Press, 1973). Sulekh Chandra Gupta, *Agrarian Relations and Early British Rule in India: A Case Study of Ceded and Conquered Provinces: Uttar Pradesh, 1801–1833* (London: Asia Publishing House, 1963).

15. Inderjit Sharma, *Land Revenue Administration in the Punjab, 1849–1901* (New Delhi: Atlantic Publishers and Distributors, 1985).

16. Ratnalekha Ray, *Change in Bengal Agrarian Society, c. 1760–1850* (New Delhi: Manohar, 1979) 282–83.

17. F. Balfour to J. E. Colebrooke and J. Deane, April 5, 1808, Pre-Mutiny: Revenue—Collector's Office, Gorakhpur: Revenue Letters Issued to the Board of Commissioners, Vol. 117, Basta 17, June 1807–July 1809 (Regional State Archives, Allahabad).

18. Mufti Ghulam Hazarat, "Kawa-if-i Zila-i Gorakhpur," (India Office Library, London, A.D. 1810).

19. See Meena Bhargava, *State, Society, and Ecology: Gorakhpur in Transition, 1750–1830* (New Delhi: Manohar, 1999). Also see Meena Bhargava, "Perception

and Classification of the Rights of the Social Classes: Gorakhpur and the East India Company in the Late Eighteenth and Early Nineteenth Centuries," *Indian Economic and Social History Review* 30, no 2, 1993, 215–37.

20. *Report on the Settlement of Goruckpore-Bustee District* II, Allahabad, 1871, 205, para. 27.

21. Irfan Habib, *The Agrarian System of Mughal India* (Bombay, 1963), 131.

22. See Meena Bhargava, "Landed Property Rights in Transition: A Note on Cultivators and Agricultural Labourers in Gorakhpur in the Late Eighteenth and Nineteenth Centuries," *Studies in History* 12, no. 2, 1996, 243–53.

23. Mufti Ghulam Hazarat, "Kawa-if-i Zila-i Gorakhpur," (India Office Library, London, A.D. 1810).

24. Proceedings held in the *kutcherry* of Collector Gorakhpur between the Collector and Devi Prasad, *Mukhtar* of Raja Sobheraj Singh of *pargana* Mansur Nagar Basti (undated), Proceedings, Board of Revenue: Fort William, Vol. 33, May 1807 (Uttar Pradesh State Archives, Lucknow).

25. *Report on the Settlement of Goruckpore-Bustee District* I, Allahabad, 1871, 49, para. 89.

26. To, F. Balfour, Consultation, May 10, 1808, Pre-Mutiny: Revenue— Commissioner's Office, Gorakhpur, Vol. 3, Misl 8 (Regional State Archives, Allahabad).

27. Buchanan-Hamilton, "An Account of the Northern Part of the District of Gorakhpur," Book IV, MSS. EUR. D92, 57 (India Office Library, London).

28. Extract from a memorandum by Holt Mackenzie, October 19, 1826, *Selections from Revenue Records: NorthWest Provinces*, A.D. *1822–1833*, Allahabad, 1872.

29. I. Carter to H. Newnham, January 4, 1819, Pre-Mutiny Records: Office of the Board of Revenue— Letters issued to the Collectors of Gorakhpur by the Board of Commissioners and the Board of Revenue, Vol. 38, 1801–1820 (Uttar Pradesh State Archives, Lucknow).

30. Extract of a letter from the Secretary to Government to the Court of Directors, October 4, 1815, Pre-Mutiny: Revenue Correspondence—Letters received from Government by the Board of Revenue, Vol. I, 1810–1816 (Uttar Pradesh State Archives, Lucknow).

31. A.D. 1821 Regulation, Territorial Department, and Secretary to Government, Pre-Mutiny: Revenue Correspondence—Letters Received from Government by the Board of Revenue, Vol. IV, 1820–1822 (Uttar Pradesh State Archives, Lucknow).

32. James Rennell, *Memoirs of a Map of Hindustan*, reprint, Patna, 1975.

33. H. R. Nevill, *District Gazetteers of the United Provinces of Agra and Oudh— Gorakhpur* 31, Allahabad, 1909, 19.

34. Ibid., 20.

35. Report on the Gorakhpur forests by Major G. F. Pearson, conservator of forests, North-West Provinces, *Selections from the Records of Government—North-West Provinces* 4, no. 1, Allahabad, 1870.

36. Translation of a report from the *qanungos* of *pargana* Anowlah, Enclosure in, Acting Collector, Gorakhpur to Charles Buller, October 24, 1803, Proceedings, Board of Revenue: Fort William, Vol. 11, January–February, 1805 (Uttar Pradesh State Archives, Lucknow).

9

State Property Rights in Nature (with Special Reference to India)

RONALD J. HERRING

PROPERTY RIGHTS, INTERESTS, AND VALUE: THE GREAT TRANSFORMATION

Among the many and overlapping causes of environmental degradation, is there a role to assign the system of property rights? Since property systems organize incentives and distribute consequences of economic activity, a plausible case can be made ex ante. Moreover, one of the most powerful organizing frames for discussing environmental degradation is the "tragedy of the commons," which is about collective failure to create property systems from open-access situations, resulting in degradation. This chapter argues that one of the most important forms of property in this discussion must be state property in nature. The dynamics of states and environments illustrate both why state property in nature is necessary in market society and why it frequently fails.

For market society to work, there must be both property and commodities. The sharpest observer of the making of market society, Karl Polanyi, wrote in 1944 (1957, 130): "Production is interaction of man and nature; if this process is to be organized through a self-regulating mechanism of barter and exchange, then man and nature must be brought into its orbit; they must be subject to supply and demand, this is, be dealt with as commodities, as goods produced for sale." But if the development of property systems and commodification of land and labor are necessary for economic growth, as both Marxists and mainstream economists agree, the residues of social dislocations and externalities created in the transition fall somewhere else—often by default on the state. This is the general problematic of Polanyi's "great transformation."

The specific tension in property systems *in nature*[1] is the disputed telos of the system: Accumulation and strategic imperatives[2] compete with preservation and conservation. The fundamental political-economic project for societies is sorting out rules for using and distributing scarce things in the face of conflicting interests. Human interests in nature are most visible in nature appropriated for human use; appropriated nature generates livelihoods and use values, as conceptualized in both mainstream and Marxian economic logic. The collective objective (and intermittently subjective) human interest in nature *for itself* posits imperatives of ecological integrity as a public good, independent of use values—introducing the conflict between conservationist and preservationist agendas. Internationally, the latter has been identified with rich nations, whereas the public good itself has been held to be disproportionately located in poorer nations; distribution of remnants of the natural world—within and across nations—then introduces differing objective interests. Though natural systems are decidedly nonterritorial, territoriality is thus introduced into the morphology of human interests by natural facts.

Karl Polanyi (1957, 34, 41) subtitled a section of Chapter 3 of *The Great Transformation* "Habitation Versus Improvement," borrowing from an official English document of 1607; the great transformation was in part the substitution of "habitation," which we now call "subsistence," as telos with "improvement," or in contemporary language "development." Polanyi was no dreamer, nor a complete romanticist; as he said (1957, 250–51): ". . . [T]he restoration of the past is as impossible as the transferring of our troubles to another planet." Yet he insists on the systemic nature of the troubles, and uses the problems as analytical tools. These tools help us understand the origins of state property in nature as well as its deficiencies as a conservation mechanism.

Individuated and state-guaranteed property rights almost certainly increase the probability that land will be "developed," as Douglass North (1990) argues persuasively. Changes in property relations in the direction of greater conduciveness to "development" simultaneously increase the likelihood of resistance from losers. The literature on "defensive reactions" derives from unresolved conflicts in Polanyi's great transformation. Polanyi noted (1957, 71):

> But land and labor are no other than the human beings themselves
> of which every society consists and the natural surroundings in

which it exists. To include them in the market mechanism is to subordinate the substance of society to the laws of the market.

In analyzing the defeat of "Indians" by colonists in the New England portion of North America, William Cronon (1983, 166–167) noted a fundamental difference in respective moral economies. "Indians" perceived a much broader range of "resources" because they knew nature—that is, they knew how to use so many more things—but they perceived a very limited range of commodities, because they had no way to accumulate wealth. Here their need for mobility mattered; but they also had no need to accumulate, as the cultural system of hierarchy and rewards made impossible any movement upward simply by becoming richer. Colonists perceived far fewer resources—they did not know how to transform so large a percentage of the landscape into use values—but far more commodities; and they were tied into larger networks in which the commodities could bring utility—a global capitalist economy. For this reason the needs of Indians in the ecosystem were limited, and thus the damage was in theory limited (population pressure notwithstanding, or bracketed for a moment); but the colonists could accumulate endlessly. Money, now also a commodity, allowed accumulation, and thus the further development of commoditization. Novel laws enabling ownership of land transformed a world of forests to one of fences, in Cronon's metaphor. In his concluding chapter of *Changes in the Land*, which he titles "That Wilderness Should Turn a Mart," Cronon notes both the contemporary astonishment that such a transformation occurred and our own retrospective surprise that it happened so fast. This was a great transformation on forced march, propelled by colonial power.

When Polanyi conceptualized the commoditization of nature a central element in the "great transformation" to market society, he likewise had in mind a process much broader than mere enclosures of the classic form: "What we call land is an element of nature inextricably interwoven with man's institutions. To isolate it and form a market out of it was perhaps the weirdest of all undertakings of our ancestors (Polanyi 1957, 178)." In his formulation, premarket economic relations, norms, and outcomes were "embedded" or "submerged" in social relations generally; the extraction and elevation of market-driven dynamics from their social mooring produces significant social conflicts and centrally involves the state (compare Neale 1988). There is nothing "natural" about the market as arbiter of allocative decisions; challenges to market allocative rules evoked the use rights established by custom and common law as bases for opposition (for example, K. S. Singh 1986; Guha 1989). For Polanyi, market society was inherently destabilizing: Its "self-regulating" character was a "myth." The state was central.

Polanyi generalized this dialectic in his postulation of a "double movement" (1957, 130):

> For a century the dynamics of modern society was governed by a
> double movement: the market expanded continuously but this
> movement was met by a countermovement checking the expan-
> sion in definite directions. Vital though such a countermovement
> was for the protection of society, in the last analysis it was incom-
> patible with the self-regulation of the market, and thus with the
> market system itself.

This simultaneous "countermovement" to the dislocations induced by
the commoditization of everything "was more than the usual defensive
behavior of a society faced with change; it was a reaction against a dislocation which attacked the fabric of society, and which would have destroyed
the very organization of production that the market had called into being."

Much of the conflict over "the commons" (see "Common Property"
section that follows) is ideologically a conflict between alternative
meanings of property, the appropriate limits to markets, and the rights of
states to impose novel proprietary claims to "protect society" from the
implications of the market-driven growth process that is part of state legitimation. Popular conceptualizations of property in India insisted on
recognition of a socially defined (and disputed) "bundle of rights" (Baden-
Powell 1892, V.I, 216 passim; Herring 1983) in land. The making of market
society entails the long process of collapsing differentiated use rights into a
system of ownership in which property rights are located concretely and
specified precisely—in general rendered more "legible" in James Scott's formulation (1998).

In the Indian subcontinent, for example, the effect of colonial law was
to simplify, collapse, and locate concretely the bundle of rights in land with
the objective of creating property rights in the sense of market society (for
example, Logan 1887, I, 670–96; Neale 1988). Simultaneously, vast tracts
were "reserved" for the state on the claim that unused "waste" land had
traditionaly been "the property of the state" (Baden-Powell 1892, I, 236).
The privatization of property went hand in hand with the creation of state
property. In this transformation, the use rights of subordinate strata were
nominally curtailed but on the ground depended more on the capacity to
exert local power or evade regulation than on law per se. Defensive reactions were set in motion by attempts of the state to claim and manage
nature previously claimed as a matter of local right (for example, Guha
1985, 1989, 1990; K. S. Singh 1986; Omvedt 1987).

The colonial state's marriage of revenue/developmental imperatives (plantations, logging, railroads) with an emerging scientific discourse of forest management and conservation established both an internal dialectic of colonial policy debates on land use (cf. Presler 1987; Tucker 1984), and a continuing confrontation with local societies' definitions of the local rights in what were held to be commons. As the imperatives of developing states are constant over time, this conflict survived the demise of colonial rule, and continues to be manifest in resistance to state encroachment for "development projects"—for example, the resistance of upstream forest communities to the state's claim to develop hydroelectric and irrigation potential through dam construction (CSE 1986, 99–120; Kothari 1995a). The scope for conflict is large; the Forest Department alone administers 23 percent of the Indian surface area (Madsen 1995, 3).

Despite overwhelming pressure to locate property rights with the state and individual, commons remain in India, though dwindling in incidence. Nevertheless, N. S. Jodha, in a path-breaking empirical analysis, has documented the importance of common-property resources to the village poor in India (Jodha 1986). His survey found that the economic benefits of using the commons were greater for the village poor than were the benefits of government programs targeted for their welfare. Privatization of village commons in India has constricted further the survival options of the poorest villagers. Moreover, the commons remains part of the ideology of resistance to encroachment by state and market. Finally, of the possible strong statements linking forms of property to environmental degradation, the most influential has of course concerned the "tragedy of the commons."

COMMON PROPERTY

Much modern discourse on environmental degradation and property systems takes place under the shadow of the "tragedy of the commons," a simple and influential model that explained why maximization of individual interests in resource use could result in catastrophe (for example, Ostrom 1990). The logic of that argument has been used by states as legitimation for seizing control of local commons on grounds of conservation; Leviathan may not be popular, but it putatively acts in the general interest when individuals cannot generate the collective action necessary to provide public goods. This construction has perhaps been so successful because it resonates with a common-sensical aphorism ([wrongly] attributed to Aristotle): "that which is everyone's concern is in practice no one's concern."

Perhaps the tragedy of the commons has been discussed to the point of diminishing returns. Yet it seems important to consider the commons as a property form because of the increasing theoretical and *political* arguments for the superiority of local commons over the state leviathan in managing natural resources (see next section, "Leviathan: Real-World States and Meta-Commons Dilemmas"). "Our rule in our village" is the political expression of the current fascination with decentralization as the solution to environmental degradation (Kothari and Parajuli 1993; Parajuli 2000).

In a deceptively simple and influential analytical move in the "tragedy" logic, maximization of individual material interests was held to produce suboptimal, perhaps disastrous, consequences for that terrain: "the tragedy of the commons" (Hardin 1968; cf. Feeny et al. 1990; Ostrom 1990; Shiva 1986). But "tragedy" is only a part of the puzzles surrounding the commons.[3] Robert Wade's formulation (1988, 184) distinguishes between commons situations and commons dilemmas:

> The exploitation of a common-pool resource is always a commons situation, in the sense that any resource characterized by joint use and subtractive benefits is *potentially* subject to crowding, deple-tion and degradation. But only some commons situations become commons dilemmas: those where joint use and subtractive benefits are combined with scarcity, and where in consequence joint users start to interfere with each other's use.

Properties of scarcity and subtractive benefits are largely properties of particular ecologies, given exogenous human demand. Prevention of esca-lation from commons situation to dilemma to tragedy is a function of property systems: institutionalized patterns of rights and obligations. Hardin's tragedy resulted not from a failure *of* common property, but rather a failure to preserve common-pool resources precisely because no common-property arrangements to limit use evolved. It is here that some overarching authority—such as that of the state—seems logically neces-sary, to prevent escalation to full tragedy. States certainly legitimate themselves in these terms: the provision of public goods.

Meta-Commons Dilemmas

The logic in the tragedy-of-the-commons literature assumes that the value of the commons is instrumental. This notion carries over in the dominant policy language of common-property *resources;* the natural is valuable insofar as it constitutes a resource, something to be exploited. Grazing lands in the original paradigm have value because they form the foundation for livelihoods; concrete material interests are identifiable. This instrumental view of nature in market economics is shared by the Marxian tradition.[4]

This perspective presupposes a nature already appropriated and altered for human use. When Blaikie and Brookfield (1987, 1–7) discuss land "degradation," they use the Latin etymology of "rank," as though assigning ranks to capacities of the physical surface of the planet were unproblematic; they (knowingly) reduce "land" to soil.[5] If ecology has taught us anything, it is the irreducible interdependence of systems. To take but one example, soil conservation locally may be futile in the face of soil contamination from acid rain or water depletion from climatic change or flooding from upstream deforestation.

The tragedy of the meta-commons is the failure of collective action to preserve the integrity of nature itself: the common biophysical systems which support and depend on a full complement of species and not merely our own. Even the most "rational," conserving use of pastures would be ruinous to the global commons if all forests were converted to pastures. As Blaikie and Brookfield understand, one person's environmental degradation is another's bonanza; wetlands regularly turn into meadows over time, which is good for agriculturalists, bad for biodiversity. Cronon described the vision of the colonists in North America as follows (1983, 5): ". . . [T]he transformation of wilderness betokened the planting of a garden, not the fall from one; any change in the New England environment was divinely ordained and wholly positive." Richard Eaton's (1990, 1993) study of the expanding frontier of cultivation at the expense of wetland forests in Bengal circa 1200–1760 illustrates this process: Islamic "saint-entrepreneurs" made use of symbolic appeals, underwritten by the space provided by superior authorities, to mobilize for collective action which achieved some public good for participants (additional agricultural land) but simultaneously destroyed the mangrove wetlands in a piecemeal fashion at the margins.

The perception of conservation of a usable resource as a collective good is not nearly so problematic as conceptualizing preservation of ecosystems as a public good independently of their utility as resources. This is the classic Pinchot-Muir controversy of American historical experience, representing the struggle between meaning systems privileging conservation in opposition to those centered on preservation, or the conflict between social ecology and "deep" ecology (Herring 1991).

The political argument for conservation depends on the commercial value of that which is to be conserved; conservation law in colonial India was generated by the imperatives of long-term access to forest products for export, military uses, and construction of rail nets (for example, Guha 1989, 37–61). The politics of *preservation* must be rooted in more tenuous values of aesthetics, risk, or species ethics (derived from the reality of species mastery). Responding collectively to the meta-commons dilemma requires recognition of interests which are temporally removed, collective in the broadest sense (specieswide), and embedded in the uncertainty of a technical discourse which can be evaluated only by a tiny elite.

It is true, as Robert Wade concludes in *Village Republics,* that our models of collective action often lack utility in dealing with real cases.[6] Nevertheless, the motivational base of the model is plausible so long as we can safely assume material interests as a driving force. Wade shows that collective action to preserve common resources and increase production varies directly with material benefits entailed in the public good.[7] Ostrom's (for example, 1990) work illustrates the conditions under which user groups may collectively preserve a usable resource. The conditions are difficult to meet, but there are many cases, across time and space. Staying within the logic of methodological individualism, meta-commons dilemmas present far more formidable obstacles to local collective action. The argument for state intervention to prevent a tragedy of the natural commons is correspondingly stronger.

LEVIATHAN: REAL-WORLD STATES AND META-COMMONS DILEMMAS

The original "tragedy" model assumed that no cooperative strategies would emerge among graziers maximizing their individual gains from a common pasture. One solution was then private property.[8] No rational person would degrade his/her own land by overgrazing, and therefore the division of common pasture into individually owned plots would avert the destruction of a common resource (cf. Ostrom 1986, 8).

But individuated property rights are useful only for ensuring that the level of exploitation does not measurably degrade the resource any further than the value of the short-term benefits of exploitation—as determined by market forces. Conservation will, even in the best-case scenario, be limited to the very loose constraint that degradation does not interfere with market rationality. Market rationality, in turn, will only incidentally coincide with ecological rationality (compare Singh 1976; Nadkarni 1987). Ecosystems are large and complex; individually rational behaviors (diversion of surface water, draining of wetlands, clearing of forests) produce the likelihood of counterfinality in a context which is extralocal and extended in time. As importantly, human lives are short in terms of the evolution of ecosystems; it is difficult to imagine a fit between short-term interests and intergenerational "rationality," or justice, being generated by the market (Nadkarni 1987, 360–61 et passim).

As a consequence, one solution is that of Thomas Hobbes (and the much earlier Indian political philosopher Kautilya[9]): a powerful state which could impose its will on subjects for their own (common) good. Kautilya noted that in the absence of a strong state, the large eat the small and all order and justice are lost.

State-centric developmental processes accentuated the proprietary role of the state. State-led economic change in India and extensive claims to property took form with colonial rule, but were presaged by the *vedic*, *puranic*, and state-craft literature of India long before (Raghunandan 1987, 545). Much of the debate at the intellectual and regime level (for example, Guha 1990) centered on how much can be assumed about local capacity to manage local commons dilemmas, preventing their escalation to tragedy. The dominant understanding in policy craft for a very long time has been that of Kautilya: "Villages" (and "villagers") need Leviathan.

In talking with state managers about the reasons for success and failure in state control of nature, I have found a number of discrete, though sometimes commingling, themes consistent with the academic literature. First, there are the *Incompetent Villagers*. Robert Wade (1988) is certainly right in arguing that much has been assumed by the powerful about the incapacity of Indian villages for collective action, but very little has been established empirically. Second, there are the *Lamentably Desperate Villagers*. In this view, congruent with the Maslovian hierarchy of needs and postindustrial society worldview, pervasive destitution drives villagers to acts of ecocide which, if not justifiable, are at least understandable. Blaikie and Brookfield (1987, 48) make the case more generically: ". . . [P]overty is the basic cause of poor management and the consequence of poor management is deepening poverty." There is a cultural predisposition, now politically incorrect, but persistent: the *Backward Villagers*. Jawaharlal Nehru said: "A village, normally speaking, is backward intellectually and culturally and no progress can be made from a backward environment." Dr. B. R. Ambedkar, a prime drafter of the Constitution of newly independent India, said: "What is the village but a sink of localism, a den of ignorance, narrow-mindedness and communalism? . . . I hold these village republics have been the ruination of India" (Mitra 1997, 3–4). In all scenarios, villagers need guidance, control, and development from the Center.

Leviathan as solution to commons dilemmas is problematic, however, even in political theory. Messy problems of policy formulation—in a sense, another form of the collective action problem—render expression of general will problematic. There is as well the absence of a guarantee, or even a likelihood, that the state will not behave in the same self-seeking, social-disregarding manner as individuals (cf. Ostrom 1986). Developmental states have historically behaved precisely in this fashion (for example, Kothari 1995a).

Leviathan as metaphor conveniently links will and implementation in one capable actor. States of the subcontinental region are (selectively) "soft" (in Gunnar Myrdal's memorable formulation). Real states in the subcontinental region demonstrate not only the permeability and bureaucratic pathologies which generate "softness," but also both vertical and horizontal incoherence; as lower levels of the state ramify into society, they become less and less distinguishable *from* society, much as blood vessels ramify into capillaries and finally disappear into tissue. Nancy Peluso's (1992) study of Java concludes in a similar vein that villagers' access depends on individual negotiations with forest officers. As the state seeks to change its relations to villagers and to development generally, it has to work through local patrons via an exchange logic—to get things done, you work through the power structure at the village level (for example, 237, 240–241). Neither political will at the top nor transmission capacity through the system can be assumed. More importantly, real implementation must take place on the ground, where the local state exhibits the permeability, incapacity, and embeddedness characteristics in extreme form.

The permeability of the state to powerful interests bent on exploitation—or "development"—is a pervasive phenomenon in South Asia and the source of significant environmental degradation (see, for example, CSE 1986, 353–82). Even assuming relative autonomy and capacity, structural pressures for tax revenue and hard currency earnings have abetted environmental degradation throughout the subcontinent (see, for example, Agarwal 1985, 363–66). But most importantly, Leviathan is not a stable configuration; exclusion and control evoke the politics of opposition and evasion, reducing state capacity. The conflict between the Bodos and the state over one of India's World Heritage Convention natural sites (see later section, "Sequestering Nature and Rigging Markets in India") is illustrative of this conflict, which continues in more or less overt form throughout the world.

Enhanced in scope by these property rights, the state itself becomes increasingly subject to creation of new property forms. Madhu Kishwar writes of "'Naukri as Property,'" reflecting the common view in the subcontinent that the state can be possessed not by the public but by public servants—who are neither "public" (in terms of transparency and account-ability) nor "servants" in any meaningful sense. Kishwar (1997, 16) argues that "the entire bureaucracy and the political class have come to believe that a government job is indeed the most inviolate form of private prop-erty." As a consequence: "Appointments, postings and transfers are in fact a big industry . . ." and are "actually purchased in the same way as one would buy a piece of property." Sinecures then can be leased like any other piece of property, and are expected to yield a rent—that is, corruption pay-ments.[10] As the state is colonized by rent seekers and patronage networks, its capacity to manage property in the public interest declines precipitously.

For these reasons, creation of "public" property resolves little. New political conflicts around defining the public and determining its collective "interests" are structurally inevitable. Reserved forest lands are not "pri-vate" property, but de jure prohibited use rights are often for sale (illegally) in practice. Legal definition of reservation for a public purpose merely introduces a conflict between the state's historically contingent claims on monopoly of definition of the public good and those of inhabitants and users of forests. With the globalization of environmental policy, the con-tingent nature of state property claims becomes even more compromised as the definition of public good moves even further from the proximate users of nature.[11]

The tragedy of the commons in South Asia is then a more serious case of counterfinality than even Hardin's pessimism implied. This is true because the theoretically possible solutions apply better to appropriated nature than to nature for itself and because states are even theoretically unlikely to behave as benevolent Leviathans. In practice, Leviathans evoke resistance on the ground for their paramilitary occupation of nature, criminalization of subsistence routines, and ineffectiveness. Writing on Java, Nancy Peluso excoriates the "custodial paramilitary" model of state resource control which produces "secret wars and silent insurgency" inim-ical to conservation (1992, 235, 236).

Enforcement of state property claims presupposes state capacity. At the point of contact with people, the state is a bureaucrat, an individual, however much an instantiation of structure. Individuals are not perfectly substitutable—not only do they differ in terms of values, commitment, integrity, and energy, but even more crucially in their connections, and hence potential for effectiveness and the personalistic constraints under which they act. Threat of transfer is a very real consideration of officials attempting to carry out policy in the face of local political opposition. Some courageous individuals resist these pressures; some even die as a result. Others, being more rational, go along in order to get along.[12]

Governance rather than management becomes the issue; and here the question is less the form of property than property's relational character.

When the state is more enemy than public trust, confrontation and evasion are more likely than cooperation; governance gives way to coercion. Protected areas are attractive to guerrilla forces, smugglers, drug merchants, and bandits for the same reason that they are attractive to preservationists: They are isolated and undeveloped. The famous poacher and smuggler Veerappan is archetypal. For more than a decade, he smuggled ivory from South India and, when tuskers became rare, turned to sandalwood. Efforts to track and capture Veerappan led to police personnel being killed in ambushes and encounters: six individuals in 1993 alone, including senior officers. He knew the terrain, had kinship connections among the Padiyachi Gounder community, and moved easily among the villages, where police are feared and distrusted. In 1993, the job of catching Veerappan was transferred from police to the paramilitary Border Security Force (BSF). Their tactics treated all villagers as suspected criminals; those suspected of withholding information or aiding Veerappan were threatened or tortured.[13] In Karnataka and Tamilnadu, at least ninety-seven people have been arrested and twenty killed in "encounters."

The cognitive world of the police and the BSF demarcates easily members of a gang, informants, and supporters: all legitimate targets of suppression and coercion. The villagers themselves have a more nuanced notion of what "support" for Veerappan means. Many simply fear the smuggler. One man who was tortured into talking by the police said: "Veerappan had threatened he would cut me into fine pieces if I talked to the police" (*India Today* 7-31-93, 34). Others consider support an obligation of kinship. The relational world between state and society is thus not simply one of power and authority, but also a cognitive one. Failing to apprehend this, repression of the sea in which outlaws swim builds additional opposition to the state, undermining authority and hence proprietary claims.

Veerappan gives news conferences and in 1996 demanded the granite concession—the right to sell the stone—from the state as a price for ceasing his other illegal activities. The state's claim that certain stretches of terrain and certain components of ecosystems are state property, to be neither commoditized nor encroached, has little deterred his livelihood, though overharvesting (the slaughter of tuskers) did.

Assertion of state property rights then comes alive or perishes on the ground, in the concrete relations between social actors and bearers of authority. When wildlife trade is connected to socially ensconced bandits, kidnappers, and insurgents (as in the case of the Bodos in Manas), the inability of the state to enforce its claims in nature is merely a reflection of the larger phenomenon of parallel power beyond the reach of state authority. More mundane considerations of compliance enforcement include the structure of incentives for enforcers. The Tiwari Report, which recommended establishment of a Ministry of Environment (India 1980, 90), noted that because of the "lower emoluments" of Wildlife Guards compared to those of the police (but facing similar dangers), "guards rather tend to associate with poachers than resist them."

An officer of long field experience explained to me that politicization of public service has reached such a level that even the lowest level of forest guard is considered a patronage resource, resulting in a cadre of enforcers who have little interest or expertise in natural-resource issues. His conclusion on the prospects for enforcement is that individual officers matter greatly and that trusting relations between the state and the local society, though rare, are the only means to enforcement ends.

In these cases, local enforcement of property claims bends back on macropolitical culture and practice—politicization of the public service, salaries, and emoluments (on which, see India 1996). Enforcement of state property claims turns on the local legitimacy of the state. In India, this legitimacy is low because of people's experience with the minions of the Forest Department. The argument for a capable state presupposes a legitimate state; legitimacy turns on the crucial question of whose interests Leviathan will serve, or is perceived locally to be serving. In a hierarchical world economic system, state legitimacy may well be grounded first in precisely that form of development which has devastated so much of the global environment. The growth-legitimized state can hardly be the legitimate demander of sacrifices to preserve as nature space and commodities desperately needed by poor people.

From the "Idiocy of Village Life" to Local Knowledge

Understanding that paramilitary command and control systems of arrogant states have often served neither conservation nor people, a discernible, and plausible, promotion of localism in scale and indigeneity in knowledge has taken the field. A fortuitous confluence of local knowledge, local practice, local institutions, and local communities in environmental policy now constitutes a "celebration of the local" (Herring 1998). State denigration coincides with the liberalization Zeitgeist that constituted the "Washington consensus" on development; the counterreaction displaces the question of authority by changing its locus—from bad states to good localities. This reversal of fortune of the state in the field of nature is ironic, for it threatens to obscure the core meaning of ecology itself—the interconnectedness of processes across levels and units of social organization.

Contributing to the elevation of community solutions were dramatic instances of local resistance to mega-development and its ecological damages, as well as critiques by intellectuals and activists of externally imposed and alien knowledge systems—resonating with centuries of intellectual tradition in the "North" as well as the contemporary "South." Ideologies of empowerment for poor people and goals of social equity converged with heightened respect for local knowledge, conservation ethics, and administration by communities. There are convinced scholars with a wealth of ethnographic confirmation.[14]

Localism then presents a powerful, in places hegemonic, vision of conditions for the preservation and restoration of nature: a robust triad of indigenous knowledge (ecological, institutional, and ethical), effective (and affective) community, and decentralized political institutions. The countervailing view questions the romanticization of "local knowledge" on epistemological grounds, the assumption of "community" as social reality, the reality and stability of values rooted in local nature, and the dangers inherent in ceding public authority to local power.[15] The paradox is that ecological dynamics simultaneously push up and down the scale ladder: up because ever-larger nets of authority are necessary to cope with the complexity of systems and down because of the dismal history of command and control systems in nature.

New currents in participatory and local environmental protection are responding to a considerable history. The notion that natural systems will be degraded by human use absent centralized political authority has long been dominant. States from the ancient to the colonial to the contemporary have used the presumed tragedy of the commons as legitimation for intervention, command, and control; these systems are now almost universally under attack as elitist and undemocratic (in Oregon as in Assam). Arguably, such systems of control by necessity reduce diversity of cultural and institutional forms and of the knowledge embedded therein. This reduction in diversity may be as dangerous in the social sphere as in the biological. But is the obverse true: Does taking power from a central state enhance prospects for preserving natural system functions? Decay of the state, and of authority generally in Russia, for example, seems not to enhance freedom the way advocates of laissez-faire would argue, nor does it improve substantive outcomes in public health or provision of social overhead capital or other common-good functions. Denigration of state power does not produce a reflexive solution in decentralization—or anarchy.

Community has a wholesome ring, far better than state or bureaucracy. Yet in critiques of a misconstrued romanticization, "community" also receives a harder look. The theoretical critique may take the form of methodological individualism or structural stratification theory. From the view of methodological individualism, communities are unlikely to form themselves, for reasons of collective action problems (Wade 1988). From the viewpoint of stratification theorists, communities may be well formed; but for purposes of dominant fragments, however defined—in Rousseau's terms, the expression of will in such communities does not represent the "general" will, only the dominant. The empirical critique is that comparatively communities exhibit quite a range of environmental values and knowledge; scale is no guarantee of either process or substantive outcomes (Herring 1998). The property rights/wise use movement in the United States uses terror against the state and environmentalists in defense of their claim ("right") to use public lands for private advantage (see David Helvaarg's *War against the Greens*).

The critique of localism from ecological science has to do with the scale of ecological systems—inevitably supralocal and therefore necessitating supralocal vision, monitoring, and institutions. The normative critique is that local claims to autonomy preclude spreading the benefits of use of nature to a larger population—justice, either intergenerational or cross-sectional, is not necessarily served if locality implies ownership. If community A's traditional terrain (which may well have been taken from community B centuries back) contains gold, and community B's turf only sagebrush and scrub thorn, is the windfall legitimately the property of A based on territorial propinquity? Is there no larger interest? Where would the authority to adjudicate reside?

Whatever one's normative position on localism, the reality is that property rights are necessarily local in character, though nested in complex systems. In a number of Indian languages, there is an aphorism which runs roughly: "Above there is god, and below the keeper of land records" (*patwari* and so on) (Herring 1983). The implication is that no one in between matters much. Local keepers of records of rights in land are, of course, and have always been in theory part of "the state." In fact, they are very much embedded in local society. One's rights in land depend on what the patwari says, on who can pressure or intimidate the patwari, on the courts' interpretation of the law, the differential staying power of parties to the dispute, perhaps the Supreme Court's decision, and ultimately on the local state's will and capacity to implement the courts' decision. Just as "all politics is local," all rights are ultimately local. State claims to property in nature depend in the last instance on someone at the level of the patwari.

Property rights in India are embedded in a very complicated political structure. The political system is federal; much that happens at the Center cannot be assumed to effect policy in the States. The form of federalism itself is under continuous renegotiation.[16] An appendix to the Tiwari Report, which recommended the creation of a separate Ministry of Environment, commented, for example: "State governments are not interested in preserving wildlife" (India 1980, 91). The Ministry of Environments and Forests (MOEF) report for the World Bank on *Environmental Action Programmes-India* (India 1992a, 24) was sweeping in its condemnation of the "low priority" accorded environmental protection in many States. Moreover, the Center's political complexion has undergone significant alteration, moving from single-party dominance in the first two decades of independence to considerable instability in recent decades. An unstable Center in turn means that bargaining with the States becomes more decisive; the Center husbands its political capital for issues of great urgency (such as maintaining a fragile coalition government).

But governments can hardly go to conferences abroad and plead incapacity and fragmentation of authority; international negotiations are displays of stateness. Agreements reached assume real capacity on the ground. International treaties in practice demonstrate the reasons for fragility in the state's claim to property rights in nature. State capacity is limited, and local populations have strong normative and political claims against enforcement. These ground realities, as much as sovereignty claims, hinder the formation of real international proprietary claims.

PROPERTY CLAIMS IN INTERNATIONAL SOFT LAW: THE DOUBLE MOVEMENT

Karl Polanyi concluded presciently in the pre-ecological age of 1944 (1957, 184):

> The economic argument could be easily expanded so as to include the conditions of safety and security attached to the integrity of the soil and its resources—such as the vigor and stamina of the population, the abundance of food supplies, the amount and character of defense materials, even the climate of the country which might suffer from the denudation of forests, from erosions and dust bowls, all of which, ultimately, depend upon the factor land, yet none of which respond to the supply-and-demand mechanism of the market. Given a system entirely dependent upon market functions for the safeguarding of its existential needs, confidence will

naturally turn to such forces outside the market system which are capable of ensuring common interests jeopardized by the system.

Just as the embeddedness of local commons logically necessitated a larger scale of authority, only cooperation at the international level would address the potentially global tragedy of the meta-commons. A species-level learning process has dramatically expanded not only the scale over which control of environmental processes must be exercised, but the breadth of implications for economic life. Killing of endangered species in India, for example, indicates a world market which can be controlled only through international collective action to establish authority.

Emergence of a global nature regime with state-like properties is a genuinely new manifestation of Polanyi's "double movement." It coexists uneasily with a global neoliberal economic regime. This simultaneous emergence seemingly reflects Polanyi's historical observation and theoretical expectation: "Markets and regulation grew up together." There is a contradictory dialectic in the global demand that the international system become more a market, absent state meddling, and the simultaneous global demand that market failures and externalities (of which ecological integrity is perhaps the most egregious) be considered in global terms.

Global neoliberalism, which is not about justice or ecological integrity but about growth, may prove unhealthy for global environmental cooperation and success. Globalization of markets and market reforms in the former socialist bloc have had a perverse effect on the Convention on International Trade in Endangered Species of Flora and Fauna (CITES) in India, for example. Eastern European and Russian entry into the market, operating with hard currency and fewer constraints on trade, has accelerated depletion of endangered species in India (Herring and Bharucha 1999).[17] Truly global free trade looks better if you are not a tiger.

The late twentieth century witnessed a sea change in the valence attached to state intervention by mass publics and intellectuals. States are increasingly seen as more a part of the problem (any problem) than of the solution. Yet the character of meta-commons dilemmas makes a strong case for larger than local authority, even though the state's role to date frequently has been destructive. It was centralized authority which protected "Silent Valley"—the last rainforest in the Western Ghats—from a (democratic, representative) state legislature bent on "development," but the Indian state has also pressed for destruction in numerous other cases. State property—which Silent Valley eventually became—offers a means to an end, but it is an end in competition with often more powerful interests and values.

SEQUESTERING NATURE AND
RIGGING MARKETS IN INDIA

Sequestering Nature

In an investigation on the destruction of wildlife in India, the high-level Subramanian Committee used a telling metaphor (1994, 23): "To use a common analogy, we have kept our valuables—the wildlife, in a bank—in protected areas, and unless we take steps to prevent the bank from being robbed, we are likely to lose all our valuables." That is precisely the analogy that captures the essence of command and control, and the logic of local resistance: "Our valuables" assumes and confirms state property; use of wildlife is equated with being "robbed"—the criminalization of subsistence routines. And the bank—which everywhere in India has armed guards highly visible—implies exclusion on penalty of force.

The global equivalent of "banks" is the World Heritage Convention (WHC). The WHC removes tracts of land from the market to preserve globally valuable ecosystems, whether Yosemite in the United States or Manas in India. This regime involves mutual, voluntary national removal of land from highest-value use for the sake of global preservation goals. Land always has opportunity costs; set-asides involve politically expensive rigging of the land market. India's proportion of protected areas is about the same as that of the United States, just under 5 percent, one-fifth that of Costa Rica. India's system of biosphere reserves and national parks provides the same level of legal and administrative protection as that provided to World Heritage Sites. There are now about 500 Protected Areas in the country, and five WHC natural sites (Herring and Bharucha, 1999).

Of India's five natural heritage sites, two—Manas and Kaziranga—have been intermittently under serious threat. Both are in the Northeast, where challenges to the authority of the central state have been endemic; both biodiversity and political insurgency characterize the region.

Manas is one of India's largest (2,837 sq. km.) and richest protected areas, containing twenty-two known endangered species; it became a WHC site in 1986. Agitation by the Bodos for a separate state began March 2, 1987; in addition to autonomy, their demands included an end to plantation monoculture in the area, prohibition of foreign liquor, prevention of exploitation by middlemen in forest products, expulsion of ethnic Assamese, and withdrawal of the paramilitary Central Reserve Police. Guerrillas of the Bodo Security Force found sanctuary in the park. Structures were burned and field officers were evacuated after a number were killed; much of the area was in effect surrendered to guerrillas. As staff departed, the "wildlife and timber mafia" moved in without restraint. Wildlife were destroyed, including threatened species such as the swamp deer. The grasslands, which are the last refuge of the floricans, hisped hare, pygmy hog, and other species, were extensively burned; timber was felled.

The state's response to Bodo demands was a typical developmentalist program. Announced in 1990 and funded by the World Wide Fund for Nature–India (WWF–I), it was meant to defuse tensions with segmentation of space and alternative livelihoods: development of the buffer zone with cooperatives, apiculture, pisciculture, and so on. A Memorandum of Settlement creating a Bodo Autonomous Council, covering 2,000 villages, was signed in 1993.[18] Nevertheless, the conflict is not resolved; guerrillas remain active, but increased staff with more firepower reestablished tenuous state control over most of the park.

Kaziranga has been threatened by both large-scale poaching and development. As in Manas, gangs of poachers outgunned forest guards. The State government blamed the Center for inadequate funding; the Center countered that allocated funds were underutilized. In 1990 Kaziranga was placed on the threatened list of the International Union for Conservation of Nature; Manas was already on the list. Kaziranga had been listed previously because of poaching and plans for rail connections; it was removed from the list and then placed on it again as plans for an oil refinery nearby were announced.[19] As in Manas, there have been cycles of threat and response, Center-State conflicts over responsibility, and speculation among wildlife activists that timber and poaching gangs could not thrive without political connections.

Though Manas and Kaziranga have received special attention because of their international status, all protected areas are susceptible to people-state conflicts. The Bodo movement is fighting for autonomous statehood, challenging not only the Indian state's property claim to protected natural area, but its territorial claim as well. In the Sunderbans WHC site, conflicts involve tigers that kill people. The widely publicized "tiger widows" of the area demand compensation from the state for depredations of animals which the state has in effect declared its property.[20]

The Bharatpur WHC site presents a paradox of the preservationist mission in biological terms. By legal notification, no grazing is now permissible in a national park. In the past, domestic buffaloes used to maintain Bharatpur as a wetland by constant grazing. Removal of the buffaloes has not only led to a conflict between park authorities and local graziers, but has created an ecologically unsuitable area for waterfowl. The ungrazed wetland is now choked with weeds and paspallum grass, which was once kept in check by buffaloes. The wetland, which is an ecologically sensitive area, is now changing into a grassland, creating suboptimal habitat for birds (many migratory, and thus a genuinely global concern) for which the area was made a WHC site. Global biodiversity in this case would be better served by preserving the site in an unnatural state (much desired by local agriculturalists). State rules have the science wrong. Compromises with villagers have allowed human removal of grasses. Threats to delist Bharatpur have been resisted by the government of India.[21]

Rigging Markets

Sequestering nature is one means of preserving biodiversity; it typically entails creation and maintenance of state property rights in nature. These rights are difficult to establish and enforce because of the embedded character of nature in subsistence routines and the historical resistance to the paramilitary pretensions of the state. If nature cannot be effectively sequestered, but has already entered into commodity circuits, an alternative state response is market rigging.

Restricting trade in species curbs the commoditization of specific species. CITES addresses the global biodiversity commons problem by imposing constraints on trade. It applies to those discrete pieces of nature already commoditized through international channels of supply and demand. Chapter XVI of India's Import-Export Policy (1993) prohibits exports of "all forms of wildlife including parts and products [p. 74]." Wildlife is defined as "all plants and animals,"[22] but flora are accorded less importance as elements of nature than are fauna.

Not surprisingly, rigging the market for species is difficult. High-value products, whether prohibited or not, will find a market. Borders are porous, enforcement personnel are often outnumbered and/or outgunned, corruption is always possible in a high-value game, and the miscreants are part of local society, which understands their motives and claims and distrusts minions of the state. The parallel to control of illegal drugs is obvious.

But a more fundamental issue is the legal challenge brought by dealers in animal products: Does the state have the authority to deprive citizens of livelihood in order to protect nature? The primary means of controlling *internal* trafficking in endangered species has been called into question by a ruling of the Delhi High Court on January 23, 1987 (PAT 5-24-93). The Wild Life (Preservation) Act of 1972 had been amended through the addition of Chapter VA notified November 25, 1986. Fur and ivory traders challenged the act on the grounds that Chapter VA violated their rights under Article 19g of the Constitution, the right to earn a livelihood.[23] They claimed that they had the right to sell legal stocks; the government claimed that they had been selling all along and that the stocks were bogus.

The Court ordered the government to buy the stocks of the traders at their market value, which the government argued it could not do. In a sense, the government had to deny the commoditization of illegal commodities.[24] The resolution has been a clear statement by the judicial system that right to livelihood is secondary to the state's interest in nature (Herring and Bharucha 1999).

The antinomies of local interests and state authority can be captured by looking at one example of a common pattern; it usefully blurs the boundaries we have been taking as given. There is an almost universal understanding of the problem of local complicity in violation of international soft-law regimes of both sequestered nature and protected species by organized criminal activity. International law is meaningless without local cooperation. Writing of the critically endangered one-horned rhinoceros protected by international agreement under CITES and within a World Heritage Convention (Natural) Site, Vivek Menon (1996, 65) concludes:

> As most poachers come from far-off villages, they need a fringe village in which to wait and bide their time, as well as to return to after the poaching. Also, there is a need for a local person who has knowledge of routes, location of anti-poaching camps, patrol times and routes, etc. Further, if arms are to be stored for some time . . . again a local is ideally involved. This local could be a corrupt employee of the Forest Department or a villager; examples of both cases are known and not uncommon. It is stressed, however, that to malign the entire Forest Department or body of villagers local to rhinoceros reserves would be most inappropriate and undesirable. Indeed, it is only with the full co-operation of these groups that poachers' assistants can be identified from among them and extracted.

Vivek Menon's disaggregation is necessary and valuable. There is a difference between subsistence routines and slaughter—one locally recognized. CITES and WHC as global soft law depend fundamentally on the local state, which is inevitably embedded in local society. The global is then local, as is the state in any meaningful sense; the surveillance of local state and society is mutual. The robust implications of Menon's poignant example are obscured by demonizing either the state or international environmental regimes and celebrating the local.

As CITES restrains the market in commoditized species, driven by the science of ecology, the International Tropical Timber Agreement (ITTA) attempts to order the market in commoditized trees—originally to sustain the global supply over time, now with a "sustainable" component. As with CITES, Indian law can be read to be much stronger than the ITTA. Chapter XVI of the Import-Export Policy (1993, Section 7) prohibits export of "wood and wood products in the form of logs, timber, stumps, roots, barks, chips, powder, flakes, dust, pulp and charcoal." The only explicit exception to this very thorough cataloguing is sandalwood handi-crafts (Section 9). India is not in any meaningful sense an exporter of "tropical timber" (to which official exception is taken).[25] But it does export value-added products which are forest based,[26] exempted on grounds of protection of "handicrafts," and is a relatively small importer of timber. Like much of the rest of the world, India consciously uses imports of timber to counteract or delay its own deforestation; globally this strategy is disas-trous, of course. Trade management does, however, substitute for the more politically difficult task of reordering internal forest-people configurations.

India's National Conservation Strategy lists multiple causes of forest destruction (1992, 3): ". . . over-grazing, over-exploitation both for com-mercial and house-hold needs, encroachments, unsustainable practices including certain practices of shifting cultivation and developmental activities such as roads, buildings, irrigation and power projects." Relative weighting of these causes evokes intense controversy, as it has historically. Continuation of the colonial system of command and control in state property is increasingly attacked as ineffective, unjust, and undemocratic (Hiremath, Kanwalli, and Kulkarni 1994), though some forestry officials worry that democracy in the forests is a recipe for anarchy. A new National Forest Policy (through amendment of the Forest [Conservation] Act in 1988) began with recognition that the 1952 Forest Policy's goal of restor-ing forest coverage to 33 percent had failed and that destruction of "genetic diversity" had been extensive. The new policy envisioned joint manage-ment, power sharing between villagers and forestry officials, compensatory afforestation for developmental diversions of forests, and eco-restoration with joint usufruct. In theory, the inadequacy of the command and control logic of colonial forestry was appreciated, though working out new institu-tional arrangements in the face of suspicious citizens and recalcitrant officials will require commitment and creativity (on which, see Guha 1994).

Despite official gestures toward participatory forest management, policy to ensure "sustainable use" remains controversial. Politically, the contradiction is between centralized bureaucratic control and devolution to States and communities. Normatively, there is conflict over conceptual-ization of forest dwellers' daily practices as "concessions and privileges" (granted by the state) as opposed to rights inherently vested in local people. Environmentally, the conflict is between preservationist "deep ecology" and the social ecology of development favored by most activist nongovernmental organizations (NGOs) (Herring 1991). Empirically, in terms of forest conservation, there are no easy conclusions and deep disagreements.[27] Conflicting claims to resource stewardship, conservation values, employment, and social justice are no easier to resolve in India than in the old-growth forests of the United States. Certainly state property alone has not generally protected forests. Nevertheless, some of India's finest biological systems are protected by state property in nature. What are emerging are new forms of institutional systems in which the bundle of rights we call property is disentangled and shared among those with claims, both local and national. The answer in forest policy has thus not been to reject state property but to reform what and who the state is, what it means locally, and what it does.

THE SECOND GREAT TRANSFORMATION: RE-EMBEDDING MARKETS

Karl Polanyi (1957, 184) argued that in the face of market failure—of which class of events environmental degradation is one of the most dramatic: ". . . [C]onfidence will naturally turn to such forces outside the market system which are capable of ensuring common interests jeopardized by the system." For Polanyi, "society" was an actor, its interests were clear, and the mechanism for moving to "such forces outside the market system" was basically unproblematized. Real world states have claimed this role, but as agents for "society" meet none of these conditions.

Nevertheless, state property in nature serves one great function: removing landscapes from market dynamics. With adequate funding and proper management, protected areas offer some refuge from the destructive commoditization of everything. Given the developmental imperatives and legitimation needs of regimes, state property is not enough.

Indeed, resistance to state property in nature, and its often inconsistent results as a conservation tool, has led to growing consensus on devolution, decentralization, and local participation as antidote to centralized state control. The move to the local is celebrated prematurely, however; the reality is that authority in natural systems is hard to establish, for all the reasons of multiple human interests in landscapes. Moving the scale of control often simply displaces the problem of authority.[28] As a result, in preventing environmental degradation through public authority, at whatever level, we are better off speaking the language of governance rather than the language of property.

Authority is at the bottom of much of the debate *about* nature as well
as the conflict in and around natural systems, even if buried in the currently fashionable discussions of "stakeholders" and institutional design.
Conflicts derive from two interdependent but distinct problems of authority: as legitimated power, in the ordinary language sense of political
authority, and in the epistemological sense, as in "scientific authority." The
conceptual flattening of science to state claims of authoritative knowledge
endangers both scientific authority and state legitimacy as manager of
nature. States claim more than they know, and mass publics know it. To
take but one example, Blaikie and Brookfield (1987, 37–49) discuss erosion
in mountain Nepal under the heading: "A crisis of the environment or
a crisis of explanation?" They convincingly demonstrate the latter.
Catastrophic erosion was caused not by bad farmers, or inadequate local
knowledge, as reams of literature had diagnosed and government officers
had tried to redress, but plate tectonics, over which there is no policy
domain. Social scientists tend to find social causes; governments tend to
find causes amenable to policy.

Consistent with the anti-state mood of our time, celebration of localism is paired with globalism. The "international system" is proposed as a
more appropriate level of governing nature than the nation-state. At
the international level, soft law promises governance coterminous with a
planetary ecosystem—a (decidedly imaginary) "global community." The
implications for local governance of nature are profound and often opaque
to state officials who, claiming to represent nation-states, sign documents
in large foreign cities. The distinction in CITES between endangered and
other species is premised on the existence of a public good (ultimately
derived from the value of biodiversity) which public authority pursues; but
it is one poorly received, or actively contested, by people whose livelihoods
are affected (for example, Kothari 1997; Herring and Bharucha, 1998).
What is globally scarce may be locally commonplace, even pesky.

One consequence of efforts to enforce such laws is violence between
bearers of national and local public authority and hunters, traders, herders,
and smugglers. It is not clear that states are winning. Nevertheless, states
sign on to global soft-law regimes as representatives of their respective societies and then set about answering the countervailing claims to authority
in their own periphery. At the extreme, conflicts over landscape autonomy
feed redefinitions of community, turf, and rights to secession. Governance
at the local level seems undermined by attempts of states to fulfill obligations accepted as global citizens: the rise of bioregionalism, "ecological
ethnicity" (Parajuli 2000), sagebrush rebellions, and wise use movements
(Helvaarg 1994).

Governance is a relational construct; it presupposes some workable relationship between various levels of state and society implying some form of legitimacy over power—that is, authority. Effective governance is then relational in a cultural as well as structural sense. When Robert Wade (1988) writes of the economic conditions for collective action at the local level (in the aptly titled *Village Republics*), he finds precisely what is missing from the institutional and economistic perspectives. Successful village republics tend to work on issues of clear public good absent redistributive conflicts; expanding pie possibilities create community. Nature seldom cooperates; evaluations contend rather than converge. Moreover, crosscutting arenas—inevitable in natural systems—render governance problematic in both its structural and cultural dimensions.

Expansion of centralized state claims has historically reduced the institutional and cultural diversity of local arrangements. The state's pernicious effect on local accommodations to natural systems may then be both structural and cultural; centralized states reduce both the political space within which local communities can work institutional solutions to perceived problems and the authority of existing institutions. Just as reduction of biodiversity precludes options, traditional state control of nature reduces the richness of institutional and cultural diversity from which governance can be constructed. Yet if ecological systems impel ever higher levels of articulation, reconstitution of the nation-state system itself may be the necessary condition for global authority in nature.

The global-local problematic is then indissoluble, just as the bumper stickers say. Global governance presupposes local governance. Yet global governance depends on—works through, reinforces, legitimates—nation-states in the first instance, reinforcing the centralism legitimated by scientific forestry more than a century ago. Paramilitary command and control systems have not only failed but have fed the ethnoregionalism that ironically undermines stateness, while simultaneously low-intensity conflict defeats conservationist goals. Yet the formation of global environmental regimes presupposes nation-states in the current structure of the international system.

CONCLUSIONS

This essay began with the question of the effect of property rights on environmental degradation. It concludes that the first task is to operationalize property rights—and this is not so simple. Property rights are both nested and contested. Despite the collapsing of dimensions of property claims—the "bundle of rights"—through the great transformation, on the ground the strands come apart again in practice, in accretions to case law: fee simple property in nature is no longer so simple. Real property rights are inevitably local; a right means what the claimant can make it mean, with or without the state's help. The state, though with more resources, faces the same contingency in its property claims—particularly those in nature. Clarification and strengthening of property rights facilitates both "development"—that is, destruction—and investment in protection of ecological systems.

Environmental degradation is so overdetermined a phenomenon that property rights per se are unlikely to be decisive. In Chapter 2 of *Land Degradation and Society*, Blaikie and Brookfield (1987) provide a model of the complexity. Thinking of Nepal, they conclude that everything ultimately rests on the decisions of the "land manager." But as in all reasonable accounts which privilege the individual actor, they recognize that choice implies constraint—thus structure (and culture, I would add). The structural variables in their account include the structure of the state and its revenue imperative, a set of taxes and an income distribution and class structure coproducing extensive poverty, a property structure evolving from the prebendal, a global structure in which hard currency for fuel and fertilizer is unequally distributed, and perhaps other factors not captured in this already daunting list. They go on to note the unsettling fact that much of the degradation social scientists have attributed to social causes is in fact geophysically driven, in part because social scientists need to find social causation or delegitimize themselves, and in part because of the prevalence of what Robert Chambers called "development tourism" masquerading as social science.

Because of the complexity of the decision tree of landscape management, it seems clear that neither public property nor individuated private property per se guarantees environmental protection, especially when we admit to the slippery slope of meta-commons dilemmas. It also seems clear that the "tragedy of the commons" does not delegitimize collective property rights as environmental policy, just as common property is no guarantee of sustainability. States have had, and will continue to have, mixed motives in declaring segments of nature their own property; their protective *effect* is determined by a very situationally contingent mix of capacity and will.

The role of the state and markets in destroying local commons and local environments, whatever the local configuration of culture and interests, is well documented (though the romanticized notion that the ancients were incapable of destruction is clearly wrong[29]). It may well be that this effect is a product of state property claims through both structural and cultural dynamics. Modern states reduce the political space within which local communities can work institutional solutions to perceived problems, as well as the authority of existing institutions; simultaneously, "development" hurries the "great transformation," creating intense pressures for the commoditization of everything and the individuation of interests.[30] Polanyi himself noted that "no misreading of the past" ever proved so prophetic.

NOTES

1. For the purposes of this chapter, nature will be essentialized and uninterrogated, though certainly it should be understood, in the words of Lukacs (1923, 234): "Nature is a societal category . . . whatever is held to be natural at any given stage of social development, however this nature is related to man [sic] and whatever form his involvement with it takes, i.e. nature's form, its content, its range and its objectivity are all socially conditioned."

2. For example, see Schama 1996 on eighteenth-century England and France. For all the differences in cultural construction of landscapes, deforestation and periodic bouts of conservation were both driven by different perceptions of naval construction needs. Also, Polanyi 1957, 184.

3. Nor is the outcome limited to land use dilemmas. The "tragedy" is simply another, though one of the most dramatic, example of what Sartre calls "counter-finality": the unintended negative consequences at the collective level of individually "rational" decisions (cf. Elster 1985, 24).

4. Scattered exceptions may be found in the works of Marx, for example in the discussion of agriculture in *Capital* I. Raghunandan (1987, 546) points to exceptions in Engels' "Dialectics of Nature." Nevertheless, the weight of the Marxian tradition is clearly as indicated in the text.

5. Tellingly, Blaikie and Brookfield mention "invasion of weeds" as an indicator of land degradation (1987, 5). To be fair, there is a biological meaning to weed; but here I think they mean, as we usually do, a plant which is growing where a human being does not want it to grow.

6. The logic of collective action is ambiguous on "small" aggregates. Villages may have more potential for collective action than much smaller aggregates in industrial society because of (a) the greater continuity of relationships over time; (b) the greater information about the character of other individuals; (c) the multidimensionality of relationships, such that "side-payments" and sanctions can be managed in spheres other than that to which collective action directly applies.

7. There is a small puzzle here, which we may note in passing: Why do villages seem capable throughout India (and in much of the world) of collective action in cases where there are arguably *no* material benefits involved? That is, collective religious observances are organized even in villages which fail to act collectively for production bonuses. A materialist explanation can be conjured, but it is clearly an

act of conjuring: Local belief systems hold that appeasing or pleasing some deity is likely to have greater material benefits than rationally using water (for example).

8. There is nothing in logic which prevents privatization from meaning devolution to local corporate bodies rather than individuals; as Bromley and Chapagian (1984, 870) note: "[T]he matter of private control over resources refers to the ability to exclude others, not to how many individuals share in the decision making by those not excluded." That extremely large and complex social organizations such as business corporations should be considered individual actors in theory and law whereas villages are a priori held to be incapable of rational action does seem bizarre.

9. Kautilya argues in the *Artha Sastra* that "the means of ensuring the pursuit of philosophy, the three Vedas and economics is the Rod [wielded by the King]; its administration constitutes the science of politics. . . . On it is dependent the orderly maintenance of worldly life. . . . If not used, it gives rise to the law of the fishes. For the stronger swallows the weak in the absence of the wielder of the Rod." (From Robinson 1988, preface). The doctrine of *matsya-nyaya*, or "law of the fishes," implies that in a state of nature anarchy prevails, providing the justification for a strong and interventionist state. So strongly is the state associated with "the Rod" (*danda*) that Kautilya calls the science of politics, or kingship, *dandaniti* (a useful corrective, more rooted in realism than the more usual *rajniti*, or the science of rule).

10. The classic statement is Anne Krueger, "The Political Economy of the Rent-Seeking Society," *American Economic Review* 64, no. 3 (June 1974): 291–303.

11. Indeed, having the state weigh in on the side of preservation may prove counterproductive, so deeply is it compromised in local political perceptions. In the case of "Silent Valley" in South India, Delhi's intervention on the side of preservation aided in transforming political dynamics in the direction of local people vs. the state, periphery vs. center, and, in a curious twist, Bharat vs. India. The Center's preservationist mission was badly damaged in local perceptions because it coincided with powerful international actors from the North and West. See Herring 1991.

12. The empirical base of much of the following rests on interviews in India 1993–1997, 1996; and MOEF 1994, 1996. For elaboration, see Herring and Bharucha 1999.

13. Police in Karnataka and Tamilnadu have arrested ninety-seven people and killed twenty in "encounters" (*India Today* 31-7-93, 24–26). This section is based on press reports, for example, *Times of India* 30-7-93; *Hindustan Times* 5-8-93, 14-8-93; and interviews with officials in the Ministry of Environment and Forests.

14. See for example the contributors to Poffenberger and McGean, eds., 1996. A powerful statement of the conventional critical wisdom is Peet and Watts 1996. On theoretical reasons for participatory success, see Uphoff 1992. Note that Uphoff's great success story of new identity formation as "farmers" rather than as ethnic partisans, in the midst of a local and national civil war of great violence, was *not* based on community but on practiced organic solidarity in face-to-face social

relations—a building realization that convergent interests as farmers were more important than divergent interests as Sinhala or Tamil.

15. On the power of environmental narratives, see Dryzek 1997; also, Sinha et al. 1997. A superb precis of the noble ecological other view is contained in Baviskar (1995, 44–47). Arun Agrawal (1995) terms the local knowledge community the "neo-indigenistas." For a summary of the critical arguments, see Herring 1998.

16. Most issues of environmental importance—water, land, forests, fisheries, public health, agriculture, wildlife—were constitutionally subjects reserved to the States before recent legislation added some to the concurrent list of joint Center-state responsibility. Forests were added to the concurrent list by the 42nd amendment to the Constitution in 1976 (India 1980, Entry 17A).

17. Infiltrators for TRAFFIC-India (WWF) who are British nationals got only so far in investigating smuggling in Nepal. They could not penetrate the inner sanctum where really big deals were done. They were finally informed that as their accents were not Italian or Slavic, no one took them seriously. Italy served as the entry point for European distribution of illegal furs and skins.

18. "Mafia" designation by Sanjay Deb Roy (1994, 2), the lead conservation official in the area. Also, WWF–I 1992–93; Telegraph (Calcutta) 18-12-89; Assam Tribune 21-2-93; Statesman (Calcutta) 21-2-93; Economic Times 11-6-90; India Today 31-8-92; STM 18-10-90; Times of India 12-08-89; PAT 22-01-90; AST 11-01-93; IED 9-5-89; and interviews in the MOEF and wildlife community.

19. Accounts in Times of India 30-11-1990; AST 1-4-90; TEL 12-12-92; NEO 6-4-93; DH 6-8-89; NWT 27-5-91; and interviews. The central government's position was explained in 1991 RSQ* 394 May 1991: a centrally sponsored scheme for rhino protection, with Rs. 5 crores in the 7th Plan, for more protection staff, vehicles, arms and wireless sets in addition to the Centrally Sponsored Scheme for the Control of Poaching and Illegal Trade in Wildlife. These schemes allow 50 percent cost sharing for the state government of Assam.

20. Wildlife officials who work in the area are convinced that press reports overstate the killings, but emphasize that recurrent deaths of people and livestock from wildlife are a large and intractable problem.

21. See Madsen 1995. Pioneer (11-2-95) carried a front-page story on the threatened delisting, citing the WHC Secretariat concern that the endangered Siberian cranes no longer visit Bharatpur. The ministry had been in contact with the BNHS and WWF-I to formulate a response.

22. A review of legal exports listed in the 1991 Annual Report of CITES shows that a lion was exported to Switzerland and blood constituents of a tiger and leopard were exported to the United States for scientific research. The list of the export of flora for purposes of trade shows a majority of live plants, mostly orchids in quantities ranging from 1 to 300 in consignments with a specific CITES permit number. Most quantities, however, are small in number; and their most common

destinations are Japan, the United States, and Great Britain. India imported three cockatoos, a pygmy hippopotamus, a jaguar, a gray parrot, and 14 kgs. of Dendrobium flowers during 1991 from either the United States or Singapore.

23. Simultaneously, the Ivory Traders and Manufacturers Association raised a similar challenge to the Wild Life Act. The stay granted by the Court was taken advantage of by nearly 300 petitioners along with the cottage industries association. The stay order was finally vacated on May 22 by the Chief Justice, but the issue of the contradiction between the amended act and the right to livelihood remains unresolved.

24. People who bring tips on customs violations are rewarded with a share (usually 25 percent) of the illegal booty confiscated. CITES enforcers recognize that this incentive will help them identify smugglers. But the government will not put a price on wildlife products, a necessary condition for the mechanism. The government's position is that pricing animal products is legitimating the market for them.

25. India was insulted by the categorization at the 1993 meeting in Kuala Lumpur as an exporter/producer, whereas the United States was categorized as a consumer/importer; the reality is just the opposite. Imports of timber are part of a conscious policy of preserving India's forests. In Parliamentary questions about what is being done about deforestation, *imports* (largely from Southeast Asia) are invariably given as the solution. Though perhaps cheaper than forest protection/regeneration strategies, this is a clear example of a beggar-thy-neighbor policy in global terms.

26. The value-added concession is legitimated as an antipoverty measure, to spur "handicrafts" which are produced by "weaker sectors." By chance, a timber exporter shared our interview space with the official in charge of certifying exceptions. He explained to us (when the official stepped out) that the loophole was used by big timber contractors to reduce sandalwood logs to dust and chips, claim these as byproducts of handicraft productions, and then export them for extraction of oil. As the regulatory regime has been tightened, the number of timber-exporting firms fell from three to one. The last exporter had to spend a lot of time in Delhi lobbying for exceptions.

27. In 1994, the government proposed the "Conservation of Forests and Natural Ecosystems Bill," which became known to NGOs through leaks from the ministry. This bill, meant to replace the 1927 colonial Forest Act, is widely perceived to represent a strengthening of the centralized command and control logic. NGO resistance prevented the bill from going immediately to Parliament; an alternative NGO bill was circulated and discussed. For commentaries by leading activists and scholars, see Hiremath, Kanwalli, and Kulkarni 1994; the government's draft bill is reproduced, pp. 91–222; see also, Guha 1994; *Times of India* 1-2-1995.

28. Declining capacity for governance endangers broader societal values, as recognized most forcefully by the 1997 *World Development Report* from the World Bank. Even the most relentlessly technocratic of global institutions has broached

the messy and expansive question of public authority as a sine qua non condition for "development." The Bank discovers a dilemma in the scale of public authority: Hegemonic Leviathan states are dysfunctional, yet "certain dangers are inherent in any strategy aimed at opening and decentralizing government . . . [including] the risk of gridlock or of capture by . . . interest groups." Conceivably, "the crisis of governance that now afflicts many centralized governments will simply be passed down to lower levels" (1997, 130).

29. To take but one example, Raghunandan (1987, 545) notes the case of a ninth-century Pallava king who was given the honorific *Kaduvetti* (one who clears forests) for presiding over the rapid conversion of forests to cultivated land. See also Eaton 1990, 1993.

30. For an expanded treatment, and discussion of conference papers pointing in this direction, see Sinha and Herring, "Common Property, Collective Action, and Ecology," *Economic and Political Weekly* July 1993.

BIBLIOGRAPHY

Agarwal, Anil. 1985. "Politics of Environment II," in *The State of India's Environment 1984–85* New Delhi: Centre for Science and Environment.

Agarwal, Anil, and Sunita Narain. 1992. *Toward a Green World* New Delhi: Centre for Science and Environment.

Agrawal, Arun. 1995. "Dismantling the Divide between Indigenous and Scientific Knowledge," *Development and Change* 26:413–39.

Ayyar, R. S. Vadyanatha. 1976. *Manu's Land and Trade Laws* Delhi: Oriental.

Baden-Powell, B. H. 1892. *The Land Systems of British India*. 3 vols. Oxford: Clarendon Press.

Bandyopadhyay, Jayanta, and Vandana Shiva. 1988. "Political Economy of Ecology Movements." *Economic and Political Weekly*. (June 11), 1223–332.

Baviskar, Amita. 1995. *In the Belly of the River*. Delhi: Oxford University.

Blaikie, Piers, and Harold Brookfield. 1987. *Land Degradation and Society*. London: Methuen.

Bromley, Daniel W., and Devendra P. Chapagian. 1984. "The Village against the Center: Resource Depletion in South Asia." *American Journal of Agricultural Economics*. (December), 868–73.

Callister, Debra. 1992. *Illegal Tropical Timber Trade: Asia-Pacific*. Traffic Network Report 1992. WWF–Oceana.

Centre for Science and Environment (CSE). 1986. *The State of India's Environment, 1984–85: The Second Citizen's Report*. New Delhi: Ravi Chopra.

Cronon, William. 1983. *Changes in the Land: Indians, Colonists, and the Ecology of New England*. New York: Hill and Wang.

Dryzek, John. 1997. *The Politics of the Earth*. New York: Oxford University Press.

Eaton, Richard M. 1990. "Human Settlement and Colonization of the Sundarbans, 1200–1750." *Agriculture and Human Values* VII (2): 6–16.

Eaton, Richard. 1993. *The Rise of Islam and the Bengal Frontier: 1204–1760*. Berkeley: University of California Press.

Elster, Jon. 1985. *Making Sense of Marx*. Cambridge: Cambridge University Press.

"Endangered Species: Targets of Asia's Affluent." 1993. *Far Eastern Economic Review*. (August 19), 23–27.

ENVIS Centre 07, World Wide Fund for Nature–India. 1993. *Annual Report*. New Delhi: Submitted to the Ministry of Environment and Forest.

Feeny, David, Fikret Birkes, Bonnie J. McCay, and James M. Acheson. 1990. "The Tragedy of the Commons: Twenty-Two Years Later." *Human Ecology* 18 (1).

Gadgil, Madhav, and Ramachandra Guha. 1995. *Ecology and Equity*. New York: Penguin Books.

Gruisen, Joanna Van, and Toby Sinclair. 1992. "Fur Trade in Kathmandu: Implications for India." New Delhi: TRAFFIC-India.

Guha, Ramachandra. 1985. "Forestry and Social Protest in British Kumaun, c. 1893–1921." *Subaltern Studies* IV:54–100.

———. 1989. *The Unquiet Woods: Ecological Change and Peasant Resistance in the Himalaya*. Delhi: Oxford University Press.

———. 1990. "An Early Environmental Debate: The Making of the 1878 Forest Act." *The Indian Economic and Social History Review* 27 (1).

———. 1994. "Switching on the Green Light." *Telegraph* 25-10-94 (October 25). Calcutta.

Hardin, Garrett. 1968. "The Tragedy of the Commons." *Science*, 1243–48.

Helvaarg, David. 1994. *The War against the Greens*. San Francisco: Sierra Club Books.

Herring, Ronald J. 1980. Review of Popkin. *The Rational Peasant, American Political Science Review* 74, no. 2 (June).

———. 1983. *Land to the Tiller*. New Haven: Yale University Press.

———. 1991. "Politics of Nature: Commons Interests, Dilemmas, and the State." Harvard Center for Population and Development Studies, Working Paper Series no. 106 (October).

———. 1998. "Celebrating the Local: Scale and Orthodoxy in Political Ecology," in *Governance Issues in Conservation and Development*, Goren Hyden, ed. Conservation and Development Forum. Gainesville.

Herring, Ronald and Eric Bharucha. 1998. "Embedded Capacities: India's Compliance with International Accords," in *Engaging Countries: Strengthening Compliance with International Accords*, eds. Edith Brown Weiss and Harold Jacobson. Cambridge: MIT Press.

Hiremath, S. R., Sadanand Kanwalli, and Sharad Kulkarni, eds. 1994. *All about Draft Forest Bill and Forest Lands*. Dharawad: Samaj Parivartana Samudaya.

India, Government of. 1980. Department of Science and Technology, *Report of the Committee for Recommending Legislative Measures and Administrative Machinery for Ensuring Environmental Protection.* New Delhi (September 15).

———. 1991. *The State of the Forest Report* New Delhi: Ministry of Environment and Forest.

———. 1992a. *Environmental Action Programmes-India* Interim Document. New Delhi: Ministry of Environment and Forests (November).

———. 1992b. *The Wildlife (Protection) Act, 1972* (as amended up to 1991). Dehradun: Natraj.

———. 1993. *Export-Import Policy 1 April–31 March 1997(with Amendments up to 31 March 1993).* New Delhi: Ministry of Commerce.

———. 1994. *Report of the Committee on Prevention of Illegal Trade in Wildlife and its Products.* New Delhi: Ministry of Environment and Forests.

———. 1996. *Recommendations of the Committee Appointed by the Hon'ble High Court of Delhi on Wildlife Preservation, Protection, and Laws.* New Delhi. (February 1996).

———. 1996. *Report of the High Powered Committee Constituted on the Recommendation of the Department Related Parliamentary Committee on Environment and Forests to 'Undertake a Review of the Project Tiger; Carry-out Evaluation and Suggest Ways and Means to Make the Project Tiger More Meaningful and Result Oriented.'* New Delhi: Ministry of Environment and Forests (Project Tiger). (January).

Jodha, N. S. 1985. "Population Growth and the Decline of Common Property Resources in Rajasthan, India," *Population and Development Review* 11, no. 2 (June).

———. 1986. "Common Property Resources and Rural Poor in Dry Regions of India." *Economic and Political Weekly* xxi, no. 27 (July).

Kishwar, Madhu. 1997. "'*Naukri*' as Property." *Manushi* no. 100: 13–24.

Kothari, Ashish. 1996. "Structural Adjustment vs. India's Environment." Paper presented at the Annual Meetings, Association for Asian Studies, Honolulu (April).

Kothari, Ashish, et al., ed. 1997. *Building Bridges for Conservation: Toward Joint Management of Protected Areas in India.* New Delhi: Indian Institute of Public Administration.

Kothari, Smitu. 1995a. "Whose Nation is It? The Displaced as Victims of Development." *Lokayan Bulletin* 11, no. 5 (March/April): 1–8.

———. 1995b. "Developmental Displacement and Official Policies: A Critical Review." *Lokayan Bulletin* 11, no. 5 (March/April): 9–28.

Kothari, Smitu, and Pramod Parajuli. 1993. "No Nature without Social Justice: A Plea for Cultural and Ecological Pluralism in India." In *Global Ecology: A New Arena of Political Conflict,* Wolfgang Sachs, ed. London: Zed.

Logan, William. 1887. *Malabar Manual*. 2 vols. Trivandrum: Charitharam. 1981 facsimile reprint.

Lukacs, Georg. 1971. *History and Class Consciousness*. London: Merlin. (First published 1923).

Madsen, Stig Toft. 1995. "Recent Changes in India's Forest Policy." Paper presented to the Conference on Rural and Urban Environments, Nordic Association for South Asian Studies. Oslo. (May 18–22).

Menon, Vivek. 1996. *Under Siege: Poaching and Protection of the Greater One-Horned Rhinoceroses in India*. New Delhi: Traffic, World Wide Fund for Nature, India.

Mitra, Subrata. 1997. "Making Local Government Work: Rural Elites, Panchayati Raj, and Legitimacy in India." Presented at the conference on "Against the Odds: Fifty Years of Democracy in India," Princeton University.

Nadkarni, M. V. 1987. "Agricultural Development and Ecology: An Economist's View." *Indian Journal of Agricultural Economics* 42, no. 3 (July): 359–75.

Nandy, Ashis. 1988. *Science, Hegemony, and Violence*. Delhi: Oxford University Press.

Neale, Walter C. 1988. "Exposure and Protection: The Double Movement in the Economic History of Rural India." Paper presented to the Second International Karl Polanyi Conference. Montreal. (November).

North, Douglass Cecil. 1990. *Institutions, Institutional Change, and Economic Performance*. Cambridge and New York: Cambridge University Press.

Omvedt, Gail. 1987. "India's Green Movements." *Race and Class* XXVIII (4): 29–38.

Ostrom, Elinor. 1986. "How Inexorable is the 'Tragedy of the Commons'?" Distinguished Faculty Research Lecture, Indiana University (Bloomington, April 3).

———. 1990. *Governing the Commons: The Evolution of Institutions for Collective Action*. Cambridge: Cambridge University Press.

Parajuli, Pramod. 2000. "No Nature Apart: Adivasi Cosmovision and Ecological Discourses in Jharkhand, India," in *Sacred Landscapes and Cultural Politics*, ed. by Philip Arnold and Ann Grodzins Gold. Aldershot, Hampshire, UK and Brookfield, Vt.: Ashgate Publishing.

Peet, Richard and Michael Watts, ed. 1996. *Liberation Ecologies: Environment, Development, and Social Movements*. London and New York: Routledge.

Peluso, Nancy. 1992. *Rich Forests and Poor People: Resource Control and Resistance in Java*. Berkeley: University of California Press.

Poffenberger, Mark and Betsy McGean. 1996. *Village Voices, Forest Choices*. Delhi: Oxford University Press.

Polanyi, Karl. 1957. *The Great Transformation*. Boston: Beacon Press.

Presler, Franklin A. 1987. "Forest Management in the Sunderbans, 1875–1952."

Paper presented at the Smithsonian Institution in the workshop "The Commons in South Asia." Washington, D.C.

Raghunandan, D. 1987. "Ecology and Consciousness." *Economic and Political Weekly* XXII, no. 13 (March 28): 545–49.

Robinson, Marguerite S. 1988. *Local Politics: The Law of the Fishes* Delhi: Oxford University Press.

Rosencranz, A., and R. Milligan. 1990. "CFC Abatement: The Needs of Developing Countries." *Ambio* xix, no. 6–7 (October): 312–16.

Roy, Sanjay Deb. 1994. "Manas National Park: A Status Report." New Delhi: World Wide Fund for Nature.

Runge, C. F. 1986. "Common Property and Collective Action in Economic Development." *World Development* 14.

Schama, Simon. 1996. *Landscape and Memory.* New York: Vantage.

Schenk-Sandbergen, Loes. 1988. "People, Trees, and Forest in India." Annex 2, *Report of the Mission of the Netherlands on the Identification of the Scope for Forestry Development Corporation in India.* Amsterdam.

Scott, James C. 1998. *Seeing Like a State: How Certain Schemes to Improve the Human Condition Have Failed.* New Haven: Yale University Press.

Shiva, Vandana. 1986. "Coming Tragedy of the Commons." *Economic and Political Weekly* 21, no. 15 (April 12): 613–15.

Singh, Narindar. 1976. *Economics and the Crisis of Ecology* Delhi: Oxford University Press.

Singh, Chhatrapati. 1986. *Common Property and Common Poverty: India's Forests, Forest Dwellers, and the Law* Delhi: Oxford University Press.

Singh, K. S. 1986. "Agrarian Dimension of Tribal Movements." In *Agrarian Struggles in India after Independence*, A. R. Desai, ed. Delhi: Oxford University Press.

Singh, Samar. 1986. *Conserving India's Natural Heritage.* Dehradun: Nataraj.

Sinha, Subir, Shubhra Gururani, and Brian Greenberg. 1997. "The 'New Traditionalist' Discourse of Indian Environmentalist." *Journal of Peasant Studies* 24, no. 3 (April): 65–99.

Tucker, R. P. 1984. "The Historical Context of Social Forestry in the Kumaon Himalayas." *Journal of Developing Areas* 18:3, 341–46.

Uphoff, Norman. 1992. *Learning from Gal Oya: Possibilities for a Participatory Development and Post-Newtonian Social Science.* Ithaca: Cornell University Press.

Wade, Robert. 1988. *Village Republics.* Cambridge: Cambridge University Press.

The World Commission on Environment and Development. 1987. *Our Common Future.* New Delhi: Oxford University Press.

World Wide Fund for Nature-India (WWF-I). 1992–93. *The Conservation Plan 1992–93.* New Delhi: WWF.

10

Water Rights in South Asia and the United States: Comparative Perspectives, 1873–2000

JAMES L. WESCOAT, JR

The water must go with the land,
and the land must carry the water.[1]

Water resources have served historically as both an object and context for broad social experiments in regional development. Water development has been a vehicle for dramatic transformation of land resources through irrigation, drainage, flood control, and municipal water supply. Transformations of hydrologic systems cascade through regional aquatic and terrestrial ecosystems, in ways that affect the management and condition of land as well as water resources.

Over the past century, river basins and watersheds have also served as the context for experiments in land settlement, energy development, and regional economic development. At times, river basins have been regarded as a "planning region," almost as jurisdictions for the comprehensive coordination of competing resource uses. That vision rarely endures, however, as communities reassert their local interests in water and established political jurisdictions reassert their sovereignty over water and land resources.

The design of allocative institutions, including property rights, for water resources has been an important dimension of these experiments and struggles. In some periods and places, water rights have served as a key institution for allocating and developing regional land resources. In other contexts, water rights have had limited importance for regional development and environmental change, relative to landed property rights and other allocative institutions for water development (for example, state policies and community organizations). In some places, as the opening quotation from George Davidson asserts, "the water must go with the land"; while in other places, such as the western United States, the two types of property are fully severable. Specific water rights regimes have been evaluated alternately as efficient and flexible institutions or as hopelessly primitive and unresponsive to environmental and social change (National Research Council 1992). In the western United States, for example, the prior appropriation doctrine is often blamed for the depletion and degradation of streams, the promotion of wasteful water use in urban and agricultural landscapes, and the destruction of community-based systems of collective water management (for example, Brown and Ingram 1987; Worster 1985).

To understand the environmental and social consequences of water rights, and their relations with landed property regimes, it is useful to compare their development and diffusion in different regions of the world. This chapter focuses on South Asia and the United States, in part because comparisons of their water rights have sometimes influenced the path of water development in those regions.

The challenges of broad regional and historical comparisons are many. In the western United States, for example, water rights vary widely in form and authority, ranging from "absolute ownership" in Texas groundwater law to a limited usufruct of navigable rivers, from private shares in a water supply organization to a state-supplied good appurtenant to federal reclamation project lands. Geographically, water rights have more salience in Colorado than in California, and more significance in the United States generally than in India or Pakistan. Water rights regimes can change quickly or with aggravating slowness. After decades of inconsequential tinkering (and the threat of a federal funding cutoff of the Central Arizona project), for example, Arizona abandoned its hopelessly weak groundwater law, based on a rule of "reasonable use," and adopted the strictest state-regulated system in the country.

South Asia has often been regarded as a region with inadequate institutions for private ownership of land and water (from Kinney 1912, to Singh 1991). By contrast, the United States has been perceived in South Asia as a nation overly concerned with private property rights and individualism (Beer 1979, 14). At times, these two regions have distinguished themselves from one another on the basis of their presumed differences in land and water rights. At other times, they have borrowed property rights institutions from one another.

This history of macroregional distinction and diffusion has had practical, as well as intellectual, significance. The diffusion of water rights
institutions is linked with, but by no means fully determined by, large-scale
patterns of land and water development and their associated environmental and social impacts. The conscious rejection of water rights principles
from another region sometimes reflects an effort to avoid that pattern of
development and impacts.

To understand how property rights institutions have been transferred,
rejected, and adapted from one region to another, we need to focus on the
geographical logic of those events: for example, the regional circumstances,
forces, and interactions that drive them. The key source of evidence in
this study comes from *previous comparisons* of water rights systems. Representatives from South Asia and the United States have, at various times,
studied each other's water policies in order to address their own problems.
This chapter examines the nature, contexts, and consequences of water
rights comparisons from the late nineteenth century to the present. The
study has several sections. The first section, "Framing the Comparative
Water Rights Problem," situates water rights within the broader context
of "landed property rights," thereby clarifying the aims of this chapter in
relation to other chapters of this book. The second section, "Conceptual
Framework," presents a set of basic propositions about the content, context, and impacts of comparative water rights research. The third section,
"Historical and Geographic Scope of Inquiry," describes the historical and
geographic scope of comparative studies between the United States and
South Asia. It briefly discusses the theoretical debates that have informed
comparative water rights research. The final sections then use these propositions to survey the record of comparative water rights research in the
United States and South Asia.

FRAMING THE COMPARATIVE
WATER RIGHTS PROBLEM

Water rights are a type of property right that aims, along with other water
institutions and "landed property rights," to assign access, use, liability,
and control over water for some persons and social groups relative to
others. Water rights, in the narrow sense of the term, should not be con-
founded with other allocative institutions (for example, preference
doctrines that favor one type of use over another, interstate compacts that
divide waters among states, or treaty rights among nation states). The content and limits of a water right are affected by those other institutions; and

the environmental effects of water rights may functionally resemble those of other institutions). But these relationships between water rights and other institutions should be clearly distinguished for two reasons. First, the institutional logic of water rights (that is, their scope, justification, administration, and alteration) differs in important ways from those of other water institutions and other types of landed property. Second, the relationships between water rights and these other institutions are often the focus of disputes among rival social groups.

Water rights operate within an evolving context, or what may be regarded as a "dynamic nested hierarchy," of water and related land management institutions. Historically, this hierarchy of institutions has evolved from the local community scale up through state and international scales. Although water rights may be individually held, they are created and enforced by the state. When state regimes are strong, higher levels of control constrain local community-based institutions, including common property rights to water. But in federated (or faltering) state systems, local water organizations strive to either manipulate or ignore higher-level institutions (Maass and Anderson 1978).

Comparing water rights systems in South Asia and the United States contributes to the comparative examination of landed property rights in several ways. Water rights shed light on the meaning and extension of the term "landed property rights." "Land" in the broadest sense of the term encompasses all of the waters that flow on and through it except those that are explicitly reserved as private or public water rights. Similarly, ownership of land often includes rights to the rainfall on that land, soil moisture, intermittent flows, and sometimes groundwater.

Conversely, control over water may convey control over land, as in local real estate development that depends upon a secure water supply. In the American West, battles over land have often been fought in the water courts. However, one should be cautious about presuming a strong connection between water laws and land use control. Many local governments have failed, for example, to control land use by restricting water and sewer services. In India and Pakistan, where canal water is a state-supplied good for private land and groundwater is privately captured, battles over water often play themselves out in disputes over land.

In both regions, water rights affect the use, value, and condition of the land. They were designed to facilitate certain types of land use change—for example, irrigation and mining—which have profound impacts on environmental quality. To this day, one hears assertions that "without water, the land is worthless," which usually means "worth less for me."[2] But the continuing appropriation and use of water in both regions has contributed to waterlogging, salinity, erosion, stream channel changes, and non–point source pollution, making the land worth less for society as well. Concentrating on these *connections* between land and water rights can help us assess their environmental and social consequences.

Comparison can also help us clarify the *differences* between rights to land (that is, solum and space) and water. It is often asserted (and denied) that "water is different" from other resources subject to ownership. One group, whom we might call the "differentiators," appeals to the life-sustaining character of water and its fluid, transboundary characteristics to justify distinctions between water and other goods.

For at least six decades, critics (mainly economists) have argued that "water is no different" from other resources. They insist that water is one of many inputs for production and one of many vital commodities for consumption—and that it should be treated like any other input. They point to the problems that arise when the role of water (for example, in irrigation agriculture) is given special treatment compared with other inputs of greater economic value, or when it is given greater emphasis than the value of the crops produced (that is, the purpose of water use) and the value of water left in the stream (that is, the opportunity cost and environmental cost of use).

Underlying this "water is different" dispute are three normative issues: (1) whether water rights should have the same attributes as other types of landed property (for example, unlimited ownership or waste); (2) whether water should be subject to private ownership at all; and (3) whether water should be treated, in a legal sense, as a commodity. As might be imagined, the scientific and legal literatures on these three issues are voluminous. Both sides have a strong normative thrust in contrast to which it is useful to consider, in an empirical way, how and why land and water rights have been distinguished from one another in specific places and times.

For example, some parts of the world that have strong traditions of private ownership in land, such as the American West, paradoxically have strong public and community-based traditions of water control which restrain private ownership of water. It is also interesting to note that private rights to water were first recognized by the California Supreme Court on federal public lands! (*Irwin v. Phillips*, 5 Cal. 140 [1855]).

In both the United States and South Asia, there has been greater experimentation with public control of property rights in water than in land. Analyzing this rich record of water rights experiments may thus suggest analogues for experimentation with landed property rights. Similarly, experiments with landed rights may offer analogues for experiments in private and community water ownership. In this chapter, however, the exploration of analogies between land and water rights is limited, for the main aim is to examine the history of water rights comparisons between the two major regions.

CONCEPTUAL FRAMEWORK

Comparative water rights studies draw their ideas and methods from two broad-ranging, but rather sparsely populated, fields: (1) comparative social science research on irrigation systems; and (2) comparative water law. The most lively theoretical debates have occurred in the first of these fields, where social theorists from Montesquieu (1949) to Wittfogel (1981) and their critics, have debated the causal relations between climate, irrigation, political regimes, social organization, and property rights. I touch briefly upon these debates in a section of the chapter that examines how debates about Wittfogel's "hydraulic hypothesis" influenced social research on water rights during the second half of the twentieth century (Wescoat 2000).

The chapter concentrates, however, on the more prosaic field of international comparative water law, a field driven by concrete social policy problems.[3] It derives its ideas and methods from experience in a practical incremental way, as well as from the professional development of comparative law and international water resources management. The first of these subfields, comparative law, has historically emphasized substantive over theoretical issues, which has led some to question its philosophical contribution and purpose (Frankenburg 1985; Kahn-Freund 1974; and Markesinis 1990; Verzijl 1970). Such questioning is notably absent, however, in research on "legal pluralism" and "transplants," where comparison has helped discern continuing legal problems associated with colonialism, cultural contact, trade, and other processes of geographic interaction.[4]

The field of international water resources management has also been less concerned with theoretical questions than practical approaches to problems of water supply, quality, and conflict. Although decried as atheoretical, this field has contributed to the pragmatic tradition of inquiry.[5]

Comparative research on water law has included major taxonomic surveys by the Food and Agriculture Organization (FAO) (Caponera 1973, 1980) and the United Nations (1967, 1968, 1974). Other surveys have focused on river basin institutions (Teclaff 1967, 1972, 1991). The codification of international water law has been advanced by the International Law Association, the legislative branch of the FAO, and specialized agencies of the United Nations. Legal studies have also played a small but important role in bilateral and multilateral water projects (for example, Radosevich and Kirkwood 1975). Because previous comparative research has often been associated with international and national organizations, it tends to have a strong statist perspective. There are some exceptions. Ford Foundation projects, for example, have recently emphasized community-based water rights and water management in both India and the United States.[6] But neither state- nor community-based studies have formally studied the evolution of international interests in water rights.

To redress this neglect, it is useful to begin with some formal propositions about the likely content, context, and consequences of water rights comparisons. These propositions are tested with historical evidence from South Asia and the United States and are revisited at the end of the chapter.

Descriptive Propositions

A first set of propositions concerns the likely historical frequency and geographic scope of water rights comparisons. Drawing on criticism of comparative international law (Markesinis 1990), we may hypothesize that international water rights comparisons are rarely undertaken at all because states rarely seek to borrow legal principles established elsewhere. Hydrologic phenomena, water resources engineering methods, and even water policy approaches which are less subject to these political constraints are more likely to be the subject of comparative inquiry.

Water rights comparisons that do occur are likely to involve areas within a single country, that is, "one-region comparisons" (*Punjab v. Sind* or *Colorado v. California*). "Two-region comparisons," such as this study, occur in association with bilateral development projects. Because comparative law generally uses qualitative methods, the upper bound of multiregion case studies is likely to be ten to fifteen cases, after which comparative inquiry gives way to cataloguing (Caponera 1973). We may also hypothesize that water rights comparisons focus on places with historically established and formally documented water rights regimes, rather than places with customary rights.

Given these limitations on the frequency and scope of comparison, it would not be surprising if most comparisons involved simple juxtapositions of cases, followed by informal inferences drawn by the analyst (for example, Ali, Radosevich, and Khan 1987). In addition, we would expect most comparisons to be asymmetrical, where an author from one country either seeks to promote the diffusion of a water rights practice from that country or, less commonly, to promote the adoption of a water rights practice from another country.

Contextual Propositions

Although few would argue that context is unimportant to the evolution of water rights systems, comparative legal research often focuses on formal principles rather than the political, economic, or cultural context of water law. When analyzing the record of historical comparison of water rights in the United States and South Asia, six key contextual issues seem pertinent.

First, we would expect international comparisons to be prompted by pressing water problems, for example, recent or anticipated hazards. If comparative water law research is more often problem based than discipline based, we would expect less attention to philosophical debates than expected outcomes.

A second key contextual issue concerns the aim of comparison, and in particular whether it aims to "import" or "export" a water rights practice. If the region that has a water problem sponsors the comparison, its action resembles an "import." Imports tend to reduce the differences between national water laws; but, as noted earlier, wholesale imports are probably rare and likely to be qualified by assertions about the foreign water rights principles that are not adopted.

A region may also seek to "export" its water rights institutions. Exports may be induced or coerced. If the export is driven by geopolitical issues unrelated to water, the context is voluntary. If it is driven by international water project investment, finance, or repayment, however, the context of the comparison may involve some coercion. Exports may also aim to "eradicate difference," for example, in the promotion of water markets and water rights transfers.

Presumably, multilateralism would encourage imports as well as exports and thus support multicountry comparisons, codification, and, ultimately, model water codes. However, as suggested earlier, concerns about sovereignty may lead national water organizations to have an ambivalent attitude toward comparative water law. If correct, multilateral organizations would tend to regard water law as a necessary but contentious and frustrating aspect of water management to be avoided rather than promoted.

We would thus expect academic research on the broader context of water rights regimes to rely upon historical evidence and to be relatively distant from contemporary policy debates. If true, Henry Sumner Maine's thesis that law lags behind social change might be amended to acknowledge that comparative inquiry also lags behind legal change. Academic research on legal policy alternatives is often funded by bilateral or multilateral organizations, and presumably serves their goals.

Propositions about Impacts

Our overall project on landed property rights is deeply concerned with the environmental and social impacts of those rights. The null hypothesis for this chapter is that international water rights *comparisons* have no impact on water management, and thus no social or environmental impacts as well. This possibility may be regarded as discouraging or encouraging, depending upon the situation and impacts involved. Comparisons undertaken in situations of coercion, such as conquest or colonization, may facilitate the imposition of foreign or regressive institutions that do harm to land and people (Wescoat 1996).

In voluntary situations, comparisons are less likely to have any discernible impacts, except in cases where water managers are actively seeking to import and adapt water institutions that speak to pressing water problems. Comparisons by importing countries are most influential at the outset of the process of property rights definition, when they help clarify an ill-defined problem.[7] Attempts to export property rights institutions, by contrast, bear little fruit except when strongly linked with broader processes of trade.

Finally, it also seems likely that the regions and peoples most vulnerable to disruptive property rights imports or exports are those which have the least well documented and established systems of ownership.[8] The tendency in such regions is to oversimplify rules of customary ownership and to displace or overlay existing traditions of ownership with foreign institutions.

These propositions about the patterns, context, and impacts of water rights comparisons will recur throughout the case study of South Asia and the United States. Collectively, they provide a template for assessing the record and consequences of international water rights research.

HISTORICAL AND
GEOGRAPHIC SCOPE OF INQUIRY

In 1873, the government of India passed the Northern India Canal and Drainage Act, which replaced much simpler legislation on water rents and became the foundation for water management in India and Pakistan up to the present day.[9] In the same year, 1873, the U.S. Congress appointed a Board of Commissioners to assess the prospect for large-scale irrigation agriculture in the Central Valley of California. One of the commissioners, an astronomer named George Davidson, who was seconded from the Coast

Survey happened to be going on a government trip to Japan "to observe the transit of Venus." It was deemed worthwhile for him to pass through India on his way home to examine irrigation works there. Because this trip led to the first comparative assessment of water rights and regional development in India and the United States, it is a fitting start for this paper. In the 120 years that followed, there were only a few major water rights comparisons, so the survey is carried up to the present day.

The geographic scope of investigation is complicated by both territorial restructuring in the regions and by the inherently local scale of water rights allocation and administration. In both regions, customary and community forms of water rights coexist with those defined by the state. National governments also claim special types of water rights, and they assert a host of policies that limit the water rights of others. These national institutions are themselves restricted by international water treaties and policies.

This study limits itself to the continental United States, India, and Pakistan. The number of comparative investigations involving the United States, India, and Pakistan is relatively small, and they tend to concentrate on a few subregions of those countries. In the field of water rights, California, Colorado, and the Punjab stand out, for reasons that will be discussed later.

Water rights comparisons must be considered in relation to three associated water institutions, namely, river basin planning, international water laws, and local water management. River basin development sought, in part, to surmount the obstacles of factious land and water laws. Some comparisons have been drawn between the Tennessee Valley Authority (TVA), Damodar Valley, Gal Oya, and Mahaveli projects. International water law occasionally also has a bearing on the exercise of water rights. Geographically, treaties on the Indus, Columbia, and Colorado rivers have previously been compared with one another. But the primary focus in recent comparative research has been on local water management, which has had the aim of strengthening local institutions including water rights.

The account that follows is organized in three major sections that retrace the diffusion of water rights institutions, first from British India to the western United States in the late nineteenth century, followed by a dramatic reversal in the flow of influence from the United States to the newly independent nations of South Asia in the mid–twentieth century, and concluding with the current cross-currents of comparison and influence in the late twentieth century.

TROUBLE IN CALIFORNIA: EARLY COMPARISONS BETWEEN INDIA AND THE UNITED STATES

Early international interest in water rights stemmed from the physical and economic expansion of irrigation agriculture in the second half of the nineteenth century (Whitcombe 1983). Scientific and popular articles on Indian irrigation began to appear in the American press by midcentury, and consular reports were solicited by the U.S. Congress (Norton 1855; Poston 1867–68; Skinner 1849; Smith 1860).

The American Civil War temporarily suspended interactions between these two regions, but it also fueled the expansion of irrigated cotton in the Indus and Nile valleys to replace the embargoed American cotton supplies to the Lancaster mills (Harnetty 1972; McHenry 1863). Initially, Indian irrigated cotton competed favorably with dryland cotton production in the southern United States, so there was not much the British sought to learn from American irrigation which could not be more clearly discerned from Spain and the Middle East (from which early irrigation systems in the western United States also descended). Mormon irrigators made important innovations, but their success was attributable in part to the religious organization of Mormon society and was not widely known outside the United States (Powell 1878).

The main mid–nineteenth-century issue in Indian irrigation concerned the role of the state in infrastructure development, a question discussed by distinguished scholar-administrators such as John Stuart Mill, Jeremy Bentham, and Henry Sumner Maine, as well as scores of civil servants. Mill wrote about the expansion of public works investment in India, while Maine compared Roman, feudal, and Indian forms of property.[10]

After the 1857 rebellion, the British Crown took over the territorial responsibilities of the East India Company, and issues of land and water ownership and public finance became even more pressing. Some of these issues were addressed through comparative inquiry. For example, the government of India sent Lt. Colin Campbell Scott-Moncrief (1868) to study irrigation systems and laws in southern Europe and the Middle East, but not America. Scott-Moncrief admired the local works, careful management, and community-based institutions of Spain and Italy, although they stood in sharp contrast with the large-scale imperial works in India. Neither he, nor other contemporary British analysts, mentioned irrigation experiments in the United States.

Americans began to study Scott-Moncrief's report and other British documents on irrigation in India as irrigation problems arose in California.

The first state engineer, William Hammond Hall, described the situation in California as follows:

> Here have met . . . customs of the civil law countries of southern Europe, as modified by Mexican practice; the common law watercourse rulings of English courts; and a mining water-right jurisprudence, with customs locally evolved under new conditions. Here also have met, to develop this industry and make laws for its governance, people from all parts of the world and in all grades of circumstances, hardly any of whom had the slightest idea of water-right systems or irrigation customs, legislation, administration or practice. (Hall 1886, 5)

> Varied and many as were the questions . . . they were few and simple as compared to the propositions which were made for their solution. (ibid., 6)

In addition to local institutional problems, there was growing interest in the large-scale irrigation potential of the San Joaquin and Sacramento Valleys. In 1873, the U.S. Congress appointed a Board of Commissioners to assess the financial viability, technical obstacles, and public role of irrigation development. As noted in the introduction to this chapter, Commissioner George Davidson was sent on a fact-finding mission to India, which was perceived to be the closest analogue to the Central Valley of California.[11]

Davidson arrived in India soon after passage of the Northern India Canal and Drainage Act of 1873. Like others who followed, he began his discussion of water rights in India by quoting the Preamble to that act, which read:

> Whereas, throughout the territories to which this Act extends, the Provincial Government is entitled to use and control for public purposes the water of all rivers and streams flowing in natural channels, and of all lakes, sub-soil water and other natural collections of still water . . . it is hereby enacted as follows. . . . (Masood ul Hassan 1992, 1)

Davidson was astonished by this wholesale assumption of public water control, which was further magnified by the sweeping administrative and magisterial powers assigned to canal officers. On the first point, however, he and other professional commentators who traveled briefly in India

seriously misinterpreted the 1873 act. In taking the Preamble literally, they
failed to recognize that customary water rights had been documented and
recognized and that the act applied to unappropriated waters, as did contemporary constitutional clauses in states of the western United States
(Gilmartin, 1994, 1998). The act did give provincial governments powers
to allocate remaining waters to landlords and to appropriate water for government lands and projects, but those powers fell far short of the authority
inferred by U.S. commentators.

A similar pattern of exaggeration and distinction occurred in
Davidson's interpretation of "takings" of land and water rights in India.

> The government of India exercises the absolute right to use and
> control the waters of all streams and lakes, without compensation.
> The compensation for entry upon private lands is arbitrary and
> minimum. . . . *It is utterly impossible that such conditions could exist
> in the United States except where the Government entered new terri-
> tory.* . . . (Davidson 1875, 39, emphasis added)

But once again, the similarity between what is criticized in India and
recommended for adoption in the United States is striking, for Davidson
and others did regard the Central Valley of California as something of a
"new territory" to be publicly reclaimed, notwithstanding a welter of local
and inefficient private uses. He went on to argue that:

> The urgency of a system of irrigation is great, and should be
> developed before the country is densely populated, and before con-
> flicting rights are too great. . . . The whole system of irrigation
> should be designed and projected by the Government and main-
> tained under the direction of the Government. . . . The subject of
> the 'rights to water' involving the cost of claims thereto, and the
> claims for entry, financially overshadow the whole scheme [in
> California]; and they utterly forbid it as a commercial enterprise.
> (Davidson 1875, 40)

> As compared with the Italian system, the greater undertakings of
> India and their whole system of distribution seem more analogous
> to what is required in the United States. . . . The Indian enter-
> prises are not cramped by existing systems; but in Italy such an
> undertaking as the Cavour had to consider the rights and condi-
> tions of all existing works for irrigation; there is thus in the former,
> as there would be in the United States, a comparatively untouched

field, a greater breadth of view, a larger freedom of plan and action. (Davidson 1875, 40)

Like Scott-Moncrief before him, Davidson admired the efficiency and sophistication of Italian water systems but saw a closer analogy with the large-scale and paternally financed, administered, and constructed systems of India. Government was portrayed, in the 1890s at least, as the advocate and protector of small farmers against exploitation by private capital and corporations, a theme that persisted through the first decade of the twentieth century but collapsed quickly, and most dramatically, in California (Pisani 1984, 1992).

Failing to anticipate these events, the Board of Commissioners naively stated:

> It was generally held that the property in water could not safely be entrusted to private hands; that the ignorant cultivators would, without the intervention of the government, be helpless against a powerful corporation; and that any supervision by the government, to be effectual in protecting the cultivators, would interfere with the freedom of the enterprise, and, therefore, with its prosperity and success. . . .
>
> At this time it was thought by the government that the profits of irrigation were great and immediate, and that they should inure to the government and not to a corporation. (Commissioners 1894, 55)

Finally, George Davidson dashed off some suggested principles for water ownership in California.[12]

> Where irrigation is a necessity, all the irrigable land should have equal rights to the water available for that purpose; and the land should be so wedded to the water that the fee-simple of the former should include the latter; their bond should be indissoluble under any process of law. The water must go with the land, and the land must carry the water. The full development of many of our broad valleys depends wholly and solely upon the adoption of some of these propositions. (Davidson 1875, 69)

These principles coincide point for point with those prevailing in the Punjab.

Although influential, the Board of Commissioners' report did not settle the question of water rights for large-scale irrigation in California.

The first California state engineer, William Hammond Hall, surveyed the water law proposals that had been proposed for the state. The first option was:

> . . . for the United States government to purchase all water-rights
> and canals in the state, construct great works of storage, diversion,
> and distribution, and sell the water to consumers . . . there was
> ample precedent in the action of the English government in India
> . . . and it would be vain to attempt widespread irrigation in the
> state under any other auspices. (Hall 1886, 6)

The second option merely substituted the state of California for the United States government. Other options transferred riparian rights to prior appropriators, or proposed a combination of solutions for different parts of the state.

Like Davidson and others, Hall believed it would be useful to study the history, customs, laws, and administrative systems of other countries. But he turned away from India and toward France, Italy, and Spain.

> These are the countries where irrigation has developed under con-
> ditions such that we may expect to derive some useful lessons in
> public policy and private enterprise from its study. (Hall 1886, 15)

His review established a template that others would follow: He began with Roman water law and proceeded to describe contemporary systems of water law and administration in southern Europe (cf. Kinney 1912).

The U.S. Congress also compiled disparate reports from travelers and consuls in various countries including China, Russia, Afghanistan, and Egypt. The influence of these documents is unclear; some of them quoted classical authors (for example, Cato and Varro 1934) or eastern travel accounts in ways that had more literary than practical value (Poston 1867–68; Skinner 1849; Smith 1860–61; and U.S. Congress 1868, 1890).[13]

Engineers were awed by irrigation works underway in India (Brown 1904). The most prolific analyst was Herbert M. Wilson (1890, 1890–91, 1894) who prepared two major reports and several short articles that compared India and the United States. He wrote entirely about perennial canal systems, however, ignoring delta and inundation canals, noting:

> The great similarity between the climate and topography of the
> great northern plains of India and portions of our arid west, espe-
> cially the eastern slope of the Rocky mountains and the great

California Valley. Central India and the Deccan have many features in common with the central arid territories, particularly portions of northern Arizona and southern Utah. (Wilson 1890–91, 369)

Like Davidson, he stressed the role of water rights institutions in land settlement. Although he traveled to Italy, he was most impressed by the civil service and public works departments of India: ". . . the government of India has entire control over all sources of water supply and so exercise it as to make it the greatest benefit to the community at large. The powers of control over the waters for irrigation are entirely centralized." (ibid. 409)

Wilson's short article in 1894 brought the water rights comparison into sharper focus. Of six key points, "the first point of difference is dependent chiefly on the fact that in India all land and all water belong to the government, and that all irrigation works are designed, constructed and maintained by the government."[14] In India, legal disputes over water were few. In the American West, by contrast:

The priority of right to appropriate water and the ownership thereof give rise to some of the most troublesome and expensive legal complications with which the Western people have to deal. In this country the laws relating to the ownership of irrigable lands and works . . . have become so voluminous and differ so greatly in the various states as to create one of the most serious impediments to the inception of irrigation enterprises. (Wilson 1894, 107)

Among the adverse economic consequences of these laws, Wilson complained, "Direct money profit . . . has as yet been chiefly realized from the sale and ownership of land, the value of which has been increased by furnishing it with a water supply, rather than from the sale of water developed by the project" (ibid. 107). Wealth rose more from the appreciation of land values than from the value added by irrigation.

Frederick Haynes Newell, who later became the first U.S. commissioner of reclamation, made two key comments on Wilson's studies in India. He was particularly concerned about the dynamics of institutional development:

The history of other nations has shown that an irrigation canal or system of ditches once developed—whether located poorly or not—is rarely improved, and if at all, with the greatest difficulty and expense. All rights, individual, corporate, or municipal, quickly become clustered around that system of water distribution and he who would better it must literally buy out the whole country before it can be changed, for in arid regions running water is the one thing which gives value to the land. (Newell in Wilson 1890, 256–57)

Newell combined the engineer's desire for a "clean slate" with the progressive battle against private monopolies over natural resources:

The essential difference between irrigation in India and in the United States is, that while there the canals are owned and built by government, and regulated not for profit alone, but directly for the benefit of the people and protection from famine, in the United States irrigation has sprung from private enterprise, and the government has, as yet, in legislation hardly recognized its [irrigation's] existence. . . . Water appropriation has gone on unchecked and unregulated, apparently under the motto of each man for himself. (ibid. 259)

Like many of the progressive engineers of his day, Newell believed that wasteful litigation over water necessitated local and federal legislation— "all engineers concede . . . this" (ibid. 259).

Summary

These early comparative investigations support some of the propositions listed earlier, but not all of them. Comparison was prompted by pressing water problems in California, which led to an import situation. The geographic areas compared were limited and asymmetrical. The water rights comparisons involved more than simple juxtaposition, but stopped short of detailed analysis. It is not clear whether Californians were seriously interested in importing British institutions vis-à-vis their irrigation technology.

The main items of trade at this time were technological, for example, in hydraulic and earthwork engineering. Detailed technical reports on Indian canals, weirs, and diversion structures were published (Buckley 1880). However, British engineering journals also published information on emerging tubewell technologies in the United States. At about the same time, agricultural scientists began to have concerns about the environmental consequences of large-scale irrigation based on comparison of India and the American West (for example, Hilgard 1886 on soil degradation in India and California).

As cited above, ambivalence toward water rights of all sorts was expressed. Some of the most influential British treatises on Indian irrigation did not even mention water rights (for example, Buckley 1880).

The impact of British irrigation in California has yet to be fully assessed; but it does seem to have included a strong connection between state property and large-scale water projects, such as the Central Valley and State Water Projects, and exclusion of Punjabi immigrants from small-scale landownership rights (Leonard 1989). Although these California projects seem to share common characteristics with Indian irrigation projects and policies, they also reflect several decades of federal water development in the United States, which would eventually be exported back to India.

FROM IMPORTS TO EXPORTS—AND WATER RIGHTS TO RIVER BASINS

International comparisons had little influence on the elaboration of state water rights systems in the United States during the twentieth century.[15] A review of water law by the U.S. President's Water Policy Commission (1950) exemplified the new pattern of thought: It began with provisions of the U.S. Constitution relevant to water law, and then examined state water laws. It did not make one reference to water laws outside the United States.

Instead, river basin development became the main object of international exchange and comparative research. Development of major rivers such as the Colorado, Tennessee, and Indus was hampered by interstate conflicts, discordant water laws, and narrow river engineering methods that failed to consider the basin as a planning region.

With the advent of river basin planning and development in the United States, the flow of international comparisons with India reversed direction. During the 1930s and 1940s, for example, the governments of Punjab and Sind cited interstate case law from the United States (Government of Sind 1944). It seems extraordinary to imagine the government of Sind citing *Hinderlider v. LaPlata & Cherry Creek Ditch Co.* (304 US 92, 58 SCt 803, 82 LEd 1202 [1938]), a precedent-setting case on a tributary of a tributary of the Colorado River, when the entire Colorado River carries only 10 percent of the flow of the Indus. Nevertheless, upon the partition of India and Pakistan, Gulhati observed:

This study [by Sikri], based on such literature as was then available in India, did not reveal any defined principles of international law that could be applied to the new problem on the Indus; there was plenty of literature, however, on inter-State practice in the U.S.A. (Gulhati 1973, 324)

Gulhati (1972) himself wrote a book on interstate water law in India, the United States, and other countries.[16] On the use of international analogies, he wrote:

> Obviously, any analogy from another federated country would be relevant in the Indian context only to the extent that the law in that other country conforms to the law in India. (Gulhati 1972, 68)

Interestingly, he primarily drew upon a compilation of American water law that had been prepared by the National Reclamation Association, a partisan organization known for its advocacy of states' rights and federal spending!

A more powerful set of institutions for water development arose in the Tennessee valley as part of President Franklin D. Roosevelt's New Deal program for mobilizing domestic resources. The Tennessee Valley Authority (TVA) was created in 1933 as a semiautonomous federal corporation and utility with broad administrative powers. The TVA concept was imported, and expanded in scope, by the Damodar Valley Authority of India in 1947 and subsequently in other basins of South Asia (White 1957; United Nations 1970). National governments in both regions sought to transcend the welter of local and state institutions by creating basin organizations with unified administrative power and substantial financial resources.[17]

Immediately following World War II, the U.S. government began to actively export concepts and methods of river basin development. In 1948, for example, the first United Nations conference on natural resources was convened at Lake Success, New York. Of its two sessions on water, the first dealt with river basin development and the second with the TVA.

In 1958, Pakistan established a national Water and Power Development ment Authority (WAPDA) to supervise the planning, construction, and operation of a system of reservoirs and hydroelectric facilities for the entire Indus valley. Although WAPDA was a TVA on a national scale, with enormous stature and authority, provincial governments retained full responsibility for water rights and canal irrigation management.[18] But by assuming status and resources formerly concentrated at the provincial level, the new national institutions weakened water rights administration at the local and provincial levels (WAPDA 1990).

River basin development acquired special salience in the Indus Basin, which was divided between India and Pakistan in 1947. International water conflicts surfaced almost immediately in 1948 (Gulhati 1973; Michel 1967). Pakistan claimed "proprietary rights" to historical canal deliveries in the Punjab while India asserted that partition created "sovereign territorial rights" over the waters within its borders. An interdominion agreement in 1948 brought temporary stability to the situation. Pakistan sought arbitration from the International Court of Justice; codification by international water law by the UN International Law Commission; and support from the UN General Assembly—all to no effect.

Longer-term negotiations were facilitated in 1951 by a proposal from David Lilienthal, former director of the TVA, who advocated cooperative river basin administration as a way to reduce water conflict, alleviate tensions over Kashmir, and strengthen democracy in the region.[19] The World Bank provided its "good offices" and financial encouragement for the treaty negotiations.

As the Indian technical representative, N. D. Gulhati noted the literature on international water law was limited. Little of it spoke to the problems of new nations and multilateralism in the post–World War II period. So India retained F. J. Berber, a German international law specialist, while Pakistan obtained legal counsel from John Laylin of the United States; and the World Bank involved its legal department. Berber and Gulhati toured Europe and the United States, collecting legal and technical information at The Hague, Rome, Ottawa, and elsewhere. On the basis of these comparative investigations, Berber (1959) wrote an influential treatise on international water law.

Of principal interest here, however, is the role that comparative legal investigations played at various stages of the negotiations. From the detailed accounts of Gulhati (1973) and Michel (1967), it appears that comparison was an important tool at the onset of negotiations. It provided an orientation to the issues, and a source of broad principles and alternatives. Even then, it was regarded with caution and ambivalence. It was agreed that legal rights should "not be affected" by the negotiations (Gulhati 1973, 99).

The president of the World Bank, Eugene R. Black, opened the Indus Basin treaty negotiations by stating:

> I would not, for a moment, under-estimate the difficulties that lie before the Working Party. . . . We know that they can be solved if tackled by the right people and in the right spirit. The people to do this kind of a job are technicians, who can approach the problem on a functional rather than a political basis. . . .
>
> . . . [T]he Indus problem is an engineering problem and should be dealt with by engineers. One of the strengths of the engineering profession is that, all over the world, engineers speak the same

language and approach problems with common standards of judgement. (In Gulhati 1973, 104–105)

Interestingly, the legal issues were handled by foreign consultants to South Asian negotiators, many of whom were engineers. Very quickly, attention narrowed from international comparisons to specific issues, situations, and negotiating positions in the Indus Basin. Comparative investigation continued to operate implicitly in the drafting of treaty articles, and explicitly in Indian and Pakistani contributions to the International Law Association's work on international water law (Wescoat 1992b).

Summary

During the twentieth century, the United States moved from being an importer to an exporter of water resources institutions, including water laws and river basin management. These interstate, regional, and international institutions redefined the role of "water rights" relative to other allocative institutions, both in the United States and South Asia. However, almost no attention was given to indigenous cultural traditions of ownership vis-à-vis broad international principles based on European and U.S. experience. The geographic scope of comparative studies thus reflected a handful of national and international experiments in river basin development, rather than a broad range of institutional approaches to regional water management. Comparative legal investigation occurred only at the onset of a problem, after which it was embedded in the negotiations or abandoned. The logic of river basin comparisons went beyond simple juxtapositions to identify common principles and traits, but it stopped short of examining the diffusion of river basin institutions or their relations with water rights regimes.

In summary, legal comparisons between the United States and India had some influence in pre-independence disputes between Punjab and Sind; and they had considerable value at the beginning of the Indus Waters Treaty negotiations. However, in each of these cases there was only grudging consideration of water rights per se and a sense that local ownership issues could and should give way to larger regional and national interests.[20]

WATER RIGHTS IN A MULTILATERAL CONTEXT

Disintegration of colonial regimes opened the door to increased U.S. and multilateral influence in water sector programs. The United States had a heavy but diminishing influence in the multilateral water programs of the

United Nations and World Bank in the 1950s through 1980s. Multilateral development of the Indus and Mekong river basins in the 1960s raised great expectations about the role of international organizations and the need for detailed comparative inquiry. Bilateral water programs were also prominent in the work of the U.S. Agency for International Development. Many of these programs evaded property rights issues, but there were some important exceptions.

Toward a Model Water Code: Multilateral Initiatives

Upon independence, many new nations lacked adequate or coherent water laws. Institutions for water allocation, administration, planning, and management were viewed as prerequisites for sound national and international investment. Three organizations began to compile and compare national water laws. The FAO Legislative Branch, for example, published an early compilation of *Water Laws in Moslem Countries* (Caponera 1954 [1973]).

The next major compilation was prepared by the Economic Commission for Asia and the Far East (ECAFE), a regional organization of the United Nations (1967, 1968). The impetus for this compilation was the belief that ". . . water had become a critical factor dictating or limiting the nature and extent of further development" (United Nations 1968, 161). ECAFE surveyed water laws in South and Southeast Asian nations, including India and Pakistan, to identify broad principles for preparing national water codes. The United States, United Kingdom, and France also participated, but their laws were not included in the survey. The aim of the comparison was to ". . . study the principal subjects which should be included in a comprehensive water code" (United Nations 1967, iii). Survey results were organized as follows:

1. Legislation in force
2. Ownership and right to use water
3. Order of priorities
4. Legislation on beneficial uses and harmful effects
5. Water wastage, quality, and pollution control
6. Underground waters
7. Water rights administration and supervision
8. Special water development agencies
9. Control of hydraulic structures
10. Declaration of protected zones or areas
11. Implementation of water legislation
12. Comments on existing legislation

Items two and seven focused on property rights. Special consideration was given to the distinction between "public" and "private" waters. The survey noted that state control over "public waters" in India did not imply state ownership of those waters (ibid. 163). Private ownership was regarded in most ECAFE countries as a *residuum* of water control, that is, after state interests and management capacity have been taken into account. However, there was little consensus on the actual or proper relations between public and private control:

> . . . the Working Group noted that no two countries appeared to agree exactly on those waters which should be regarded as public and those which should be private. However, all participants regarded navigable rivers and major streams as public water, and all regarded water lawfully reduced into certain receptacles, or collected from the eaves of a house, as permitting of private ownership by person [sic], communities, or corporations. Beyond this, generalization was found to be difficult. (ibid. 163)

The difficulty would have been even more keenly appreciated if community perceptions of ownership had been examined. The Working Group was not able to identify clear or consistent criteria for distinguishing public and private waters; nor did it consider that such formal distinctions might be of limited significance (see Wescoat 1984, ch. 8).

The Working Group had somewhat more success on the topic of water rights. It began with basic rights:

> . . . all countries recognized certain limited rights of all members of the public to use water from public sources without seeking specific administrative permission. . . . All recognized that private persons might take public water to quench their thirst and for certain domestic or household purposes. Some also acknowledged the right to water domestic animals and to irrigate household gardens. Although some participants were of the opinion that these rights were so fundamental that they did not require legislative recognition, the opinion was expressed that a code should reaffirm such customary rights.

It is worth noting, however, that the alleged consensus on basic rights to water is not formally recognized or enforced in the United States or South Asia (Gleick 1998; McCaffrey 1992; Wescoat 1995). It is also noteworthy, in light of past efforts to export U.S. water laws, that the prior appropriation doctrine was only mentioned once in the ECAFE survey; and even then it was simply to note that it does not apply in the region (UN 1968, 180). The ECAFE survey also neglected to consider how water laws have been affected by international relations and multilateral organizations.

Soon after the ECAFE studies, specialized agencies at UN headquarters began to compile materials on national systems of water administration and management (United Nations 1974). The FAO Legislative Branch published comparisons of groundwater law and international water law. Ongoing coverage of international water issues was provided by the UN Department for Technical Cooperation and Development (UNDTCD), which published a newsletter titled *Rivers and Lakes* on international water issues, as well as occasional monographs (Wolf 1999). See also two Internet websites on international water law at http://terra.geo.orst.edu/users/tfdd (the URL for the Transboundary Freshwater Dispute Database) and http://home.att.net/~intlh2olaw/ (the URL for the International Water Law Project).

These broad-scale legal surveys paralleled escalating water sector investment programs. Unlike comparisons that were driven by specific projects and problems, these surveys were prompted by long-term development programs. The aim of "Model Water Codes," for example, was to distill common principles for the "progressive development" of national water laws.

There have been no detailed ex post analyses of these multilateral water studies. It is not clear whether these compilations of water law have been used to address national water problems. Their effect on water laws in India and Pakistan, for example, seems to have been negligible, though some recent studies draw upon property rights information compiled from other countries.[21]

From Multilateral to Nongovernmental Initiatives

Multilateral river basin development dramatically transformed many river ecosystems and the societies that depend upon them. In addition to their environmental and social impacts, large water projects and programs did not yield the economic benefits expected of them, in part because the needs of local water users were largely ignored. Criticism was ignored by development agencies, leading to increasingly strident protests, not just of the projects and their impacts but also of the essential character of state involvement in water development.

These practical criticisms of water projects coincided with academic debates about the relations between irrigation and social organization sparked by Karl Wittfogel's *Oriental Despotism: A Comparative Study of Total Power* (1981). Wittfogel had little interest in water management per se, but he had strong views about the connections between aridity, irrigation works, bureaucracy, and despotism (as well as the Soviet threat to democracy!). The first wave of scholarly criticism of Wittfogel involved anthropologists and cultural historians who had no practical involvement in water management (see O'Leary [1989] for the latest in this genre). A second generation of scholars focused on irrigation in modern states and communities (for example, Geertz 1983). A third generation included scholar-practitioners working for development organizations like the Ford Foundation and the U.S. Agency for International Development (USAID 1992).[22]

This last group called for wholesale reform of water sector investment programs in Asia (see Coward 1980; Freeman 1989; Lansing 1991; Uphoff 1992). A major component of reform involved a shift from large-scale public works to improved "management" of supplies and systems. The key challenges of management were: (1) equitable access to water (especially by those at the tail end of canals); (2) efficient physical use and adminis- tration of supplies; (3) conjunctive management of surface and groundwater supplies of varying quality; and (4) increased authority and institutional capacity for community water management organizations. Property rights to water were sometimes implicit but not central in this program of institutional reform. Their limited treatment reflects, once again, historical ambivalence toward water law and concerns about the inefficiency and divisiveness of property rights transactions.

Ford Foundation Programs. From the 1970s to the present, the Ford Foundation has sponsored innovative research on water management in both the western United States and India.[23] The U.S. program included comparisons of water rights issues in the western states, extending occa- sionally into Mexico and Canada, but not to Asia. The Ford Foundation program in India, by contrast, has funded the Indian Law Institute to examine U.S. and other water laws (Singh 1991; Vani 1992). There have been no formal comparisons of Ford's water law studies in India and the United States.

USAID Programs. USAID has sponsored several important compara- tive studies. For example, USAID funded massive irrigation management programs in Pakistan, which were directed for some years by Colorado State University.[24] Thousands of references to water institutions and laws were compiled in a bibliographic monograph series (Jones 1971, 1972; Jones et al. 1974).

Three water development projects in Pakistan stand out for their use of comparative investigation. The On-Farm Water Management Program included an analysis of water users associations at the watercourse level (Mirza, Freeman, and Eckert 1975). Radosevich and Kirkwood (1975), for example, explored organizational alternatives for on-farm water management by compiling examples from the United States, Spain, Argentina, Turkey, and Taiwan. Although they appreciated the challenges of institutional transfers (even quoting Montesquieu on the uniqueness of laws adapted to each land), they went so far as to reproduce the Colorado Uniform Corporation Code, bylaws for the Grand Valley [Colorado] Irrigation Company, the Grand Valley Water Users Association, the Idaho Irrigation District Law, and documents from the other countries noted. These efforts also supported the institutional components of two other USAID projects in Pakistan—the Water Management Synthesis project and Command Water Management.

All of these bilateral projects operated within what we might call a "weak export" context. Management approaches were exported to Pakistan within a broader geopolitical context that had little to do with water. Project evaluations repeatedly noted the entrenched institutional barriers to reform, for example, bureaucratic resistance to the devolution of authority; the decline of water users associations and local institutions soon after construction of physical works; and cultural traditions of competition and conflict.

On the latter point, Merrey (1979) emphasized the calculus of honor (*izzat*), vis-à-vis cooperative management. Honor depended upon a willingness to use force to maintain one's social position relative to others, willingness to use influence, willingness to entertain lavishly and engage in private generosity, desire to win regardless of the collective consequences, and the aptness of such maxims as "Who holds the stick, owns the buffalo." Mirza and Merrey (1979) concluded that substantial changes were needed in Punjab water law to turn these cultural traditions toward a beneficial, or less harmful, direction, but such changes would not be advanced by USAID programs.

USAID programs in South Asia and elsewhere are generally fragmented among individual country missions. One experiment was designed to coordinate country irrigation programs. It involved a comparative assessment of irrigation projects and programs known as ISPAN, the Irrigation Support Program for Asia and the Near East. ISPAN prepared water sector strategy papers for its country missions in Asia and the Near East (USAID 1992, 1993). Thoughtfully assembled and produced, these regional studies were printed shortly before the completion of the ISPAN contract and closure of its office. Unless picked up by some other USAID program or put to use at the mission level, these regional efforts will have little impact.

The World Bank. The World Bank sponsored a comparative study of irrigation systems by Anthony Bottrall in 1981, which like many reports of the "irrigation management movement" stressed the need for equitable water distribution (that is, enforceable water rights) for tail enders. The bank's Operations Evaluation Department has also prepared project appraisals that would permit comparative institutional assessments; but project imperatives seem to leave bank staff, consultants, and borrowers with little time, energy, incentives, or resources for comparative analysis. More recently, some offices in the World Bank have strongly advocated privatization of water services and the establishment of private property rights in water, for example, in the Indus Basin of Pakistan (World Bank 1994; Mumtaz 1996). Although modeled after arguments for water rights and markets in Western countries, they have not acknowledged either the limited progress toward water markets in those countries, or the full historical record of public and private performance in providing water services (Mustafa 2000).

International Irrigation Management Institute. Among the many nongovernmental organizations involved in water management, the International Irrigation Management Institute (IIMI) has gone furthest toward comparative institutional analysis of water systems in South Asia and other regions. IIMI has sought to integrate the technical, environmental, social, and institutional dimensions of management. Although multiregional in scope, its core program has focused on South Asian countries. Through workshops and publications, IIMI has made important substantive contributions to comparative irrigation studies (for example, IIMI 1991).

Interestingly, the legal definition of rights has not figured prominently in the IIMI agenda. Water rights have been regarded as a necessary, but not focal, aspect of privatization, local control, and irrigation efficiency. Greater emphasis has been placed on the strengthening of community and bureaucratic organizations than the articulation and implementation of legal institutions (Bhutta and Vander Velde 1992; cf. Ostrom 1992).

Law Associations. However, comparative legal research has been advanced by some international nongovernmental organizations (INGOs), such as the International Water Law Association. As in many other fields, INGOs have proceeded more rapidly than international governmental organizations (IGOs).[25] George Radosevich (1975) organized the first global conference on water law in Valencia, Spain. Although the proceedings from that conference have not received the attention or circulation they deserve, subsequent proceedings have been used by the Indian Law Institute in its Water Project Series (for example, Singh 1991).

Summary

Multilateral and nongovernmental initiatives have been both import- and export-driven in recent decades, and American-trained social scientists have had a significant influence in both processes. The "water management movement," which partially arose in response to problems generated by river basin development, has now taken root in multilateral water programs. It has been embraced in some South Asian water programs and resisted in others—just as it has been adopted by some U.S. water groups and not others.

The turn toward water management has also yielded a limited body of multidisciplinary property rights research. But comparative research on South Asian, U.S., and other water rights institutions deserves further attention. Marcus Moench (1991) has recently conducted a major comparison of groundwater management institutions in India and the United States (see also Moench 1999; and National Research Council 1996). These studies suggest that an aim for future comparative research may once again be to seek out lessons from Asian water management experience for adaptation and application in the United States—as occurred with different problems and alternatives in the late nineteenth century.

CONCLUSIONS

With this historical-geographic perspective on water rights in South Asia and the United States in mind, we may now return to the theoretical propositions that were made about the nature, context, and impact of comparative inquiry.

The Changing Nature of Water Rights Comparisons

As hypothesized, international water rights comparisons were infrequent relative to research on other aspects of water resources science, technology, and management during the period from 1873 to 1998. International water research has been dominated by civil engineers with increasing, but still limited, involvement by environmental scientists, economists, and other social scientists. Water rights comparisons, when they have occurred, have generally been conducted by this last group, which treats water rights within a much broader class of water management "institutions." The main explanations for this low frequency of comparison are the slow pace and political constraints on comparative legal inquiry (Wescoat 1992b). However, this case study revealed two additional factors: first, the importance of recognizing when a region is prepared to consider property rights practices in other regions; and, second, understanding how to design comparisons that have salience in those situations.

This case study also revealed that while scholars in the United States have focused in recent decades on domestic (that is, interstate) comparisons, scholars working in South Asia have been less parochial in their outlook. Multilateral and nongovernmental comparative studies have concentrated on moderate numbers of country case studies (five to fifteen). Bilateral projects have had smaller samples of two to five cases. Large-scale compilations of water laws have been compiled by the UN International Law Commission, the International Water Law Association, and the Food and Agriculture Organization.

Within individual countries, water rights comparisons have also been narrow. In the United States, Colorado and California are often selected; while in South Asia, the Punjab and northern India are most commonly discussed. In international comparisons, emphasis has also been given to state laws and surface water laws, to the neglect of water laws in remote, mountainous, pastoral, groundwater, or urban regions. More systematic sampling and coverage is needed in comparative water rights research.

As hypothesized, most comparisons involve simple juxtapositions from which broader, often tenuous, practical inferences are drawn using a logic that is often vague or implicit and sometimes tautological. Bilateral comparisons have been particularly unbalanced, reflecting (but not critically examining) an import or export mode of comparison. Although multilateral comparisons by the UN are more comprehensive and balanced, they have had less effect upon water policies and projects.

The Changing Context of Water Rights Comparison

The evidence compiled in this research confirms that the most consequential comparisons have been those that were driven by immediate water problems. Multilateral efforts, by contrast, have concentrated on longer-term and less-well-defined water problems. The dominant role of engineering and its ambivalence toward legal inquiry help explain this problem orientation and limited use of comparative law. Scholarly comparisons (for example, of "hydraulic societies"), by contrast, have been driven by entirely different concerns only distantly related to the problems faced by water managers. Most strikingly, by the end of the twentieth century, there was greater integration of scholarly and applied social research on water law and institutions in South Asia than in the United States.

The initial propositions in this paper distinguished situations conducive to the import and export of water laws. Importing regions have, by definition, a practical interest in studying the water rights experience of other regions. They make both positive and negative judgments about that experience, as evidenced by California in the 1880s and India in the 1990s. Such judgments may contribute to the diffusion or differentiation of water rights regimes. An import context occurs at the beginning of the policy analysis. It does not carry through to the drafting or implementation of new property rights institutions.

Colonial imposition of water rights institutions in British India was the clearest case of executive fiat and force in this case study (cf. Wescoat 1996). The export of U.S. water rights institutions, by contrast, was a post–World War II phenomenon coincident with bilateral and multilateral water sector programs. Although largely voluntary, it has been linked with larger geopolitical agendas and political-economic ideologies. The linkages between the international export of institutions and domestic coercion to implement them deserves closer attention.

Postwar international organization has been a major stimulus for comparative water policy studies. Initially, comparative studies sought common concepts, methods, and principles for national water resources administration. As the limits and problems of state water control became clear, greater attention focused on water rights at the community and non-governmental level. However, the continuing role of multilateralism in supporting comparative inquiry and exchange in these local and non-governmental arenas remains unclear, especially in the post–Cold War era and its ongoing restructuring of bilateral and multilateral water programs.

Comparative academic research on water rights was supported in part by these international water development programs and projects that have subsided in recent years. But scholars have also continued to pursue topics of "Oriental despotism" and "hydraulic societies." It remains to be seen whether the intellectual vitality of and institutional support for these fields of comparative institutional research will be sustained and, more importantly, whether the research will be translated into practical water management programs, as occurred in the 1970s and 1980s (Ostrom 1992).

The ambivalent attitude toward legal issues and inquiry among water resources engineers and policy analysts helps explain the limited record and accomplishments of comparative water rights research to date. Comparative legal studies have had higher status in certain scholarly arenas—but less practical impact on water use and management.

The Changing Impacts of Water Resources Comparisons

The extreme examples of legal coercion that occurred in the colonization of the western United States and South Asia had the most dramatic impacts on the semi-arid environments of those regions and the mixed pastoral and cultivating social groups that occupied them. In South Asia, this process led to the 1873 Canal and Drainage Act, which reinforced state control over water resources. Expansion of state control ran contrary to the findings of early comparative studies with southern Europe by Scott-Moncrief and others. However, it was consonant with some principles of Roman law, and it also influenced state water development in central California.

Export of property rights has had severe impacts on certain types of regions and peoples vulnerable to state expansion. Large, sparsely settled regions, such as the Punjab and Central Valley of California, are good examples. More remote, localized environments and communities (for example, in mountainous areas), although vulnerable in other ways, have not experienced the same degree of "legal transplants" and "legal pluralism" (Hooker 1975; Watson 1974). Social groups which have written water (and other property) laws suffer less than those without written laws, in part because the former may be legally recognized in peace treaties and other agreements.

It seems clear from this survey that comparisons driven by import situations have had more nuanced impacts than those driven by coercive, voluntary, or even cooperative exports. The positive influence of imports is greatest at the outset of seemingly intractable problems when analysts are likely to look beyond their borders and generate alternatives that might otherwise be neglected. Although the fundamental misinterpretation of state water rights in India by U.S. commentators in the late nineteenth century reminds us of the serious errors that have occurred, the Wittfogel legacy indicates the potential fruits of such errors. Greater errors probably arise from ignoring water rights practices and innovations in other regions, as occurred in the United States in the second half of the twentieth century, compared with creative comparative research in South Asia from the 1970s to the present. Perhaps the main conclusion to be drawn from comparative research on water and related land rights in South Asia and the United States over the period from 1873 to 2000 is the importance of cultivating an attitude that continually seeks practical lessons from institutions crafted in different regions of the world (Wescoat 2000). Although I have referred to that as an import attitude, the case study reveals that it entails more of an openness to foreign approaches than a slavish adoption of them. American water planners and scholars, in particular, might once again consider shifting from an export to an import attitude to address emerging water problems of the twenty-first century, both in the United States and internationally.

NOTES

1. Principles drawn from the first official U.S. government study of irrigation in India (Davidson 1875, 69).

2. One of the most vivid examples is a speech by Zulficar Ali Bhutto to the United Nations in which he reportedly said, "If there is any interference in the normal and assured supply of irrigation waters, my country would face the threat of *total* annihilation. It would create widespread famine and frustration. It would make it virtually impossible for any authority to control civil strife and bloodshed. Starvation would compel civilized human beings to resort to cannibalism" (Cited in Gulhati 1973, 328, emphasis added).

3. International comparative water law examines water laws within different fields, while comparative international water law focuses on agreements among countries.

4. Good reviews of comparative law include Watson 1974; Markesinis 1990; Kahn-Freund 1974; and Frankenburg 1985. Theoretical work is more central in specific regional and historical contexts, for example, on colonial India, Hooker 1975; Kolff 1992; Price 1992; and Cohn 1989. For the postcolonial context, see Baxi 1985; Beer 1979; and Galanter 1992.

5. In the pragmatic philosophy, theory is not the aim or end of research; it is a tool that becomes refined through use. For its role and character in water resources research, see Wescoat (1992a).

6. See Bates 1993; Singh 1991; and Vani 1992.

7. The best contemporary example is the international research by the Republic of South Africa which seeks to rewrite its water code drawing upon lessons gained from water rights regimes around the world. See the resultant National Water Act (Act no. 36 of 1998), assented to August 20, 1998.

8. A good example is the differential impact of U.S. annexation of New Mexico on Hispanic peoples, whose property rights were formally documented and recognized though not adequately protected, and Pueblo peoples, whose claims to water were not recognized (Clark 1987).

9. Parallel legislation was adopted in 1879 by the Bombay presidency for Sind. After the independence of India and Pakistan, these acts were continued by the provinces of Punjab and Sind (Masood-ul-Hassan 1992).

10. Maine, H. S. 1870. *Ancient Law.* New York: Charles Scribner and Co.; Mill, J. S. 1858. "Memorandum of the Improvements in the Administration of India during the Last Thirty Years." In *Collected Works of John Stuart Mill*, ed. J. M. Robson, M. Moir, and Z. Moir, 91–160. Toronto: University of Toronto Press, 1990.

11. Davidson was instructed to pass through Egypt, France, and Holland if possible. Cf. Alfred Deakin's (1893) travels on behalf of Australia.

12. Late nineteenth-century writers from both the United States and British India use the term "duty of water," which refers to the amount of land that can be reasonably irrigated with a given quantity or flow of water, and which therefore should constitute the upper limit of a water right.

13. For example, Poston (1867–68, 198) quotes without attribution the statement: "In India the law directs that 'on both sides of the canal trees of every description, both for shade and blossom, be planted, so as to make it like the canal under the trees in Paradise, that the sweet flavor of rare fruits may reach the mouth of every one, and that from these luxuries a voice may go forth to travellers, calling them to rest in the cities where their every want will be supplied.'"

14. Wilson 1894, 107. The other five differences included ignorance and poverty (in India); climate; engineering methods; haste and cheapness (in the United States); and maintenance and supervision (again, better in India than the United States). Although Wilson's mistake about landownership was not a common occurrence, it is interesting that American water specialists did not examine land tenancy laws associated with irrigated lands in India (cf. Aggarwala 1991; Ali 1989).

15. Kinney's 1912 treatise on irrigation law was the only one to include chapters on irrigation in Egypt, India, Australia, South Africa, Italy, and Canada. Otherwise, the legal literature is dominated by local comparisons, for example, between Colorado and Utah. The story developed, and persists, that the "Colorado" and "California" doctrines are home grown.

16. American influence extended into the field of constitutional law as well (Barrier 1986; Baxi 1985; Beer 1979; Galanter 1992).

17. Water law received limited consideration in early UN documents on river basin development.

18. It is telling that almost none of the U.S. literature on Indus Basin development or national economic planning considered property rights issues (for example, Lieftinck 1969; Rosen 1985; White House 1964).

19. This combination of water resource management and geopolitics became a central theme in U.S. foreign policy (cf. also the Mekong Basin program). The main concerns were not to "lose India," as China had allegedly been "lost," and to develop a close strategic alliance with Pakistan.

20. Gulhati (1973, 313–14) noted that water apportionment had been a stumbling block for the U.S.-Canada International Joint Commission for decades.

21. Singh (1991, 58), for example, uses FAO sources to compare the outcome of conflicts among water laws in India with those in Africa. The government of Iran solicited ECAFE advice on a draft of its water code in 1967.

22. For a sense of the academic vitality of this work, see W. Coward, ed., *Irrigation and Agricultural Development in Asia: Perspectives from the Social Sciences* (Ithaca, N.Y.: Cornell University Press, 1980).

23. Grantees focusing on water rights, and their relationship with law and management, include the Natural Resources Law Center at the University of Colorado and the Indian Law Institute (ILI) in New Delhi. The ILI proposal to Ford is reprinted in Singh 1991, App. A.

24. Although the record of U.S. development assistance to Pakistan lies beyond the scope of this paper, geopolitics did have a strong effect on Indus Basin water programs and reduced the effectiveness of bilateral water programs (Wescoat, Smith, and Schaad 1992).

25. A good illustration is the contrast between the International Law Association (ILA) and the UN International Law Commission (ILC). The ILA developed the path-breaking "Helsinki rules" in twelve years, while the ILC continues to revise draft articles on the same subject after twenty years (Wescoat 1992a).

BIBLIOGRAPHY

Aggarwala, O. P. 1991. *The Manual of Tenancy Laws (in Pakistan)*. Lahore, Pakistan: Khyber Law Publishers.

Ali, I. 1989. *Punjab under Imperialism, 1885–1947*. New Delhi: Oxford University Press.

Ali, M., G. E. Radosevich, and A. A. Khan. 1987. *Water Resource Policy for Asia*. Proceedings of a symposium in Dhaka, Bangladesh. Rotterdam, Netherlands: Balkema.

Barrier, N. G. 1986. *India and America: American Publishing on India, 1930–1985*. New Delhi: American Institute of Indian Studies.

Bates, Sarah F. 1993. *Searching Out the Headwaters: Change and Rediscovery in Western Water Policy*. Covelo, Calif.: Island Press.

Baxi, U. 1985. "Understanding the Traffic of 'Ideas' in Law between America and India." In *Traffic of Ideas between India and America*, ed. R. Crunden. Delhi: Chanakya Publications.

Beer, L. W., ed. 1979. *Constitutionalism in Asia: Asian Views of the American Influence*. Berkeley: University of California Press.

Berber, F. J. 1959. *Rivers in International Law,*. translated by R. K. Batstone. New York: Oceana, (first published 1955).

Bhutta, M. and E. Vander Velde, Jr. 1992. "Equity of Water Distribution along Secondary Canals in Punjab, Pakistan." *Irrigation and Drainage Systems* 6:161–77.

Bottrall, A. F. 1981. "Comparative Study of the Management and Organization of Irrigation Projects." *Staff Working Paper no. 458*. Washington, D.C.: World Bank.

Braibanti, R., ed. 1966. *Asian Bureaucratic Systems Emergent from the British Imperial Tradition*. Durham, N.C.: Duke University Press.

Brown, F. Lee, and Ingram, Helen. 1987. *Water and Poverty in the Southwest*. Tucson: University of Arizona Press.

Brown, H. 1904. "Irrigation under British Engineers." *Transactions, American Society of Civil Engineers*, no. 31:3–31.

Buckley, R. B. 1880. *The Irrigation Works of India and Their Financial Results*. London: W. H. Allen and Co.

Caponera, D. 1973. *Water Laws of Muslim Countries*. 2 vols. FAO.

———. 1980. *The Law of International Water Resources*, FAO Legislative Study, no. 23. Rome.

Cato, Marcus Porcius and Marcus Terentius Varro. 1934. *Cato and Varro on Agriculture*. Trans. W. D. Hooper and H. B. Ash. Cambridge, Mass.: Harvard University Press.

Clark, I. G. 1987. *Water in New Mexico: A History of Its Management and Use*. Albuquerque: University of New Mexico Press.

Cohn, B. 1989. "Law and the Colonial State in India." In *History and Power in the Study of Law: New Directions in Legal Anthropology*, ed. J. Starr and J. F. Collier, 131–52. Ithaca, N.Y.: Cornell University Press.

Commissioners on the Irrigation of the San Joaquin, Tulare, and Sacramento Valleys. 1894. *Irrigation of the San Joaquin, Tulare and Sacramento Valleys, California*. U.S. House of Representatives, 43d Cong., 1st sess., Ex. Doc. 290.

Coward, W. 1980. *Irrigation and Agricultural Development in Asia*. Ithaca, N.Y.: Cornell University Press.

Davidson, G. 1875. *Irrigation and Reclamation of Land for Agricultural Purposes in India, Egypt, Italy, etc.* U.S. Senate, 44th Cong., Ex. Doc. 94. Washington, D.C.

Deakin, Alfred. 1893. *Irrigated India*. London: W. Thacker & Co.

Frankenburg, G. 1985. "Critical Comparisons: Re-thinking Comparative Law." *Harvard International Law Journal* 26:411.

Freeman, David M. 1989. *Local Organizations for Social Development: Concepts and Cases of Irrigation Organization*. Boulder, Colo.: Westview Press.

Galanter, M. 1992. *Law and Society in Modern India*. New Delhi: Oxford University Press.

Geertz, C. 1983. "Local Knowledge: Fact and Law in Comparative Perspective." *Local Knowledge: Further Essays in Interpretive Anthropology*, 167–234. New York: Basic Books.

Gilmartin, D. 1994. "Scientific Empire and Imperial Science: Colonialism and Irrigation Technology in the Indus Basin." *Journal of Asian Studies* 53:1127–49.

Gilmartin, David. 1998. "Custom, Reason and Property: British Irrigation in the Indus Basin." Delhi: Oxford University Press.

Gleick, P. 1998. "The Human Right to Water." *Water Policy* 1:487–503.

Government of Sind. 1944. *Rejoinder of the Government of Sind to the Representations of the Punjab and other Unites on the Report of the Indus Commission.* Karachi, Pakistan: Government Press.

Gulhati, N. D. 1972. *Development of Inter-State Rivers: Law and Practice in India.* Bombay: Allied Publishers.

———. 1973. *Indus Waters Treaty: An Exercise in International Mediation.* Bombay: Allied Publishers Ltd. Pvt.

Hall, William H. 1886. *Irrigation Development.* Sacramento, Calif.: State Office.

Harnetty, Peter. 1972. *Imperialism and Free Trade: Lancashire and India in the Mid-Nineteenth Century.* Vancouver: University of British Columbia Press.

Hilgard, E. W. 1886. *Alkali Lands.* College of Agriculture, University of California, app. 7.

Hooker, M. B. 1975. *Legal Pluralism: An Introduction to Colonial and Neo-Colonial Laws.* Oxford: Clarendon Press.

International Irrigation Management Institute (IIMI). 1991. "Thematic Research Programs." *Annual Report, 1991.* Colombo, Sri Lanka: IIMI, 1–7.

Jones, Garth N. 1971. *Pakistan Government and Administration: A Comprehensive Bibliography.* Water Management Technical Report no. 6. Fort Collins: Colorado State University (CSU).

———. 1972. *Pakistan Government and Administration: A Comprehensive Bibliography,* Vol. 3. Water Management Technical Report no. 23. Fort Collins: CSU.

Jones, G. N., A. R. Rizwani, M. B. Malik, and R. F. Schmidt. 1974. *Informational Sources on Water Management for Agricultural Production in Pakistan with Special Reference to Institutional and Human Factors.* Water Management Technical Report no. 31. 2 vols. Fort Collins: CSU.

Kahn-Freund, O. 1974. "On the Uses and Misuses of Comparative Law." *Modern Law Review* 37:1–27.

Kinney, C. S. 1912. *A Treatise on the Law of Irrigation and Water Rights etc.* 2nd ed. 4 vols. San Francisco: Bender-Moss Company.

Kolff, D. 1992. "The Indian and British Law Machines: Some Remarks on Law and Society in British India." In *European Expansion and Law: The Encounter of European and Indigenous Law in 19th and 20th-Century Africa and Asia,* ed. W. J. Mommsen and J. A. de Moor, 201–35. Oxford: Berg.

Lansing, J. Stephen. 1991. *Priests and Programmers: Technologies of Power in the Engineered Landscape of Bali.* Princeton, N.J.: Princeton University Press.

Leonard, Karen. 1989. "Punjabi Pioneers in California: Political Skills on a New Frontier." *South Asia* XII:69–81.

Lieftinck, P. et al. 1969. *Water and Power Resources of West Pakistan.* 3 vols. Baltimore, Md.: Johns Hopkins University Press.

Maass, A., and R. L. Anderson. 1978. *. . . and the Desert Shall Rejoice: Conflict, Growth and Justice in Arid Environments*. Cambridge, Mass.: MIT Press.

Maine, H. S. 1870. *Ancient Law*. New York: Charles Scribner and Co.

Markesinis, B. 1990. "Comparative Law—A Subject in Search of an Audience." *Modern Law Review* 53:1–21.

Masood-ul-Hassan, S. ed, 1992. *The Manual of Canal and Drainage Laws*. Lahore, Pakistan: Irfan Law Book House.

McCaffrey, S. 1992. "A Human Right to Water: Domestic and International Implications." *The Georgetown International Environmental Law Review* 5:1–24.

McHenry, George. 1863 (reprint 1969). *The Cotton Trade . . . Considered in Connection with the System of Negro Slavery*. New York: Negro Universities Press.

Merrey, D. 1979. "Irrigation and Honor: Cultural Impediments to Improvement of Local Level Water Management in Punjab Pakistan." *Water Management Technical Report no. 53*. Fort Collins: CSU.

Michel, A. 1967. *The Indus Rivers*. New Haven, Conn.: Yale University Press.

Mirza, A. H., D. Freeman, and J. B. Eckert. 1975. *Village Organizational Factors Affecting Water Management Decision-making among Punjabi Farmers*. Water Management Technical Report no. 35. Fort Collins: CSU.

Mirza, A. H., and D. J. Merrey. 1979. *Organizational Problems and Their Consequences on Improved Watercourses in Punjab*. Water Management Technical Report no. 55. Fort Collins: CSU.

Moench, Marcus. 1991. "Sustainability, Efficiency, and Equity in Groundwater Development: Issues in India and Comparisons with the Western United States." Berkeley, Calif.: Pacific Institute for Studies in Environment, Development, and Security.

Moench, Marcus, ed. 1999. *Rethinking the Mosaic: Investigations into Local Water Management*. Kathmandu: Nepal Water Conservation Foundation.

Montesquieu, Baron de. 1949. *The Spirit of the Laws*, translated by T. Nugent. 2 vols in 1. New York: Hafner Publishing Co.

Mumtaz, Ashraf. 1996. "World Bank Wants Terms Met Before Loan Talks." *Pakistan News Service* 10:no. 1010 (electronic, no page numbers). Thursday, April 11.

Mustafa, Daanish. 2000. "State, Property, and Power in the Geography of Access to Irrigation Water and Vulnerability to Flood Hazard in Pakistan." Ph.D. dissertation. Department of Geography. Boulder: University of Colorado.

National Research Council. 1996. *A New Era for Irrigation*. Washington, D.C.: National Academy Press, pp. 20–45.

Norton, C. E. 1855. "Irrigation in India." *North American Review* 77:439.

O'Leary, B. 1989. *The Asiatic Mode of Production: Oriental Despotism, Historical Materialism, and Indian History*. London: Basil Blackwell.

Ostrom, Elinor. 1992. *Crafting Institutions for Self-Governing Irrigation Systems*. San Francisco: ICS Press.

Pisani, Donald J. 1984. *From Family Farm to Agribusiness*. Berkeley: University of California Press.

———. 1992. *To Reclaim a Divided West: Water, Law and Public Policy 1848–1902*. Albuquerque: University of New Mexico Press.

Poston, C. D. 1867–68. "Irrigation." U.S. House of Representatives. 40th Cong. 2d sess. H. Ex. Doc. 293, U.S. Commission of Agriculture Report 1867.

Powell, John Wesley. 1878. *Report on the Lands of the Arid Region*. 1st ed. Printed as U.S. House of Representatives. 45th Cong. 2d sess. Ex. Doc. 73.

Price, P. G. 1992. "The 'Popularity' of the Imperial Courts of Law: Three Views of the Anglo-Indian Legal Encounter." In *European Expansion and Law: The Encounter of European and Indigenous Law in 19th and 20th-Century Africa and Asia*, ed. W. J. Mommsen and J. A. de Moor, 179–200. Oxford: Berg.

Radosevich, G. and C. Kirkwood. 1975. *Organizational Alternatives to Improve On-Farm Water Management in Pakistan*. Water Management Technical Report no. 36. Fort Collins: CSU.

Radosevich, G. E., ed. 1975. *Proceedings of an International Conference on Global Water Law Systems*. Valencia, Spain. 4 vols. in 2. Fort Collins: CSU.

Rosen, G. 1985. *Western Economists and Eastern Societies: Agents of Change in South Asia, 1950–1970*. Baltimore, Md.: Johns Hopkins University Press.

Scott-Moncrief, C. C. 1868. *Irrigation in Southern Europe: Being the Report of a Tour of Inspection of the Irrigation Works of France, Spain, and Italy, Undertaken in 1867–68 for the Government of India*. London: E. & F. N. Spon.

Singh, Chhatrapati. 1991. *Water Rights and Principles of Water Resources Management*. Water Project Series, Indian Law Institute. With "Research Programme" by U. Baxi. Bombay: N. M. Tripathi Pvt Ltd.

Skinner, F. G. 1849. "Irrigation." *Report of the Commissioner of Patents, 1849*. U.S. House of Representatives. 31st Cong. 1st Sess. H. Ex. Doc. 20.

Smith, E. G. 1860–61. "Irrigation." U.S. House of Representatives. 36th Cong. 2d sess. H. Ex. Doc. 48, Commissioner of Patents Report. Washington, D.C.: Government Printing Office.

Steward, J. et al. 1955. *Irrigation Civilizations: A Comparative Study*. Pan American Union, Social Science Monographs no. 1. Washington, D.C.

Teclaff, L. 1967. *The River Basin in History and Law*. The Hague: Martinus Nijhoff.

———. 1972. *Abstraction and Use of Water: A Comparison of Legal Regimes* UN, ST/ECA/154.

———. 1991. "Fiat or Custom: The Checkered Development of International Water Law." *Natural Resources Journal* 31:45.

United Nations. 1970. *Integrated River Basin Development*. New York.

United Nations Department of Economic and Social Affairs. 1974. *National Systems of Water Administration*. E.74.II.A.10.

United Nations Economic Commission for Asia and the Far East. 1967. *Water Legislation in Asia and the Far East, Part 1*. Water Resource Series, no. 31. Bangkok.

United Nations Economic Commission for Asia and the Far East (ECAFE). 1968. *Water Legislation in Asia and the Far East, Part 2a; 2b*. Water Resource Series, no. 35. Bangkok.

United States Agency for International Development (USAID and ISPAN). 1992. *Draft Water Resources Strategy Bureau for Asia*. Washington, D.C.

———. 1993. *Water Resources Action Plan for the Near East: Background, Issues, and Options*. Washington, D.C.

United States President's Water Resources Policy Commission. 1950. *Water Resources Law 3*. Washington, D.C.

U.S. Congress. 1868. "Irrigation of Public Lands." Correspondence with Egypt, China, Russia, and British Columbia. U.S. House of Representatives. 40th Cong. 2d sess. Ex. Doc. 293. Washington, D.C.: Government Printing Office.

———. 1890. "Report of the Special Committee of the United States Senate on the Irrigation and Reclamation of Arid Lands: Reports on Irrigation from Consuls of the United States." U.S. House of Representatives. 51st Cong. 1st sess. S. Rept. 928, pt. 5, 249–97. Washington, D.C.: Government Printing Office.

Uphoff, Norman. 1992. *Learning from Gal Oya: Possibilities for Participatory Development and Post-Newtonian Science*. Ithaca, N.Y.: Cornell University Press.

Vani, M. S. 1992. *Role of Panchayat Institutions in Irrigation Management: Law and Policy*. Water Project Series, Indian Law Institute. New Delhi: Indian Law Institute.

Verzijl, J. H. W. 1970. *International Law in Historical Perspective, Part III: State Territory*. Leiden, Netherlands: A. W. Sijthoff.

Water and Power Development Authority (WAPDA). 1990. *Water Sector Investment Planning Study*. 5 vols. Lahore, Pakistan: WAPDA.

Watson, A. 1974. *Legal Transplants: An Approach to Comparative Law*. Charlottesville: University Press of Virginia.

Wescoat, J. L., Jr. 1984. *Integrated Water Development: Water Use and Conservation Practice in Western Colorado*. Research Paper no. 210. Chicago: University of Chicago, Department of Geography.

Wescoat, J. L. 1992a. "Common Themes in the Work of Gilbert White and John Dewey." *Annals of the Association of American Geographers* 82:587–607.

Wescoat, J. L., Jr. 1992b. "Beyond the River Basin: The Changing Geography of International Water Problems and International Watercourse Law." *Colorado Journal of International Environmental Law and Policy* 3:301–30.

Wescoat, J. L., Jr. 1995. "The 'Right of Thirst' for Animals in Islamic Law: A Comparative Approach." *Environment and Planning D: Society and Space* 13:637–54.

———. Jr. 1996. "Main Currents in Multilateral Water Agreements: A Historical-Geographic Perspective, 1648–1948," *Colorado Journal of International Environmental Law and Policy* 7:39–74.

———. Jr. 2000. "Wittfogel East and West: Changing Perspectives on Water Development in South Asia and the United States, 1670–2000." In *Cultural Encounters with the Government: Enduring and Evolving Geographic Themes*, ed. A. B. Murphy and D. L. Johnson. Lanham, Md.: Rowman and Littlefield, 109–32.

Wescoat, J. L., Jr., S. Halvorson, and D. Mustafa. 2000. "Water Management in the Indus Basin of Pakistan: A Half-Century Perspective." *Water Resources Development* 16:391–406.

Wescoat, J. L., Jr., R. Smith, and D. Schaad. 1992. "Visits to the U.S. Bureau of Reclamation from South Asia and the Middle East, 1946–1990: An Indicator of Changing International Programs and Politics." *Irrigation and Drainage Systems* 6:55–67.

Whitcombe, E. 1983. "Irrigation." In *The Cambridge Economic History of India, v. 2, c. 1757–1970*, ed. D. Kumar, 677–737. Cambridge: Cambridge University Press.

White, G. F. 1957. "A Perspective of River Basin Development." *Law and Contemporary Problems* 22:157–84.

White House. 1964. *The White House, Report on Land and Water Development in the Indus Plain*. Washington, D.C.: Government Printing Office.

Wilson, H. M. 1890. "Irrigation in India." *Transactions, American Society of Civil Engineers*. no. 454. XXIII:217–60.

Wilson, Herbert M. 1890–91. *Irrigation in India*. 12th Annual Report, U.S. Geological Survey, Part II, Irrigation. Washington, D.C.

Wilson, H. M. 1894. "American and Indian Irrigation Works." *Irrigation Age*, 107–109.

Wittfogel, K. 1981. *Oriental Despotism: A Comparative Study of Total Power*. New York: Vintage (first published 1957).

Wolf, Aaron T. 1999. "Criteria for Equitable Allocations: The Heart of International Water Conflict." *Natural Resources Forum* 23: 3–30.

World Bank. 1994. *Pakistan Irrigation and Drainage: Issues and Options*. Report no. 11884-PAK (restricted). Washington, D.C.

Worster, D. 1985. *Rivers of Empire: Water, Aridity and the Growth of the American West*. New York: Pantheon Press.

11

Property Regimes for Sustainable Resource Management

DANIEL W. BROMLEY

The idea of sustainable resource management now seems to enjoy general acceptance among scholars and development practitioners. Less clear, it seems, is an understanding of how property regimes relate to the important task of implementing sustainability at the local level. That understanding requires some clarification of concepts and language.

The early concern for the so-called "tragedy of the commons" is now understood to reference instead the various problems associated with "open-access resources" (Berkes 1989; Berkes et al. 1989; Bromley 1989a, 1991, 1992a, 1992b; Bromley and Cernea 1989; McCay and Acheson 1987; Ostrom 1990). However, implicit in this newfound clarity about common property remains a lingering difficulty that calls for some further elaboration. Specifically, there is the notion that simply giving people something called *property rights* will automatically result in wise resource management decisions; and, presumably, "wise" resource management is consistent with sustainability.

We see this most recently from the "property rights" movement in the United States. In some instances, the arguments have become somewhat strident. Part of the contemporary message is about creating property rights so as to "protect" environmental resources. Another part of the message is about reasserting the protection of those individuals who happen to possess private property rights in land. In its most extreme form, the property rights approach offers a range of claimed social benefits—protecting endangered species, curing air and water pollution, and protecting old-growth timber,

338

to name just a few. The property rights approach, in its individualistic form, brings together the possessive individualism of contemporary economics with the legal fiction that ownership implies autonomy and free choice. The hoped-for implication of this blend is that individual owners will behave in socially acceptable ways with respect to land and natural resources. But of course individual owners of land have never been in absolute control of their assets, nor do their decisions always assure proper stewardship of land and related resources.

The point here is that implementing sustainability requires that we move beyond the general celebration of property rights and seek, instead, clarity in the specific institutional arrangements associated with various property regimes. In other words, we must abandon the simplistic idea that particular property regimes—private property, state property, common property—bear any clear and decisive relation to the way in which land and related resources are used and managed. The argument here shall be that the particular property regime over a parcel of land and related natural resources is not a very decisive explanatory variable for whether or not that parcel will be used wisely or will fall into disrepair. In the language of lawyers, property regimes are simply not dispositive.

The reason for this agnosticism is not difficult to find. Private property regimes exist in which land is both well managed, but also destroyed—the Dust Bowl in the United States, and farm and forest land around the world come immediately to mind. Government-owned lands (state property) have been protected from devastation (the national parks and wilderness areas), but other government land has not fared so well (forested areas in the United States and elsewhere). Some common-property regimes are the epitome of wise management (the Swiss Alps), and some common property regimes have fallen into serious degradation (some forests and grazing areas in the developing world).

This should not be surprising. After all, a particular property regime is only as good as the institutional structures which give that regime protection from encroachment by others, and which underpin its internal authority with respect to the legitimate co-owners. In other words, one should not expect property regimes to work well when the political systems of which they are a part are largely dysfunctional.

ON INSTITUTIONAL COHERENCE

Recall that all coherent and functioning societies are defined by a set of institutional arrangements that both liberate and constrain individual actions. Think of these institutional arrangements as the "working rules" of the nation-state (Bromley 1989b). The significance of these working rules can best be appreciated by considering conditions when such structures are absent or dysfunctional. Consider Haiti, Somalia, Zaire, Rwanda, or the former Soviet Union. The common element in these disparate places is precisely the lack of a coherent nation-state owing to the absence of decisive working rules. It is often said that some of these nations have fallen into civil war and unrest, but those circumstances of internal strife are simply the logical culmination of societies that have lost—or failed to create—a clear set of institutional arrangements that define choice domains for individuals within the society. The philosopher might refer to such circumstances as a *state of nature*. Political scientists might label the situation as one of *anarchy*. Economists refer to the *soft state*.

The sustainable management of biological systems in the developing countries is threatened for two related reasons: (1) unclear institutional arrangements—of which property rights are an important part; and (2) a breakdown in the authority systems that give meaning to those very institutional arrangements. The first reason speaks to the lack of clear rules that comprise the essence of property rights. The second reason speaks to the failure of authority systems—governments—to provide coherent protection for the extant property regimes.

The various news media stress the serious problems of overgrazing and deforestation in the Tropics. It will often be said that these destructive practices are the result of expanding populations. The policy response to this problem will be misdirected, however, if the cause is laid at the feet of population growth. By blaming population growth—and the subsequent land clearing for agriculture and scavenging for fuelwood by the masses— the public focus will be shifted away from the real cause of natural resource destruction in the developing nations. That cause is most often ineffective governments with little interest in preserving natural resources (Bromley 1998). While population growth is indeed a contributory cause of much deforestation and accelerated soil erosion, it is often not the *primary* cause. Until various governments are understood to share much of the blame for the natural resource degradation now so prevalent in the Tropics, the proper solutions will be difficult to effect.

Some governments may have a vested interest in perpetuating the belief that population growth is to blame for natural resource destruction. If the problem can be blamed on prolific peasants, then it is far easier to avoid being held responsible. By allowing population growth to become a convenient scapegoat, governments are then free to proceed with their weak and often-perverse policies. Blaming population growth also helps governments to attract development assistance programs to replant trees or rehabilitate rangeland that they have been unwilling to protect in the first instance. These rehabilitation programs often employ large numbers of the poor and unemployed, thereby providing external funds for a potentially serious socioeconomic problem beyond the capacity of many governments to solve.

In fairness it must be emphasized that colonialism left its victims with very serious governance problems. Once colonialism gave way to national independence, the imposed systems of authority at the village level were once again in need of modification and realignment with the new imperatives and interests of a fledgling national government. These disruptions destroyed, yet again, evolved relationships of power, influence, and authority. During these eras of creation and modification of local-level systems of authority and control, populations were expanding rapidly, and technology was altering the way in which people used their natural environment. At the very time when the ability to control individual behavior at the village level was at its lowest point, populations were expanding and the pressure on the natural resource base was increasing. Degradation of natural resources was the predictable outcome.

Many of the newly independent nation-states have shown little interest in revitalizing local-level systems of authority. As with previous rulers and colonial administrators, the governments of these nation-states are often suspicious of local political forces that might challenge the legitimacy and authority of the center. This means that natural resources have become the property of the national governments in acts of outright expropriation when viewed from the perspective of the residents of millions of villages. This expropriation is all the more damaging when national governments lack the rudiments of a natural resource management capability. These new governments are struggling with the problems of governance, economic development, self-sufficiency, and political stability. In this setting, natural resource destruction continues, and even accelerates, with only a very indirect causal link to population growth.

REVITALIZING PROPERTY REGIMES

There are two essential tasks in creating resource management regimes that have some hope of preserving biological diversity. The first task pertains to establishing the legitimacy of a particular natural resource management regime in the eyes of others who may covet the assets under control of the right holder(s). This is essential in private property regimes, in common-property regimes, and in state property regimes. I call this the problem of establishing *external legitimacy*. The second task pertains to establishing legitimacy and authority within particular resource management regimes. I call this the problem of establishing *internal authority*.

Fostering External Legitimacy

The history of much natural resource policy in the developing countries has been one of persistent governmental interference in—or indifference toward—local-level natural resource management regimes. This interference, or this indifference, has meant that external threats to such regimes by squatters—and by the spread of sedentary agriculture—have been either promoted or tolerated by the central government.

In 1957 the government of Nepal expropriated forest lands under the administration of local jurisdictions—mostly village governments. The Nepalese government is now embarked on a program to return management control over these forests to the villages. This pattern has been repeated elsewhere. These transitions in perceptions of legitimacy of local-level resource management regimes by central governments are profoundly destructive of the management regimes they hope to supplant. Once the habit of management—and the expectation of compliance with local-level institutional arrangements—is lost at the local level, it is not easily restored.

The willingness of the state to legitimize certain resource management regimes is partly explained by the state's perception of the importance of the individuals or groups who make up the constituents for those regimes. If pastoralists are regarded as politically unimportant, then those resource management regimes central to pastoralism are vulnerable. If those threatening pastoralist regimes have more favor from the state, then protection of pastoralist regimes will be indifferent. If it is the poor who are inordinately dependent upon the village commons, then governmental indifference to the plight of the poor will mean that the village commons is available for others to plunder with impunity. A common-property resource becomes, in the absence of external legitimacy, an open-access resource.

Here the central government could empower (even demand) local jurisdictions to undertake collective management of nonprivate lands. In most settings national governments do not have the requisite staff to manage these lands as state property, and the absence of effective administration means that resource management is absent.

There is, of course, evidence to suggest that local units may be no better at innovating and maintaining successful management regimes than central governments have been. Knowing this, however, does not help us to explain the causes of failures of local-level management systems. Did they fail because of internal contradictions and pressures? Or did they fail because of systematic breakdown of critical relations in the larger economy and polity? The answer to this question is central to the probable success of new local resource management regimes. In the absence of that answer, it is insufficient simply to point to past problems as evidence of the inevitability of future failures. Analysis of both failed and successful resource management regimes is the prerequisite to informed policy advice in the Tropics.

Fostering Internal Authority

The internal authority of a resource management regime affects the degree of compliance with the evolved institutions that define that regime. This is most apparent with common-property and state property regimes. Compliance is, to a certain extent, a matter of expectations regarding the actions of others. If the expectation begins to form that others are not abiding by the understood norms and conventions of the regime, there will be a diminished incentive on the part of any one agent to continue to abide by the rules of the regime. Once this perception spreads, and in the absence of aggressive enforcement, it will be only a matter of time before the regime degrades into anarchy. A common-property regime, or a state property regime, will become de facto open access. A situation of positive reciprocity in terms of mutually reinforcing conservation behavior soon degenerates into negative reciprocity in which a free-for-all emerges as the dominant behavioral norm.

It is necessary to point out that even private property regimes require "internal" authority. That is, the presumption of private property regimes is that the owner exercises socially acceptable behavior with respect to the privately held object. A farmer's management practices hold implications for soil erosion, and the presumption of private ownership is that the actual rate of soil erosion in a private property regime is the "socially acceptable" erosion rate. However, when that erosion begins to foul downstream rivers and lakes, then the putative optimality of that particular property regime is called into question. While such concerns do not undermine the external legitimacy of private property in general, these concerns do undermine the legitimacy of certain behaviors on erosion-prone agricultural lands. The matter of internal authority here concerns the behavior of an asset owner in a property regime that has external legitimacy. As with state property regimes and common-property regimes, there are norms of behavior that attend a private property regime. When behaviors violate those norms, the internal legitimacy of the regime is challenged. In essence, all rights are conditional and derivative. . . . They are derived from the end or purpose of the society in which they exist. They are conditional on being used to the attainment of that end, not to thwart it (Tawney 1920, 51).

In many parts of the developing world, the effort to revitalize internal authority may well focus on establishing or reinvigorating common-property resource management regimes. This may seem paradoxical since some will imagine that the original problem arose because of "common property." However, the earlier discussion of the distinction between common property and open access should dispel that confusion. It is now well recognized that while an open-access regime is one without rules of entry or behavior, a common-property regime is defined by group ownership in which the behaviors of all members of the group are controlled by the co-owners. Individual behaviors are collectively observed. In the developing countries, it is reasonable to suppose that conformity with group norms is an important sanction against antisocial behavior (as defined by the group). These conformity norms do not always work well, to be sure. But there is social pressure in that direction. An effective common-property regime thus has a built-in incentive structure that encourages compliance with existing conventions and institutions. Another way to put the matter is to point out that in social settings in which individual conformity to group norms is the dominant ethic, common-property regimes offer a vital incentive structure for effective performance. This is the idea of *positive reciprocity* discussed previously.

The essence of any property regime is an authority system that can assure that the expectations of rights holders are met. The presence of compliance through the expedient of an authority system is a necessary condition for the viability of any property regime. Private property would not "work" without the requisite authority system that makes certain the rights and duties are adhered to. This same situation exists for common property. When the authority system breaks down for whatever reason, then common property—as with private property—is converted into open access.

As suggested at the outset, it is not the property regime that explains sustainable natural resource use. It is, instead, the authority system that ensures that the institutional arrangements central to any particular property regime are adhered to.

In most common-property regimes in the developing world, two problems have arisen. The first is that a breakdown in compliance by co-owners has occurred because of the loss of opportunity arising from changes elsewhere in the economy. With scant economic opportunity to attract away population growth, the numbers of individuals being sustained by a fixed resource base grow until degradation is the inevitable outcome. The second problem arises if privatization is occurring in the immediate area, which then precludes seasonal adjustments to highly variable resource conditions. Ultimate degradation of the resource may result if the users have no other alternatives.

The investment in—or improvement of—dysfunctional resource management regimes must first focus on the institutional dimension. If property and management arrangements are not established and secured through a meaningful authority system, and if there is investment in the form of a capital asset such as improved tree species or range revegetation, the institutional vacuum of the *status quo ante* will practically ensure that individual resource use rates will eventually deplete the asset.

Recall that open access is characterized by the absence of an authority system whose purpose is to assure compliance with a set of behavioral conditions with respect to the natural resource. Valuable natural resources available to the first party to effect capture are de facto open-access resources through a series of institutional failures that have undermined former collective management regimes. In a situation of dysfunctional common property, each potential user has complete autonomy with respect to use of the resource since no one has the legal ability to keep others out. That is, the natural resource is subject to the rule of capture and belongs to no one until it is in someone's physical possession. No property rights exist in this situation; there is only a quest for possession.

Recall that property rights—a social contract that defines an individual and an object of value vis-à-vis all other individuals—cannot exist when an individual must physically capture the object before he or she can exercise effective control. Having *property rights* means not having to stand guard over something. The social recognition that gives property its content means that others have a duty to respect the owner's interest in the thing owned. Hence with many institutionally and physically degraded resource regimes, the necessary precondition for any successful management of biological resources is that the property regime be converted from open access. Recall that a common-property regime at the village level constitutes *private property* for the group, with the attendant co-equal rights and duties for the individual members.

The dismal record of natural resource management in many developing countries leads to the obvious question as to whether or not there are alternative institutional arrangements that offer some promise. That is, the widespread nationalization of forested areas has exceeded the capacity of many governments to implement effective managerial systems and so forests are often "national" in name only. Reestablishing community-based management of forests raises the question of whether villagers can be "trusted" with resource management.

WHO SHALL MANAGE BIOLOGICAL RESOURCES?[1]

The idea of community-based programs for conservation of biological resources has spurred much recent interest. The idea seems compelling because it starts from the most fundamental principle (individuals will take care of those things in which they have a long-run, sustained interest). The traditional model of national preserves violates this principle by driving a legal and bureaucratic wedge between local people and the resource base in need of protection. Think of such preserves as *ecological apartheid*. Community-based conservation seeks to locate arenas of mutuality between those who wish for biological resources to be managed on a sustained basis and those who must rely on these same biological resources for the bulk of their livelihood.

In considering the idea of community-based conservation, many leaders in the international conservation community now appear to accept the fact that not all biological resources are equally essential to the long-run sustainability of particular ecosystems. Put somewhat differently, people and their livestock interacting with a particularly esteemed ecosystem may imply that certain plant species are utilized beyond the level that some preservationists may prefer. Yet, in the larger picture, the grazing pressure on these species may allow an ecosystem of greater social value to thrive. The acceptance of this idea has made it possible to consider the feasibility of community-based conservation.

The problem to be addressed in community-based conservation is one of how the working rules of such resource management regimes can be structured such that local people have a robust and durable interest in the conservation of biological resources of interest to the larger international community? The answer, in brief, is to be found in the structure of entitlements (property rights) and in the constellation of incentives and sanctions that emanate from those entitlement structures. If these new entitlement structures are thought of as resource management regimes, then the incentives and sanctions constitute the *working rules* of those regimes. These working rules define domains of choice for local people as participants in the sustainable management of biological resources. The economic problem is to craft working rules that are incentive-compatible for community-based conservation.

Two general property regimes are pertinent to such programs. The first, and the traditional way in which biological resources are protected, is to create national parks or national reserves for this purpose. These are *state property regimes*. In these regimes, ownership and control over environmental resources rests with the state, while management is carried out through its agents (government). Individuals and groups may be able to make use of the environmental resources, but only at the forbearance of the administrative agency charged with carrying out the wishes of the larger political community. The state may either directly manage and control the use of state-owned environmental resources through government agencies, or it may lease the resources to groups or individuals who are then given usufruct rights for a specified period of time. In the extreme, state property regimes result in the complete eviction of those with customary use rights.

State property regimes remove most managerial discretion from the user, and generally convey no long-run expectations in terms of tenure security. To be successful, such regimes require governmental structures and functions that can match policy pronouncements with meaningful administrative reach.

The conservation community seems divided about the record of such regimes. A state property regime is an example of compulsion. Those who live in or near such areas are generally prevented from using most parts of the local ecosystem. This exclusion is certainly not conducive to the alignment of interest of the local inhabitants with long-run conservation. Indeed, it is generally recognized that such property regimes are not sustainable precisely because local people are dispossessed from traditional areas. The usual pattern is then one of spiraling enforcement efforts (and costs), followed by a subsequent erosion of compliance with the rules of the regime, which is then followed by yet-heightened enforcement efforts.

Recently, there have been efforts to establish buffer zones around some biological reserves. The intention is, evidently, that if the local inhabitants can be reincorporated into the ecosystem on the fringes of globally significant preserves, then they will become part of the enforcement mechanism rather than part of the poaching problem. These buffer zones still operate as examples of state property regimes, with the provision that certain uses are allowed. It is still a regime of compulsion in which strict rules from outside the group of locals prescribe acceptable resource use patterns and rates of resource use.

While buffer zones were thought to represent a solution to the enforcement problems associated with the social artificiality of preserves, this solution is only partial. The next logical step is to recognize that conservation may best be enhanced if local individuals can be incorporated directly into the ecosystem as part of the management regime. Indeed, at the extreme, conservation is often enhanced to the extent that local peoples can be vested with a long-run interest in resource management.

Two approaches may be pursued. The first, as illustrated in the case of the Kakadu National Park in northern Australia, is to create a state property regime on lands that are acknowledged to belong to local peoples (Western and Wright 1994). Kakadu National Park encompasses Aboriginal land under lease, and Commonwealth land. Along with this joint ownership of land, there is a system of joint decision making over many aspects of park use and management. Under this institutional arrangement, local people become an integral part of the structure of resource use.

Where this option is not available, one can rely on the development of an alternative ownership regime that gives locals a stake in the future benefit streams arising from the ecosystem. This ownership structure would resemble a *common-property regime*. Of course many common-property regimes around the world have been destroyed as a result of the relentless march of "modernization" and individualization. However, as suggested earlier, the essence of a common-property regime is that it strives to get the incentives right in a most fundamental way. By granting ownership rights to a group of local inhabitants, and by allowing them to craft a set of management rules for controlling use of those biological resources, one has potentially solved much of the conflict of interest in the preservation of local biological resources. Whereas state property regimes evict individuals and alienate them from the resource, common-property regimes incorporate (or reincorporate) individuals into the ecosystem through an ownership interest.

The feasibility of common-property regimes has sparked a great deal of discussion in the literature. Much of this literature addresses the *robustness* of the regime against competing claims from those outside of the group of co-owners. As with private property, a common-property regime requires willing legitimation by the political hierarchy in which it is located. Private property would be nothing without the capacity of the owner(s) to call upon some authority system to enforce the sanctity of that property regime. The same condition of authority must also exist for common-property regimes to survive. There appears to be a difference of opinion on this fact. Some will suggest that community-based tenure systems obtain their primary legitimacy from the community in which they operate and not from the nation-state in which they are located. In other words, local participants are the primary allocators and enforcers of local rights to natural resources, not the national government.

Two ideas arise here. First, local participants (really the co-owners) are the ones who make and enforce the rules of use of the resources. This idea is widely shared among those who write about common-property regimes. However, implicit here is a second idea regarding the sanctity of the regime against outside claimants—this too is an "enforcement" problem. Here, the implication seems not to go far enough. Left unaddressed is the fundamental problem of to whom shall those in the local community turn when the legitimacy of the external boundary of that "community-based tenure" is challenged by outsiders? It is not enough to argue that legitimacy rests with the locals when the very security of that local natural resource is under threat from others who covet its bounty. While armed conflict might reinforce the local legitimacy of the communal tenure, coherent conservation requires alternative sources of conflict resolution.

The position that communities possess property rights in biological resources addresses only the *origins* of the ownership interest of local people, while it is silent on the fundamental dynamic element of how that alleged property right is to be upheld against potential incursions by others. To whom are the local "owners" to turn for protection of their property interest? It is not enough to appeal to reason based on the original legitimacy of that regime under customary occupancy. If logging interests want in, there is only one place to turn for protection of the boundary of that property regime. The only authority system available for that task is the nation-state and its government. Indeed, the breakdown of many common-property regimes is traceable to the fact that the nation-state regarded the occupants of such regimes as politically marginal and therefore not worthy of the effective protection that only the state can bring to such disputes. Individuals only have those effective rights that the nation-state agrees to protect with its monopoly on coercion. No rights exist in a state of nature—rights only exist in the presence of an authority system that agrees to protect, with violence if necessary, those interests it finds legitimate. The protection brought to those interests by the state consists of *duties* for nonowners. Only with effective duties on others can rights exist. Recall that to have a right is to possess that wonderful capacity to *compel* the state to intervene to protect your interests against the predations of others. That protection by the state is precisely the imposition of duties on those who would contravene your interests (Bromley 1991).

The "community reserves" of the Peruvian Amazon appear to meet this condition of external legitimacy for the common-property regime. They also appear to have internal authority for rule making by the management group (Western and Wright 1994). In these systems, efforts were made to incorporate local people into the decision making about how the resources were to be used. The local people have the opportunity and the authority to develop and implement management rules for the subsistence zone in which they reside, and then protect the core area with its valuable ecological diversity. The government acts as an authorizing agent to these management regimes, but seems to rely on the local inhabitants to operate the regime. This decision was apparently the foundation of a renewed commitment on the part of the locals to manage the resource base in a sustainable fashion.

The impetus for the community management scheme came from locals reacting to the extraction of natural resources they regarded as their own. With external legitimacy recognized by the nation-state, the way was clear for the locals to undertake the hard work of crafting improved management rules that would conduce to enhanced resource management over the long run. With protection against encroachment assured by this recognition of external legitimacy, the necessary though not sufficient conditions for coherent management were in place. Internal authority could then emerge to satisfy the sufficient conditions.

IMPLICATIONS FOR CONSERVATION OF BIOLOGICAL RESOURCES

In formulating policies to enhance the management of biological resources, it is essential that careful analysis be undertaken of the feasibility of rehabilitating common-property regimes. Before that is considered, however, it is necessary to recall that policy requires more than good intentions. Coherent environmental policy also requires rules of implementation and rules of enforcement. The history of destruction of common-property regimes is dominated by failures of rules and by failures of enforcement mechanisms. While there have assuredly been instances in which public policy was formulated with the explicit intent of destroying local resource management regimes, many such regimes have simply been undermined by the gradual breakdown of the endogenous rule structure, by the breakdown of rules at the boundary of such regimes (rules governing who might enter the area), and by the failure of enforcement mechanisms pertaining to both constellations of rules.

This history notwithstanding, a focus on local-level resource management will need to recognize the ecological, economic, and social legitimacy of common-property regimes. In one important respect, common property (res communes) is identical to private property for the group of co-owners because nonowners are excluded from use and decision making. Each of the co-owners in a common-property regime has structured rights and duties inside the regime. A true common-property regime requires, at minimum, the same thing as private property: exclusion of nonowners. While property-owning groups vary in nature, size, and internal structure across a broad spectrum, they are all social units with: (1) definite membership and boundaries; (2) certain common interests; (3) some interaction among members; (4) some common cultural norms; and (5) their own endogenous authority systems. Tribal groups and subgroups, sub-villages, neighborhoods, small transhumant groups, kin systems, or extended families are all possible examples of meaningful authority systems within common-property regimes. These groupings hold customary ownership of certain natural resources such as farmland, grazing land, and water sources.

It is important to recognize that group property regimes are quite compatible with distinct individual use of one or another segment of the resources held under common property. For instance, in customary tenure systems throughout much of the world, the ownership of certain farmland may be vested in a group. The group's leaders then allocate use rights on portions of the land to various individuals or families. As long as those individuals cultivate their plot, no other person has the right to use it or to benefit from its produce; tenure security is present. But note that the cultivator holds use rights (usufruct) only, and is unable to alienate or transfer either the ownership or the use of that land to another individual. Sometimes there will be provisions for permission to be granted by those in a position of authority, but the decision is a collective one as opposed to an individual one. Once the current user ceases to put the land to beneficial use as defined by the authority system, then the usufruct reverts to the jurisdiction of the corporate ownership of the group. Contrary to regimes of state ownership, the customary common-property regimes throughout the world are usually characterized by group-corporate ownership with management authority vested in the respective group or its leaders.

An essential element of enhanced biological conservation is to determine which areas should remain in the freehold (private) domain, which areas should remain in state property, and which areas should be restored to common-property regimes. In some places it will be necessary for national governments to declare their commitment to own and manage certain critical areas. Existing national parks and preserves fit this notion. But state property regimes may be created, as well, where several competing user groups are unable to reach sustainable agreements among themselves.

In other areas, governments will need only to assure external legitimacy of boundaries, thus allowing the evolution of common-property regimes over large expanses of important biological resources. Note that the national government may be required to protect the new common-property regimes from intrusion by others, but can then delegate management to the users themselves. Under this assured protection of the boundary of the regime, the co-owners are presumed to be able to innovate institutional arrangements for managing the natural resources on a sustainable basis. This management, in addition to concern for the nature and extent of natural resource use, would also be concerned with mobilizing and implementing investments in the natural resource. Such investments would, in all probability, constitute joint property among the co-owners of the regime.

Community-based conservation strategies will only be successful with the recognition that the local management entities (communities) are themselves embedded in a political regime that may be indifferent to conservation, and to the role of local communities in that process. At this stage, therefore, one must presume that national governments have agreed to a program of enhanced biological conservation and the problem is how to devolve that new (or enhanced) interest down to the local community whose actions will be central to successful conservation outcomes. In other words, national governments will face the problem of determining the best locus for: (1) engaging in a particular policy discussion about biological conservation; (2) formulating particular policies that will bring about enhanced biological conservation; and (3) implementing the working rules and enforcement mechanisms associated with a particular policy.

A need remains to develop criteria whereby the policy dialogue on biological conservation can be properly located in a vertical dimension. The failure in most environmental policy discussions is that they fail to start with a logic for identifying which level in the political hierarchy is the *necessary and sufficient* one for choice about particular environmental matters. By the political hierarchy I mean: (1) the national level; (2) the regional level; and (3) the local level. Most environmental policy fails to articulate a coherent reason why practically all policy dialogue is presumed to be at the national level, while the regional and local levels are ignored or assumed subservient to the national level. It is this failure that has led to the traditional approach in which national governments presumed that they were the only entity competent to protect and manage biological resources.

The task, therefore, is to develop criteria that will help national governments to understand that some environmental issues are best addressed at a local level, some are best addressed at a regional level, and some are best addressed at a national level. Given the extreme sensitivity to local and regional concerns in many nations, these issues will continue to plague the development of conservation policy.

In summary, the efficacy of any particular property regime for the sustainable management of biological resources is secondary to the existence of a functioning authority system. All coherent and operational property regimes require the presence of Kantian intelligible possession in which ownership depends, not on the assertion of the putative owner, but rather on the agreement—indeed the forbearance—of nonowners. What a single individual "owns" depends on what others in the community assent to, not what that individual claims to "own."

No property regime can function in a state of nature. The problems of sustainable management of biological resources require a coherent authority system capable of defining and enforcing constellations of rights and duties. Only then does it make sense to worry about the particulars—whether private property, state property, or common property.

Thus, while one can be encouraged by the newfound interest in property regimes, the discourse about property *regimes* has been both distorted and undermined by the language of property *rights*. The conservation and wise management of biological resources will not improve until analytical attention is shifted away from rights and toward duties that are embedded in property regimes. Furthermore, because only meaningful authority systems can impose duties, it will be necessary to address the existing institutional incoherence in most developing countries if there is to be any hope for the sustainable management of biodiversity.

NOTES

An earlier version of this paper was presented to the First Open Meeting of the Human Dimensions of Global Environmental Change Community, Duke University, June 1–3, 1995.

1. Portions of this and the following section are taken from my chapter (15) in Western and Wright 1994.

BIBLIOGRAPHY

Berkes, Fikret, ed. 1989. *Common Property Resources: Ecology and Community-Based Sustainable Development.* London: Belhaven Press.

Berkes, Fikret, David Feeny, Bonnie McCay, and James M. Acheson. 1989. "The Benefit of the Commons." *Nature* 340 (6229): 91–93, July 13.

Bromley, Daniel W. 1989a. "Property Relations and Economic Development: The Other Land Reform." *World Development* 17 (6): 867–77.

———. 1989b. *Economic Interests and Institutions: The Conceptual Foundations of Public Policy.* Oxford: Blackwell.

———. 1991. *Environment and Economy: Property Rights and Public Policy.* Oxford: Blackwell.

———. 1992a. "The Commons, Common Property, and Environmental Policy," *Environmental and Resource Economics* 2:1–17.

———, ed. 1992b. *Making the Commons Work.* San Francisco: ICS Press.

———. 1998. "Deforestation: Institutional Causes and Solutions." In *World Forests, Society, and Environment,* ed. by Matti Palo and Juusi Ussivouri. Boston: Kluwer.

Bromley, Daniel W. and Michael M. Cernea. 1989. *The Management of Common Property Natural Resources: Some Conceptual and Operational Fallacies.* Washington, D.C.: World Bank Discussion Paper 57.

McCay, Bonnie and James M. Acheson. 1987. *The Question of the Commons.* Tucson: University of Arizona Press.

Ostrom, Elinor. 1990. *Governing the Commons.* Cambridge, England: Cambridge University Press.

Tawney, R. H. 1920. *The Acquisitive Society.* New York: Harvest Books.

Western, David and R. Michael Wright. 1994. *Natural Connections: Perspectives in Community-Based Conservation.* Washington, D.C.: Island Press.

12

Sustaining the Community, Resisting the Market: Guatemalan Perspectives

STEPHEN GUDEMAN AND ALBERTO RIVERA

A s the century drew to a close, the evidence of environmental degradation was mounting. Global warming, desertification, water
pollution, and depletion of the earth's stocks of resources attest to the
planet's fragility. Few deny the evidence of these processes, but there is
little agreement about their sources and severity. In this essay, we propose
that modern market activities heighten spoliation of the material world,
and suggest the process can be resisted and slowed by strengthening and
expanding the community dimension of economy. Market practices are not
the sole source of severe environmental change; explosive population
growth and the workings of other economic formations including socialist
systems have taken their toll. But we argue for strengthening the role
of human association in economy and the morality it offers in managing
the world's physical heritage and countering some of the dynamics of
market systems.

In the spring of 1994, and earlier years, we carried out fieldwork in
various locales of Guatemala exploring ways different communities
manage their environment. The communities we examined ranged from
relatively isolated Indian groups in highland regions to seacoast villages
and collections of small-scale agriculturalists, urban groups, and private
organizations. Each community is organized around enduring social relationships and holds something in common, although they differ widely.
Some represent a precolonial, colonial, or postcolonial heritage; others are
informed by the ideal of market transactions or the language of ecological

movements. All demonstrate how humans make and remake communities in relation to market practices. In approaching the problem of environment this way, and by starting with practices, we are suggesting that one set of solutions to contemporary environmental problems may need to come from "outside" the realm of the market and the institution of private property, and that "the economy," as described and delimited by much contemporary discourse, does not encompass all forms of material behavior.

THE TWO SPHERES OF MATERIAL LIFE

All economies are built on the interacting realms of communal and commercial value.[1] Material life is double-sided, for humans harbor feelings of both mutuality and self-interest. For simplicity, we label these two spheres, *community* and *market* (or trade). A communal value is a common or shared interest that may or may not have a material form. Market value is represented by price in money, although by an older terminology *value* (the underlying measure) and *price* (its financial expression) were distinguished.The first—the communal realm—placing each of us within a matrix of social relationships that mediate material life in which communal projects take precedence over self-interest, offers a degree of predictability and provides one bulwark against material uncertainty. The second—trade realm—situates individuals and groups as separate actors in material life, and represents an opening to the world of fortune, although ways of managing contingency are developed in this realm, too. In the market, self-interest of the unit—whether an individual, family, or corporation—is a primary motive and value. In practice, most institutions and actions are mixtures of the two spheres, but they are constructed of just these two.

One realm consists of short-term material relationships that are undertaken *for the sake of* achieving a project or securing a good. In the other, material goods are exchanged through relationships that are kept *for their own sake*. Sometimes the two spheres are separated in acts, institutions, and sectors. Sometimes they complement and join one another in unpredictable ways, but with one or the other dominant; sometimes the modes envelop or interpenetrate so that features of one are categorized as if they were part of the other, yet retain their original sense as well.

Each domain is partial; neither is a total system. For example, material life based on the regime of social value can lead to self-sufficiency or autarky, but even in small house economies—as in Latin America—the complementary sphere of trade is part of material life. Conversely, no pure trade or market system exists without the support of communal agreements, such as shared languages, mutual ways of interacting, and implicit under-standings. Communities are inside markets, as households, corporations, unions, guilds, and oligopolies, and contain them as nation-states that pro-vide a legal structure for contracts and material infrastructure.

Many combined patterns have been recorded. There are dualistic or parallel systems as in the case of colonial regimes when a cross-national corporation makes use of a local, community economy through political power; likewise, ports-of-trade—such as Portobelo in old Panama—are international marketplaces that have been given a special time and quar-antined place in a local economy (Boeke 1942; Geertz 1963; Polanyi, Arensberg, and Pearson 1957). There exist inner/outer relationships when a house economy is contained within a market economy as in rural Panama or the United States (although we now increasingly marketize transactions within the domestic family: For example, both the affluent and less wealthy may pay for childcare providers, use premarital contracts, or employ low-paid migrants to provide domestic services). Sometimes a market draws a surplus from a community economy, when subsistence farming supports cash cropping or when people undertake piecework or telemarketing from their homes at very low rates of remuneration. In the West, too, there has been a long-term shift from community to market that is often described as modernization, progress, and the triumph of rationality.

The two spheres may be institutionally and tactically interwoven, as in a "trade partnership"—found in many parts of the world—in which two members of different groups located in different areas maintain an endur-ing relationship (communal) yet each aims to secure a monetary profit from the other (commercial).[2] Similarly, in the "trader's dilemma" (Evers 1994), a local merchant is caught between the aims of maximizing profit in selling and maintaining relationships with customers with whom he shares kinship, residential, or social ties. Likewise, the house business in Latin America that combines the two modes is neither transitional nor on the road to modernization but lasting under certain conditions.

Most of us use both strategies every day. Some days we buy at an imper-sonal superstore that has no clerks and uses automatic checkouts, taking pleasure in anonymity, not having to talk with others, and securing a low price. Other days we buy at a small, nearby store so that we can support a business community or chat for a moment with a clerk or cashier, though at the cost of paying higher prices. Sometimes we go to both stores within the same hour, as if to seek a psychic balance; and some of us—ill-mannered or confused by this realm of social tactics—seek social contact in the anonymous store or avoid it in the communal one, thus producing quizzical if not curt responses in both.[3]

The marking and balance of community and market differs in each example, but the two spheres are involved in all. Seemingly anonymous market transactions are always dependent on prior communities; church potluck suppers are no less expressions of market.

Material life is always double: Communities generate anonymous exchanges inside themselves and at their borders; impersonal interactions presuppose and may nourish mutuality. The interplay is continual, and the relative importance of the two domains varies widely.

In contrast to this intertwining of trade and mutuality in everyday life, the two usually are separated by our knowledge systems or discourses. Most of standard economics, although it makes claims to universality, focuses on the commercial dimension only, thereby equating economy with market and defining material life in community as noneconomic, and thus falling outside the domain to be explained.[4]

Throughout Western history, various discourses about these two domains have been constructed from Aristotle (1984) on the polis or purely communal economy to contemporary neoclassical economics on the market. Most of these discourses part the linked domains and highlight one while marginalizing and obscuring the presence of the other. Today the language of neoclassical economics is dominant especially because it promises efficiency in the allocation of product, distribution of resources, and production of goods and services through markets. Communal transactions may achieve equity or other moral outcomes, but they cannot assure efficiency. In contrast to such pure discourses which dominate our thinking, we hold that most material practices are combinations along a continuum; economies are complex mixes, separations, and negotiations of the two spheres.

Both dimensions of material life have their attractions, though today the market sphere dominates for the freedom and lifestyle it offers as well as the potential for accumulating wealth and dominating others in a competition. Our purpose in exploring the community side of material life is not to propose a specific alternative to market life but to provide a language and examples of this sphere, and point to its changing presence and forms so that a wider range of choice in managing the environment and formulating property rights may be considered.

COMMONS AND CAPITAL

Social and natural relationships have a very different cast and temporality in market and community. Communities, as we use the term, may be face-to-face, as in the case of the household, or imagined as in the nation-state (Anderson 1991). They rarely encompass a person's total life or make complete entities themselves. Often communities are organized around specific activities, and people participate in many different ones in their daily living. Communities may be hierarchically arranged, embedded, or overlapping. For example, cities comprise many communities, variously based on ethnicity, religion, school districts, wealth, recreational zones, and commerce—each linked to a different social identity. The same principle holds in so-called small-scale societies. A matrilineal group in northern Colombia, for example, is made up of crosscutting matricentral units, homesteads, uterine kin, females who garden together, males who herd together, and trekking groups (Rivera Gutiérrez 1986). The composition of communities also shifts as affiliations are changed in authorized ways or by manipulating qualifications of membership, based on genealogy, marital status, language spoken, and place of birth. In modern times especially, "racial" purity has been invoked to constrict membership in private clubs, nation-states, and the human race. The rules of inclusion also may be contested and altered as in the case of political struggles in the United States over which age groups and citizens qualify for community-supported welfare and health care. In the contemporary world, communities cross national borders sometimes with the goal of resisting market forces: Animal rights groups, drawing on membership from around the world, slice the nets of fishing boats from one or another nation; money and help from different countries flow to victims of floods in the Midwest of the United States or in South Asia. Such acts depend on imagined commonality.

The community realm of economy has several distinctive features: (1) a base or *commons*, and ways of maintaining the base through time; (2) the circulation of goods through processes of *allotment* that encode and ensure enduring moralities; (3) reliance on *situated*, contextual, or local *reasoning*, (4) a degree of *self-sufficiency* that becomes part of its identity; (5) an emphasis on "living well" or flourishing by maintaining social relationships; and (6) the use and control of external trade.

A community economy, above all, makes and shares a commons. We also term this feature the *base* or *foundation*, adapting some terms from Latin America. The commons is a shared interest or value. It is the patrimony or legacy of a community and refers to anything that contributes to the material and social sustenance of a people with a shared identity: land, buildings, seed stock, knowledge of practices, a transportation network, an educational system, or rituals. As the lasting core, though changeable over time, the base represents temporality and continuity. Without a commons, there is no community; without a community, there is no commons.

Most modern economists—after Galileo, Descartes, and Locke—interpret the material commons of a people as an independent, objective entity that can be properly managed only by having expressly stated rights of access (Ostrom 1990). They re-read the commons as something separate from a human community, perhaps as a symbol of community but not the community itself. This market and modernist reading separates objects from subjects.

In our view, the commons is the material thing or knowledge a people have in common, what they share, so that what happens to a commons is not a physical incident but a social event. Taking away the commons destroys community, and destroying a complex of relationships demolishes a commons. Likewise, denying others access to the commons denies community with them, which is exactly what the assertion of private property rights does. The so-called "tragedy of the commons" (Hardin 1968), which refers to destruction of a resource through unlimited use by individuals, is a tragedy not of a physical commons but of a human community, because of the failure of its members to treat one another as communicants and because of its transformation to a competitive situation.

Our use of the term *commons* is different from that of most contemporary economists and political scientists in another way. For them, a commons is real property used by market agents and contained within a market; a commons is either an open-access resource, freely available to all, or a common-pool resource, regulated by rules of use (Ostrom 1990). These theorists would show how control of certain scarce resources through social rules rather than competitive exchange supports market ends and the achievement of efficiency; thus, they argue, market actors sometimes agree for reasons of self-interest to form limited economic communities with a commons. We think this formulation represents a misunderstanding of the social sphere of value, reduces the social to self-interest, and conflates community and market through the misapplication or imperialist use of the language of trade. Communities of the form we describe are not devised to serve market life; irreducibly social, they operate for themselves as they relate to self-interests and the world of trade.

Often a community economy does not despoil the environment as rapidly as a market economy does, because in doing so it despoils itself. A commons is regulated through moral obligations that have the backing of powerful sanctions. But communities are hardly homes of equality and altruism, and they provide ample space for the assertion of power and exploitation from patriarchy to feudal servitude. As expressed in European writing from Locke through Mill, one attraction of arranging society through exchanges born of private property and individual contract, and liberated of persisting social claims and ties, lies in the freedom it offers to all members to engage in economic and political transactions that are advantageous to them as individuals.

The substance of the base or commons varies widely, comprising more than real and productive property. For example, by communicating and sharing knowledge, scholars make a community. They hold and enjoy knowledge in common which sustains both community and individual goals. The base may be composed of land, natural resources such as water or minerals, or a fishing or hunting domain. The commons may be a stand of trees kept from human entry, held for recreational enjoyment, or maintained for long-term use. In Latin American cities, squatter settlements may form around a water supply, and then local associations begin to demand sewage and electricity services which become their commons. When Indian communities on Guatemala's Lake Atitlán reserve forest land from individual use, in order to preserve their water sources and keep wood for communal use, they add to their material commons and to their community. Communities are made around a commons that can be land, trees, animals, saints, dolphins, organic foods, ancestors, or the refusal to buy green grapes or redwood hot tubs.

The contrast of market and community is well captured by the opposition of capital and commons. If a key feature of market capitalism is making profits and their accumulation as capital, a central characteristic of community is making and sustaining its commons. We suggest that capital and commons are not only homologues but closely connected, which leads us to argue for the importance of establishing community ties to protect the environment.

Measured in money, profit—which may be accumulated as capital—arises through market transactions. But it is created by innovations which, in Joseph Schumpeter's expression, constitute "creative destruction." An innovation destroys the accepted or traditional—that which is common—as it creates the new (Schumpeter 1934). In this process, as new goods are introduced, value is created; and the heritage or legacy of market participants is expanded. On the Schumpeterian argument, the increment of new value created is initially embodied in a surplus of money which is secured by the "innovator" or entrepreneur. Money profit constitutes the return for the creative, accepted, and purchased addition to the commonweal. It is also private property as well as capital.

Like profit and capital, a commons is made and remade through innovations. For a community, innovations expand the heritage or patrimony. But these tokens at the margin are not held by individuals, they are shared. Yet, what begins as profit in a market system eventually does become the "commons," for when a profitable innovation is broadly produced and held, it becomes a component of the general welfare or well-being through the new consumer goods, higher wages, and lower prices it brings. Conversely, as we shall suggest later, innovations for profit depend on the existence of a cultural legacy. In these respects, capital and commons are closely connected.

But what are the environmental implications of innovations and the expansion of value as capital or commons? In general, an innovation may or may not have a direct effect on the use of resources: Sometimes a particular innovation saves, sometimes it maintains, and sometimes it increases the use of material resources. But spurred by competition, the quest for innovations has become perpetual in the contemporary market economy; and when innovations themselves spread and become common coin, so use of the living and inanimate worlds is heightened. Certainly, innovations may be labor- or land saving; but their elaboration and dispersion, stimulated by competition and the search for profits, and manifested as the desire for increased living standards and heightened consumption, almost always lead to greater use of the ambient.

We are suggesting that market economy affects community and environment in a triple way.

- Innovation for profit often draws upon and "creatively destroys" a cultural heritage.
- Profit making may draw upon human effort previously directed to creating commensality, bringing it to account.
- Profit making may draw upon a physical resource such as a private holding, turning it from a potential or current use in the commons.

But communities within or without the market also contest and circumscribe market activity. People everywhere, now and in the past, have drawn on their communities to create and support, to set boundaries upon, to resist, and to dissent from the market: Zoning laws, architectural stipulations, and the rejection of shopping malls or mass retailers are some examples of the latter. Similarly, when an association of people makes land or another resource into a commons, they are not just acting on "nature" as an object but changing its context of use and meaning from being an objective and separate input for the market to being part of a seamless community of a people in a place. A community economy is built upon the commitment to care for, maintain, and hold together an association of humans and their commons, which is a different project from individual acquisition and accumulation. Our suggestion, then, is that a principal way people have managed nature is not only by using the tools of the market system, such as valuing the "objective" resources of nature by extending market calculations (Repetto 1992), calculating externalities and converting them to a property rights system (Demsetz 1964, 1967), and figuring the entropic costs and effects of economic behavior (Daly and Townsend 1993; Georgescu-Roegen 1971)—all methods constructed within the modernist framework—but human groups also manage environmental problems through community and its morality, and by judiciously mixing market and community economies. It is the existence and potential of this complementary discourse and set of practices that we want to explore.

TWO COMMUNITIES AND MARKET CONTAINMENT

Guatemala is an extraordinarily varied nation. With twenty-one Mayan languages (plus Garifuna and Spanish), marked and tense ethnic divisions, a colonial past, archeological riches, and a highly varied topography, it provides a context for the development of many different types of community and their interactions with markets. Some communities involve activist intellectuals, and some native groups; some preserve the environment as an end, and some maintain resources to meet human needs. To illustrate these several ways profit making affects community life, we provide a selection from the stories we heard in different parts of the country.

An initial tale of two communities that has nothing to do with material resources illustrates how a people may struggle to maintain their heritage or patrimony, their identity, and commons. In each of these cases, the patrimonies are expensive to maintain and so each community has had to make its adjustments with the market. The different adaptations illustrate how communities both resist and use the market to keep themselves.

Each community is actually a collection of *cofradías* or religious brotherhoods. Both are located in large cities, one about an hour from Guatemala City itself, the other some three to four hours away. Every cofradía possesses a saint's idol in whose honor it mounts a procession on the saint's day and other feast days. A common practice in the past, processions today are usually found in small communities. The festivities, which feature bands, dancers, and a well-appointed float for the saint, are expensive to produce. Male members of a cofradía take turns organizing and collecting funds for each year's festivities. The work, unpaid, is regarded as a service for the saint and the community, and an honor, just as its performance is considered an end itself. In both of the urban areas, the costs of the processions have risen dramatically in recent years, and the cofradías are in danger of financial collapse. The performances are well attended, however; and they draw tourists, which benefits local businesses. This financial gain has opened up new possibilities of support for the cofradías, but their responses have been cautious and divergent.

In one city, the municipal authorities—at the urging of local businesses—offered financial support for the processions; but they asked the cofradías to play music and perform on nonreligious days for tourists, who would be charged for the entertainment. In response, the cofradías suggested that for religious processions they would collect less than their expenses, because these performances were a service and a community commitment; however, for tourist performances, they would charge the city a higher rate. The cofradías distinguished between community commitment and market performance. Both practices maintain the patrimony; but the cofradías used the market, via local businesses, to earn a profit for their heritage. They perpetuated their community by both limiting and drawing on the market, making their accord with it.

The happenings in the second town were different. Religious processions there also are drawing tourists; and hotels, restaurants, and shops that benefit agreed to pay the cofradías for the performances. The cofradías responded that they were not charging for their service to the saints and the community. They proposed that the businesses offer them alms (*limosna*), though not specifying the amount. The people's response again differentiated between community and market economy. A community is supported by alms, donations, gifts, and services, and not by the purchase of its performances with payments. What a person offers is determined by commitment not by competition. As the people say, a donation is given "in accord with one's heart." In this second case, the cofradías drew the hotels and others into their way of life; they asked the market actors to transform their behavior from market to community, and in so doing they incorporated the wealth of the market into the community.

In both cities, the cofradías provide a service and add to well-being through a self-fulfilling activity. Because participants must feed and clothe themselves, pay for their musical instruments, and purchase market goods, each community must make its accords with the market. Both have refused to sell their community service: In one case, the people separate unpaid community and paid market performance; in the other, they ask market actors to transform their behavior by offering alms instead of wages. Market and community are separated yet combined. Neither community response indicates ignorance of the market value of religious performances; they signal commitment to resist, circumscribe, and use the market.

SUPPORT OF THE COMMONS

For our third example, we turn to a small Indian village, located on rela-tively marginal land in a highland area to the west of Guatemala City. Many men of the community seek wage labor outside its borders, at least part of the year; and most people are only partly dependent on local resources. The case illustrates the way a community in a town manages, holds, and defends a commons. In this instance, a cofradía sustains both a religious patrimony and a material resource that together compose its shared commons.

In the larger town, most land is held privately, whereas all commons land is owned by one or another cofradía. Each brotherhood contains households and composes a community within a larger one, the town. Each cofradía requires member participation in its festivities and donations to its saint. In the people's formulation, the productivity of the land and crops is a divine blessing that depends on honoring the saint, because humans, the saint, and God are all co-owners of the earth. Soil fertility signifies the divine presence. By this metaphoric or analogical construction, productivity is made mean-ingful and seen through divine grace (Gudeman 1986; Mirowski 1989).

The brotherhood we studied has both a highland commons, consisting of a forest, and a lowland commons, used for agriculture. Members' families cannot fully sustain themselves from either region or in combination, and most hold private land as well. Both commons are divided into plots to which individual families have exclusive access. On the lowland commons, the people make *milpa*, meaning they grow maize, beans, and other crops for home consumption. Members also grow coffee, which is a cash crop; but they use the returns to buy goods for "maintaining the house" and "meet-ing its needs." The highland forest is carefully managed and may be cut only to meet the needs of a house for firewood or construction materials. Effectively, both commons are used to meet domestic necessities or to maintain the base of the household.

Cofradía control of the commons is illustrated by the story the people tell of when a mayor of the town, without consultation or warning, tried to sell seventy-two trees from their stand to an outside contractor. Upon seeing the marked timber and learning of his plans, the people marched to the forest and physically stopped the process. In recounting the story, they stated that the trees were for use not sale, that the cofradía had not been consulted, that the mayor did not have the right to sell from the commons, that they did not know how money from the sale would be used, and that plots of trees were held by families, anyway. Effectively, the mayor acted as if the commons were capital and not a heritage and integral part of the cofradía. In the telling, the people added that when the town church had needed timber for a new roof a few years prior, several families offered trees from their plots.

Cofradía members were not only protecting material goods but their social interactions. Rights to shares in their patrimony, realized as plots in the forest and farmland, are passed from father to child. But the cofradía holds title, and inheritance and retention of plots are not automatic; they depend on providing cofradía service. For example, on the saint's day, the cofradía sponsors a procession, ritual, and commensal celebration. The ritual leader of this service, known as the principal, keeps the saint's idol in his house and offers food to cofradía members on the fiesta day. When the saint is at his house, the people say that the saint is the owner of the principal's house, as is the human owner; and both are patrons just as the saint is co-owner of the land. The position of principal is very costly and rotates yearly; and everyone must take a turn. But the people have little difficulty recruiting leaders because if a man refuses to serve and offer time, goods, and money that honor the saint, he loses the right to use the commons and to pass his usufruct rights to his children. If a man moves away and cannot participate in the cofradía's work, his rights in the commons also lapse. In such cases, the cofradía redistributes the resources to new members. The commons, thus, helps to support community members just as they support the saint and community.

This case shows how a community defends its commons. A community economy represents a form of life in which humans achieve well-being (*bienestar*) not by continuously acquiring goods but by participating with others. Managing a cofradía requires time—there is a transaction cost—but the people do not count this an expense. Serving the saint is said to be a pleasure and leads to reinforcing social, political, and economic ties with others while preserving these bonds for one's offspring. A community of this form operates with a longer time perspective than a competitive market unit: It hoards or saves (*hacer economías*) land and trees for future use and not as investments designed to secure a financial return. The example illustrates how communities may be embedded in larger ones and in markets, yet defend important spheres of life from the latter. The material and ideological are here welded in a way that is hardly understandable through a discourse which separates rational subjects from material objects.

COMMUNITY STRUGGLES

The expression, "Life is a struggle," heard frequently in many regions of Latin America, is well illustrated by accounts from two villages in

Guatemala that have struggled to defend their commons. In these secular communities, the shared resources are devoted to everyday maintenance, importantly so in one of them.

One village held title to a stand of trees. Rights to cut timber were occasionally sold to outsiders with the revenues flowing to the municipality. Recently, two roads were built near the forest, which allowed for the easy, illegal stealing of wood, often by the truckload. Municipal police caught some invaders; but enforcement proved to be costly, and the forest was rapidly depleted. This loss of the commons was not simply a function of the high cost of guarding and the low cost of stealing; no community actually shared it. The trees were a town resource of which occasional use yielded a revenue disbursed by the mayor. The benefit never flowed to a collectivity. We might say that the trees were never actually a commons or that the community, which the commons serves, consists of those who cut the trees! The forest was an open-access resource.

The commons of the neighboring community presents a very different story. This municipality of more than 2,000 persons holds 6 *caballerías* of land (1 *caballería* equals 40.94 hectares). One-half of this land is forest, one-half is farmland. The entirety is used by 200 renters who are the poorest folk in town. The renters say that the land is blessed, because its productivity constitutes their only source of maintenance. They have formed a committee, led by seven men, to protect the commons.

One afternoon, when we met the renters' group, consisting of males, they recounted their struggles. The committee of seven consists of several elders plus some young men, including one who is unmarried; they reach decisions through consensus after everyone has given voice. The men explained that each renter made milpa and was permitted to sell the produce, hold it for domestic consumption, or do both in combination. Disposal of the product was no concern of the community, but holding the patrimony was.

Long in the telling, the story of their fights to keep the land can be separated into several stages. The struggles began some years ago when the town's mayor tried to sell some of the trees on the reserved land to a contractor in order to raise money for the municipality. A few trees in wetlands and around springs were cut. The renters' community immediately complained, however, that much of the forest also protected the municipality's water sources and that the woods were meant for household use. The mayor canceled the contract but then tried to sell some of the agricultural plots to an outsider. Instantly, the struggle between the renters and the mayor intensified, armed fights broke out, and several renters lost their lives. Eventually, the mayor backed down. Following this conflict, he offered to sell the land to the renters, with the capital value to be paid to the municipality over time.

The offer seemed attractive, because individuals would hold personal title to the land they used. The renters discussed the offer at length and then refused because—as one after another explained—whereas each might gain access to sufficient land, when they had children and their children had children, there would not be enough land for everyone. They needed to think of the "future" and "the children." On the face of it, their argument against privatization of the land was hardly convincing, for the same demographic pressures affect a commons. But the leaders explained that a community would not let its commons be divided into ever smaller plots, because its purpose is to maintain people sufficiently for their well-being. They knew also that if privatized the land might be sold to complete outsiders. In their explanations the leaders pitted community against market, commons against capital. Kept as a community holding, the land would not be used to secure short-term gains.

The people's refusal to convert the land into a commodity produced another response from the mayor. He decided to raise the land rent. Many years ago, the charge was 50 cents (Guatemalan) per *cuerda*, but this had risen to 5 quetzals or ten times the first amount. (One *cuerda* equals approximately one-tenth hectare; 400 cuerdas equal one caballería.) By his latest offer, the mayor would increase the rent fifteen times to 75 quetzals per cuerda. The renters' community complained, but not for the reason one might expect. They were willing to pay a higher rent, but wanted to see a plan for use of the money; and the rental receipts had to be used for the benefit of the municipality, such as improving its water supply or repairing the streets. Community members suspected that the mayor would use some of the returns personally, but their main desire was that any rents they paid for use of the commons be expended for the benefit of the larger municipality. To underline their convictions, nearly half the renters marched on the mayor's office; and he agreed to keep the rent at its current level.

After hearing that the community was willing to pay an increased land rent, we wondered what level they considered to be appropriate. Drawing on our experience in the uplands of Colombia—where local folk speak of the "just price"—we asked the Guatemalan renters what they thought a just rent would be. They understood the meaning. A just rent had nothing to do with a market price or an "honest" price, as it once meant to post-Aristotleans. The people also were not concerned to find out what the rents were for comparable pieces of land. A just rent was the return needed to "meet the necessities" of a community. In the highlands of Colombia, a "just price" is one that meets the needs of both parties to the exchange; anything charged above or below the just price signals the taking of a gain or profit by one and the rejection of mutuality. In Guatemala, a just rent for individual use of the commons may be any amount as long as it is used to meet the needs of the receiving community. The level of the just rent has nothing to do with market forces and the equilibration of supply and demand but with community maintenance.

In these four successive struggles, the community placed boundaries on the market, that is, on the commodification of pieces of land and trees. The agent against whom the renters' community struggled was an elected official; however, he was selected by the broader municipality, did not represent the renters, and seemed to be using his political position to seek rents for himself. Adopting a market perspective, he valued the land, forest, and water as if each had a monetary price determined by its potential market uses. In response to the mayor's incursions, the people drew on a different discourse. Certainly, the resisting renters had an interest in not purchasing the land and in keeping the rent low, but they also were saying that the land was not for sale, even by them. It constituted their "base," the foundation by which they lived, and fell outside market evaluation. In opposing the initial sale of forest products, then the sale of land to outsiders, subsequently the sale of land to themselves, and finally a rise in rents, the renters voiced a community model that legitimated their practices to themselves as well as the larger market and polity.

This sequence of struggles also raised a question about community legitimacy in the larger legal framework. Since their last struggle with the mayor, the renters' group has been trying to secure title to the agricultural land. The process has been stalled by political impediments, and a new fact has emerged: The forest land, consisting of 3 caballerías, is owned by the municipality, but the 3 caballerías of farmland have no official owner and so are possessed by the state. Yet, the municipality has been acting as owner of this state land and collecting rents for years, and the people have been transmitting their use rights to offspring. This complicated situation, which has its origins in the conquest and colonial times, raises the question: What makes a land claim legitimate? The case suggests that a community's holding of a commons, its moral claim to a part of the environment, is partly a matter of persuasion and possession made through actions, such as demonstrating in front of a mayor's office. Communities make themselves—often today, through struggles with market forces.

WHO IS SUBSIDIZING WHOM?

Community formation is often hard to achieve, especially when a material commons providing immediate sustenance is not possessed. We saw this problem in relation to environmental protection.

In an attempt to help defend the environment, Guatemala has created a number of national park reserves. We visited one, located in a wetlands area adjacent to a Pacific coast village. The town has grown dramatically in the last decade due to population pressures and the search for arable land in other parts of the nation. Hardly a community, the town is a collection of people, from various strata of life, who pursue different strategies of living. Ambient problems in the area are many, including loss of timber, wetlands, and the sand beach. Due to extensive fishing, marine life, from sharks to corvina and turtles, is being seriously depleted as well. Underfunded and struggling against overpowering forces, the park staff focuses its efforts on a few problems. For example, the park keeps tanks and cages for reproducing some of the endangered animals, and it carries out educational functions in the town and at its visitor center.

Officials at the park are concerned about the disappearance of large sea turtles. Hunted for their meat and fed as bait to sharks which also are prized, the turtles are doubly in danger because their eggs are considered a delicacy and aphrodisiac. The turtles lay eggs on the town's beach, but residential and hotel expansion has narrowed the sand strip; night lights also confuse the turtles, which sometimes lose their way and turn back to the ocean without laying. Egg collectors, who sell their booty, are the major danger. National laws prohibit taking eggs and killing turtles; but enforcement problems, including understaffed and underpaid police, are many. One of the park employees lamented that many in the local village had become "predators," who did not think of their children. Despite the bleak prospect, he often spoke with the villagers about the turtle problem and requested that they contribute one-tenth of their collected eggs to the reserve so that it might hatch them, raise the baby turtles in its tanks, and release grown ones in the ocean. The park employee tried to persuade his neighbors by saying this payment would be a "donation" or "alms," and in fact the amount he requested equaled the tithe. Some villagers refused, saying they would not donate because others would not; but many responded positively, and the park has been able to stock its tanks. A member of the village itself, the park worker appealed, as he explained, to the people's *consciencia*—roughly, to their community sentiment or social consciousness. He used a community lexicon to help persuade them to make a "commons" of turtle eggs.

The story is hardly straightforward, however, for this small enactment of community economy is set within a larger market economy. The turtle commons and park, sponsored by the local village and the state, subsidize market actors by reproducing turtles whose meat will be hunted and eggs will be scavenged for profit. Still, in the midst of the predation, a few of the collectors with a social consciousness are willing to set aside (*guardar*) a tithe for the commons, even if their own behavior—shifting from market to commons to market—is double-sided, dialogic, almost schizophrenic in its contradictory nature.

We learned about other ways of rescuing turtle eggs when we talked with a young man involved in plant and animal conservation projects. In our conversation with him, we came to understand even more clearly the dual and divided economic life that everyone leads. This energetic organizer works saving species and developing educational programs on conservation. Protecting species, he says, is impossible without involving local communities and demonstrating the "benefits" of conservation. He adds that successful programs meet the "needs" of the people involved—his language draws heavily on the community lexicon. But he voices a different side as well. He recounted how he served as consultant to a leather factory that was polluting a town's river with waste materials. The problem was that the factory provided about 90 percent of the employment in the area. If it were shut down, he said, who would lose but the community? And who really lost, he added, by the unsafe discharge? He claimed to have solved the problem by explaining to the owners of the factory, whose main customers are in the United States, that there is a demand for environmentally safe products in the North. If the factory were to clean up its waste, it could advertise that it sold green products only, and the subsequent increase in demand would cover the cleanup costs.

The young man then spoke of other ways to attack environmental pollution; all were market solutions and employed the concepts of externalities, opportunity costs, and demand. He turned to the turtle problem, saying that the national law against the taking of eggs should be strictly applied in the area we visited and that the local reserve officials "lacked the balls" to enforce the law. Furthermore, their practices, relying on community sentiment, were "half-assed." He told about a different way of solving the problem. Elsewhere along the beach, a small store—affiliated with a reserve—bartered used clothing from the United States for turtle eggs. Local people were enthusiastically responding, and the store was providing many more eggs to its park reserve than the one we visited was receiving from the community donations. Here, said he, was an ingenious, market solution to problems of the environment.

But his market story omitted discussion of the source of the used clothing, which in fact further involves the dialogical relation of market and community. Much used clothing in Guatemala comes from organizations in the United States, such as Goodwill Industries. Donations to Goodwill and other charitable agencies are leftovers of the household economy.

Frequently, Goodwill sells these gifts at auction; and entrepreneurs purchase large quantities which they transport south and sell to others, such as marketeers in Guatemala and nonprofit organizations that operate beach stores. Establishing a commons of turtle eggs through the barter of clothes, thus, has a complicated place in the global economy. First, clothing is produced (sometimes in Guatemala itself) for sale in the United States; after a period of use, it becomes a donation (and a tax deduction) to a community organization; the recipient or charitable organization returns the clothing to the market sphere by selling it at a low rate; the purchased clothing then is transported to Guatemala by entrepreneurs where it is bought with community funds to trade it, at below-market rates, for turtle eggs, which then are removed from the market sphere but ultimately returned to it free of charge. In this sequence, that cycles from market to community and back, community economy subsidizes the market, but only because people seem easily to shift their practices and discourse between the two domains.

DOUBLE LIVES AND UNCERTAINTY

The commons, as a holding or savings, constitutes one bulwark against uncertainty, which seems clear by the frequency with which people talk about holding land or another resource "for the future." Given this propensity to hoard in community, we sought situations in which people were conserving and preserving a resource to find how they imagined and verbalized their actions, especially in relation to the uncertainty of living by the market.

One Saturday we made our way to an inaccessible-by-road Indian village to learn about the large forest the inhabitants were preserving in the mountains above the town. We found over a hundred people building a new church in the village center. Men were digging trenches, women were carting water, and children were involved in tasks everywhere. As the people explained, in a language now familiar to us, they were performing a *service* in which one *collaborated*. No one was paid money, so the community had no financial costs (*costos*), although the work was a personal expenditure (*un gasto*) of effort. The organizers, who were members of Catholic Action, had sought and received permission from the mayor to cut designated trees in the community's forest for use in building the church.

We found the mayor sick in bed. He explained that the forest, which was inaccessible by road and half-a-day's walk from the village, constituted a "fund" or "bottom" (*fondo*) for the community. Before anyone could cut a tree, she had to ask the mayor and he in turn consulted with town elders. If permission was given, ten new trees had to be planted for each one cut in order to preserve both the timber and the watershed. The mayor, proud of the forest and a commons land kept for domestic crops, talked at length about several communal groups that were run by unpaid collaboration and cooperation.

He then switched topics and said that young men in the community were earning cash by winding string balls used in a kicking game popular in the United States. He had encouraged the young men to undertake this wage work but suggested that they keep "making milpa" in case the work stopped. The mayor continued that he was spending considerable time urging government agencies to complete the building of a new road to the village. With a proper road, he thought, maize could be brought in and sold to people in the town, even though the villagers raised it in their milpas; he surmised that tourists would also visit, and so stimulate local arts, trade, and more cash work. The mayor did not express concern about a conflict between maintaining community—such as building a church on Saturdays, caring for the communal forest, and holding a commons for farming—and augmenting market interactions through tourism, wage work, and greater dependence on purchased commodities. He lived a double economic life, as signaled by his shifting use of community and market discourses, and visualized no clash of the two.

Several days later we had another double-sided conversation that was different from the mayor's. This one illustrated more sharply the limits of market rationality in coping with uncertainty. When we met the head of a wildlife foundation, he talked at length about Guatemala's bleak ecological situation. The Petén jungle was a frontier zone—out of control and subject to the usual wave of destruction: First, contractors cut wood for sale; *colonos* then burned the remainder in order to seed subsistence crops; next, cattle-men took over the land and the colonos moved further into the jungle; finally, the land was seeded in export crops. The process, destructive and irreversible, was hard to stop given the land and economic pressures in the nation which were erupting in political struggles. In parts of the country, he continued, cadastral surveys were inadequate, and the land titling system was a mess: One plot title had been granted on top of another. Regardless of production system or tenure rules, the loss of topsoil continued.

He then told about his foundation's attempt to convince political authorities to protect one forest region in Guatemala. The foundation had undertaken studies comparing the revenues produced by sale of the timber with the costs of cutting and damage to the watershed; the research showed that levelling the forest was not profitable. His group had found some success in convincing the government to protect the region, because the study, drawing on numerical calculations, accounting techniques, and modern economics, had been stated in a language officials understood.[5]

With a smile, our conversant then added, "This is not all." He was conscious of using a discourse about benefits and costs to persuade others of the value of preserving the forest; however, he recognized there were limits to this language. He knew that one could never be certain of selecting the right discount rate to evalute the future flow of timber or water, and his forestry study could always be improved and made more accurate. But in stating, "This is not all," he was also saying something about the discourse he had employed. The market model had limits; it was incomplete; and there was a nonquantifiable element he had not included. Explaining that alternative ways of constructing the environment must always exist, our discussant concluded that he did not see "the environment" as something separate from humans, as an object characterized by mechanical laws and consisting of discrete elements such as water, wood, and leaves. Yet, he was not totally clear in what he was trying to say: Did he believe that his discourse created a realm of uncertainty or did he think that a domain of uncertainty remained outside any discourse? Perhaps he expected that his knowledge system would itself change in time. Certainly, he lacked an alternative or supplementary discourse.

Then, as an afterthought, he produced another study his group had commissioned; it described the practices and ideas of the people who had for centuries been living in the region his foundation had studied. Filled with local metaphors and imagery, this second study set forth the local people's perspective of the forest and environment. Our conversationalist did not know what to do with this study and had not presented it to the government.

How should we appreciate and understand his partly split, partly incomplete discourse? We suggest that his statement, "This is not all," marks the boundary between the market discourse, which constructs probabilistic outcomes, and what we will call uncertainty (Dewey 1929; Knight 1971). Uncertainty, in our view, concerns our lack of knowledge (1) about the future, (2) about what is "really there," (3) about the knowledge formulations we may someday use, and (4) about where the limits of our knowledge lie. This undetermined space cannot be quantified and tamed through the construction and projection of probability distributions and risk calculations. These latter are constructs in our discourse and partly manufacture the idea of uncertainty itself (Hacking 1975). Our coping tool of "instrumental rationality" may not be capable of dealing with uncertainty as opposed to risk. Coping with uncertainty sometimes requires that we make savings or hoards not profit, and that we preserve a commons and not build capital, because we cannot know what will happen.

PROFITS AND COMMUNITY

The small, independent house-business in Latin America, straddling community and market, illustrates how profits, built by innovation in conditions of uncertainty, draw on community and its base. Consider the case of a successful woman potter outside Guatemala City, who was crafting new figurines for sale. She worked in a corner of her kitchen but had a separate store that was stocked with finished pieces. Buyers came from the city to purchase in quantity, her husband spent much of his time overseeing the practical arrangements, and the woman had accumulated enough money to make other small investments in her village. The woman's items were selling well, but she liked to make new pieces and was experimenting with figures of angels. Each figurine emerged from the potter's hands with a slightly different form as the woman made adjustments to achieve greater balance or more stability. Looking at earlier angel figures, one could also see that the overall design had been evolving. The figures had taken well to the firing, and the results were generally good. As the potter explained, all her work was done by touch and testing (*tantear*), or contextual reason.

Feeling one's way also characterized the potter's pricing. For a batch of figures, she knew what quantity of clay was used and the time she spent. Each new figurine had a real cost basis derived from the cost of the raw materials and labor return the potter had been receiving. (Unlike some household workers, the potter considered that her labor was a monetary "cost" and not an unpriced "expense of the house" that supported production of the market commodity through the use of "unaccounted" house work). Still, the sum of her material costs and labor, a calculation the potter made with a high degree of precision, was not the price she charged. For pricing, the ceramic artist would also feel her way; depending on what the market would bear, she raised or lowered her price—and would or would not make a profit above costs. Her expenditures were calculable and predictable for every angel figure, but her profit was not; it was always uncertain, depending on the market.

The ceramic artist's profit also was temporary for a double reason. If her product continued to sell well, eventually she would recalculate the gain as an augmentation to the "value of her work"; she increased the figured return to her own labor, and this could have a long-term effect on what she charged for her other pieces. But other potters in the community would also see what she had done, how the figure was made, and whether it drew buyers. They were adept artisans, too, and would quickly copy her figurine if it became popular. Still, the potter said that even with competition the eventual sale price of a new figure usually did not fall to its original cost of production (and she added that as she made more angel figures she would find ways to produce them better and more quickly). Although the price of new ceramic pieces might decline through competition, the remuneration for her own labor almost always increased: Even with competition, she was able to absorb some of the initial profit as a return to her labor. Over time, the value of all her work efforts had in fact been rising; she had observed, for example, that although she had learned her craft directly from her mother at home, her standard of living was appreciably higher than that of her parent.

In minature the potter's case neatly displays the foundation, course, and effects of profit making. The new product, as well as the pricing, was established by trial and error. The angel figure as a material creation in the household of the woman initially was an uncertain product. Then its price was uncertain, as was its profit. Even so, profit on the innovation was temporary. But as it disappeared, it was distributed as a higher imputed wage to the original maker, lower prices to consumers, and increased returns to other potters; what had been profit became higher wages and lower prices. The woman potter fits Schumpeter's classic model: The entrepreneur invents a new process, introduces it to the market, and holds a short-term monopoly; eventually, the improvement is distributed one way or another within the system and alters economic development.

The potter's example shows how the market relies on community. The figurines themselves were suggested by media and other sources; as products, they varied with the batches of clay, the characteristics of the oven, and the skills of the potter in relation to these. But the woman learned her skills by watching and working in her mother's kitchen, just as she continued to work in her own kitchen and her offspring learned from her. In addition, she added to this legacy or commons, because her neighbors who were also "competitors" would visit, watch, and copy her work just as she could benefit from their innovations. The series of innovations that emerged from and circulated among all the potters added to the village heritage. Artisanship was sustained by house and village communities, as were the practices of trial and error in conditions of uncertainty. The innovations lay in the entire communal situation, including practiced hands, clay, and other people. The potter's case suggests how innovation— that engages uncertainty, alters a heritage, draws a profit, and raises the standard of living—depends on and flourishes in the communal dimension of economy.

TELLING TALES

In Guatemala, we conversed with many people who talked in terms of risks and probabilities. For them, solutions to the problems of the environment had to be found within the market and market theory. For example, most contemporary economists agree that if people desire "green products," demand them, and pay for them, this preference will lead suppliers to change their ways. On this view, community morality influences the market through demand. But if a product supplied by two vendors appears the same to sensory experience and one is less expensive than the other, most market participants will choose the cheaper to preserve capital. The ordinary argument leaves out the quest for profit and the power of capital as well as the pervasiveness of imperfect information and the fact that almost no market is perfectly competitive. Some might also argue that if we priced all environmental expenditures in production and the full cost of waste, then even in market terms, corporations could never make a profit or the standard of living would drop. They might suggest that we live on borrowed time because the world's stocks of resources are being turned into flows for the market (Daly and Townsend 1993).

We invoke a different story. The market may be a competition, a game of winning and losing as the Spanish word for profit (*ganar*) suggests. But who shall be the umpire, who shall set the rules of the game? Players cannot also be referee (*juez y parte*). The market has never been "self-regulating" (Polanyi 1944); the rules about what can and cannot enter the market game, and what the exits must look like, are set externally. Communities situate a market, and support it by yielding their leftovers as uncosted gains and accepting its garbage as uncosted waste. Communities define what domain the market shall occupy, and they struggle with the market over this space. To phrase this in a language from Latin America, the market deals with numerical *costs (costos)* determined in *exchange,* the community copes with incommensurate *expenditures (gastos)* of materials and work. Entries to and exits from the market—which support profit making and have to do with using community *expenditures* in place of market *costs,* and with converting market *costs* to community *expenditures*— are determined by a community placing boundaries on the market.

Our Guatemalan cases suggest that such assertions of community are made and remade, by acts such as demonstrating in front of a mayor's office.

But communities, such as those protecting turtles, need not be locally based or face-to-face (Anderson 1991); in today's global market, communities cross national borders, assume new forms, and place new limits on transnational actors.

The "environmental problem," covering much, can refer to using up limited resources, generating excessive waste, degrading the planet's environment and living conditions, or all three. Certainly, demographic growth leads to environmental pressures; and human life and the making of social agreements are entropic activities. But we view the environmental problem through the lens of the dual model of economy, as part of the struggle between market and community, or capital and base. Let us return to the central act of making a profit by innovation.

Some innovations are thrifty or have a negligible effect on the use of materials. A smaller computer chip is thrifty; the potter who made angel figurines sold new ones in place of others; automobiles may be made with lighter materials or designed to use less gasoline; tires may be manufactured to last longer. Innovations also may revolve about recycling, a common practice in less capitalized sectors: In many parts of Latin America, used tires are first mended and remade, then fashioned into sandals or used for cushioning boats at docks and piers.

But profit making through innovations and their spread can have the reverse effect. What had been used to sustain community by its base may be diverted to the market. This debasement process is part of the environmental problem not because a community conserves resources better than market participants but because a commons or base is part of a market's environment. The physical environment is our shared heritage—sometimes unseen. Transforming this patrimony changes a people's identity by altering the base of their community and the possibilities it affords for future practices.

For this reason, although economists and others factor in environmental effects through cost/benefit analyses, they may be part of the problem they would eradicate. With heroic assumptions, we may price the value of an unused forest by figuring the monetary value of all its previously uncounted benefits, arranging these as a stream of wealth that accrues over time, and discounting this flow to capture its current capital value which can then be weighed against alternative uses. But this impeccable technique uses the logic of market activity to save the environment from that same activity!

Making things commensurate through the market is an exercise in eradicating unpredictability and denying the human desire to innovate and encounter uncertainty. A community's commons, even if fuzzy-edged, offers a base for exploration and discovery. We can never know how the environ‐ment will be used in one‐thousand or even fifty years. To price a forest, river, air, or lake implies that its long‐term value is determinable now and not sub‐ject to future discovery. By pricing the environment and assigning it a capital value—even for the sake of preserving it—we limit the legacy for our successors while contradicting our status as legatees of a base, not capital.

The ambient is in part a realm of uncertainty. How should we act in the face of such true uncertainty—by supporting systems of growth and claims that our knowledge system can encompass this darkness, or by main‐taining communities and the commons on which they depend, because in these ways of living nature is not divided from human society, the human is not seen as holding a position superordinate to a purely rule‐governed environment, and people cannot destroy the externality except at peril to themselves. The commons is the savings or the holding space for the incommensurate, castoffs, and unused materials. In these places, humans cope by trial‐and‐error practices. We can value the environment also by making it part of community.

The environmental issue, thus, has to be discussed partly within a com‐munity language. We do not presume that the spread of the market is bad or good, or that a community will manage the environment well. We pre‐serve our environment for the future, however, because we cannot predict the meanings, values, and uses that may be supported by a base. Times to come are incalculable, and potential uses of our shared base must be addressed in light of economy's totality or two sides.[6]

Tomorrow's struggles over use of the environment and human labor—or tomorrow's political economy—we surmise will take the form of community versus market, and perhaps this negotiation will supersede the class struggle that itself may now be reread as one between communities in relation to market interests.

NOTES

We wish to thank John Richards for his encouragement and comments in the preparation of this essay.

1. This same theme informs much of John Richards' introductory essay to this book.

2. One example is the pratik relationship in Haiti, as described by Mintz (1961).

3. Humans also invent, make sense of, and interpret many micro‐behaviors by projecting these building blocks onto practical action. Consider opening a

door. Sometimes one does it for oneself: This is individual self-sufficiency. But sometimes one does it for another as an act of communality or social connection. Here the complications start. The communal courtesy can be an act of friendship; but until recently it was for males a gendered act indicating dominance, although one sometimes opens a door for a banker, businessman, or president, as an expression of submission. Nonetheless, all are acts within community indicating social connection.

Conversely, a doorman at a hotel or restaurant may open doors, which is a market act, especially since the prices of the establishment will be raised to cover the doorman's pay. This act may be seen as a projection of communal relations, for the restaurant or hotel sells itself as an establishment of community, although the doorman may depend on communal tips for survival. Are the tips a market repayment for a service, a communal act of friendship that converts a market gain to community, a mystification of community relationships—or does their interpretation depend on the local context?

Women today are suing to be able to practice this male profession, which is an apt illustration of the way the realm of community helps structure market participation. Because part of the significance of the doorman's act is its gendered nature, contestation against this power and the closed labor market must originate in shifting communal expectations. From gender to tips to the projected sense of mutuality, the significance of the doorperson's act depends on its place as a material service within a community and market that interact in shifting ways.

4. But nonmarket behaviors also may be modeled through a market lens (Becker 1976, 1981).

5. For a discussion of the evaluation of forest products using local or ethnographic information, see Godoy and Lubowski 1992.

6. See also Richards' introduction in this book.

BIBLIOGRAPHY

Anderson, Benedict. 1991. *Imagined Communities*. Rev. ed. London: Verso.

Aristotle. 1984. *The Politics*. Cambridge, England: Cambridge University Press.

Becker, Gary S. 1976. *The Economic Approach to Human Behavior*. Chicago: University of Chicago Press.

———. 1981. *A Treatise on the Family*. Cambridge, Mass.: Harvard University Press.

Boeke, J. H. 1942. *The Structure of Netherlands Indian Economy*. New York: Institute of Pacific Relations.

Daly, Herman, and Kenneth Townsend. 1993. *Valuing the Earth*. Cambridge, Mass.: MIT Press.

Dewey, John. 1929. *The Quest for Certainty.* New York: Minton, Balch, and Co.

Demsetz, Harold. 1964. "The Exchange and Enforcement of Property Rights." *Journal of Law and Economics* 7:11–26.

———. 1967. "Toward a Theory of Property Rights." *American Economic Review* LVII: 347–59.

Evers, Hans-Dieter. 1994. "The Trader's Dilemma." In *The Moral Economy of Trade,* ed. Hans-Dieter Evers and Heiko Schrader, 7–14. London: Routledge.

Geertz, Clifford. 1963. *Agricultural Involution.* Berkeley: University of California Press.

Georgescu-Roegen, Nicholas. 1971. *The Entropy Law and the Economic Process.* Cambridge, Mass.: Harvard University Press.

Godoy, Ricardo, and Ruben Lubowski. 1992. "Guidelines for the Economic Valuation of Nontimber Tropical-Forest Products." *Current Anthropology* 33:423–33.

Gudeman, Stephen. 1986. *Economics as Culture.* London: Routledge.

Hacking, Ian. 1975. *The Emergence of Probability.* Cambridge, England: Cambridge University Press.

Hardin, G. 1968. "The Tragedy of the Commons." *Science* 162:1243–48.

Knight, Frank H. 1971. *Risk, Uncertainty and Profit.* Chicago: University of Chicago Press. (First published 1921).

Mintz, Sidney W. 1961. *Pratik:* Haitian Personal Economic Relationships, Symposium: Patterns of Land Utilization and Other Papers, 54–63. Seattle: American Ethnological Society.

Mirowski, Philip. 1989. *More Heat than Light.* Cambridge, England: Cambridge University Press.

Ostrom, Elinor. 1990. *Governing the Commons.* Cambridge, England: Cambridge University Press.

Polanyi, Karl, Conrad Arensberg, and Harry Pearson, eds. 1957. *Trade and Market in the Early Empires.* Glencoe, Scotland: Free Press.

Repetto, Robert. 1992. "Accounting for Environmental Assets." *Scientific American* (June), 94–100.

Rivera Gutiérrez, Alberto. 1986. "Material Life and Social Metaphor." Ph.D. thesis. University of Minnesota.

Schumpeter, Joseph. 1934. *The Theory of Economic Development.* Cambridge, Mass.: Harvard University Press. (First published 1926).

13

Community and the Market in Modern American Property Law

ERIC T. FREYFOGLE

The economic success of the United States over the past century has prompted observers around the world to look to it for lessons on stimulating growth. Compared with many countries, the United States is plainly doing something right in terms of fostering the energies of its people. One cause of the United States's success has been the fertile land of central North America, and no study can overlook that unearned natural blessing. Still, American culture and its many institutions have played chief roles in the nation's cornucopia. Somewhere in the American story are useful lessons, however hard they may be to find and transport.

One American institution that has rightly drawn attention is the system of private property, particularly the private ownership of land. Economic enterprises commonly take place on land and entail the mixing of labor and capital with land. Much land is used directly to produce food, fiber, and minerals; other lands become sites for enterprises less dependent on a land parcel's particular natural features. In all cases, investment is needed for economic gains to flow. Both economic theory and common sense give guidance on what it takes to stimulate such investments in land. One requirement is that people have secure land tenure. Mine shafts will not be dug, nor office buildings constructed, when entrepreneurs risk losing their investments because of unstable property rights. Another requirement, less necessary but still important, is the ability to transfer property freely. People are more likely to invest when they can exit an enterprise by selling to others. Free transferability also facilitates the shift of assets to their mostly highly valued uses. When property is easily transferred, markets soon develop, and assets in time move to owners able to use them for the greatest gain.

These familiar points sometimes lead observers to conclude that property rights best promote growth when they are (1) legally secure against interference, particularly governmental interference; (2) clearly defined, so that people know who owns what; and (3) readily transferable. As some see it, the more that a property rights regime reflects these principles, the more growth it stimulates. Best of all is a system in which everything is privately owned and transferable. Then, the market's reach is complete and all resources can flow to their highest valued uses.

In this era of transition for so many countries, it is pertinent to ask: Do these characteristics describe property rights in the United States, particularly landed property rights? Would a property rights regime based on these principles help foster elsewhere the kind of economic success the United States has enjoyed?

Questions like these are difficult to answer. Elementary economic models produce answers that are clear and simple, but models operate only by reducing and portraying crudely a vast complexity. In the case of landed property rights, it turns out, the American story is far too nuanced and contradictory to capture adequately with this model, or any other simple one. The United States has long embraced a market economy, and that market has had much to do with the nation's economic success. Moreover, the market's reach does extend to nature, and property rights are tailored in part to meet market needs. Yet the economic success of the United States has also come from quite different cultural tendencies and pressures. Markets in land and natural resources are checked in many ways, and nonmarket factors play key roles in the definition and allocation of landed property rights. Considered as a whole, the U.S. regime of property rights deviates markedly and increasingly from the simple vision of land as a secure, clearly defined, transferable commodity, vested in a single private owner. At one point in its history (the late nineteenth century), the United States seemed headed toward this approach. But its shortcomings soon became apparent, including the environmental degradation it unleashed; and ownership norms were recast considerably in response.

Over the past century, U.S. laws and regulations have increasingly re-embedded property rights in a communal order, aimed in important part at protecting the natural environment. Property law continues to recognize and protect individual rights, as it has for generations; but it recognizes other aims as well, and constraints on the market are pervasive. Aggregate calculations are hard to undertake, yet plentiful evidence suggests that these constraints have served not to contain economic growth but to help fuel it, both by correcting the market's flaws in pricing and allocation and by fostering the kind of trust, social cohesiveness, and civic stability that any market needs to work well. In the ongoing drama of private property in America, the market is only one of the lead characters.

The thesis of this chapter stems from a form of macroanalysis that is engaged in only with trepidation, for it necessarily entails generalizations painted with a broad brush. Generalizations obscure details and inevitably emphasize a few aspects of life at the expense of others. Landed property rights in the United States have always been characterized by contradictory impulses—between individual autonomy and community wants, for instance; between the protection of existing uses and the stimulation of new ones; and between organic, status rules aimed at social cohesion and contract rules aimed at maximizing flexibility. Beset with such tensions, American property law defies easy summary.

Yet treacherous though they are, generalizations have their place, if only to qualify simple models that distort even more the complex, unfolding story of landed property rights in the United States. Private property in America has long been a battleground of conflicting interests, a center of power struggles on a variety of social and spatial scales—from the individual family and neighborhood to the watershed, the bioregion, the state economy and polity, and upward to the nation-state and global community. Americans may stand united in their fondness for private property over socialist alternatives. But they have argued ceaselessly about what ownership ought to mean. From these arguments has come a complex set of ownership norms, continually evolving in response to changing values and circumstances.

NINETEENTH-CENTURY TRENDS

To understand landed property rights at the beginning of the twenty-first century, it is useful to back up and review briefly some of the experiences and trends that led the United States a century ago to increase constraints on the market's operation.

Expanding the Market

Many of the trends affecting landed property rights during the nineteenth century were ones with broad social and economic impacts. One dominant trend, permeating many aspects of life, was the continued expansion of the market's domain. Labor was increasingly performed, and goods increasingly produced, not for direct use and consumption but for sale in the market. Agricultural production became more specialized, increasingly focusing on staple crops and responding to market prices. Particularly in settled areas and cities, transactions more often took the form of monetary deals rather than exchanges or gifts. As the market expanded, local economies became linked into ever larger ones, and transactions commonly occurred among people who knew each other only in the market.

As the market waxed in importance, it both reflected and propelled the evolving ways that people perceived the natural world and valued it. Nature became, more than ever, a fragmented collection of market commodities rather than an organic whole. Valuation increasingly was set by market forces, with an item gaining value because a person could sell it for cash or use it to produce marketable things. This sense of value was hardly new, but it gained strength during the era, pushing to the side older notions of value that paid attention to the land's direct usefulness to the owner and to the status and political relationships centered on land. With this accentuated market emphasis, land was increasingly viewed as an income-generating asset—something that helped an owner succeed in the market—rather than a source of independence that allowed an owner to live apart from the communal order. By no means completely but nonetheless perceptibly, land became a source for generating wealth; and it was the generated wealth itself, not the land, that provided independence and perpetuated a family's fortune.

Trends in landed property rights were part and parcel of the nation's waxing enthusiasm for economic development—for plowing fields, sinking mines, building factories, and constructing various means of transport, communication, and trade. In several critical ways, law and government affirmatively aided this enthusiastic transformation of the landscape: by vesting broad legal powers in corporations and other large-scale organizations; by overtly subsidizing costly and risky ventures; and by pruning liability rules and other laws that either added costs to large-scale enterprises or that unduly restricted contractual freedom. In the property realm, land was surveyed as quickly as funding and sectional politics would allow; and land title recording systems were instituted everywhere to make titles more secure and to enable buyers and sellers to know who owned what—a critical step in the development of land markets. In many small ways, the law struck down long-term restraints on the alienation of land and otherwise cooperated in the push to make nature a more readily marketable commodity.

When the nineteenth century began, most land not yet in private hands was owned by the federal government. Throughout the century, the government's policy toward that land was guided by a single aim: to get it into the hands of productive users as quickly as possible. Disputes about public lands policy were heated and endless, decade upon decade, particularly when sectional politics intervened. But arguments were chiefly about who would gain from land distributions and by how much, not about disposition as the overall goal. In the case of Indian lands, treaties and reservation policies brought more and more land into the hands of white settlers.

Property Rights and the Intensification of Land Uses

One vital shift in this release of entrepreneurial energy (as historian Willard Hurst would call it) took place in the legal definition of what it meant to own land. This was probably the most important shift that occurred in property law, and it requires careful study, both because of its importance at the time and because so much change in the twentieth century is best understood as a counterreaction to it.

When the nineteenth century began, the common law displayed a deep concern for the right of a property holder to remain undisturbed in his quiet possession of the land. State governments, to be sure, occasionally took property without paying for it; and the nation by then already had extensive experience with land use regulation. Still, private property enjoyed a legal protection that befitted its practical and mythical importance in the ways Americans thought about their nation and understood their liberty.

In time, the new class of industrial entrepreneurs would share this enthusiasm for secure property rights, but early in the nineteenth century, ironically, they often found that secure property stood as a roadblock for their plans.

When courts of the era described what it meant to own land, they typically portrayed the institution in natural terms. The right to use land in the Anglo-American common law was the right to live on it peacefully and to remain undisturbed in its quiet enjoyment. A nineteenth-century English court offered a particularly lyrical rendition of this early understanding of private ownership:

> What then is the right of land and its owner or occupier? It is to have all natural incidents and advantages as nature would produce them. There is a right to all the light and heat that would come, to all the rain that would fall, to all the wind that would blow; a right that the rain which would pass over the land should not be stopped and made to fall on it, a right that the heat from the sun

should not be stopped and reflected on it, a right that the wind should not be checked, but should be able to escape freely; and if it were possible that these rights were interfered with by one having no right, no doubt an action would lie.[1]

Private land was protected by laws against trespass, which barred all unconsented physical entries, and by nuisance law, which prohibited neighbors from engaging in acts that indirectly harmed an owner's use and enjoyment of land. A landowner could not disturb the land's natural drainage in a way that harmed neighbors. Water in flowing rivers was available for use by a landowner, but except to fulfill elementary needs no owner could use it in a way that diminished its quality or quantity—its natural incidents, that is—for a downstream user. Under the doctrine of ancient lights, an owner who made extended use of sunlight reaching his land could halt a neighbor's interference with that light, even when caused by an ordinary building or fence.

Property rights were secure enough in this farm-centered legal scheme, but they were defined in ways that industrializing America increasingly deemed unacceptable. Industrial landowners needed to use land more intensively than did their agrarian forebears. Small-scale farmers might enjoy water laws that protected a stream's natural flow, but industries wanted to use water intensively, altering the flow and degrading its quality. They needed the right to emit smoke and odors bothersome to surrounding households, to make noises that scared horses, and even to emit sparks that occasionally set wheat fields on fire. Water wheels necessarily disrupted migratory fish patterns. Tall buildings necessarily blocked sunlight and healthful air. The old law, by protecting an owner's right to the land's "natural incidents," stood as a barrier to industrial-style progress.

Over the course of the nineteenth century, American lawmakers materially changed the meaning of landownership to facilitate these newer, intensive land uses. As they did so, sensitive, agrarian landowners suffered in that they lost some of their legal rights of protection. The doctrine of ancient lights was one of the first to go; as it did, landowners could no longer complain about the blockage of natural light. Courts continued to talk about a landowner's right to enjoy quietly the "natural incidents" of the land, but that right increasingly was qualified by the neighboring landowner's right to make "ordinary" and "customary" uses of the land— uses that were, increasingly, anything but quiet.

As many courts cast the issue, the key legal question was not whether a neighbor caused harm but whether the neighbor's activities were reasonable under the circumstances, or whether they were conducted in ways typical of the industry or trade that the neighbor conducted. Water law dropped its concern with the river's natural flow and began allowing riparian landowners to make more intensive uses of the river, even a use that drained a river dry or polluted it severely, so long as the use was deemed reasonable under the increasingly pro-development standards of the day. In the Western arid states, the riparian rights doctrine was dropped entirely, replaced by the more pro-development prior appropriation system in which downstream landowners had no rights to challenge upstream water uses—no matter how destructive—unless they possessed water rights dated earlier in time.

This shift in property rights took many forms, and while it occurred erratically and incompletely in many states the overall trend was clear. Sensitive, agrarian land uses no longer enjoyed the protection they once did. Priority in time as a principle for resolving land use disputes—a principle that typically favored the older, less intensive use—was given less and less weight, until some courts began deeming it irrelevant. Nuisance law no longer halted harmful interferences with a landowner's enjoyment of the land; increasingly it protected only against substantial interferences caused by unreasonable or negligent land uses. As many courts saw matters, mines, factories, stockyards, and the like were reasonable activities in a rapidly expanding economy. If landowners were to undertake them, benefitting the economy as well as themselves, property law should not stand in the way.

Market Individualism and the Common Good

These changes in landowner rights, diminishing the protection of sensitive uses and facilitating more intensive ones, were parts of a larger shift in cultural values and power relationships. It was a shift that exalted individual liberty and the open market while downplaying more traditional, organic visions of the social fabric.

Fading visions of a society well-ordered. By the time the nineteenth century moved toward a close, landownership commonly meant the right to use land, water, and other resources in any way that did not intentionally harm neighbors and that was not conducted in a negligent manner that caused avoidable harm. Losing ground in legal thought was the once vibrant ideal of a "well-ordered society," under which laws prescribed carefully the methods of economic enterprise for the good of the whole. Also losing ground was the line of thought that linked "property" with "propriety" and that viewed the property rights of individuals as counterbalanced by equally strong, if not overriding, rights held by the community.

Early in the century, New York Chancellor James Kent could proclaim with little debate that "private interest must be made subservient to the general interest of the community,"[2] and Justice John Woodworth of New

York could reason that "the sovereign power in the community . . . may and ought to prescribe the manner of exercising individual rights over property."[3] Even at midcentury Lemuel Shaw, chief justice of the Massachusetts Supreme Judicial Court, could state as

> a settled principle, growing out of the nature of well ordered civil society, that every holder of property, however absolute and unqualified may be his title, holds it under the implied liability that his use of it may be so regulated, that it shall not be injurious to the equal enjoyment of others having an equal right to the enjoyment of their property, nor injurious to the rights of the community.[4]

By late in the century, talk of the community's rights became less frequent, and courts referred less often to the idea of a society "well-ordered." Public interest and private interest were more intertwined for, as many people saw it, both were promoted by intensive uses of land. Indeed, courts began to show greater hostility to land use regulations, particularly restraints on industrial land uses, and occasionally struck them down as improper interferences with private rights. The entire body of law known as public nuisance weakened and nearly disappeared, as courts raised the burden of proof needed to show that a landowner's activity unlawfully disrupted public rights.

The impotence of local government. Since early colonial days, land use laws had largely originated at the local level, and so did other economic regulations. But so potent had the market become by the late nineteenth century that local communities found themselves less and less able to contain it, even when they wanted to do so. Businesses were simply too big. Goods moved too freely through the national economy. Competing to have railroads lay tracks to them, local communities and even states were hard pressed to complain when railroads damaged farms and towns. By late century, businesses became big enough to manipulate national markets through monopolistic practices. Within local economies centered on a single commodity such as timber or silver, residents were too dependent on the commodity to challenge its methods of extraction.

The obvious answer for these various problems was for higher levels of government to become involved, particularly the federal government. But the nation's tradition of economic regulation was all at the state and local level. It was a new thing for the federal government to become involved, and its intervention in the market was slow. Only gradually, over a period of generations, did it become clear that big-scale businesses created a need for big-scale government to contain the ills of industrialism and concentrated, amoral private power.

The rhetoric of individualism. A related reason why governments addressed mounting problems so slowly and reluctantly stemmed from the rhetorical power of individual liberty and property rights. America was founded on notions of liberty and property, and possessive individualism had become a potent ideological force. The Civil War, fought in part to aid the most downtrodden, paradoxically also aided big business, as the rhetoric of liberty that helped free slaves carried over easily to the liberty arguments of entrepreneurs anxious to avoid regulation. As business apologists saw it, liberty meant freedom from governmental restraint. It meant negative liberty—not the more positive liberty, implemented and secured by law, that late eighteenth-century theorists had had in mind.

The abstraction of private rights. With land speculation such a popular pastime, Americans paid heightened attention to the protection of land's market value. So focused were property theorists on land as commodity that they paid less and less attention to a given land parcel's natural features. In legal thought, scholars like Christopher Columbus Langdell, dean of the Harvard Law School, pushed hard to transform law into a science, as rigidly logical (and hence as entitled to academic respect) as chemistry and physics. The upshot, in the case of property law, was that a parcel of land became viewed at law as an abstraction—as the hypothetical Blackacre, as it was often called—and the landowner's rights became abstractly defined. The right to use land was conceived and defined in a way that paid little attention to the land's natural features. Whether flat or hilly, wet or dry, fragile or stable, land parcels were largely equated. Land surveys followed rectangular grid lines, and the law treated a section of land in one place like a section elsewhere.

Dividing the private and public realms. By late century, the rhetoric of individual liberty, and the public's dismay over governmental corruption, lent strength to another idea that influenced profoundly how people understood landownership—the distinction between the public and private realms in modern life. For Jefferson and other late eighteenth-century theorists, property was linked to the civic order. Landownership gave a person sufficient independence to rise above self-interest and act for the common good. Property was thus inextricably linked to the good ordering and governance of society, and both the distribution of land and patterns of settlement and land use were matters of vital public moment. A century later, however, property was understood differently. Not statesmen but captains of industry were the honored leaders of the day, and industry magnates operated in a realm that appeared distinct from the public, governmental one of Jefferson and other landholding aristocrats. Property, too, seemed to exist more in this private realm rather than in the public one. Public officials might intervene to halt a land use that amounted to a nuisance. Otherwise, a landowner held the right to be left alone. Far from being the link to full participation in civic society, private property became a shield to keep the public realm in check. With liberty defined in this negative way, as the right to be left alone, regulation became more a threat to liberty than, as it once had been, a vital means to secure it.

The competitive society. By the end of the nineteenth century, American law had come to embrace a new concept of society. The old organic vision of a structured, well-ordered society, containing and controlling the market, had given way to a more fluid, competitive society in which the market supplied the chief means for achieving public goals. Society had become more fragmented. With market forces so influential, the land too had become more fragmented, with each land parcel conceptually distinct from the next and with landowner rights described abstractly, with little regard for context. Private land existed within the private, market realm. Its ownership brought economic power and privacy, rather than virtue and a commitment to the common good.

THE GATHERING STRENGTH OF CONTRARY FORCES

Although the property-as-commodity vision of property dominated American legal culture in the waning years of the century, it never really displaced older, more community-based ideals, nor did it displace the notion that when public need required, the law-making community could subject property to extensive regulation. The longstanding tradition of regulating land uses, present from the first days of settlement, never disappeared completely—particularly in urban areas, where governments controlled tanneries, slaughterhouses, mortuaries, prostitution houses, and other annoying activities. Also as an important counterbalance to private rights, courts gradually developed the legal doctrine that the state possessed broad "police powers" to regulate economic activities in the public interest. This was not the era of complete laissez-faire that popular histories have sometimes described.

Also retaining flexibility in the face of waxing property rights was the idea of land use "harm," which limited what landowners could do. Harm—which the law had always banned—was a culturally dependent idea, one that derived its meaning from the values that prevailed in a particular time and place. With economic development enjoying such widespread support, many damaging land uses were not deemed harmful overall, given the benefits they generated. Still, the ban on harmful activities remained a living element of property law, powerful enough to contain disruptive land uses when the day came that public sentiment softened its pro-development tilt.

The Downside of Industrialism

Industrialization had never enjoyed complete support in the United States; and as the century came to a close, its critics became more vocal, both in urban areas beset with pollution and in rural areas where industrial forces squeezed farm families off the land and left widespread scars. Many Americans responded by way of escape, turning back nostalgically to older times and mimicking primitive ways in architecture and arts and crafts. Others, though, rose up to challenge the market and to insist that government subject it to greater control.

By the waning years of the nineteenth century, many people recognized that a market freed from social control brought widespread devastation, along with economic gain. Industrialization brought great wealth, to visible families like the Carnegies, Rockefellers, and Vanderbilts, but it brought poverty and destruction too, including destruction to the land community. Chicago was marred by smoky skies and a river burdened with wastes from meat packing plants. In the north woods, deforestation occurred at frightening rates. Soil erosion and exhaustion afflicted farms all across the country. Mining tailings were dumped wherever convenient, often next to waterways that were soon polluted. With the development of the steam shovel, drainage became a crusade, diminishing waterfowl habitat, disrupting hydrologic cycles, and fostering widespread flooding. Passenger pigeons were shot to extinction by market hunters, and other migratory birds suffered. So haphazard were urban land use patterns that many residential areas were hardly fit for habitation. On Western lands, bison were slaughtered wholesale, and grasslands were degraded by excessive and insensitive grazing. Along with this destruction came a nagging sense that the nation was losing something vital—not just its frontier, but its connection to the land, particularly to wildlands. John Muir drew upon this sense of loss with his popular writings on the Sierra Nevadas and Alaska. Hiking and camping clubs flourished, and children rushed to join the new-formed Boy Scouts and Campfire Girls.

The Benefits and Limits of Private Rights

Some of the land degradation that occurred during this period was due not to market forces but to the federal government's failure to police its lands and to the incomplete definition of private property rights in land

and other resources. Public grazing lands often went unmanaged and unregulated, operating as a true open-access commons with the predictable tragic consequences. In the case of other public lands, rules commonly went unenforced; timber companies, for instance, clearcut vast areas under the guise of mining and homesteading. In the private-land realm, ownership interests in oil and gas deposits were governed by a rule of capture, which rewarded the oil producer who drained fields quickly without regard for waste or market prices. Rivers and air sheds, like public grazing lands, were largely open-use commons in that polluters could degrade them almost at will. Without sharply crafted, legally secure rights, users of nature had no incentive to take care, and no right to complain, of land abuse by others.

Looking back, it is clear that much land degradation came about because of nonexistent property rights or ill-defined property rights—just as economic theory would now predict. But much of the degradation took place because of behavior that the market deemed rational, even on secure private land. With virgin forests abundant, reforestation simply was not worth the cost. With crop and livestock prices low, farmers had to exhaust land just to get by. Drainage made good economic sense, and its ill effects were too widespread and subtle to trace back to the source. Property rights could have reduced overgrazing on the public domain, but it was infeasible to use property rights to help migratory birds or fish. Private rights also could not remedy environmental problems that no single owner acting alone could halt or redress, such as the degradation of riparian corridors and the decline of game populations. Then there were the many parts of nature that simply had no market value and that were pushed aside, or that were affirmatively killed (like wolves) because they posed threats. In the market's scheme of values, the health of the land as a whole simply did not count.

Resisting the Market

Reactions to market forces took many forms in late nineteenth- and early twentieth-century America. In rural areas, farm groups such as the Grange and Farmers Alliance arose to combat market manipulations by railroads and other corporations. Farm-run cooperatives flourished as alternatives to big business. Grain elevators faced regulation to contain their abusive practices; like other public utilities, they became seen as a special form of property, privately owned yet "vested with a public interest." Resistance to monopolies and trusts fueled successful pushes for new federal laws. At the state level, oil and gas laws gave birth to regulatory commissions charged with reducing the wastefulness of unbridled competition. In urban areas, community leaders increasingly recognized the need for land use regulation on a communitywide basis to segregate inconsistent activities and make cities more livable. After initial hesitation, the U.S. Supreme Court upheld early zoning laws, and did so with language that acknowledged the practical need for governments to wield broad regulatory powers to protect the public health, safety, and welfare against the gain-driven market.

In the case of public lands, an alarmed citizenry was increasingly unwilling to allow the continued excesses of commodity-focused market forces. Public forests were set aside to protect them from private clearcutting, millions of acres at a time, and majestic natural areas gained protection as parks. Valuable oil and gas reserves were placed off limits, no longer available to the first comer. The federal land-disposition policy slowed and, in the 1930s, largely halted, as reasons mounted to keep land in public hands. Private ownership had become a more ambiguous institution, and long-term public ownership began to make sense for many lands. In the West, grazing lands were subjected to regulation, however poorly enforced and grazier-dominated. In the East, the federal government bought back cutover timber lands to create national forests in an attempt to remedy the market's failure to promote reforestation and to protect watersheds. Public ownership and public subsidies were also used to address the market's widespread lack of concern for soil erosion—a problem that no one could ignore when Dust Bowl silt in the 1930s coated the Eastern seaboard.

By the mid–twentieth century, American industry still enjoyed prestige and economic development remained an unquestioned goal, particularly with memories of the Great Depression so vivid. Industry still wielded considerable political clout, in some cases (such as Kentucky's coal industry) so much clout that it could capture and manipulate law-making processes. Even when law making remained more legitimate, "price of progress" arguments carried weight. In 1953, for instance, the Supreme Court of Pennsylvania turned aside a homeowner's nuisance suit against a coal-processing operation that caused his white house to turn black in a single year and rendered his home almost unlivable. "One's bread is more important than landscape or clear skies," the court responded. "Without smoke, Pittsburgh would have remained a very pretty *village*."[5] A decade or two later, when the first wetlands preservation laws were challenged, some courts reiterated this pro-development bias. Laws prohibiting wetlands drainage were not aimed at halting a harmful activity, courts announced. They forced landowners to turn their lands into parklike nature preserves, and landowners deserved compensation.

Yet pro-development reasoning like this was clearly becoming a thing of the past, at least when couched so extremely. New environmental measures, to be sure, would encounter resistance, yet nearly everyone recognized that tradeoffs were involved. Intensive land uses could be bad overall, and laws were needed to limit them.

CONTEMPORARY TRENDS

As the twenty-first century begins, landed property rights in the United States are moving in many directions. Private rights remain important, and loud calls are heard both to expand private rights into new realms and to make private rights more clear, secure, and transferable. Yet other pressures and trends are also visible, some pushing in opposing directions, toward property rights that are less clear, more restricted, and more subject to group rather than individual control. As a whole, property law displays continuing struggles, most vividly between private rights and communal interests and between a fragmented, commodity view of land and more holistic views that emphasize ethics, aesthetics, and ecology.

To survey the landscape of property rights is to see ongoing negotiations and struggles, with no end in sight. On the surface, disputes center on resource use options and on who holds the reins of decision-making power. Beneath these issues are fundamental questions about values and human nature, as well as how individual humans might best fit into their social and land communities.

Though the contemporary scene is distinctly messy, it is possible to identify six major themes or trends in contemporary landed property rights.[6] Briefly stated, they are as follows:

1. Landowner rights to use land are increasingly tailored to the land and to the surrounding social context; that is, rights to use land are becoming more context dependent. In a related shift, rights to use land intensively are being reduced, with corresponding increases in the protections landowners enjoy against disruptive land uses by neighbors.
2. Old categories of private ownership versus public ownership are being blurred, with more instances of intermediate ownership forms that mix the categories. Increasingly, rights in a single piece of land are fragmented among various "owners," with some rights held by the prime user of the land while other rights are held by neighbors, private entities, and government bodies.
3. Land use planning is taking place on larger spatial scales and covering rural lands, aimed chiefly (although not solely) at urban sprawl, quality-of-life issues, and various land use–related environmental problems.

4. American law has made substantial progress toward a complex reconciliation of the unending conflict between the private owner's desire for clearly defined, stable property norms and the community's contrasting need to retain power to redefine ownership rights in light of shifting conditions and values. The reconciliation offers substantial protection for existing land uses but far less protection for landowner desires to devote land to new uses.

5. Governments at all levels, from the most local to the national and even global, are becoming involved in the processes of defining and controlling land use rights, albeit with little consensus and much experimentation on how best to allocate power and responsibility among the various governing levels.

6. In the vitally important rhetorical battleground over the meaning of private property, individualistic, commodity-focused images of ownership have gained prominence; and they have significantly impeded efforts to address rural land use problems, particularly land degradation caused by agriculture and other commodity-production activities. Though conservation advocates have been slow to develop alternative images of ownership—ones that draw upon organic, communal understandings of ownership—alternative images are emerging, thus joining the contest over private property as cultural emblem.

The remainder of this study explores in order these six dominant trends in American property law. Collectively, these trends reveal the peculiar shape of private landownership in the United States. Embedded within them, more than in any simple model, lie the lessons that the United States may offer to other legal systems.

Emphasizing Context and Protecting Sensitive Uses

Limiting pollution. By the end of the third quarter of the twentieth century, American law was well on its way toward requiring landowners to reduce their pollution and otherwise pay attention to the visible external harms that they caused. Some pollution-control laws operated by mandatory fiat; others simply imposed liability or fines; still others worked through economic incentives. Early efforts typically required industry groups as a whole to make across-the-board cutbacks. In recent years, regulators have acted more flexibly, tailoring permits to a polluter's particular context in such a way that rights to pollute are more dependent on surrounding conditions.

The most conspicuous deviation in American law from the "polluter pays" principle occurs in the case of water pollution caused by commodity-production land use activities, particularly agriculture. In that setting, political alliances, aided by the rhetoric of liberty and private property rights, have combined to resist meaningful regulatory limits on land use practices. The continuing degradation of many farm-dominated landscapes provides a reminder of the typical impacts of an unfettered market.

Tailoring private rights to the land. The tailoring of landowner rights to the land has been even more pronounced in the case of laws restricting development activities in ecologically sensitive areas, such as wetlands, endangered species habitat, floodplains, aquifer recharge areas, and highly erodible hillsides. For landscapes as a whole to become (or remain) healthy, such sensitive lands require some form of legal protection.

Thus far in the United States, laws protecting sensitive lands have typically addressed only a single category of land (for example, floodplains, sensitive aquifers), and they are understood as discrete measures. But when such laws are assessed together, as a new trend in landed property rights, they show how a landowner's use rights are no longer so abstractly defined. The land's peculiarities are being taken into account in defining the owner's right to use it. Western water rights, for instance, entitle owners to use water only in ways that are "beneficial"; and the term's definition increasingly pays attention to ecological impacts. Nuisance law works similarly, by limiting land uses to those that are reasonable in a given place. Under the Endangered Species Act, habitat conservation plans effectively tailor a landowner's development options so as to minimize adverse impacts on protected species. Incentive programs also play a role here: The federal conservation reserve program for farmlands, for instance, pays landowners to devote ecologically sensitive lands to conservation purposes. By accepting payment, owners voluntarily reduce and tailor their land use rights.

Redefining "harm." The move to tailor private property rights is closely related to the important, ongoing shift in the idea of land use "harm," and to the increased legal protection afforded sensitive activities. In many ways, this twentieth-century trend has reversed the tendency a century earlier to sanction intensive uses. Cultural values have shifted, and the reasonableness of land uses is being reassessed. Noisy, smelly, polluting, and disrupting land uses are increasingly banned as harmful. Wetlands-protection laws restrict drainage rights while protecting downstream owners against flooding. Wildlife-protection laws restrict development in sensitive habitats while offering landowners in exchange a more biologically diverse landscape. Laws such as these are often criticized as *reductions* in property rights, but they are more accurately understood as *reconfigurations* of those rights: Intensive land use options have been reduced, but landowners gain in exchange greater rights of protection for their sensitive uses of land. Out of the confluence of these trends is emerging an image of landownership that deviates widely from the abstract bundle-of-rights image so popular in the late nineteenth century.

The Communal Role

Writing in the nineteenth century, historian Sir Henry Maine claimed that advancing societies typically shift from a scheme of common or shared property to individual private rights. Whatever the truth of Maine's observation for particular development stages, the recent trend in America has been far different, toward an increase in shared or communally managed property and toward a blurring of the public-private line.

From individual to shared rights. One small chapter in this story occurred in 1988, when the Supreme Court of Illinois heard a case dealing with rights to use the surface of Lake Zurich, a nonnavigable lake outside Chicago. The governing common law rule for such a dispute was that each owner of part of the lake bed controlled the water surface above his or her part. That rule, though, divided the lake surface into individual pieces, with no one able to use the entire lake's surface. Disturbed by this outcome, the court abandoned the common law in favor of what it termed the "civil law" rule—the rule that each owner of lakefront land has rights to make reasonable use of the entire lake surface, in common with the rights of other owners to do the same.

This Illinois ruling illustrates a pronounced willingness in American culture to abandon old practices of dividing nature into distinct individual pieces and to consider instead possibilities for shared or communally managed rights. Lake Zurich did not become public property, usable by anyone; it became a type of closed-access commons, usable only by landowners and their guests. Ownership rights were shared, with the court reserving ultimate power to decide whether particular surface uses are reasonable.

The result in the Illinois case caused little controversy, mostly because it fit so readily into an already familiar trend toward shared ownership rights. Condominiums and cooperatives provide a prime example of this trend. In them, buyers obtain both exclusive rights to particular living spaces and rights to the shared use of commonly owned facilities. Common facilities are typically managed by a homeowners' association or other entity; they are a form of jointly owned property. Even the separately owned units, however, are regulated by the collective group, and the regulatory control of the group effectively gives it a nonpossessory ownership stake. Single-family homes and even office buildings are similarly arranged in common-interest ownership schemes that empower an owners' association, or other private governance entity, to provide common services, regulate activities, and manage common spaces. Mineral extraction in oil and gas fields is often done under pooling and unitization schemes in which numerous private parcels are united into a single operating scheme. In coal districts, landowners sometimes organize themselves into associations to make their lands more attractive to potential lessees. Many irrigated lands are indirectly managed by irrigation districts or membership organizations that control essential water flows.

Private land planning. Along with these and other instances of shared or pooled resources are the many cases of private land use planning—another form of private rights mingled with group control. Residential developments for decades have included land use restrictions—restrictive covenants or equitable servitudes, as they are commonly termed—that limit private land use options. Restrictive covenants first became popular in urban residential areas, and have since spread to developments everywhere, residential and commercial. So restrictive are many covenant schemes that owners effectively hold only the right to make a single use of the land, typically single-family residential use. The remaining rights in the land are, in effect, held by other landowners, who are empowered to enforce the covenant restrictions. Because all landowners are typically both restricted and given enforcement powers against their neighbors, landed property rights are intertwined.

In recent decades, private land use planning has often taken the form of negative easements, in which development rights are given or sold to a preservation-oriented entity. Some easements preserve historic structures. Others keep land in farming, ranching, and other low-intensity uses. Many conservation easements are held by land trusts specifically set up for that purpose. Less restrictive than conservation easements are arrangements in which private conservation groups such as Pheasants Forever supply seed and assistance to landowners to improve wildlife habitat, in exchange for agreements to maintain land in conservation status. In all such cases, ownership rights are shared.

By all appearances this trend toward shared ownership and private land planning is expanding in scale, with new land trusts arising weekly and individual conservation transactions sometimes involving thousands of acres at a time. In Western arid grazing regions, proposals are under consideration to combine private ranches into single management units, covering hundreds or thousands of square miles, to allow for grazing practices that better mimic the wandering habits of native bison. Other proposals would allow for the initiation of semicoercive private land planning in already developed areas—a practice now impossible without the unanimous consent of all landowners.

The blurring of public and private. In urban areas, and increasingly in rural areas too, private land planning supplements public, government-run processes, which also arise because of the interconnection of land uses and the need to mitigate the ill effects of fragmented decision making. Under zoning laws that became widespread in the 1920s, a government body typically prepared a comprehensive land use plan, dividing an area into land use zones, and then made decisions based on that plan. In the decades since then, planning has become a more fluid process, as formal plans have proven insufficiently flexible. Zoning ordinances have become less a clear set of rules, mechanically applied, and more a set of norms that are tailored to a project through negotiation between private developers and government land planners. Public input is sought and often heeded; and developers are commonly asked to mitigate the ill effects of a project, either by providing cash payments to the government or by dedicating land and improvements for public use. At the same time, communities often recognize the beneficial spillover effects of certain developments, and they offer tax rebates and other incentives to attract them.

The end result of these various government actions is that the right to develop, and the development process itself, blend private rights and public interests. In practice, a landowner typically holds only vague, uncertain rights to develop a land parcel. In recent decades these rights have become more vague and more uncertain with heightened public concerns over congestion and land degradation.

This blurring of public and private interest occurs, not just on land that is nominally private, but on public land as well. Governments in the United States own a full 40 percent of all land, with the percentage rising slowly through the continued purchase of lands for recreation and conservation aims. Many public lands, however, are subject to legally binding claims by miners, timber harvesters, graziers, ski-resort owners, and others, who hold protected rights to use public property for private gain. Such use rights are crafted and regulated by statute and regulatory action. With the exception of hard-rock mining claims on federal lands, they are typically allocated to private parties through competitive bid systems.

In the 1970s, many Western states called loudly for the federal government to divest its massive landholdings. That movement soon withered, however, in part because it became clear that the ultimate ownership of land, in the sense of holding title, is often less important than are the rights to use land and gain income from it—rights that are severable from the land title itself. In the West, much land remains federally owned; but state and local governments, as well as commodity industry groups, play important roles in deciding who uses the land and on what terms, and they have captured much of the income generated by these lands. Under federal laws promoted by Western interests, most royalty and rental payments on public lands are turned over to states and local governments. In addition, states have the power to tax private activities (such as mining) conducted on public lands, thereby capturing an even greater share of the overall gain; and they are empowered legally to regulate federal lands for environmental ends. As a matter of practical politics, extractive industries are part owners of these lands as well, given their considerable influence over government decision making at all levels. The upshot, as in the case of private land, is that public and private interests are intermingled; and decisions are made through negotiated, public-private processes.

Taken together, these various trends reveal that private land in America is not well presented by the image of a single land parcel managed by a single landowner. Land use is very much a communal concern, and in important ways the people affected by land use decisions have a voice in making them.

Expanding the Scale of Land Planning

One of the most prominent trends in landed property law is the increasing spatial scale of land use regulation. For decades, communities regulated their lands independently, with only minimal concern over spillover effects at a community's edge. By the end of the twentieth century, much land planning was occurring on regional and even statewide scales, in addition to traditional local-level work.

Planning for conservation. Much of this regional planning was done to contain the ill effects of urban sprawl. Acting alone, suburban cities and even entire counties lack the power to contain the market pressures propelling expansion: Only by acting in concert can lawmakers take control. Wisely done, regional planning can reduce the costs of highways and other infrastructure improvements, mitigate traffic and commuting times, preserve open spaces and greenways, protect floodplains and other ecologically sensitive lands, and otherwise improve the quality of suburban life. Other regional planning efforts have aimed more expressly at ecological conservation. Land use activities are sometimes controlled in areas that overlie sensitive drinking water aquifers, such as New Jersey's Pine Barrens. Development is similarly constrained in treasured forests like New York's Adirondack Mountains, and in watersheds that supply drinking water to major cities. Sensitive ecological regions in Florida, including the Everglades area, are subject to regional plans that require careful assessments of the ecological impacts of major construction projects. Nearly all coastal states have special regulations protecting coastal zones.

Specific federal statutes have encouraged states to deal with particular ecological problems through wide-scale planning, sometimes referred to as watershed planning or ecosystem management. The Clean Water Act, for instance, requires states to address the problem of polluted runoff—what the statute terms "nonpoint source" pollution—and this is often possible only by influencing regional land use practices through incentives and regulation. The Safe Drinking Water Act encourages states to protect drinking water supplies and expresses a preference for protection that reduces problems at their source, usually widespread land use practices. The Endangered Species Act indirectly promotes regional habitat conservation planning as a means of balancing development pressures and the needs of imperiled species.

Development rights in the regional context. One of the special challenges that arises in efforts to limit overall development is the need to avoid unfairness in deciding who gets to develop. U.S. law has only begun to address the issue. Many damaging land uses are harmful, not in isolation, but only when too many landowners engage in them. Drainage on one farm rarely causes damage; the drainage of an entire watershed can yield flooding, drought, and streambank erosion. Habitat modification that has little impact on a modest scale can, on a larger scale, materially disrupt a biological community. Pesticides and fertilizers used in abundance can disturb aquatic ecosystems and render water undrinkable.

One way to deal with such "carrying capacity harms" is to allow damaging uses to continue rising until the point is reached when further harm is intolerable. By allowing development to occur freely and then halting it abruptly, this approach effectively allocates development rights based on a first-in-time system. Because many people perceive this approach as unfair—and because communities have trouble drawing a line and sticking with it—communities have sought alternative methods to cap overall alteration. One method, little used yet highly promising, entails the use of transferable development rights (TDRs), in which all landowners in a region receive limited rights to develop, which they can either exercise or sell. TDRs are allocated so that overall development stays within acceptable limits. Owners of ecologically sensitive lands are often banned from developing their own lands, but they participate nonetheless in the gains of development by receiving development rights that they can sell for cash to owners of land that is suitable for development.

The rise of community-based conservation. Because land use regulation has long been a local prerogative, many landowners resist regulation that originates from a distant government, particularly the federal government. Disproportionately, criticism of regulation centers on federal laws protecting wetlands and endangered species habitat, even though the federal government plays only a minor role in the overall regulatory scheme. Conservation groups have responded by trying to work more with and through local communities, using bottom-up processes that encourage landowners to understand and help solve land use challenges. Community-based conservation, as it is often termed, focuses on such problems as nonpoint source water pollution, excessive modification of hydrologic cycles, loss of wildlife habitat, and the disappearance of open space.

A major challenge to such work, aside from the widespread rural suspicion of land use limits, is the long-term decline of rural communities, economically, socially, and psychologically. The market has helped bring on that decline by reducing the need for farmers and shifting jobs to cities. It has also corroded senses of community by promoting competitiveness and individualism. By instilling a commodity-centered view of nature, it has reduced the ability of landowners to perceive the land, and their place on the land, in ecological terms.

What the trends illustrate is the growing recognition that land parcels are interconnected, not just neighbor-to-neighbor but at the landscape level. Many environmental problems are only addressable at that level, and beginning steps are being taken to do so.

Pressures for Stability and Change

The norms governing landownership in the United States have always evolved in response to changing conditions and values, which is to say that private property has always been a living, evolving institution. Change, though, meets resistance from landowners adversely affected by it, just as it is promoted by landowners who stand to benefit. Dealing with this tension is a central challenge for any private property regime.

For generations, the existence and pace of legal change in the United States was masked because change occurred largely within the common law tradition. Judges used a conservative writing style that concealed change by presenting new rules as logical outgrowths of earlier rulings. Change was even harder to note when it occurred not by explicit rephrasings of legal rules but by shifts in their application. A court could consistently require land uses to be "reasonable," while significantly altering the meaning of the term as applied.

From common law to statutory change. By the mid–twentieth century, changes in laws governing private land were largely being made by lawmakers writing statutes and regulations—legal expressions that were more precise in their terms than common law rules and that changed the law more visibly—rather than by courts adjudicating common law disputes. Overt, distinct changes are easier to criticize as unfair disruptions of landowner rights and expectations. Several factors late in the twentieth century fostered heightened concern over the perceived unfairness of many of these new laws: an increasing hostility toward government generally; the rise of free-market, libertarian thought; and the expansion of land use limits to address ecological disruptions that many citizens did not perceive as harmful. Among the institutions showing new hostility toward shifts in landed property rights was the U.S. Supreme Court, which in a series of rulings scrutinized new regulations and, in several cases, struck them down as unlawful interferences with vested property rights.

By century's end, governments at all levels were struggling to accommodate the desire of most landowners for clear, stable property rights with their own need, as community guardians, to reshape laws to accommodate new problems and new values. Arguments about the issue often took the form of lawsuits claiming that particular regulations amounted to unlawful "takings" of private property, without the payment of just compensation.

The benefits of vagueness. Governments continue to negotiate this never-ending conflict in several ways. Many have learned that clear, precise rules, prescribing what landowners can and cannot do, soon become out of date and cause problems when changed. One solution is to shift to regulatory approaches more similar to the old common law, which defined landowner rights vaguely and hence left enforcers with room to maneuver. Water law reformers, for instance, have worked to graft a "public trust" notion on to water rights so that courts have a vague but potent tool to prod water users to mend bad practices. The common law itself has revived in importance, as more land use disputes are brought as nuisance cases with citizen-jurors judging disputes using vague standards and by drawing upon evolving, contemporary values. When precise rules are inescapable, governments often leave room for negotiation, including possibilities for variances and adjusted standards. Flexible standards hold particular appeal because they allow room to tailor rules to a specific setting.

Protecting expectations: existing versus new land uses. By and large, landowners in the United States enjoy widespread protection for current land uses, which are allowed to continue unless they are nuisances. Regulations banning particular activities almost always contain "grandfather" clauses, which permit the continuation of preexisting violations. Such protection is needed, to one degree or another, if landowners are to make valuable investments. On the other hand, much less protection is needed for landowners who want to develop bare land or to change current uses, and American law affords them less protection. Under prevailing constitutional law, for instance, a regulation that prohibits development or new activities on a parcel is unlikely to trigger the duty to compensate so long as it allows continuation of an existing, profitable land use.

Several reasons explain this lessened protection for changes in current uses. Land speculation is so uncertain already that legal uncertainty is easier to accommodate. Moreover, an increase in the value of bare land often comes about not through any landowner action but from roads, sewers, and other public and private investments. Landowners have less forceful claims for protection when the value they want to protect was not created by them. Finally, land development has so many spillover impacts that it is inevitably a quasi-public activity, and landowners have abundant notice of the public's oversight role.

Compensation to smooth transitions. One final piece in this complex reconciliation of landowner desires and public needs is the regulatory takings doctrine itself. Although commonly understood as a firm protection against regulation that "goes too far"—as the Supreme Court famously put it in a 1920 decision—the doctrine in practice operates chiefly to protect landowners only in times of legal transition. As an institution, private property can function well under legal regimes with widely varied ownership norms. What owners need is stability in those norms. Takings challenges have typically succeeded only when a landowner is surprised by a new legal rule. Landowners who acquire property after a specific law has taken effect have little chance of challenging it successfully. What these legal pieces reveal, once assembled, is a recognition in American law of both the benefits of clarity and security in private rights and the equally vital benefits of vagueness and flexibility.

Getting the Institutions Right

By the late twentieth century, it had become clear that all levels of government—from the most local to the national—needed to play roles in addressing land use environmental problems. Early in the 1970s, the federal government considered various proposals for national land use planning, but the entire idea met great resistance. Two decades later, when heated controversy broke out over environmental land use controls, the prime targets of attack were the few federal regulations, not the more numerous state and local laws. The federal government, it was plain, was simply too far from the people to regulate land successfully. At the same time, conservation interests were becoming frustrated by the inability of most states to deal with land use environmental challenges such as polluted runoff and declining endangered species habitat. Too many states would act, it seemed, only if pushed hard from above. Conservation interests also came to realize that the public would support needed regulation only if local communities had greater involvement in the process.

All levels of government. The overriding conclusion that has emerged from these assessments is that all levels of government must become involved if the land community is to regain health. Also, among the several levels of government, power and responsibility should be allocated pragmatically, rather than based on any theoretical vision of federalism. Although American lawmakers rarely look to international law for guidance, policy makers are increasingly espousing positions roughly similar to the subsidiarity principle in international environmental law: The lowest level of government that can handle a problem responsibly should do so, recognizing, however, that higher levels of government are commonly needed to set expectations, to equalize competitive conditions for business, and to ensure that state and local governments do not push their problems downstream or downwind.

In free-market thought, attention is often paid to the need to "get the prices right," so that goods and services are priced to reflect true overall costs. When it comes to embedding the market in the social order and protecting community interests, the comparable need is to get the institutions right. Allocating power and responsibility among levels of government is part of that need. Another part is to overcome the fragmentation of governing bodies in settings where coordinated action is needed to address landscape-scale problems.

Containing big business. Getting the institutions right means, in part, finding ways to counteract the power that vested market interests enjoy in influencing government processes. Government actions that promote the common good benefit many people in small ways. Individually, however, beneficiaries have little motive to protect their interests, particularly on complex issues; and high costs are involved in organizing them into effective pressure groups. Economic analyses of "free riders," and the related theory known as public choice, explain why the pro-conservation side of disputes is typically underrepresented.

Progress in addressing environmental problems has come about in large part because conservation interests have nonetheless been strong enough to raise the conservation banner. Without them little progress would have occurred, and further progress depends importantly on their continued vitality. Conservation groups typically focus their resources at the national level, and their impact there, accordingly, has been greatest. Resources are much thinner at the state and local level, where development interests typically exert great influence. Not surprisingly, the United

States has made far less progress on environmental problems that states and local governments are left to address, a fact that doubtless explains the enthusiasm of many business groups for shifting environmental management to the state level.

The special challenges of subtle declines. As the twenty-first century begins, perhaps the prime challenge in U.S. landed property law is to get the institutions right with respect to decision-making processes aimed at addressing gradual, subtle, yet ultimately debilitating land abuses. Interest in community-based conservation is directed in part toward this aim. The motivating hope is that organized market forces, such as agribusiness industries and large timber companies, will be less effective in dealing with widely scattered groups of citizens who come together to learn about their local lands and to make decisions about it as citizens rather than consumers. Vested economic interests most often succeed in derailing effective land use regulation by portraying such regulation as an unwanted interference with local activities. Particularly in rural areas, support for land use regulation increases markedly when regulation is viewed instead as a tool for a community to use in defending itself against destructive market forces. Thus, rural support for regulation is high when it provides a tool to ward off unwanted landfills or confined animal feeding operations.

As a means of getting institutions right, community-based conservation remains in its infancy. It may or may not prove effective as a means of helping local citizens learn about subtle, destructive land uses that erode and degrade soil and otherwise sap the land's health. It also may or may not prove effective in getting local communities to act as responsible members of larger regional and interstate communities.

The fallacy of neutrality. One final point about getting the institutions right has to do with the policy orientation of government. A longstanding ideal within liberal thought is that of the neutral, "night watchman" state that mediates among citizens, insisting upon fairness but not itself choosing among versions of the good life. The "neutral state" idea has been discredited, in part because neutrality is often impossible. Still, the idea lives on, and has revived in importance with the waxing strength of free-market ideology.

In the environmental arena, the market plainly has not and will not promote the overall health of the land, and deliberate communal action is essential. Although government can remain neutral in many policy arenas, sustainable living practices are achievable only through collective means—both to correct market failures and to achieve nonmarket goals. With a neutral state in charge, market deficiencies would lead quickly to a degraded land, as they have done many times in American history.

The Rhetoric of Owning

By the end of the twentieth century, much of the debate over private property in the United States was occurring not at the level of specific policy but at the level of symbol and myth. Private property is central to the self-image of the United States. It helps define the uniqueness of America and accounts, in the widely held story, for much of the nation's success. Property as symbol is particularly vital to those who strongly embrace individualism and free enterprise and who view private property as a shield against an overreaching state. In the eyes of many, environmental land use rules threaten this core institution.

Property rights and irresponsibility. On their side, conservation interests have also come to worry about private property, largely because it gives landowners a powerful tool to escape accountability for degradation. "Polluter pays" has become a widely accepted idea in American law, *except* in the case of pollution generated by rural land uses. Conservation interests are also concerned about the messages implicitly conveyed by private property in its individualistic, market-based forms: that nature is a collection of parts rather than an integrated whole; that fragmented management makes sense; and that private land creates a sphere of private interest distinct from the public realm.

These messages blend with market ideology in the popular mind to make land a market commodity, with its value set and its highest use determined by market forces. Also damaging are the market's messages about value—that most parts of nature hold no value, and that value lies entirely in the tradable parts of nature, not in the interconnected organic whole.

The ethics of owning. By the 1930s, the leading conservation figure in twentieth-century America, Aldo Leopold, was already struggling with these issues. A pioneering field ecologist, Leopold realized that the main conservation challenge of his day, as of later days, was the need to promote sensible land use by private landowners. Leopold initially rested his hope in economic incentives and in the arrangement of market forces so that good land use made economic sense. Within a few years, however, he had learned enough from various incentive-related experiments to see that incentives alone would not work, useful though they sometimes were. Yet Leopold also recognized that land use regulation alone was unlikely to work, for good land use required careful attention to the features and peculiarities of each land parcel. It required, he sensed, the knowledge and devotion of a careful land steward. Regulation, he feared, was too blunt an instrument to bring about that result.

As Leopold saw it, the key to sound land use was to expand the knowledge and redirect the ethical values of private owners. Landowners needed to see land use as a matter of ethics and aesthetics as well as economics. They needed to understand how landownership inevitably brought membership in the land community that surrounded and included the owner's land. Along with that membership, Leopold believed, came duties to promote the well-being of the entire community, duties such as protecting and enriching the soil, leaving room for wildlife, protecting the natural hydrologic cycle, and otherwise altering the land as gently as possible

Leopold's well-known "land ethic" has had a profound impact on conservation thought. Inspired by Leopold, conservation groups have recognized the need to develop within landowners stronger senses of community, both so that they are more likely to promote the common good in their land uses and so that they perceive the land more holistically. Leopold's genius lay in his ability to mix ecology with ethics and aesthetics, and conservation leaders have followed his example. In disputes over land use, they have openly pushed ethical ideas, such as the obligation to protect other species and to preserve the land for later generations. They have also encouraged landowners to consider land aesthetics, hoping to stimulate concern for all of nature's parts.

A new rhetoric of responsibility. What the contemporary conservation movement has learned is that the rhetoric of ownership counts for a great deal, and commodity-based images of ownership can provide formidable roadblocks. Better than they have, conservation groups need to develop ownership visions that allow private property to fulfill its historic functions in promoting liberty and privacy while nonetheless encouraging landowners to consider the communal context. The idea of ownership-as-stewardship has proven useful, for it encourages landowners to recognize that their tenure is necessarily limited. More such images are needed, ones that encourage landowners to become sensitive to their lands, to become more aware of ecological connections, and to show more respect for vital ecosystem processes. Above all, as Aldo Leopold put it, ownership needs to carry the sense of belonging to a community, with rights of ownership matched by duties to promote the well-being of that community. Property law plays an important role here, for the law necessarily performs an educational function. What the law ignores, landowners are encouraged to ignore.

The United States remains saddled with images of ownership that are unhelpful to the conservation cause; and one of the chief challenges of private-lands conservation in the coming century is not just to reform those images but to embed them in narrative tales about the nation, its settlement of the continent, and its long history of progress—tales that capture the popular imagination and that bring private ownership into line with vital conservation goals.

What the U.S. experience shows on this issue is the importance of understanding private property as a symbol as well as an economic and political institution, and paying careful attention to the way private ownership is described. Ownership *rights* need to marry ownership *responsibilities*. Talk of property as individual enclave needs to be matched with community-focused talk about owning as belonging.

CONCLUSION

So linked is private property to the economic, social, and intellectual strands of American history that it is hard to understand property without digging deep into American history and culture. America's economic success has been the product of a culture mixed with a favorable landscape, and no single institution, including private property, has played more than a small role. Still, private property has helped stimulate enterprise, of that there is no doubt; and secure land tenure has encouraged landowners to take care of what they own, even though the market's incentive toward care is by no means strong enough to protect the health of the overall land community. Private property is a powerful tool, but it is a tool that needs social control, not just by governments but by citizens who live in a place and who are prepared to work through public and private means to tailor landowner rights so that market forces do not undercut the collective good.

In the end, private property in the United States is a hard institution to describe. To capture it, one needs to take into account both the transferability of property and the many restraints on transfer; the clarity of individual entitlements as well as their continued vagueness; the role of individual owners in making land use decisions as well as the pervasive persistence of communal and public control; the role of contract bargaining in the reallocation of assets as well as the persistence of constraining communal norms; the pervasiveness of individual private ownership as well as the huge amounts of public land; the protection offered private expectations as well as the continued public role in reshaping operative rules. Property norms reflect market needs, yet they also and importantly reflect efforts by communities to contain the market and to remedy its shortcomings. That containment has been possible only because law-making institutions have been sufficiently democratic to respond to public concerns and because citizen groups have stepped forward to speak for the common good.

America's story, then, has been about both the market and democratic governance; about individualism as well as the community; and about abstract ideas joined with a careful attentiveness to nature's complex ways.

NOTES

1. *Bryant v. Lefever*, 4 Common Pleas Division 172, 175–76 (1879).
2. James Kent, *Commentaries on American Law* 2:265 (New York, 1826).
3. *Vanderbilt v. Adams*, 7 Cow. 349 (N.Y., 1827).
4. *Commonwealth v. Alger*, 7 Cush. 53, 84–85 (Mass., 1851).
5. *Waschak v. Moffat*, 109 A. 2d 310, 316 (Pa. 1954).
6. Because my focus here is on landed property rights and land use options, I do not consider contemporary developments relating to real estate transactions or to the relative rights of mortgagees and landlords.

SUGGESTED READING

The scholarly literature relevant to the issues considered here is vast to the point of overwhelming, and I have used far more sources than I can cite here. The most valuable works on the history of property rights in the United States over the past two centuries include: Gregory S. Alexander, *Commodity & Propriety: Competing Visions of Property in American Legal Thought, 1776–1970* (Chicago: University of Chicago Press, 1997); James W. Ely, Jr., *The Guardian of Every Other Right: A Constitutional History of Property Rights* (New York: Oxford University Press, 1992); William J. Novak, *The People's Welfare: Law & Regulation in Nineteenth-Century America* (Chapel Hill: University of North Carolina Press, 1996); Morton J. Horwitz, *The Transformation of American Law, 1780–1860* (Cambridge, Mass.: Harvard University Press, 1977); Morton J. Horwitz, *The Transformation of American Law, 1870–1960* (New York: Oxford University Press, 1992); Rutherford H. Platt, *Land Use and Society: Geography, Law, and Public Policy* (Washington, D.C.: Island Press, 1996); Richard Schlatter, *Private Property: The History of an Idea* (London: Russell & Russell, 1973); William B. Scott, *In Pursuit of Happiness: American Conceptions of Property from the Seventeenth Century to the Twentieth Century* (Bloomington, Ind.: Indiana University Press, 1977); William F. Fisher III, *The Law of the Land: An Intellectual History of American Property Doctrine, 1776–1880* (Unpublished Ph.D. thesis, Harvard University, 1991); John F. Hart, "Colonial Land Use Law and Its Significance for Modern Takings Doctrine," *Harvard Law Review* 109 (1996): 1252; Paul M. Kurtz, "Nineteenth Century Anti-Entrepreneurial Nuisance Injunctions—Avoiding the Chancellor," *William and Mary Law Review* 17 (1975): 621; Francis S. Philbrick, "Changing Conceptions of Property in Law," *University of Pennsylvania Law Review* 86 (1938): 691; William Michael Treanor, "The

Original Understanding of the Takings Clause and the Political Process,"
Columbia Law Review 95 (1995): 782; Kenneth J. Vandervelde, "The New
Property of the Nineteenth Century: The Development of the Modern
Conception of Property," *Buffalo Law Review* 29 (1980): 325.

Less focused on property issues, but nonetheless of considerable value
in interpreting the institution, are Samuel P. Hays, *Explorations in Environ-
mental History* (Pittsburgh: University of Pittsburgh Press, 1998); Samuel P.
Hays, *Conservation and the Gospel of Efficiency: The Progressive Conservation
Movement, 1890–1920* (Cambridge, Mass.: Harvard University Press,
1959); Samuel P. Hays, *The Response to Industrialism, 1885–1914* (Chicago:
University of Chicago Press, 1957); Donald Worster, *The Wealth of Nature:
Environmental History and the Ecological Imagination* (New York: Oxford
University Press, 1993).

Valuable assessments of property rights in more recent times include:
Timothy Beatley, *Ethical Land & Use: Principles of Policy and Planning* (Balti-
more: Johns Hopkins University Press, 1994); Timothy Beatley and Kristy
Manning, *The Ecology of Place: Planning for Environment, Economy, and Com-
munity* (Washington, D.C.: Island Press, 1997); Samuel Bowles and Herbert
Gintis, *Democracy and Capitalism: Property, Community, and the Contradic-
tions of Modern Social Thought* (New York: Basic Books, 1987); Lynton Keith
Caldwell and Kristin Shrader-Frechette, *Policy for Land: Law and Ethics*
(Lanham, Md.: Rowman & Littlefield, 1993); John Christman, *The Myth of
Property: Toward an Egalitarian Theory of Ownership* (New York: Oxford Uni-
versity Press, 1994); John Echeverria and Raymond Booth Eby, *Let the People
Judge: Land Use and the Private Property Rights Movement* (Washington, D.C.:
Island Press, 1995); Harvey M. Jacobs, ed., *Who Owns America? Social Con-
flict over Property Rights* (Madison: University of Wisconsin Press, 1998);
Richard F. Babcock and Duane A. Feurer, "Land as a Commodity 'Affected
with a Public Interest,'" *Washington Law Review* 52 (1977): 289; Myrl L.
Duncan, "Property as a Public Conversation, Not a Lockean Soliloquy: A
Role for Intellectual and Legal History in Takings Analysis," *Environmental
Law* 26 (1996): 1095; David B. Hunter, "An Ecological Perspective on Prop-
erty: A Call for Judicial Protection of the Public's Interest in Environmen-
tally Critical Resources," *Harvard Environmental Law Review* 12 (1988): 311;
Marc R. Poirer, "Property, Environment, Community," *Journal of Environ-
mental Law and Litigation* 12 (1997): 43; Carol M. Rose, "Property as a Key-
stone Right?" *Notre Dame Law Review* 71 (1996): 329; Joseph L. Sax,
"Property Rights and the Economy of Nature: Understanding Lucas v. South
Carolina Coastal Council," *Stanford Law Review* 45 (1993): 1433; Joseph
William Singer and Jack M. Beerman, "The Social Origins of Property,"
Canadian Journal of Law and Jurisprudence 6 (1993): 217; "Symposium:

Power, Politics, and Place—Who Holds the Reins of Environmental Regulation?" *Ecology Law Quarterly* 25 (4): 559 et seq. (1999).

I have considered in more detail in the following writings many of the specific points considered in this interpretive essay: *Bounded People, Boundless Lands: Envisioning a New Land Ethic* (Washington, D.C.: Island Press, 1998); *Justice and the Earth: Images for Our Planetary Survival* (New York: The Free Press, 1993); "A Sand County Almanac at 50: Leopold in the New Century," *Environmental Law Reporter* 30 (January 2000): 10058; "The Particulars of Owning," *Ecology Law Quarterly* 25 (1999): 574; "Owning the Land: Four Contemporary Narratives," *Journal of Land Use and Environmental Law* 13 (1998): 279; "Ethics, Community, and Private Land," *Ecology Law Quarterly* 23 (1996): 631; "The Construction of Ownership," *1996 University of Illinois Law Review* 173; "The Owning and Taking of Sensitive Lands," *U.C.L.A. Law Review* 43 (1995): 77; "Context and Accommodation in Modern Property Law," *Stanford Law Review* 41 (1989): 1529; "Land Use and the Study of Early American History," *Yale Law Journal* 94 (1985): 717.

The larger legal context is assessed in Donald Fleming and Bernard Bailyn, eds., *Law in American History* (Boston: Little, Brown and Co., 1971); Lawrence M. Friedman, *A History of American Law* (New York: Simon & Schuster, 2nd ed., 1985); Kermit L. Hall, *The Magic Mirror: Law in American History* (New York: Oxford University Press, 1989); James Willard Hurst, *Law and the Conditions of Freedom in the Nineteenth-Century United States* (Madison: University of Wisconsin Press, 1956); Leonard W. Levy, *The Law of the Commonwealth and Chief Justice Shaw* (New York: Oxford University Press, 1957). Also valuable, for historical perspective, are Allan Kulikoff, *The Agrarian Origins of American Capitalism* (Charlottesville: University Press of Virginia, 1992); Lawrence Goodman, *The Populist Movement: A Short History of the Agrarian Revolt in American History* (New York: Oxford University Press, 1978); Richard Hofstadter, *The Age of Reform* (New York: Random House, 1955); Charles Sellers, *The Market Revolution: Jacksonian America, 1815–1846* (New York: Oxford University Press, 1991); Robert H. Walker, *Life in the Age of Enterprise* (New York: G. P. Putnam's Sons, 1967); Richard Wiebe, *The Search for Order, 1877–1920* (New York: Hill and Wang, 1967);

Aldo Leopold's life, and the conservation movement during his day, are considered in Curt Meine, *Aldo Leopold: His Life and Work* (Madison: University of Wisconsin Press, 1988). Able commentary on his land ethic is set forth in J. Baird Callicott, *Beyond the Land Ethic: More Essays in Environmental Philosophy* (Albany, N.Y.: State University of New York (SUNY) Press, 1999). Among the many good studies of contemporary environmental thought and policy are Richard N. L. Andrews, *Managing the Environment, Managing Ourselves: A History of American Environmental Policy* (New Haven, Conn.: Yale University Press, 1999); Brian Donahue, *Reclaiming the Commons: Community Farms and Forests in a New England Town* (New Haven, Conn.: Yale University Press, 1999); Thomas R. Dunlap, *Saving America's Wildlife: Ecology and the American Mind* (Princeton, N.J.: Princeton University Press, 1988); Stephen Fox, *John Muir and His Legacy: The American Conservation Movement* (Boston: Little, Brown and Co., 1981); Philip Shabecoff, *A Fierce Green Fire: The American Environmental Movement* (New York: Hill and Wang, 1993). Two indispensable works in understanding economic issues are Herman E. Daly and John B. Cobb, Jr., *For the Common Good: Redirecting the Economy toward Community, the Environment, and a Sustainable Future* (Boston: Beacon Press, 1989); and Mark Sagoff, *The Economy of the Earth: Philosophy, Law, and the Environment* (Cambridge, England: Cambridge University Press, 1988).

About the Contributors

Meena Bhargava is a professor of history at Indraprastha College, University of Delhi.

Daniel W. Bromley is Anderson-Bascom Professor of Applied Economics at the University of Wisconsin–Madison.

Philip C. Brown is an associate professor in the Department of History at Ohio State University.

David Feeny is a professor of pharmacy and pharmaceutical sciences, a professor of public health sciences, and an adjunct professor of economics at the University of Alberta, as well as a fellow at the Institute of Health Economics.

Eric T. Freyfogle is Max L. Rowe Professor of Law and an affiliate professor in the Department of Natural Resources and Environmental Sciences at the University of Illinois at Urbana–Champaign.

James Giblin is a professor in the Department of History at the University of Iowa.

Stephen Gudeman is a professor in the Department of Anthropology at the University of Minnesota.

Ronald J. Herring is John S. Knight Professor of International Relations and a professor of government at Cornell University.

John R. McNeill is a professor of history in the School of Foreign Service and History Department at Georgetown University.

Peter C. Perdue is a professor of history at the Massachusetts Institute of Technology.

John F. Richards is a professor of history at Duke University.

Alberto Rivera is the academic program director at the Higher Education Consortium for Urban Affairs.

Anna Tsing is a professor in the Department of Anthropology at the University of California, Santa Cruz.

James L. Wescoat, Jr., is a professor of geography at the University of Colorado at Boulder.

Index

ABOUT ICS

Founded in 1974, the Institute for Contemporary Studies (ICS) is a nonprofit, nonpartisan policy research institute.

To fulfill its mission to promote self-governing and entrepreneurial ways of life, ICS sponsors a variety of programs and publications on key issues including education, entrepreneurship, the environment, leadership, and social policy.

Through its imprint, ICS Press, the Institute publishes innovative and readable books that will further the understanding of these issues among scholars, policy makers, and the wider community of citizens. ICS Press books include the writing of eight Nobel laureates, and have been influential in setting the nation's policy agenda.

ICS programs seek to encourage the entrepreneurial spirit not only in this country but also around the world. They include the Institute for Self-Governance (ISG) and the International Center for Self-Governance (ICSG).